THE
TEACHER
WARS

•••••••••••••

THE
TEACHER
WARS

....

A History
of America's
Most Embattled
Profession

Dana Goldstein

Doubleday

New York   London   Toronto   Sydney   Auckland

Some reporting in chapters 9 and 10 originally appeared in
*The American Prospect, Slate, The Daily Beast,
The Nation,* and *Zócalo Public Square.*

Book design by Maria Carella
Jacket design by Emily Mahon
Jacket photograph © iHennigs / Ignacio Hennigs / Getty Images

Library of Congress Cataloging-in-Publication Data
Goldstein, Dana.
The teacher wars : a history of America's most embattled profession /
Dana Goldstein.—First edition.
pages cm
ISBN 978-0-385-53695-0 (hardcover)—ISBN 978-0-385-53696-7 (eBook)
1. Teaching—United States—History. 2. Teachers—Professional relationships—
United States—History. 3. Public schools—United States—History.
4. Educational change—United States—History. I. Title.
LA212.G65 2014
371.1020973—dc23   2014007024

MANUFACTURED IN THE UNITED STATES OF AMERICA

5 7 9 10 8 6

First Edition

To my parents,
Laura Greene and Steven Goldstein

It is . . . advisable that the teacher should understand, and even be able to criticize, the general principles upon which the whole educational system is formed and administered. He is not like a private soldier in an army, expected merely to obey, or like a cog in a wheel, expected merely to respond to and transmit external energy; he must be <u>an intelligent medium of action</u>.

JOHN DEWEY, 1895

Contents

THE
TEACHER
WARS

....

Introduction

I began this book in early 2011 with a simple observation: Public school teaching had become the most controversial profession in America. Republican governors in Wisconsin, Ohio, and Indiana, and even the Democratic governor of deep blue Massachusetts, sought to diminish or eliminate teachers' rights to collectively bargain. Teacher tenure was the subject of heated debate in statehouses from Denver to Tallahassee, and President Obama swore in his State of the Union address to "stop making excuses" for bad teachers. One rising-star Republican, New Jersey governor Chris Christie, even became a conservative folk hero after appearing in a series of YouTube videos in which he excoriated individual public school teachers—all of them middle-aged women—who rose at public events to challenge him on his $1 billion in education budget cuts, even as he cut $1.6 billion in corporate taxes.

No other profession operates under this level of political scrutiny, not even those, like policing or social work, that are also tasked with public welfare and are paid for with public funds. In 2010 *Newsweek* published a cover story called "The Key to Saving American Education." The image was of a blackboard, with a single phrase chalked over and over again in a child's loopy handwriting: *We must fire bad teachers. We must fire bad teachers. We must fire bad teachers.* Wide-release movies like *Waiting for "Superman"* and *Won't Back Down,* funded by philanthropists who made their fortunes in the private sector, portray teacher tenure and its defender, teachers unions, as practically the sole causes of underperforming schools. Everywhere I traveled as a reporter, from the 2008 Democratic National Convention to the 2010 meeting of former president Bill Clinton's Clinton Global Initiative, powerful people seemed to feel indignant about the incompetence and job security of public school teachers, despite polls showing that the American public considers teachers highly respected professionals, nearly on par with medical doctors.

Anxiety about bad teaching is understandable. Teachers do work that is both personal and political. They care for and educate our children, for whom we feel a fierce and loyal love. And they prepare our nation's citizens and workers, whose wisdom and level of skill will shape our collective future. Given that teachers shoulder such an awesome responsibility, it makes sense that American politics is acutely attuned to their shortcomings. So I want to begin by acknowledging: It is true that the majority of American teachers have academically mediocre backgrounds. Most have below-average SAT scores and graduate from nonselective colleges and universities.* It is also true that one large review of practices within typical American elementary school classrooms found many children—and the majority of poor children—"sitting around, watching the teacher deal with behavioral problems, and engaging in boring and rote instructional activities such as completing worksheets and spelling tests." Another study of over a thousand urban public school classrooms found only a third of teachers conducting lessons that developed "intellectual depth" beyond rote learning.

In the Obama era, the predominant policy response to these very real problems has been a narrow one: to weaken teachers' tenure protections and then use "measures of student learning"—a euphemism for children's scores on an ever-expanding battery of hastily designed tests—to identify and fire bad teachers. One Colorado teacher told me (hyperbolically) that the disproportion-

---

* Recent data shows teachers' academic qualifications improving, but it is unclear whether this is a lasting development or a short-term trend due to weak private sector hiring during the recession.

ate focus on punishing awful teachers made her feel "I've chosen a profession that, in the public eye, is worse than prostitution." A spate of online videos and blog posts, in which angry teachers publicly quit their jobs, has gone viral. "I can no longer cooperate with a testing regime that I believe is suffocating creativity and innovation in the classroom," wrote Ron Maggiano, a Virginia high school social studies teacher and winner of two national teaching awards. In Illinois, Ellie Rubinstein tendered her resignation via YouTube, explaining, "Everything I loved about teaching is extinct. Curriculum is mandated. Minutes spent teaching subjects are audited. Schedules are dictated by administrators. The classroom teacher is no longer trusted or in control of what, when, or how she teaches." Olivia Blanchard chose to leave her Teach for America placement in Atlanta, where hundreds of thousands of dollars in merit pay bonuses had been paid to administrators and teachers who cheated by erasing and correcting students' answers on standardized tests before submitting them to be graded. After a round of indictments, those teachers who remained in the district were left demoralized and paranoid. When Blanchard clicked Send on her resignation e-mail, she was "flooded with relief," she recounted in *The Atlantic*.

Blanchard, Maggiano, and Rubinstein represent a larger trend. Polls show teachers feel more passionate and mission-driven about their careers than other American professionals. But a MetLife survey of teachers found that between 2008 and 2012, the proportion who reported being "very satisfied" with their current job plummeted from 62 to 39 percent, the lowest level in a quarter century.

I had assumed this war over teaching was new, sparked by the anxieties of the Great Recession. After all, one-fifth of all American children were growing up poor—twice the child poverty rate of England or South Korea. Young adults were suffering from a 17 percent unemployment rate, compared to less than 8 percent in Germany and Switzerland. Over half of recent college graduates were jobless or underemployed for their level of education. A threadbare social safety net, run-amok bankers, lackadaisical regulators, the globalization of manufacturing, and a culture of consumerism, credit card debt, and short-term thinking might have gotten us into this economic mess. But we'd be damned if better teachers couldn't help get us out. "Great teachers are performing miracles every single day," Secretary of Education Arne Duncan said in 2009. "An effective teacher? They walk on water." The rhetoric could provoke whiplash. Even as we were obsessed with the very worst teachers, we were worshipping an ideal, superhuman few.

This confusing dichotomy led me to wonder: Why are American teachers both resented and idealized, when teachers in other nations are much more universally respected? In South Korea, teachers are referred to as "nation builders." In Finland, both men and women name teaching as among the top three most desirable professions for a spouse. Meanwhile, that old American saw—"Those who can't do, teach"—continues to reverberate, reflecting elite condescension toward career educators.

I suspected that the key to understanding the American view of teachers lay in our history, and perhaps had something to do with the tension between our sky-high hopes for public education as the vehicle of meritocracy and our perennial unwillingness to fully invest in our public sector, teachers and schools included. For two hundred years, the American public has asked teachers to close troubling social gaps—between Catholics and Protestants; new immigrants and the American mainstream; blacks and whites; poor and rich. Yet every new era of education reform has been characterized by a political and media war on the existing teachers upon whom we rely to do this difficult work, often in the absence of the social supports for families that make teaching and learning most effective for kids, like stable jobs and affordable housing, child care, and health care. The nineteenth-century common school reformers depicted male teachers—90 percent of the classroom workforce in 1800—as sadistic, lash-wielding drunks who ought to be replaced by kinder, purer (and cheaper) women. During the Progressive Era, it was working-class female teachers who were attacked, for lacking the masculine "starch" supposedly necessary to preside over sixty-student classrooms of former child laborers. In the South during the civil rights era, *Brown v. Board of Education* prompted the racially motivated firings of tens of thousands of black teachers, as the Eisenhower, Kennedy, Johnson, and Nixon administrations looked the other way. Then, at the height of the Black Power movement in the

1960s and 1970s, it was inner-city white teachers who were vilified, for failing to embrace parental control of schools and Afrocentric pedagogical theories.

Teachers have been embattled by politicians, philanthropists, intellectuals, business leaders, social scientists, activists on both the Right and Left, parents, and even one another. (As we shall see, some of the critiques were fair, others less so.) Americans have debated who should teach public school; what should get taught; and how teachers should be educated, trained, hired, paid, evaluated, and fired. Though we've been arguing about these questions for two centuries, very little consensus has developed.

Amid these teacher wars, many extraordinary men and women worked in public school classrooms and offered powerful, grassroots ideas for how to improve American education. Henry David Thoreau, Susan B. Anthony, W. E. B. Du Bois, and Lyndon B. Johnson are just a few of the famous Americans who taught. They resisted the fantasy of educators as saints or saviors, and understood teaching as a job in which the potential for children's intellectual transcendence and social mobility, though always present, is limited by real-world concerns such as poor training, low pay, inadequate supplies, inept administration, and impoverished students and families. These teachers' stories, and those of less well-known teachers, propel this history forward and help us understand why American teaching has evolved into such a peculiar profession, one attacked and admired in equal proportion.

Today the ineffective tenured teacher has emerged as a feared character, a vampiric type who sucks tax dollars into her bloated pension and health care plans, without much regard for the children under her care. Like past conflagrations over crack babies or welfare queens, which exemplified anxiety over public spending on poor people of color, today's bad teacher scare employs all the classic features of a moral panic. According to sociologists who study these events, in a moral panic, policy makers and the media focus on a single class of people (in our case, veteran public school teachers) as emblems of a large, complex social problem (socioeconomic inequality, as evidenced by educational achievement gaps). Then the media repeats, ad nauseam, anecdotes about the most despicable examples of this type of person (such as "rubber room" teachers, who collect pay, sometimes for years, while awaiting termination hearings on accusations of corporal punishment or alcoholism). This focus on the worst of the worst misrepresents the true scale and character of what may be a genuine problem.

As a result, the public has gotten the message that public school teaching—especially urban teaching—is a broadly failed profession. The reality is concerning, but on a more modest scale: Depending on whom you ask, teacher-quality advocates estimate that somewhere between 2 and 15 percent of current teachers cannot improve their practice to an acceptable level and ought to be replaced each year. Far from confirming the perception that low-performing urban schools are uniformly bleak, talentless places, the latest "value-added" research quantifies what history shows: that even the highest-poverty neighborhood schools in cities like New York and Los Angeles employ teachers who produce among the biggest test score gains in their regions. What's more, veteran teachers who work long-term in high-poverty schools with low test scores are actually more effective at raising student achievement than is the rotating cast of inexperienced teachers who try these jobs out but flee after one to three years.

The history of American education reform shows not only recurring attacks on veteran educators, but also a number of failed ideas about teaching that keep popping up again and again, like a Whac-A-Mole game at the amusement park. Over the past ten years, cities from Atlanta to Austin to New York have experimented with paying teachers bonuses for higher student test scores. This type of merit pay was attempted in the 1920s, early 1960s, and 1980s. It never worked to broadly motivate teachers or advance outcomes for kids. For over a century, school reformers have hoped that tweaking teacher rating systems would lead to more teachers being declared unfit and getting fired, resulting in an influx of better people into the profession. But under almost every evaluation system reformers have tried—rating teachers as good, fair, or poor; A, B, C, or D; Satisfactory or Unsatisfactory; or Highly Effective, Effective,

Developing, or Ineffective—principals overburdened by paperwork and high teacher turnover ended up declaring that over 95 percent of their employees were just fine, indeed.* Fast-track teacher training programs like Teach for America, the Great Society–era Teacher Corps, and the nineteenth-century Board of National Popular Education are likewise a perennial feature of our school reform landscape. They recruit ambitious people to the classroom, but on a small scale, and do not systemically improve instruction for kids.

History also shows that teacher tenure has been widely misunderstood. It is true that tenure protections make it costly, in both time and money, for schools to fire veteran teachers. That is because due process rights allow tenured teachers accused of poor performance to "grieve" their evaluations and terminations to an arbitrator, who can rule to send them back to the classroom. Yet tenure predates collective bargaining for teachers by over half a century. Administrators granted teachers tenure as early as 1909, *before* unions were legally empowered at the negotiating table to demand this right. During the Progressive Era, both "good government" school reformers and then-nascent teachers unions supported tenure, which prevented teaching jobs from being used as political patronage and allowed teachers to challenge dismissals or demotions, once commonplace, based on gender, marital status, pregnancy, religion, ethnicity, race, sexual orientation, or political ideology. Tenure has long existed even in southern states where teachers are legally barred from collective bargaining.

Today it is usually assumed that teachers enjoy much more job security than workers in the private sector. Even if we set aside the nearly 50 percent of all beginner teachers who choose to leave the profession within five years—and ignore the evidence that those who leave are worse performers than those who stay—it is unclear whether teachers are formally terminated for *poor performance* any less frequently than are other workers. In 2007, the last year for which national data is available, 2.1 percent of American public

---

* These are the actual categories of the four rating systems used in the New York City public schools between 1898 and 2014.

school teachers were fired for cause, a figure that includes tenured teachers. Compared to federal workers, who one study found are fired at an annual rate of .02 percent, teachers are exponentially more likely to be terminated. There is no comparable data from the private sector, because the Bureau of Labor Statistics groups layoffs with firings. But in 2012, companies with over a thousand employees, the closest private counterpart to large urban school systems, lost only about 2 percent of their workforce from firings, resignations, and layoffs combined. In short, teachers are more, not less, likely than many other workers to get fired.

It may well be that we want teachers to be fired more often than other professionals because their work is so much more important. Still, the public conversation about teaching rarely offers a realistic sense of scale—of how many bad teachers there truly are, and what it would take to either improve their skills or replace them with people who are apt to perform at a higher level.

It is often said that teachers ought to be as elite and high performing as attorneys or doctors. But teaching employs roughly five times as many people as either medicine or law. There are 3.3 million American public school teachers, compared to 691,000 doctors and 728,000 attorneys. Four percent of all civilian workers are teachers.

In some recent years just as many new teachers were hired— over 200,000—as the total number of American college graduates minted by selective institutions, those that accept fewer than half of their applicants. The National Council on Teacher Quality estimates that high-poverty schools alone hire some 70,000 new teachers annually. Reformers sometimes claim that this huge demand for teachers is driven by overaggressive class-size limits, and they argue for decreasing the number of teachers while raising class sizes and recruiting a smaller, more elite group to the profession. In California and Florida, poorly designed class-size laws did lead to the overhiring of underqualified teachers. But the leading teacher demographer, Richard Ingersoll of the University of Pennsylvania, has shown that the decrease in average elementary school class sizes since 1987, from 26 to 21 children, does not fully explain the "ballooning" of the teaching force. There are two other factors that together account for a larger part of the change: first, the explosion of high-needs special-education diagnoses for students, such as those with autism-spectrum disorders, and second, the increase in the number of high school students who enroll in math and science courses. Those trends are not likely ones we can or should reverse. While teacher prep programs in regions with an oversupply of teachers should raise their admission standards or shut down, calls for 100 percent of American teachers to hail from selective colleges are, frankly, absurd, especially if we also lay off the bottom, say, 2 to 15 percent of teachers each year—66,000 to 495,000 people—as many reformers would like. Currently, just 10 percent of teachers are graduates of selective colleges. Teach for America recruited 6,000 teachers in 2013. Another elite alternative certification program, The New Teacher Project, recruited about 1,800 teaching fellows. Urban teacher residencies, which are also highly competitive, produced some 500 teachers. These are tiny numbers relative to demand.

Moreover, with the possible exception of high school–level math teachers, there is little evidence that better students make better teachers. Some nations, such as Finland, have been able to build a teaching force made up solely of star students. But other places, such as Shanghai, have made big strides in student achievement without drastically adjusting the demographics of who becomes a teacher. They do it by reshaping teachers' working days so they spend less time alone in front of kids and more time planning lessons and observing other teachers at work, sharing best practices in pedagogy and classroom management. According to Andreas Schleicher, a statistician who researches schools around the world, Shanghai "is good at attracting average people and getting enormous productivity out of them." The future of American education likely looks similar. As John Dewey noted in 1895, "Education is, and forever will be, in the hands of ordinary men and women."

I came to this project with sympathy for educators. American public school teaching has typically attracted individuals taking their first, tentative steps out of the working class, and one of them was my maternal grandfather, Harry Greene, a high school dropout. In his first career as a printer, he led a drive to organize a union at a nonunion shop, and for a while the fallout from that made it difficult for him to find work. When he was fifty-two years old, Harry finally earned an associate's degree, and in 1965 began teaching vocational courses in New York City public high schools. He benefited from the early years of teacher collective bargaining. As a teacher, my grandfather made a steady middle-class salary with periodic raises for the first time in his life. That financial stability allowed my mother, Laura Greene, to attend a four-year private college.

My dad, Steven Goldstein, was another first-generation college graduate who became a public school teacher. He attended Adelphi University on a soccer scholarship. Always the jock, my dad discovered he had a passion for history, too, and taught middle and high school social studies for ten years before going into school administration, because he wanted to earn more money. He worked in several socioeconomically integrated suburban school districts, and would sometimes say that the teachers union could be an administrator's greatest ally in removing a bad teacher from the classroom.

In addition to being the daughter and granddaughter of educators, I attended public schools in Ossining, New York, with a diverse group of white, black, Latino, and Asian classmates. A few parents, like my mom, commuted down the Hudson River to New York City for corporate jobs; others were single mothers on public assistance or line cooks in the kitchen of our town's maximum-security prison, Sing Sing. But regardless of whether they were college professors or home health aides, the most involved parents in Ossining wanted their kids in the classrooms of the most experienced teachers. My junior-year math teacher, Mr. DiCarlucci, wore a full suit and tie every day, accessorized with blingy gold jewelry. Though he taught precalculus, he assigned research papers on high-level concepts like topology, to inspire us to stick with math over the long term. The white-haired Mr. Tunney guided English classes through dense classics like *All the King's Men* with uncommon energy drawn from his infectious love for the books he taught. When teachers like that retired, the entire community mourned.

When I began reporting on education in 2007, I quickly learned how lucky I had been. Most American schools are socioeconomically segregated, very little like the integrated schools I attended in Ossining, where highly qualified teachers aspired to build long careers, and to teach both middle-class and poor children. In 2005, the average high school graduation rate in the nation's fifty largest cities was just 53 percent, compared to 71 percent in the suburbs. International assessments conducted by the Organisation for Economic Co-operation and Development, or OECD, show American schools are producing young adults who are less able than our counterparts in other developed nations to write coherently, read with understanding, and use numbers in day-to-day life. Even our most educated citizens, those with graduate degrees, are below world averages in math and computer literacy (though above average in reading). I do not believe schools are good enough the way they are. Nor do I believe that poverty and ethnic diversity prevent the United States from doing better educationally. Teachers and schools alone cannot solve our crisis of inequality and long-term unemployment, yet we know from the experience of nations like Poland that we don't have to eradicate economic insecurity to improve our schools.

What I do believe is that education reformers today should learn from the mistakes of history. We must focus less on how to rank and fire teachers and more on how to make day-to-day teaching an attractive, challenging job that intelligent, creative, and ambitious people will gravitate toward. We must quiet the teacher wars and support ordinary teachers in improving their skills, what economist Jonah Rockoff, who studies teacher quality, calls "moving the big middle" of the profession. While the ingenuity and fortitude of exemplary teachers throughout history are inspiring, many of their stories, which you will read in this book, shed light on the political irrationality of focusing obsessively on rating teachers, while paying far less attention to the design of the larger public education and social welfare systems in which they work.

To understand those systems, we will begin our historical journey in Massachusetts during the first half of the nineteenth century. Advocates for universal public education, called common schoolers, were challenged by antitax activists. The détente between these two groups redefined American teaching as low-paid (or even volunteer) missionary work for women, a reality we have lived with for two centuries—as the children of slaves and immigrants flooded into the classroom, as we struggled with and then gave up on desegregating our schools, and as we began, in the late twentieth century, to confront a future in which young Americans without college degrees were increasingly disadvantaged in the labor market and thus relied on schools and teachers, more than ever before, to help them access a middle-class life.

Chapter One

"Missionary Teachers"

THE COMMON SCHOOLS MOVEMENT
AND THE FEMINIZATION OF AMERICAN TEACHING

In 1815 a religious revival swept the Litchfield Female Academy, a private school in a genteel Connecticut town.

In those years, there were few truly "public" schools in the United States. The U.S. Constitution did not mention education as a right (it still doesn't), and school attendance was not compulsory. Schools were generally organized by town councils, local churches, urban charitable societies, or—in more remote parts of the country—ad hoc groups of neighbors. A mix of tuition payments and local tax dollars supported the schools. Two-thirds of American students attended one-room schoolhouses, where as many as seventy children from age five through sixteen were educated together, usually by just one overwhelmed schoolteacher, who was nearly always male. School was held only twelve weeks per year, six in the summer and six in the winter. There were rarely any textbooks on hand, and the most frequent assignment was to memorize and recite Bible passages. Naughty children were whipped or made to sit in the corner wearing a dunce cap.

At Litchfield, a relative island of privilege, girl after girl loudly and publicly achieved the state of "conversion" expected of all fervent Calvinists, a transcendent, nearly manic period in which God's plan for one's life would be revealed, setting an individual upon her predestined path toward heaven. Conversion tended to be catching, like the flu. But fourteen-year-old Catharine Beecher refused to convert. This made her conspicuous, because she was the daughter of a celebrity preacher.

Her father, Lyman Beecher, first came to the public's attention after he delivered a passionate sermon against dueling in the wake of Alexander Hamilton's death in 1804 at the hands of Aaron Burr. He cast himself as a moral compass on matters both religious and secular. In sermons and articles, he opposed Catholic immigration and the spread of liberal Unitarianism, supported the gradual elimination of slavery and the "re-colonization" of black Americans to Africa, and celebrated American expansion into the West as a sign that God intended the Protestant United States to lead as "a light to the nations"—a phrase he borrowed from the prophet Isaiah. In 1830 he would speak out against President Andrew Jackson's brutal relocation of Native American families from the Southeast to land west of the Mississippi River.

Those views were fairly liberal for their time. Lyman Beecher's faith was not. He preached predestination, the doctrine that holds that a baby is fated from birth for either salvation or damnation, and that his deeds on earth can hardly change the outcome. In riveting sermons, Beecher would sketch a vivid portrait of the death and perdition of sinners, their brows sweating and extremities growing cold as they sunk down to hell.

Catharine Beecher hated disappointing her father, to whom she was very close. He would even boast that Catharine was "the best boy he had"—quite a statement coming from a man with seven sons! But she found Bible study "irksome and disagreeable" and chafed against the notion of original sin. How could an unformed child be guilty of all of humanity's past corruptions? She was far more passionate about poetry than religion; several of her verses were published in journals while she was still a teenager. She earned every academic distinction and then took up the only job considered socially respectable for a young woman of her class: She worked as a finishing school teacher of the "domestic arts"—needlepoint, knitting, piano playing, and painting. In truth, Catharine hated those feminine pastimes. She would later lament the "mournful, despairing hours" she had once devoted to such activities, which were thought to raise a girl's value on the marriage market. But for Catharine, wage earning was an important goal, at least until marriage. Her mother had died when she was sixteen, and Lyman Beecher quickly remarried. The preacher had a dozen younger children to support, including the future author of *Uncle Tom's Cabin,* Harriet Beecher Stowe.

At a party in the spring of 1822, when Catharine Beecher was twenty-one years old, she met Horace Mann. He had grown up on a farm in Franklin, Massachusetts, southwest of Boston, and was at the time a twenty-six-year-old law student in Litchfield, rumored to have political ambitions. Mann had already heard of Beecher: She was the famous preacher's iconoclastic daughter, and a published poet, too. Up to this point in his life, Mann, though tall and handsome, had demonstrated almost no interest in women, even pretty ones. (His roommate at Brown University would recall Mann as someone so self-serious that he had committed "not a single instance" of youthful misbehavior.) But Beecher was different. With tightly wound curls framing a square-jawed face, she conveyed a certain harshness, which she had inherited from her father. The young teacher was fascinating not because she was beautiful, but because she was intelligent.

Beecher and Mann traded thoughts that evening on the romantic novels of Sir Walter Scott; later Mann regretted that the conversation had produced only "truisms" on his part, nothing at all "tremendous" to demonstrate the depth of his ideas. But no matter, for Beecher was already engaged to a far more accomplished man: Alexander Metcalf Fisher, a math prodigy who at the age of twenty-four had become Yale's youngest-ever tenured professor, and had already written several well-regarded textbooks. Fisher had grown up a few farms away from Mann in Franklin, and Mann gossiped in a letter home to his sister that Beecher "is reputed a lady of superior intellect" and would "probably make the Professor a very good help-mate."

Impressed as he was with Beecher, Mann had underestimated her. She was destined not to be a housewife, but to assume her father's mantle as a leading public intellectual. Together, she and Horace Mann would define public education as America's new, more gentle church, and female teachers as the ministers of American morality.

———

Less than two weeks after Beecher met Mann, her fiancé drowned in a shipwreck off the coast of Ireland. Fisher had been on his way to Europe for a yearlong tour of the continent's universities, to study alongside the leading scientists of the day. They had planned to marry the following spring. Now Beecher's future was uncertain. "I lie down in sorrow and awake in heaviness, and go mourning all day long," she wrote. Following several months of confinement in her father's home, she fled to the Fisher family farm in Franklin. Alexander's parents asked if Beecher might tutor their younger children, a teenage boy and two small girls, who had lost not only their beloved eldest brother, but also their academic mentor.

Upon her arrival, a depressed Beecher retreated to the Fisher attic, where she searched obsessively through her dead fiancé's diaries and letters. She was surprised by what she found. The couple's courtship had been stilted and almost all their time together chaperoned. It turned out she had not known her fiancé very well at all. Alexander Fisher's diaries laid bare a tortured soul who, at the age of nineteen, endured a case of "delirium," so torn was he between the obligations of religion and his attraction to his true passions, math and science. During this episode, Fisher suffered from delusions of grandiosity, believing he could deploy mathematical problem solving to save the universe from sudden destruction. When the mania passed, Fisher returned to his scientific studies at Yale, chiding himself for a lack of religious faith, which he described as "an incapacity . . . of making moral truth the subject of steady contemplation." Like Beecher, Fisher had devoted years of tedious Sundays to devotional study, only to regretfully conclude in 1819, when he was a professor, that his spiritual life was "a blank," and he would never achieve conversion. Around this time, he stopped keeping a journal and devoted himself full-time to planning lessons, writing textbooks, and counseling his Yale students.

Beecher was moved by Fisher's frustrations with traditional religion—so similar to her own—and by his eventual decision to commit himself fully to a career as a scholar and teacher. She felt certain, for the first time in her young life, that predestination was false. Fisher had been a good man—a saved man—not because he had converted, but because he had done good in his life. Beecher wrote to her father: "The heart must have something to rest upon, and if it is not God, it will be the world."

Beecher's new conviction that public works could serve society as well as private faith set her off on a career in education. As a girl, she had been denied the academic opportunities granted to Fisher to study classical languages, master higher-order mathematics, and immerse herself in contemporary political thought. The Litchfield Female Academy had been organized around religious piety, public shaming, and social positioning. Each morning, the students would queue up to submit to a barrage of leading questions posed by the commanding headmistress: *Have you been patient in acquiring your lessons? Have you spoken any indecent word or by any action discovered a want of feminine delicacy? Have you combed your hair with a fine-tooth comb and cleaned your teeth every morning? Have you eaten any green fruit during the week?* Every girl was required to keep a daily journal of her spiritual faults; entries notable for either their righteousness or depravity were read aloud to a Saturday morning general assembly—with names attached. The school's pedagogical techniques were stultifying, and entirely typical of the era. In class, the headmistress merely read aloud to her pupils; for homework, the girls regurgitated in their journals all the trivia they could remember: the longitudes and latitudes of various countries, the dates of major battles, the lineages of British kings. Math instruction ceased before algebra or trigonometry, while chemistry and physics were neglected entirely.

Poring over Fisher's notebooks and lesson plans, Beecher was exposed for the first time to philosophy and logic. With guidance from her younger brother Edward, who had been educated at Andover and Yale, she was able to grasp the challenging material quickly and impart it to her pupils. Didn't all girls deserve the opportunity Beecher was now offering Fisher's sisters—to undertake broad intellectual pursuits? And if Beecher could successfully learn and teach serious subject matter—not just the "domestic arts"—why couldn't other smart young women?

Most crucially for the history of American education, Beecher came to believe that women were likely to be the most effective teachers not only of girls, but of boys as well. A middle-class lady like herself, without immediate marriage prospects, faced a strictly limited landscape of opportunity. She could not enroll in college (Mount Holyoke and Oberlin did not become the first American colleges to admit women until the 1830s), nor study for the ministry (it was closed to women), nor train to become a doctor or lawyer (medical and law schools were male only), nor set out in business on her own (banks rarely lent to women). The more Beecher thought about it, the more it seemed that teaching was the one profession in which a woman could gain "influence, respectability, and independence" without venturing outside "the prescribed boundaries of feminine modesty," she wrote. Beecher was a lifelong opponent of women's suffrage; she thought politics a dirty game that would corrupt women's God-given virtue. But that virtue, she thought, made women the ideal educators. Beecher saw the home and the school as intertwined, two naturally feminine realms in which women could nurture the next generation. "Woman, whatever are her relations in life, is necessarily the guardian of the nursery, the companion of childhood, and the constant model of imitation," she wrote in her "Essay on the Education of Female Teachers." "It is her hand that first stamps impressions on the immortal spirit, that must remain forever." Historian Redding Sugg dubbed this the "motherteacher" ideal—the notion that teaching and mothering were much the same job, done in different settings.

Just a year after her fiancé's death, Beecher began to put her new theories into practice. In 1823 she deployed her father's social connections to establish the Hartford Female Seminary, and within a year had attracted a hundred students from throughout the eastern United States and as far away as Canada, many of whom hoped to become teachers. Beecher's school embraced a level of academic rigor unheard of at elite girls' academies of the period; students took classes in Latin, Greek, algebra, chemistry, modern languages, and moral and political philosophy. Beecher opposed rote memorization and overt academic competition; her school gave out no awards, which she believed inflated students' vanity when they should be motivated to learn by simple love for God, their parents, and their country. Beecher believed in hands-on learning, through field trips and science experiments. Her educational philosophy was far ahead of its time. It would be another seventy years before John Dewey would famously articulate similar notions about teaching the "whole child." Some of the school's graduates launched new schools based on Beecher's ideas.

The Hartford Female Seminary was controversial. Some local parents objected to the teaching of classics, which they believed inflated their daughters' expectations beyond reason, since these girls were likely to lead rather monotonous, domestic lives as wives and mothers. "I would rather my daughters would go to school and sit down and do nothing than to study philosophy," one father wrote in a letter to the *Connecticut Courant* newspaper. "These branches fill young Misses with vanity to the degree that they are above attending to the more useful parts of an education."

In her 1827 essay "Female Education," Beecher responded directly to such critics, rejecting the conventional wisdom that the only reason for a girl to attend school was to refine her deportment in order to snare a husband. "A lady should study, not to *shine,* but to *act,*" she wrote. "She is to read books, not to talk of them, but to bring the improvement they furnish. . . . The great uses of study are to enable her to regulate her own mind and to be useful to others," primarily as a teacher.

Beecher and her school attracted so much attention that by the late 1820s she was spending almost no time teaching and was instead traveling the nation on the lecture circuit, speaking to ladies' church groups and at libraries and social clubs. She had become America's first media darling school reformer. By this time, Beecher had declared she would never marry. She lived during a cultural moment of high anxiety about the proper role for unmarried women—"old maids" who, without husbands or children, were often thought to be unable to contribute productively to society. In her speeches, she would cite U.S. Census figures showing that there were 14,000 more unmarried women than unmarried men in the Northeast. At least one-quarter of these single women, Beecher guessed, might want to become "missionary teachers," migrating west to educate the two million "ignorant and neglected American children" of the frontier, whose parents presumably lacked the educational commitment of the New England elite and needed to be prodded into establishing village schools.

Well before most states or territories began raising taxes to fund education, Beecher summoned up the terrifying specter of the French Revolution to make the argument for universal schooling. In her speech "The Duty of American Women to Their Country," she described education provided by female teachers as the best bulwark against a violent uprising by the underclass. The French Revolution, she warned, had been "a war of the common people upon the classes above them" in which "the wealthy, educated, and noble are down" while "the poor, the ignorant, the base hold the offices, wealth, and power. Everything is mismanaged. Everything goes wrong." Beecher had imagined a way for elite young women to go west, not as wives or mothers, but with a patriotic duty to their young, expanding nation—to educate the masses for democracy. These lady teachers would be motivated by "energy, discretion, and self-denying benevolence," she said, taking inspiration from Catholic nuns. With teaching as an option, Beecher argued, women could choose to marry only if they fell in love, not because marriage was the only socially acceptable role.

It was radical to suggest women should teach in co-ed schools. In the early nineteenth century, only 10 percent of American women worked outside the home. Because the assumption was that public work of any kind was degrading to a middle-class woman, Beecher had to make the case that opening the teaching profession to women would be good for students and society—not just for the women themselves. Women, she posited, would make better teachers than the men currently presiding over most classrooms. In fact, she helped ignite a moral panic about male teachers. In her famous 1846 lecture, "The Evils Suffered by American Women and American Children," she enthusiastically cited a New York State report on local schools that called male teachers "incompetent" and "intemperate . . . coarse, hard, unfeeling men, too lazy or stupid" to be entrusted with the care of children. Ichabod Crane, the protagonist of Washington Irving's 1820 classic short story "The Legend of Sleepy Hollow," epitomized the type. Described as a sort of well-intentioned petty tyrant lording it over the children at a poorly maintained single-room schoolhouse through the generous use of a birch rod, Crane is "tarrying" away his youth before, he assumes, beginning a more illustrious career. He fancies himself an intellectual, but in truth, the schoolmaster is a superstitious simpleton.

Pious young women seemed preferable to the hapless Ichabod Cranes of the world. "I simply ask," Beecher said, "if it would not be better to put the thousands of men who are keeping school for young children into the mills, and employ the women to train the children?" There was another argument, too. Female workers were cheap. Beecher openly pitched hiring female teachers as a potential money-saving strategy for state and local governments launching compulsory schooling for the first time. "[A] woman needs support only for herself" while "a man requires support for himself and a family," she wrote, appealing to the stereotype that women with families did not do wage-earning work—a false assumption even in the early nineteenth century, when many working-class wives and mothers labored on family farms or took in laundry and sewing to make ends meet. Black women almost universally worked, whether as slaves in the South or as domestic servants or laundresses in the North. What was truly new about Beecher's conception of teaching was that it pushed middle-class white women, in particular, into public view as workers outside the home.

Male teachers of this period may have been less cruel or stupid than frustrated. They were struggling with educational neglect, such as the short school year and lack of funding for decent classrooms and school supplies. Many promising young men of Beecher's generation tried teaching school but quickly became disgruntled by the conditions under which they were forced to work—conditions that Beecher, who attended and then taught in elite private schools, never experienced firsthand. At the age of eighteen, Herman Melville spent a winter as a teacher in a remote part of rural Massachusetts, wrangling thirty poorly behaved students of every age and size, all of them crammed into a one-room schoolhouse that had no supplies, tiny windows, and bad ventilation. He boarded with a local family and earned $11 per month, about the same salary as a farm laborer and half that of a skilled mechanic. These conditions left Melville "anxious for some other occupation," he admitted. Henry David Thoreau found his two weeks teaching public school in Canton, Massachusetts, so bleak that he concluded that classroom education—as opposed to education from "real life"—was almost always a futile effort, one in which children were subject to "the process, not of enlightening, but of obfuscating the mind."

As much as men were frustrated with the working conditions in schools, such concerns were not the real reason the profession transitioned from college-educated males toward the young female moral educators envisioned by Catharine Beecher. Antitax sentiment played a more important role, as did the political evolution and influence of Horace Mann.

In the years after Horace Mann left Litchfield, he established a successful legal practice, and in 1827 he was elected to the lower house of the Massachusetts legislature. As part of the political movement that would become the Whig Party—a marriage between social liberals and fiscally cautious northeastern business interests—Mann supported the establishment of insane asylums and schools for the blind and deaf. He was a critic of the death penalty and wanted to shut down lotteries, which he considered unchristian. On August 11 and 12, 1834, an anti-Catholic mob torched an Ursuline convent and school in Charlestown, Massachusetts, burning it to the ground. Mann was appointed to lead a citizens committee investigating what he called the "horrible outrage" of the arson. Several months after this high-profile assignment, Mann was elected to the state senate. He had patrons in the railroad industry, as well as political support from Boston intellectuals, so he focused on social issues around which these two constituencies could converge, especially education.

Mann had become a devotee of phrenology, the analysis of people's physical characteristics, especially the sizes and shapes of their heads, in order to determine their moral and intellectual nature. Phrenologists like the Scottish philosopher George Combe (after whom Mann named one of his sons) characterized Mediterraneans as hotheaded and lazy, blacks as brutish, and northern Europeans as hardworking and intelligent. During the nineteenth century, phrenology was considered a progressive ideology. Its proponents believed that each individual's deficiencies could be identified, then ameliorated through schooling; these methods, it was thought, would eradicate poverty and crime in just a few generations.

Mann found phrenology appealing, in part as a replacement for religious doctrine. When he was a young teenager, his brother Stephen drowned horsing around in a local pond, where he was playing hooky when he was supposed to have been in church. The next Sunday the town preacher, a fire-and-brimstone Calvinist, sermonized on the incident, warning the children of Franklin that they too would die and suffer in eternal hell if they sinned as Stephen Mann had. Sitting in the pews that day were Horace, his two surviving siblings, and their mother, who during the sermon let out an audible groan of pain. Horace Mann never forgot the preacher's act of cruelty toward his grieving family, and, like Catharine Beecher, struggled to accept Puritan notions of predestination and original sin, with their implication that people could not improve themselves.

Unlike strict Puritanism, phrenology held that individuals—even the poor, the drunk, or the criminal, like those who perpetrated the convent arson—could save themselves through education. If that was true, Mann the politician could promote funding schools as the primary means of improving society, while overlooking more controversial interventions. Biographer Jonathan Messerli writes that as Mann became more and more fascinated by school reform, he largely ignored his colleagues in the state legislature who called for regulating the free market more aggressively, through preventing industrialists from seizing public land, establishing monopolies, and paying low wages. Of course, the miseries of nineteenth-century poverty had as much to do with dismal working conditions and low pay as with lack of schooling. Historian Arthur Schlesinger called Mann's impulse "moral reform." Whigs, Schlesinger stated, "saw things simply. They ignored the relationship between ethical conduct and the social setting," and believed social improvement was "a personal problem" more than an economic or structural one.

In 1837 Mann helped lead a Whig push to establish a state board of education to oversee local schools and require compulsory enrollment for all children. This was the flowering of the national common schools movement, a state-by-state effort to fund universal elementary education. From the state senate floor, Mann asked his fellow legislators to commit $2 million to achieve these goals, arguing that through education "[t]hose orders and conditions of life among us now stamped with inferiority are capable of rising to the common level, and of ascending if that level ascends." He complained that Bostonians had paid a collective $50,000 for tickets to see the European ballerina Fanny Elssler, known "for the scantiness of her wardrobe." This was the same amount of money, total, paid to Massachusetts teachers each year. What did society value more—salacious dancing or schools?

The legislature appropriated $1 million for the new board of education, half of what Mann asked for. This was an early lesson in the broad appeal of the common schools movement—as long as costs could be contained. Mann left the state senate to become Massachusetts's secretary of education, the first such position in the United States. Overflowing with enthusiasm for his new position, he undertook a self-guided study of the most important educational theories then circulating in the Western world. Like many American reformers, he was intrigued by the French philosopher Victor Cousin's 1831 report on Prussian public schools. With the goal of creating a unified, educated, and—above all—morally superior citizenry, the Prussian monarchy had prioritized improving the quality of its teacher corps. In 1811 Prussia issued a decree banning teachers from holding secondary jobs and discouraging the practice of teachers boarding with local families, which the government thought compromised teachers' dignity. (Both of these remained common practices in the United States well into the twentieth century.) By 1819, Prussian law guaranteed teachers a living wage and a pension paid to their families after their deaths. Schoolhouses were to be "properly laid out, kept in repair and warmed," and local governments were required to provide "furniture, books, pictures, instruments, and all things necessary for the lessons and exercises." To train teachers, Prussia established normal schools, which admitted both male and female students between the ages of sixteen and eighteen, called normalites. They spent two years studying pedagogy and the subjects they would teach, and then passed a third year as an apprentice teacher in a real school.

Considering the limited funds available to the Massachusetts Board of Education, Mann decided to focus on two projects: first, making sure each district school was equipped with at least a rudimentary library, and second, opening Prussian-style normal schools to train teachers. His hopes for these new teacher training academies were nearly ecstatic: "I believe Normal schools to be a new instrumentality in the advancement of the race," he wrote. By 1840 Mann had opened three normal schools, and by 1870, twenty-two states had followed suit. The best early normal school was probably the very first, in Lexington, Massachusetts (now Framingham State College). Unlike Prussian normal schools, it was open only to female applicants because they would be cheaper than men for the state to employ as teachers. The normalites were supposed to spend three years taking classes in algebra, moral philosophy, and "the art of teaching." They practiced their skills in a model classroom, with thirty real students between the ages of six and ten. A celebrated veteran teacher named Cyrus Peirce was the principal of the program. He described in his journal how he helped the apprentice teachers learn their craft:

> Twice every day the Principal of the Normal School goes into the model school for general observation and direction, spending from one half hour to one hour each visit. In these visits, I either sit and watch the general operations of the school, or listen attentively to a particular teacher and her class, or [teach] a class myself, and let the teacher be the listener and observer. After the exercises have closed, I comment upon what I have seen and heard before the teachers, telling them what I deem good, and what faulty, either in their doctrine or their practice, their theory or their manner. . . . In these several ways, I attempt to combine, as well as I can, theory and practice, precept and example.

It is uncanny how this routine describes today's acknowledged best practices in teacher training and professional development, with a mentor teacher acting as a thoughtful instructional coach. Alas, most normal schools across the United States had little of the curricular rigor of the Lexington normal school and were especially lacking in opportunities to practice teaching in real-world conditions. Up through the early twentieth century, normals were considered an alternative to academic high school or college, with far less prestige. They enrolled many young girls who were straight out of primary school themselves, with the equivalent of just a sixth- or seventh-grade education. Between the 1920s and 1960s, as the high school diploma became more universal and states passed laws requiring teachers to earn bachelor's degrees, often in education, many normal schools transitioned into regional state colleges with lower admissions standards than flagship state universities. Most American teachers continue to enter the classroom after studying education at the undergraduate level at nonselective colleges. In many ways, we are still living with the teacher training system the common schools movement created.

By the early 1840s, four times as many new Massachusetts teachers were female than male. Not everyone was happy about this shift. The Boston masters, an association of university-educated male high school teachers, complained that bringing normal school alumnae into the classroom would weaken academic standards and school discipline, and that adolescent boys would run amok. Mann responded by adopting the ideas of his old acquaintance Catharine Beecher, offering both pragmatic and idealistic arguments for employing female teachers. In his eleventh annual report as secretary of education, he noted that replacing male teachers with women had saved the state $11,000, which was "double the expense of the three State Normal Schools." Hence—a bargain for taxpayers! Mann depicted these cost-effective female educators as angelic public servants motivated by Christian faith; wholly unselfish, self-abnegating, and morally pure. He said that careers in politics, the military, and journalism ought to remain closed to women, who were too innocent to wade into those "black and sulfurous" spheres. Teaching, Mann argued, was woman's true calling, one that would take advantage of all her natural, God-given talents as a nurturer, whether or not she had biological children of her own:

> As a teacher of schools . . . how divinely does she come, her head encircled with a halo of heavenly light, her feet sweetening the earth on which she treads, and the celestial radiance of her benignity making vice begin its work of repentance through very envy of the beauty of virtue!

Mann's descriptions of the perfect female teacher sounded very much like his eulogies of his late wife, Charlotte, whom he mourned acutely for nearly a decade after her death at the age of twenty-three, just two years after their wedding. In an early letter to Mary Peabody, who would become his second wife, Mann wrote that Charlotte had "purified my conceptions of purity and beautified the ideal of every excellence . . . Her sympathy with others [sic] pain seemed to be quicker and stronger than the sensation of her own; and with a sensibility that would sigh at a crushed flower, there was a spirit of endurance, that would uphold a martyr."

This rose-tinged conception of women teachers' virtue spread from Horace Mann and Catharine Beecher throughout the common schools movement. An 1842 manual for local schools produced by an anonymous New York philanthropist was unapologetic about promoting female teachers as the cornerstone of "a cheap system," positing that the most talented women would be willing to work for half of what men of the "poorest capacity" would demand. But the authors made sure to add that "women have a native tact in the management of very young minds which is rarely possessed by men . . . they have a peculiar power of awakening the sympathies of children, and inspiring them with a desire to excel."

Given widespread nineteenth-century assumptions about women's lack of intellectual capacity, there was an explicit connection between the promotion of non-college-educated female teachers and the idea, influenced by phrenology, that American public schools should focus more on developing children's character than on increasing their academic knowledge beyond basic literacy and numeracy. Although both Mann and Beecher had enjoyed studying

Latin, Greek, and the sciences, their public pronouncements on education rarely devoted much attention to the academic curriculum, especially from the 1840s forward, as the common schools movement began to attract more support from influential politicians and business leaders, the kind of men more concerned with educating the next generation of voters and workers than in fostering intellectuals. Early in her career at the Hartford Female Seminary, Beecher had fought to win for elite young women access to the classical liberal arts curriculum. But when it came to setting the agenda for public schools for the masses, she seemed to feel differently about what the purposes of an education should be. "Education in this country will never reach its highest end," she wrote in her autobiography, "till the care of the physical, social, and moral interests shall take precedence of mere intellectual development and acquirements." Mann agreed. "The teaching of A, B, C, and the multiplication table has no quality of sacredness in it," he said in an 1839 lecture. Instead, the purpose of schooling was to lead students' "affections outward in good-will towards men, and upward in reverence to God."

This value system, in which morality was given more weight than intellect, set the new American public school system apart from some of its Western European counterparts. Between 1830 and 1900, the American teacher corps feminized much faster than did the teaching forces in Germany or France, which remained about 50 percent male. Prussia's comparatively generous teacher pay and pensions, as well as gender-segregated schools, helped keep men in the classroom (since boys' schools were more attractive to male teachers). In France, an additional factor was at play: the government's insistence that public schools maintain rigorous liberal arts standards. For the French philosopher Victor Cousin, the one failing of the Prussian system was that it was more concerned with imparting religiosity than with teaching secular knowledge of languages, literature, and history. "Classical studies," Cousin wrote, "keep alive the sacred tradition of the moral and intellectual life of the human race. To curtail or enfeeble such studies would, in my eyes, be an act of barbarism, a crime against all true and high civilization, and in some sort an act of high treason against humanity."

Horace Mann referred to this intellectual critique of moral

schooling as "the European fallacy." He considered a French-style liberal arts education irrelevant to the masses in a popular democracy, where the most important task facing any man was, as a voter, to assess the moral character of candidates for political office. As he aged, the leader of the common schools movement grew increasingly anti-intellectual in his worldview. His scorn for Nathaniel Hawthorne, author of *The Scarlet Letter* and one of the first truly great American writers, is evidence of this trait in full flower. Mann haughtily disapproved of Hawthorne, a bohemian who was in love with Mary Peabody Mann's younger sister, Sophia. The young couple scandalized Boston society by reputedly lying in bed together (albeit fully clothed) before they were married. In a letter to a friend, Mann confessed that he did not understand Hawthorne's writing, adding, "I should rather have built up the blind asylum than to have written *Hamlet*." This view of art and social good as in opposition to each other—with intellectual pursuits coded as somewhat decadent—contained more than a kernel of the Puritan ideology Mann believed he had rejected in his adolescence.

In the late 1830s, Mann and Catharine Beecher began to carry on an occasional correspondence about Beecher's newest project, the Board of National Popular Education. The Board, a sort of prototype of Teach for America, would make Beecher's vision of a corps of "missionary" female teachers a reality. It aimed to locate well-bred, evangelical young women from the Northeast and send them west to open frontier schools. It took Beecher until 1847 to raise enough philanthropic funds to recruit the Board's first class of seventy volunteer teachers. In their month-long training, conducted by Beecher, the women learned some basic pedagogy, were warned about the primitive living conditions in the West, and, most of all, were encouraged to act as "a new source of moral power" in frontier communities. If no Protestant Sunday school existed in their settlements, they were expected to establish one, in addition to teaching secular school during the week.

The young women were dispatched to Illinois, Indiana, Iowa, Wisconsin, Michigan, Minnesota, Kentucky, and Tennessee. Conditions in the territories were difficult, and during the first decade of this work, twenty-one teachers died. Some recruits found that despite their best intentions, communities were too poor to build schoolhouses or heat them in the winter. Some parents objected to religious proselytizing by Board recruits, and others complained that the young women had too little teaching experience. One recruit became the only teacher in a rural school serving children aged five through seventeen. "Not one can read intelligibly," she lamented in a letter to Beecher. "They have no idea of the proprieties of the school-room or of study, and I am often at a loss to know what to do for them. . . . Though it is winter, some are without stockings and no shoes."

Recruits boarded with local families and shared bedrooms with their students. There was little privacy, and sometimes not even candlelight or basic sanitation. Yet many of the teachers remained grateful for the opportunity and experienced modest success. One recruit reported that she was teaching forty-five students in a "small log house . . . The people here are *very* ignorant; very few of them can either read or write, but they wish to have their children taught." Religion sustained these young women. A recruit who taught both secular and Sunday school in Minnesota wrote to Beecher that despite being broke and suffering from a two-month fever, "the refinements of society, the wealth or honor of earth, cannot attract me from this isolated spot so long as God has work for me here. I have never had the first regret at having come."

After rebelling against the harsh Calvinism of their parents, the tightly knit first generation of American education reformers tended to see schools as secular churches: community centers where any child could be improved—even religiously "saved"—through education. Mann and Beecher believed it was more important to teach a child good deeds than good doctrine; to focus less on the details of literature or mathematics than to create faithful, decent, socially adept young men and women—people who would resist the mob rule represented by the French Revolution and the Ursuline convent arson. Teaching was promoted as the female equivalent of the ministry: a profession whose prestige would be rooted not in worldly rewards, such as money or political influence, but in the personal satisfaction that came from serving others.

Yet during an era of deep bias against women's intellectual and professional capabilities, the feminization of teaching wrought by the common schoolers carried an enormous cost: Teaching became understood less as a career than as a philanthropic vocation or romantic calling. The common schools movement succeeded in attracting political support in part because of its emphasis on accessible moral education over more academic concerns. But this left a number of important educational problems unresolved. Should schools prepare students for particular occupations, or give all children the exact same education? If teachers were expected to be the chief architects of their pupils' moral lives, what implications did this have for the role of parents—and was it reasonable to expect the influence of teachers to outweigh the influence of the family? How would common schools founded as purveyors of WASP morality deal with increasingly diverse student populations, soon not only Catholics but free blacks and immigrant Jews as well?

The gadfly Boston journalist Orestes Brownson proved prescient in his skepticism toward the common schools movement. A convert to Catholicism, Brownson worried about Protestant reformers' attempts to make public school teachers double as missionaries, and thought parents should exercise more control over community schools. In general, he subscribed to a more pragmatic vision of the role of the school in society, arguing it was unlikely teachers could make much headway in defeating poverty as long as workers lacked vocational training and labor rights. He wrote:

> Education, such as it is, is ever going on. Our children are educated in the streets, by the influence of their associates . . . in the bosom of the family, by the love and gentleness or wrath and fretfulness of parents, by the passions or affections they see manifested, the conversations to which they listen, and above all by the general pursuits, habits, and moral tone of the community. In all these are schoolrooms and schoolmasters sending forth scholars educated for good or for evil or, what

is more likely, for a little of both. The real question for us to ask is not, Shall our children be educated? but, To what end shall they be educated, and by what means? What is the kind of education needed, and how shall it be furnished?

Beecher and Mann believed morality was the end of public education, and female teachers were its means. In fact, there was little public consensus on what American common schooling should look like. Subsequent generations of education reformers—and women's rights leaders—would angrily challenge the status quo Mann and Beecher had wrought: of masses of low-paid, poorly educated "motherteachers," prioritizing faith over academic learning.

How much, if any, of the teacher wage shortage + fair treatment stems from this 20th + 19th century idea of education being feminine and, therefore, being cheaper or lower level? Could this be systemic sexism that has broadened to the whole teaching profession?

Chapter Two

"Repressed Indignation"

THE FEMINIST CHALLENGE TO AMERICAN EDUCATION

In 1838, eighteen-year-old Susan B. Anthony was away at Quaker boarding school when she received a letter informing her that a childhood friend had married a middle-aged widower with six children. Letters home had to be edited by a teacher for moral content, so Susan took her true feelings to her diary: "I should think any female would rather live and die an old maid."

A few months later, Anthony withdrew from school. Her father's cotton mill had gone bust, and he could no longer afford tuition. She began working as a teacher in village schools near her family's upstate New York home. By the time she moved away, eight years later, she had turned down at least two marriage proposals. She liked working and had secured an exciting new job, as head of girls' education at the Canajoharie Academy in Palatine Bridge, New York, where her uncle served on the school board. With her $110 annual salary, more money than she had ever had before, Anthony binged on high fashion, including a dress made of purple merino wool at $2 per yard, an $8 gray fox muff, and a $5.50 white silk hat that "makes the villagers stare." In a letter home she wondered (a little churlishly) if her sisters did not "feel rather sad because they are married and can not have nice clothes."

At age twenty-six, Anthony was exhilarated by life on her own, attending balls and the circus for the first time. Always a Quaker—if a somewhat lapsed one—she founded a local women's temperance organization. Yet she took her teaching job seriously and resented the fact that she earned less than her male colleagues. Anthony wrote to her mother in November 1846 that although her students' parents celebrated her "diligent" teaching, and she had recruited four new pupils to the school, she would not receive a raise. "That salary business runs in my head, I can tell you," she complained. She immersed herself in the work, giving special attention to one fifteen-year-old girl who had what Anthony considered an unfair reputation for being "unmanageable. I hope to find her otherwise." Soon enough, the child regarded her young teacher as "a sort of cousin," Anthony reported, and began to "carry herself rather strait."

Over the next two years, Anthony's enthusiasm for teaching waned. She admired the headmaster who had hired her, but when he retired in 1848, she disliked the new boss, a nineteen-year-old fond of corporal punishment. Though Anthony had been teaching for a decade, her gender disqualified her for a larger role at the school—it was unthinkable that a woman would supervise men. Her stagnant salary meant she was still living in a tiny, cold room in a relative's home. In May she wrote to her parents that she now considered teaching a "penance . . . A weariness has come over me that the short spring vacation did not in the least dispel. I have a pleasant school of 20 scholars, but I have to manufacture the interest duty compels me to exhibit. I am anxious they should learn, but feel almost to shrink from the task."

Like many extraordinary nineteenth-century women, Anthony had an unusually supportive father. "I have only to say," Daniel Anthony responded, "that when you get tired of teaching, try something else."

In 1848 Anthony moved back in with her parents and tried to figure out what that something else might be. Through her family's involvement in New York State temperance and antislavery circles, she was becoming aware of the growing women's rights movement, which had held its first national conference that summer in the Finger Lakes town of Seneca Falls.

The conference's chief organizer was a young mother named Elizabeth Cady Stanton, the daughter of an affluent and politically well-connected judge. In 1840 Stanton and her husband had traveled to the World Anti-Slavery Convention in London. She and another American female activist, Lucretia Mott, hoped to be recognized there as official delegates, but the male abolitionists refused to seat them. It was highly unusual for women to speak in front of large, mixed-gender crowds—especially on controversial topics—and many antislavery activists of both sexes worried that the radicalism of early feminism would hamstring the global abolitionist movement.

So Stanton came to the realization that without a social movement of their own, the cause of women's rights in America would not move forward. In planning the Seneca Falls Convention, she recruited not only female activists, but also important male abolitionists, including Frederick Douglass and a number of influential Quakers. The extraordinary manifesto that came out of Seneca Falls was called the Declaration of Sentiments. It borrowed the structure and vocabulary of the Declaration of Independence—"we hold these truths to be self-evident," "consent of the governed"—to argue in favor of women's suffrage, equal treatment before the law regardless of sex, and equal access to marital property and child custody.

Anthony read about the convention in her local newspaper, and for the cash-strapped young schoolteacher, so long denied raises and promotions, the Declaration's bracing opposition to gender-based pay must have been truly revelatory:

> The history of mankind is a history of repeated injuries and usurpations on the part of man toward woman, having in direct object the establishment of an absolute tyranny over her. . . .

> He has monopolized nearly all the profitable employments, and from those she is permitted to follow, she receives but a scanty remuneration.

> He closes against her all the avenues to wealth and distinction, which he considers most honorable to himself. As a teacher of theology, medicine, or law, she is not known.

He has denied her the facilities for obtaining a thorough
education—all colleges being closed against her.

The Declaration of Sentiments was a far cry from the writings of Catharine Beecher, who believed in empowering women to
teach, but who never expected—nor even wanted—women to win
broad equality with men beyond the schoolroom. By midcentury,
the terms of the debate over the so-called "Woman Question" had
changed. Women's rights activists were demanding admission to
male colleges and access to careers in medicine, the law, journalism, and even the ministry. They hoped to earn equal pay for their
efforts. For many of them, like Anthony, teaching had accelerated
their sense of outrage, by giving them a taste of independence and a
view of workplace discrimination.

In 1850, four-fifths of New York's eleven thousand teachers
were women, yet two-thirds of the state's $800,000 in teacher sala-
ries was paid to men. It was not unusual for male teachers to earn
twice as much as their female coworkers. These inequalities became
the subject of Anthony's first famous speech, which she made at age
thirty-three, at the August 1853 annual meeting of the New York
State Teachers' Association. Three hundred of the five hundred
teachers present in the Rochester convention hall were women. Yet
by the second evening of the conference, not a single woman had
risen to speak. When the conversation shifted to why teachers were
not accorded more respect by the public, Anthony could no longer
sit silently. She rose from her seat at the back of the room, cleared
her throat, and said loudly, "Mr. President."

The hall fell silent. "What will the lady have?" answered West
Point math professor Charles Davies, who was presiding over the
meeting in full military regalia, including a blue coat with conspicuous gilt buttons. He was appalled.

"I wish, sir, to speak to the question under discussion," Anthony
responded.

The hall erupted in shouts. For a half hour the male teachers
debated Anthony's simple request. The convention leaders eventually offered Anthony the floor, but only begrudgingly.

"It seems to me, gentlemen, that none of you quite comprehend the cause of the disrespect of which you complain," Anthony said. "Do you not see that so long as society says a woman is incompetent to be a lawyer, minister, or doctor, but has ample ability to be a teacher, that every man of you who chooses this profession tacitly acknowledges that he has no more brains than a woman? And this, too, is the reason that teaching is a less lucrative position, as here men must compete with the cheap labor of women?" A few other female teachers, emboldened by Anthony's performance, also rose to speak. One was Clarissa Northrop, a Rochester teacher and principal who reported that she earned $250 per year, while her brother, who held the same job at a different city public school, received $650.

As she left the hall that evening, Anthony was mobbed by well-wishers and horrified traditionalists alike; her speech made the next morning's newspapers. The *Rochester Daily Democrat* editorialized, "Whatever the schoolmasters might think of Miss Anthony, it was evident that she hit the nail on the head." On the conference's last day, Northrop introduced a resolution acknowledging women's low pay and committing the New York State Teachers Association "to remove the existing evil" of gender-based wage inequality among teachers. It narrowly passed.

Anthony became a full-time women's rights activist. When she met Beecher in 1856 at a Manhattan meeting of the American Woman's Educational Association, she found the older woman hopelessly outdated in her advocacy for women-only normal schools. Anthony believed it was critical both for women and for education that prospective teachers, no matter their sex, be trained at prestigious colleges and universities, which were then closed to women. Anthony wrote to Stanton about the frustrating encounter, calling Beecher's ideology "strange" and her rhetoric on female education "stupid" and "false"—more a play for respectability among conservative men than a serious effort to improve women's lives as teachers or raise the quality of public schools.

The differences between Beecher and the younger feminists were not just generational. Beecher had been raised by a mainstream minister. Anthony grew up among freethinking Quaker radicals. At the Quaker meetinghouse, women were allowed to preach. She had seen her father refuse to physically hand over his tax dollars when the tax collector visited, in pacifist protest against funding the U.S. military. So it was unsurprising that Anthony took a confrontational, theatrical approach to her activism.

Female teachers across New York hailed Anthony for taking on the seemingly quixotic causes of equal pay and access to male colleges for training. "I am glad that you will represent us at the Troy gathering," one wrote as another teachers conference approached. "You will bear with you the gratitude of very many teachers whose hearts are swelling with repressed indignation at the injustice which you expose." Anthony's efforts were about more than just rectifying the pay inequality she had endured as a teacher. She had noticed female educators tended to be enthusiastic about a broad array of social reform issues, not only women's rights, but also antislavery work and temperance. Yet because of their low wages, teachers had very little disposable income to donate to philanthropic causes, and local political groups founded by women often floundered. What's more, Anthony was becoming interested in labor politics. At women's rights conferences she had befriended Ernestine Rose, a Polish-born Jewish socialist whose magnetic oratory attracted attention wherever she traveled. Rose was a follower of Robert Owen, the Scottish factory owner and philosopher who believed in liberating female workers by providing them with a fair wage and full-time child care and education for their offspring. These social democratic ideas were deeply resonant for Anthony, who had always been fascinated by her father's cotton mill and the poor women who labored in it.

Being middle-class, teachers were just the most visible of a vast landscape of mistreated female workers—a group Anthony hoped would make up the core of the emerging women's suffrage movement. Women who worked outside the home had perhaps the most to gain from securing more political clout, which they could use to demand access to better jobs and higher pay. In a letter to other activists on how to advertise and promote women's rights meetings across New York, Anthony advised them to reach out to working women first. "I should like particular effort made to call out the teachers, seamstresses, and wage-earning women generally. It is for them, rather than for the wives and daughters of the rich, that I labor."

Anthony was valued in reform circles as a tireless organizer, but Stanton was considered the women's movement's true intellectual—a graceful writer and speaker who probably would have become an attorney or journalist had she been born male. Like other radical feminists who wanted to see women argue court cases, run for Congress, and launch businesses, Stanton did not bother to hide her disdain for "schoolmarms," who were doing, after all, a job that had become socially coded as demure and traditionally feminine. Teachers who defended gender-segregated normal training were "an infernal set of fools," Stanton wrote to Anthony, and the education profession was "a pool of intellectual stagnation."

Stanton was a wealthy woman who educated her own seven children at home. She did not acknowledge the pride so many female teachers took in their work, and she seemed to lack a sophisticated understanding of why so many advocates for female education, like the aging Catharine Beecher, felt attached to gender-segregated normal schools—some of the very few institutions in nineteenth-century American life that formally trained women for the workforce. Stanton often spoke about the exhaustions of her own pregnancies and child-rearing responsibilities, and she seemed to see teaching in exactly the way Beecher and Horace Mann had portrayed it—as mothering outside the home. In Stanton's popular 1880 lecture "Our Girls," she offered parents advice on the rearing of daughters, explaining that if girls were offered the same education as their brothers, they could become postal workers, preachers, physicians, or even president of the United States. "Are not any of these positions better than teaching school for a mere pittance?"

For Anthony, it was frustrating that so many female teachers did not see that coeducation would likely raise their own professional status, by ensuring teachers were trained at more elite colleges, not second-rate normal schools. But unlike Stanton, she reserved most of her ire for the male administrators who were actively preventing female colleagues from advancing in the profession, regardless of their demonstrated skill. After a particularly tiring protest at a Lockport, New York, teachers meeting in 1858, Anthony wrote to a friend that the experience was "rich. I never felt so cool and self-possessed among the plannings and plottings of the few old fogies, and they never appeared so frantic with rage. They evidently felt their reign of terror is about ended."

By 1860, Anthony's efforts to organize female teachers slowed as the nation braced for the war over slavery. In the years after the terrible conflict, she and Stanton became caught up in debates within the American Left about how to balance the all-too-often competing drives for female and African American suffrage. The two women's rights leaders were distraught when the Republican Party and former allies from the abolition movement chose to push for a Fourteenth Amendment that extended the franchise to black men, but not to women of any race. In their anger, Stanton and Anthony increasingly made common cause with outright racists, those who said educated white women were more deserving of the vote than uneducated freed slaves. The women's movement split into two hostile camps.

It would be another half century before female teachers won equal pay and access to administrative jobs in education, in part by allying themselves with male blue-collar organized labor—a constituency that, because it could vote, had the power to amplify female workers' demands for fair pay. In the meantime, the idea of teachers as non-college-educated, unmarried, low-paid mother substitutes lived on, and men continued to react by streaming out of the classroom.

By 1873, every northern state except Indiana and Missouri had more female than male teachers. In his annual report that year, federal commissioner of education John Eaton expressed muted concern about the new "difficulty . . . in finding fully educated men for the various departments of school work." But he hesitated to make any grand pronouncement on what, if anything, should be done to counteract the trend, suggesting more evidence was needed on how students performed under male versus female teachers. One Rhode Island superintendent was more forthright in stating his concerns about the feminization of teaching, claiming that because men were more intellectual and women more emotional, a well-rounded education could be provided only by both sexes working together. "The two types of mind and heart (i.e. Male and female) are distinct and were designed to have their combined effect on the youthful character," he wrote. "Any scheme of education and training that leaves out either is defective and cannot secure that symmetrical development which is possible under the other plan."

One clear downside of feminization—that, because of sexism, the political class would be unlikely to respect and thus fund a profession dominated by women—never seemed to occur to nineteenth-century male education reformers. In 1869 Charles William Eliot, a patrician Bostonian, became president of Harvard College. Eliot was an advocate for the modernization of schooling and hoped to reorganize Harvard according to the model of a German university, in which faculty performed research and undergraduates chose to major in a specific discipline. In his inaugural address, Eliot laid out this agenda, but also cautiously addressed the Woman Question. He expressed reluctance to admit female students to Harvard, noting that educating men and women of "immature character and marriageable age" together could lead to "very grave" consequences. Like John Eaton, Eliot seemed genuinely befuddled by women's recent appearance on the scene of American scholarly and professional life. "The world knows next to nothing about the natural mental capacities of the female sex," he said. "Only after generations of civil freedom and social equality will it be possible to obtain the data necessary for an adequate discussion of woman's natural tendencies, tastes, and capabilities."*

---

* It is impossible to resist comparing this comment to that of another Harvard president, Larry Summers, who in 2005 expressed confusion about why there were not more women scholars in the sciences: "There are issues of intrinsic aptitude, and particularly of the variability of aptitude . . . those considerations are reinforced by what are in fact lesser factors involving socialization and continuing discrimination. I would like nothing better than to be proved wrong, because I would like nothing better than for these problems to be addressable simply by everybody understanding what they are, and working very hard to address them."

Given his biases against working women, it is unsurprising that Eliot emerged as the nation's most influential critic of the feminization of teaching, especially at the high school level. "The average skill of the teachers in the public schools may be increased by raising the present low proportion of male teachers in the schools," he wrote. "Herein lies one of the great causes of the inferiority of the American teaching to the French and German teaching."

In a June 1875 essay in *The Atlantic,* Eliot shared a number of ideas for reforming public education. His main complaint was that local governments were too hesitant to spend tax dollars on schools, which led to classes that were too large—forty to sixty students—for anyone other than "an angel or a genius" to effectively teach. The same chronic underfunding led to low teacher salaries, which made it difficult to keep talented people in the classroom over the long haul, especially men. Eliot wrote:

> It does not matter whether the trade or occupation be printing or telegraphing or book-keeping or teaching; the average skill of the persons engaged in it will be lowered if large numbers of young people enter it for a time, with no fixed purpose of remaining in it for life. No improvement in the implements of education can make up for less skill in the teachers.

Eliot associated the problem of high teacher turnover with the influx of women into the classroom. While the common schoolers had celebrated softness and femininity as virtues, Eliot believed women were physically "weaker than men . . . more apt to be worn out by the fatiguing work of teaching," and he complained about female teachers quitting their jobs after marriage. Of course, Eliot's essay was casually sexist. Instead of questioning, as Anthony had, why school districts expected, and often actually required, women to leave their jobs after their wedding day, he took it as given that women wanted to stop working and become housewives. His assumptions about female physical capabilities were unfounded. Yet in arguing for higher teacher pay, and even "some permanence of tenure" for teachers, Eliot made a powerful case for teacher professionalization, one that reached an audience that was more mainstream than that of women's movement leaders like Anthony, who made similar points. He also pushed back against the Mann-Beecher fantasy of the "angel" teacher—a person so consumed by a spiritual calling to educate that she would labor in overcrowded, under-resourced classrooms for far less than adequate pay. Working conditions, Eliot said, do matter for teachers, just as they do for any other professional.

These warnings went unheeded by policy makers, however, and the pace of feminization quickened over the subsequent decades. In 1890 only about one-third of teachers across the nation were men. The wealthier and more developed a state became, the faster male workers fled education in search of higher-paying fields. In Massachusetts, women made up 90 percent of the teaching force, despite a statewide program in which female teachers' already unequal salaries were lowered further in order to pay male teachers more. Across New England, only 10 percent of normal school students were male. There was now powerful evidence that the lofty rhetoric of Horace Mann and Catharine Beecher had come down to earth. American public school teaching had developed less as a female ministry and more as a working-class job for young women barely out of adolescence. American teachers earned only about as much as weavers. When a teacher took a sick day, her salary was suspended and paid to her substitute.

Mann had been inspired by the Prussian school system, yet German visitors to the United States observed that American teachers were far less well trained and well respected than their European counterparts. Dr. E. Schlee, a German principal who toured American schools in 1893 on a trip organized around the Chicago World's Fair, linked the "extraordinary preponderance of female teachers" in American public schools to a general anti-intellectualism that pervaded American education. Most students never encountered algebra or a foreign language. State teacher licensing exams tested applicants less on curricular knowledge than on morality—asking them whether they agreed, for example, that alcohol and nicotine were forces of social evil. Schlee complained that too many American teachers relied solely on rote lessons from textbooks. All these problems were confounded by feminization, since "woman, by stepping out of the domestic circle to compete with man, seems to increase the unrest, precipitation, and tension in all relations of life." To attract higher-skilled men to the profession, Schlee argued that teachers would have to be paid much more.

Stephan Waetzoldt, a Berlin professor who attended the same conference, agreed that the United States needed to recruit more male teachers. But he thought this might be difficult to do, since unlike in Germany, American teachers received no uniform nationalized training; benefited from no tenure protections or retirement pension; and had no organization dedicated to representing their interests. As a result, "In many cities the teacher is a poor day-laborer who earns his bread in sorrow and fear of the Damocles sword. . . . I believe we Germans have no reason to be envious of the school system of America."

A half century after Horace Mann began to open normal schools that admitted only women, the new moral panic was less about uncaring male teachers than about undereducated female teachers.

The toxic mix of uneven, highly localized training; low pay; anti-intellectualism; and lack of social prestige pushed not just men but ambitious women, too, out of the classroom. One was Belva Lockwood, another early feminist pioneer from upstate New York. Born in 1830, she became a rural schoolteacher at age fourteen, earning $5 per month plus room and board, less than half a male teacher's salary. She married at eighteen and by twenty-three was a widow, with a three-year-old daughter to support. She returned to teaching, bringing her daughter, Lura, to the classroom each day, since she had nowhere else to put the little girl.

When she had saved up enough money, Lockwood enrolled in the Genesee Wesleyan Seminary, a college that was experimenting with coeducation, offering women the option to study serious subjects, such as science and politics, alongside men. One evening, Lockwood snuck off campus to see a "young and handsome" Susan B. Anthony address a local teachers conference. From Anthony, Lockwood heard, for the first time, the "startling heresy" that women should be able to work not only as teachers, but at any job, from selling shoes to operating printing presses.

Over the next decade, Lockwood continued to teach across New York State. But she never forgot Anthony's radical charge for women to open up the professions. In 1866 she took Lura and moved to Washington, D.C., to explore her lifelong interest in politics. She taught at a girls' school until 1 p.m., and spent the afternoons observing congressional hearings and Supreme Court arguments. Lockwood longed to play some sort of role in civic life. She applied for a job with the U.S. Foreign Service, but her application was never acknowledged. Three Washington law schools rejected her on account of her gender, so she began studying the law on her own during the evenings. Lockwood had little reason to hope she would ever practice as an attorney; the number of women admitted to the bar across the country could be counted on two hands, and it was not until 1869 that an American law school, Washington University in St. Louis, admitted women.

Her legal dreams on hold, Lockwood joined a Methodist church whose congregants were active in the women's and freedmen's rights movements. Through these new connections, Lockwood befriended two female journalists, Emily Briggs and Mary Clemmer Ames. Both wrote often about the poor treatment of female federal workers. Women had begun serving as government clerks to replace male workers who were conscripted during the Civil War. Now that men were back at work, stark, gender-based pay discrimination became clear: Women who cut and counted currency notes for the Treasury Department, for example, earned only half what men earned. In some cases, federal departments reported that women were more efficient workers than men and asked Congress permission to pay female clerks more. Lawmakers refused.

As a teacher, Lockwood had experienced pay discrimination firsthand, an offense she called "odious . . . an indignity not to be tamely borne." But rather than pursue pay equity in her own profession—which at this point in her life bored her—Lockwood proclaimed herself the advocate for female government workers. Through suffrage organizing, she had met a clerk for Tennessee congressman Samuel Arnell, the chairman of the House Committee on Education and Labor. Lockwood lobbied Arnell aggressively, and in 1870 he introduced H.R. 1571, "A bill to do justice to the female employees of the Government."

Lockwood launched a national petition drive to support the legislation, which Congress debated that spring. The Senate version of the bill would have prohibited federal agencies from sex discrimination in both hiring and pay, but in the end a weaker House version became law, guaranteeing women equal pay in the lowest federal clerk positions, but doing nothing to help them gain access to higher-level government jobs. Nevertheless, H.R. 1571 was the United States' first equal-pay law for women. After it was enacted, the number of female Treasury Department workers earning more than $900 annually increased from 4 to 20 percent—which meant some female clerks could make more than three times as much as a female teacher or even a female principal.

Lockwood eventually enrolled in the National University Law School, and in 1879 became the first woman admitted to the Supreme Court bar. In 1884 she launched a presidential run as the standard-bearer of the National Equal Rights Party, founded by feminists fed up with the Republican Party's sidelining of women's issues. She ran for president again four years later. Lockwood's rapid ascent from country schoolteacher to congressional lobbyist to trailblazing attorney provided early evidence of the complicated relationship between feminism and the teaching profession. It was through teaching that many women became aware of their talents and began to hunger for a role in the wider world. Yet when ambitious women left the underfunded, often maligned teaching profession to better their lives, public education lost powerful advocates for both teachers' and students' needs.

In the African American community, even greater barriers to employment outside education worked to keep more of the most talented black women—and men—in the classroom. There they developed a set of high ideals about the political and social power of educators, which anticipated later hopes that all teachers, regardless of their own race, would understand themselves as agents for racial justice.

Chapter Three

"No Shirking, No Skulking"

BLACK TEACHERS AND RACIAL UPLIFT
AFTER THE CIVIL WAR

O n November 7, 1861, the Union army captured the Sea Islands off the coast of South Carolina. White plantation owners fled, abandoning homes, cotton fields, and ten thousand slaves. When word of the Yankee takeover reached the mainland, more slaves arrived, runaways from parts south. By February, twelve thousand black people had gathered on the islands, at Hilton Head, St. Helena, and Port Royal. There was a lot of potential labor, and a lot of cotton, too, of a finer, more valuable quality than the cotton grown on the mainland.

The U.S. Treasury Department dispatched Edward Pierce, a thirty-two-year-old Massachusetts lawyer, to the islands to assess how they might be used in the war effort. He reported back that he was more impressed with the character of the former slaves than he thought he'd be; they harvested the cotton in their masters' absence, and were committed Christians, honest and industrious. Those who had escaped slavery had a "courage . . . worthy of heroes." What they really needed, he concluded, were teachers. In the states that became the Confederacy, it had been a crime to teach the four million enslaved men, women, and children to read or write. Pierce had met a few literate black people on the Sea Islands, but they had learned to read clandestinely and only haltingly, usually by befriending a white child. "All of proper age, when inquired of, expressed a desire to have their children taught to read and write, and to learn themselves," he wrote. "On this point, they showed more earnestness than on any other."

In part on Pierce's recommendation, the islands became the site of a massive government and philanthropic intervention, known as the Port Royal Experiment. If given an education and collective custody over their former owners' property, could freed slaves build a functioning, self-sufficient society? Pierce put out a call to the North to recruit volunteer teachers:

> There are at Port Royal and other places, many thousands of colored persons, lately slaves, who are now under the protection of the U.S. Government. They are a well-disposed people, ready to work, and eager to learn. With a moderate amount of well-directed, systematic labor, they would very soon be able to raise crops more than sufficient for their own support. But they need aid and guidance in their first steps towards the condition of self-supporting, independent laborers.
>
> These agents are called teachers, but their teaching will by no means be confined to intellectual instruction. It will include all the more important and fundamental lessons of civilization—voluntary industry, self-reliance, frugality, forethought, honesty and truthfulness, cleanliness and order. With these will be combined intellectual, moral and religious instruction.

In Philadelphia, an extraordinary young woman named Charlotte Forten was moved by this call to action. She was the fourth generation of black Fortens to be born free, the granddaughter of James Forten, a Revolutionary War veteran who was taken prisoner aboard a British ship. Many black prisoners of war were exiled to the West Indies as slaves, but James impressed the English captain with his intelligence and sense of humor and won his release. He later owned his own sail-making company and became a wealthy man. His descendants enjoyed elegant homes and private educations at a time when most black Americans lived in bondage.

By the time Charlotte was born in 1837, the Forten family had led abolition and temperance efforts in Philadelphia for several decades. Her mother died when she was three years old, and Charlotte grew into an introspective young woman, prone to waves of despondency. From her adolescence into her late twenties she kept a keenly observed, beautifully written journal, in which she recorded the contradictions of a life lived between extremes: Forten received the best education available to a girl of her race and class and met and corresponded with many of her era's most important freethinking activists and artists, including the poet John Greenleaf Whittier and the famous abolitionist orator Wendell Phillips, both of whom were white. But Forten also experienced the pain and loneliness of living as a free black woman moving alongside, if not exactly within, the American upper crust. Most of the white girls with whom she associated as a student avoided her outside the classroom. She had few intimate companions of her own age or race. At age seventeen she wrote that racism produced in her a "constant, galling sense of cruel injustice and wrong. I cannot help feeling it very often, it intrudes upon my happiest moments, and spreads a dark, deep gloom over everything." She found it incredible that "every colored person is not a misanthrope. Surely we have everything to make us hate mankind."

Throughout her life Forten struggled not to succumb to her natural pessimism. She had been raised with the expectation that she would use her relative privilege to serve the race, and because she was a girl, this meant she was expected to teach. In 1856 she became the first African American to enroll in the Salem Normal School, one of the teachers colleges founded in Massachusetts by Horace Mann. While enrolled at Salem, Forten taught herself Latin in the evenings. She submitted poems and essays to *Ladies' Home Journal* and *The Liberator,* an abolitionist newspaper. A few of her pieces were published, but Forten still considered herself a teacher first and a writer second. "I will spare no effort to become what [my father] desires that I should be," she promised her journal, "to prepare myself well for the responsible duties of a teacher, and to live for the good that I can do my oppressed and suffering fellow creatures."

Forten was appointed the first black teacher in the Salem public schools, but she was soon forced to abandon her work when she suffered a life-threatening respiratory infection. She was back in Philadelphia when the Civil War broke out, and by her twenty-fifth birthday on August 17, 1862, Forten vowed to overcome ill health in order to play her part, as a teacher, in the great unfolding drama of the war. She signed up to teach in one of the newly established Sea Islands schools for emancipated children. As Forten anticipated a physically challenging voyage into an active war zone, she prayed "that God in his goodness will make me noble enough to find my highest happiness in doing my duty."

Forten described her eighteen months teaching on St. Helena Island as "a strange, wild dream," one that challenged many of her pious preconceptions about lifting her people out of dependence and poverty. She lived with other northern volunteers and officers' wives in a drafty house abandoned by a rebel doctor and his family. There were too few blankets in the winter, and she confessed to "intense mental suffering" due to the constant threat of a Confederate invasion. Her students' lives were even more difficult. They lived in former slave quarters, typically two-room huts with open holes for windows. In winter, fire pits clogged the air with poisonous smoke. Forten longed to teach modern habits of sanitation and personal hygiene, but she admitted it would be impossible to expect much improvement under such crowded conditions, without stoves or running water.

The school met inside a one-room Baptist church, where Forten and another volunteer presided over 140 students, ranging in age from toddlers to a sixty-year-old woman who contentedly sat on the ground among her grandchildren, eager to learn her ABCs. Forten referred to them all as "my scholars," and at first she was delighted by the freed slaves' enthusiasm for learning.* "Coming to school is a constant delight and recreation to them," she wrote. "They come here as other children go to play." But she found the work "dreadfully wearying." Some of her pupils were so young that they needed babysitting more than teaching; she wrote to philanthropists in Phil-

---

* The nineteenth-century honorific for students, "scholars," is back in vogue today, especially at charter schools.

adelphia to send picture books for toddlers. The older children, who just months before had been toiling in the fields, were unaccustomed to "intellectual concentration," as Forten called it, and needed constant stimulation "in order to keep their thoughts from wandering. Teaching here is consequently far more fatiguing than at the North."

Forten created lessons meant to supplant memories of slavery with those of racial pride. She taught her students about Haitian revolutionary Toussaint L'Ouverture, who had been born a slave. "It is well that they should know what one of their own color could do for his race," she wrote in her journal. "I long to inspire them with courage and ambition." At Forten's request, the poet John Greenleaf Whittier sent the children of St. Helena a Christmas hymn he had written especially for them:

> *Oh, none in all the world before*
> *Were ever glad as we!*
> *We're free on Carolina's shore,*
> *We're all at home and free. . . .*

> *We hear no more the driver's horn,*
> *No more the whip we fear,*
> *This holy day that saw Thee born*
> *Was never half so dear. . . .*

Forten taught the children to sing Whittier's hymn and showed them the writer's picture. The reality of the students' lives was far more complicated than the poet's optimistic verse acknowledged, but knowing that such an important artist had dedicated himself to their cause made the students "very proud and happy," Forten wrote. That—as much as sharing academic knowledge—was one of her goals as a teacher.

In many ways, Forten's sojourn south was in the same spirit as the voyages of the northeastern white women who volunteered to teach in western frontier schoolhouses. But while nineteenth-century white missionary teachers were motivated largely by the desire to promulgate Protestantism, as well as their belief that women should have a socially useful alternative to marriage, Forten and the black educators who followed in her footsteps subscribed to an additional ideology: They believed it was the responsibility of more privileged African Americans to instill in their disadvantaged brothers and sisters not only knowledge, but also self-esteem and racial pride. W. E. B. Du Bois later articulated this way of thinking in *The Souls of Black Folk,* writing, "In the Black World, the Preacher and Teacher embodied once the ideals of this people—the strife for another and a juster world, the vague dream of righteousness, the mystery of knowing."

Teaching was a brave choice for Forten and other young black women and men. Before the Civil War, antitax southern state legislatures actively resisted the spread of the common schools movement, preferring to leave the education of white children in the hands of families and churches. By 1870, black activists and Reconstruction politicians had driven every state to organize at least a rudimentary public education system, with separate schools serving white and black students. Yet even with the U.S. Army garrison of the South, expanding black education remained a political lightning rod and a target for white supremacist violence. "Schoolhouses are burnt, teachers mobbed and murdered, schools broken up," Frederick Douglass reported in 1871.

Idealism and faith gave young teachers the strength to face these threats. In 1867 Robert Fitzgerald, a northern black college student, signed up with the federal Freedmen's Bureau to spend a year running a public school and Sunday school for former slaves in rural Amelia County, Virginia, outside Richmond. His experiences teaching 160 students of all ages entered family lore: The freedmen's zeal for literacy was supposedly so intense that when Fitzgerald came over a hill, eager students would run to him, pleading to borrow any book or religious pamphlet he might be carrying. Nearly a century later, Fitzgerald's granddaughter, civil rights activist Pauli Murray, recalled the stories Fitzgerald often told about instilling his students not only with book learning, but also with a sense of self-respect:

> He found . . . that in spite of the disorganization of their lives, whenever the freedmen made the effort to build a school or house of worship they tended to settle around it and their

habits showed immediate improvement. They felt it was something that they *owned* and to which they *belonged*. It made a vast difference in their lives. It would take some of them quite a while to move the awkward distance from saying "Master," to saying "Mister," but it had taken them no time at all to respond with glowing faces to "ladies" and "gentlemen" and "scholars." It gave them a new image of themselves.

Eight years later in Malden, West Virginia, a nineteen-year-old teacher who had been born into slavery, Booker T. Washington, had a similar experience. He worked from eight in the morning until ten at night teaching the children of emancipated slaves basic math and reading, as well as personal hygiene: how to comb one's hair, bathe regularly, and use a toothbrush. He established a reading room and a debating society, tutored working adults in the evenings, and prepared the village's most talented young black men and women for admission to the new colored normal schools springing up across the South. This frantic time "was one of the happiest periods of my life," Washington wrote in *Up from Slavery*. "I now felt that I had the opportunity to help the people of my home town to a higher life. . . . Without regard to pay and with little thought of it, I taught any one who wanted to learn anything I could teach him."

Many of the teachers who told the tale of education after emancipation romanticized their exhausting work. Reconstruction was a heady time for social progressives, just as the 1960s would be for a later generation of activists who went south. But there was another story to tell: how the black schools founded in the decades after the Civil War presaged a long history of entrenched poverty, racial segregation, underpaid black teachers, and lowered academic expectations for children of color.

In 1866 President Andrew Johnson allowed the former Sea Islands plantation owners to reclaim their land. The Port Royal Experiment in communal black ownership and education ended, and many of the freedmen and -women became sharecroppers. It was a sign of what was to come. The federal government had acknowledged that the education of former slaves should be one of the major goals of Reconstruction, but Congress never appropriated adequate funding for the task, nor did it compel states to do so. In total, the Freedmen's Bureau spent $5 million on southern black schools between 1865 and 1877, when federal troops left the South. The funds were used mostly to pay rents on schoolhouses, which left black communities footing the bill for up to two-thirds of the cost of running a school—costs such as teacher salaries, books, and desks. Northern charities and religious groups helped fill budget gaps, but by 1880 philanthropic interest in black common schools had greatly diminished. Then a series of state and federal court cases declared it legal for counties to spend more per pupil in white schools than in black schools. In 1899 the Supreme Court ruled in *Cumming v. Richmond County Board of Education* that Augusta, Georgia, had not defied the Constitution by shutting down its one black high school while continuing to operate its white high school.

By 1915, southern states spent three times more on the education of a white child than on the education of a black child. It was not unusual for black students to walk five miles to reach the nearest black school, or for black teachers to receive only one-third the pay of white teachers. As the decades passed, the most educated African Americans saw more and more financial incentives to abandon southern common school classrooms for more lucrative work in northern schools, black colleges, or outside education altogether.

W. E. B. Du Bois made that journey from teacher to professor to public intellectual. But despite his desire to remain involved with black public education throughout his career, his controversial critique of narrow vocational tracking of black students and teachers eventually prevented him from running the nation's largest black school system.

Du Bois was born free in the idyllic Berkshire village of Great Barrington, Massachusetts. His first close look at southern black poverty came in 1882, when he ventured out from Fisk University's Nashville campus, where he was an undergraduate, to search for a summer teaching job in a black common school. To earn his state teaching credential, he enrolled in the Lebanon Teachers' Institute, which instructed whites in the daytime and blacks in the evening.

Like Charlotte Forten, Du Bois had received a classical education at an integrated public high school. He was shocked by the rudimentary skills taught in what passed for a Tennessee normal academy: "fractions and spelling and other mysteries." His teaching certification easily won, he set out on foot to find a school willing to hire him, and eventually he secured a position in the sharecropping region of Wilson County, Tennessee, where living conditions were so severe that Du Bois felt he had "touched the very shadow of slavery."

He boarded with black families in one-room homes, and taught thirty students, including some married young adults, in an uncomfortable log hut, once the corn repository of a Confederate colonel. Du Bois loved his little school and appreciated the trust he won from the sharecropping families. "[T]he fine faith the children had in the wisdom of their teacher was truly marvelous," he wrote in an 1899 *Atlantic* essay about the experience. "We read and spelled together, wrote a little, picked flowers, sang, and listened to stories of the world beyond the hill."

Most Wilson County children attended school only sporadically. Du Bois visited their homes to check on their whereabouts, but parents informed him that they needed their children to work in the fields. Even his brightest students, Du Bois concluded, had little chance of using education to escape the circumstances into which they had been born. His *Atlantic* essay ended on an elegiac note. Though the children of sharecroppers hungered for knowledge, in reality, "their weak wings beat against their barriers;—barriers of caste, of youth, of life."

Du Bois and Booker Washington would spend years debating the proper education for the descendants of slaves—especially those who would become teachers. Both men based their careers as educational theorists in part on their own school experiences. In 1881 the white founder of Virginia's Hampton Institute, the early black normal school where Washington had trained to become a teacher, recommended Washington to the state of Alabama, which was looking for a black educator to launch a school for former slaves and their children, in the town of Tuskegee. Washington took the job. He knew that black people in the rural region surrounding the Tuskegee Institute were largely illiterate and heavily in debt. Drawing upon his own experience at Hampton, which taught only the equivalent of a modern middle-school curriculum, he believed his new students needed a basic education in reading and numeracy, as well as hands-on vocational training in brickmaking, tailoring, and carpentry—skills he hoped would inculcate personal discipline and industry. Du Bois, on the other hand, studied at Harvard and the University of Berlin. He dreamed of catapulting the most academically promising poor black children, whom he dubbed the "talented tenth," straight from abject southern poverty into the intelligentsia by providing them with a classical education in literature, history, math, Latin, and Greek. Washington rejoined: "One man may go into a community prepared to supply the people there with an analysis of Greek sentences. The community may not at that time be prepared for, or feel the need of, Greek analysis, but it may feel its need of bricks and houses and wagons."

For the black population outside the talented tenth, Du Bois came to enthusiastically support vocational education, along with a broader agenda of working-class solidarity and labor organization across racial lines. Washington, meanwhile, sent his own children to four-year liberal arts colleges and encouraged his Tuskegee students to read widely and pursue higher education if they could afford it. Most Tuskegee graduates became common school teachers, not skilled laborers. So the infamous debate between Du Bois and Washington was mostly a disagreement over emphasis: whether to focus philanthropists and policy makers on creating basic educational opportunities for the black masses, or on ensuring access to higher education for a smaller number of African Americans.* As he reflected on his Wilson County teaching experience, Du Bois often mentioned his former student Josie Dowell, a bright twenty-year-old who had dreamed of attending college, only to find herself relegated

---

* This question remains at the crux of today's debate over charter schools. The best charters demonstrate off-the-charts college attendance rates but serve only a tiny percentage of low-income students.

to domestic servitude. Du Bois's bitterness toward Washington was partly motivated by the fact that the Tuskegee founder's huge success in defining the turn-of-the-century educational philanthropic agenda as a vocational one meant there was little private money left over to provide children like Josie with access to higher education. As Presidents William McKinley and Theodore Roosevelt visited Tuskegee and magnates like Andrew Carnegie and John D. Rockefeller showered the school with praise and donations, more academically oriented black colleges such as Fisk and Atlanta University, where Du Bois taught, struggled to raise money and maintain their core programs, despite their record of success in minting black lawyers, doctors, and professors.

Another major disagreement between the two thinkers centered not so much on the role of the teacher—both men idealized the missionary black educator—as on what kind of training black teachers should receive before managing a classroom. Du Bois understood public school teachers as part of the college-going talented tenth. He was an early and prescient critic of teacher training programs that focused too much on pedagogy at the expense of content knowledge, writing, "It was not enough that the teachers of teachers should be trained in technical normal methods; they must also, so far as possible, be broad-minded, cultured men and women, to scatter civilization among a people whose ignorance was not simply of letters, but of life itself."

Washington, on the other hand, rushed to assure the Tuskegee Institute's white benefactors that black students there were *not* receiving a rigorous classical education. Henry Villard, a German-born journalist, publisher of *The Nation,* and early investor in western railroads, made at least two modest donations to Tuskegee. In 1897 he was dismayed by a letter he received from a student thanking him for his contribution; she wrote that she had studied natural philosophy, ancient history, algebra, classical music, and civil government and rhetoric. Villard fumed in a letter to Washington that black students with "immature minds" were "not prepared" to absorb this type of curriculum; he accused the Tuskegee founder of concealing the true nature of his school, which Villard thought should prepare girls exclusively for domestic service and boys for agricultural and mechanical trades. Villard's racism would have lit a fire under a man like Du Bois, but Washington, ever a pragmatist, likely hoped to secure more funding from the industrialist. He responded to Villard with a solicitous letter, explaining that "youthful ambition" had caused the student to inflate her coursework, and that "civil government" was a basic class about division of power, while "classical music" meant only that the girl sang in the school choir. If Alabama law allowed it, Washington wrote, he would have lowered the level of math taught at Tuskegee. "I would say your criticism has done us good," he closed, "and I thank you for it."

According to biographer Robert Norrell, on northern fundraising expeditions, Washington rarely mentioned that Tuskegee alumni were not only teaching common school in large numbers, but were also opening normal academies across the Black Belt, to train new generations of teachers. Tuskegee's wide circle of influence in teacher training discomfited Du Bois. Like the northern feminists who wanted female teachers to be educated at co-ed colleges, not less rigorous normal schools, Du Bois thought prospective black teachers would have received a more appropriate education at full-fledged universities. He believed black teachers should be "gifted persons" well acquainted with elite white ways of learning, so that they could decode mainstream norms for black children, helping them "to cope with the white world on its own ground and in its own thought, method and language." He worried that Tuskegee-trained teachers, who had never studied a foreign language nor struggled with calculus, would be unprepared to truly expand their pupils' minds.

Much of Du Bois's writing on teachers is deeply resonant today; many contemporary education reformers insist that public schools will not improve unless more elite college graduates are brought into the teaching profession. Washington's historical reputation, on the other hand, has always been mixed. Especially in the wake of the twentieth-century civil rights movement, many progressives came to see him as a compromised Uncle Tom figure, a self-appointed spokesman for African Americans who, in his quest for philanthropic support, went too far in bending to white racist assumptions about blacks' intellectual capabilities. "Washington stands for Negro submission and slavery," Du Bois wrote to a friend in 1910.

"Representing that, with unlimited funds, he can afford to be broad and generous and most of us must accept the generosity or starve."

In fact, both Du Bois and Washington expressed ideas that either became common practice or remain at the heart of education debates. In private Sunday evening lectures Washington girded Tuskegee students with detailed, practical advice about how to open and support new schools for black children: New teachers must seek the trust and support of local ministers and community organizations; they should go door-to-door asking black parents to enroll their children in school; through cookouts and fairs, they should raise money to extend the school year from three months to eight. More than a century later, many contemporary charter schools in black neighborhoods draw students in through door-to-door recruiting, and advocates for "extended learning time" call for (and many charters require) a longer school day, week, and year. Both men lobbied on behalf of congressional bills that would have provided supplemental federal funding to schools serving poor black children in regions with high illiteracy rates. It took until 1965, when Washington had been dead for nearly half a century and Du Bois for two years, for Congress to finally pass the Elementary and Secondary Education Act, which did exactly that.

At the turn of the century, only one predominantly black public school system in the United States received significant federal funding: the segregated colored schools of Washington, D.C. Because of extra dollars from Congress, there was no pay gap between white and black public school teachers working in the nation's capital, which made Washington a magnet for ambitious black educators.

One of them was Anna Julia Cooper, the daughter of a North Carolina slave and the white man who owned her. For six decades, from her adolescence until her retirement at age seventy-two, Cooper taught in black public schools and colleges. Her long tenure in the classroom tested many of the ideas around which Du Bois and Washington debated. Politically, the two men lobbied for higher teacher pay, yet they often advised individual young black teachers to ignore their low salaries and the day-to-day administrative headaches of their jobs, and instead to approach their work with what Washington called a "missionary spirit." When Du Bois's goddaughter complained that the rural Mississippi public school in which she taught was disorganized, "backward and dumb," he returned a loving, but stern rebuke, advising her to ignore the school's unprofessional principal and the other, less well-educated teachers. "Your real duty is, of course, to the children, and they are entirely deserving," he preached. "You ought to put your whole life and energy in stirring them out of their lethargy and carelessness."

Anna Cooper could not afford the luxury of such idealism. She was born a slave, widowed at twenty-one, and never remarried. In middle age, she essentially adopted five needy children. So teaching was not only Cooper's calling, but also her permanent livelihood. Consequently, she fought throughout her career for higher pay. And although teacher unionism did not come to Washington, D.C., until 1916, a decade earlier Cooper independently pushed an agenda that was similar to that of the northern, predominantly white teachers organizations founded at the turn of the century. She critiqued early IQ testing and resisted administrative and philanthropic efforts to direct an increasing number of poor children into purely vocational courses.

Cooper's own education had proceeded very much along the lines of Du Bois's hopes for the talented tenth. Born Annie Haywood, she was just six years old at the end of the Civil War and was lucky to live near the Saint Augustine's Normal School and Collegiate Institute in Raleigh, which had been founded by the Episcopal Church to provide former slaves with a rigorous classical education. Annie displayed an early aptitude for the written word and was soon on the school's payroll as a tutor to her fellow students. In the evenings she would teach her mother the basics of reading and writing. "My mother was a slave and the finest woman I have ever known," Cooper wrote many decades later. "It is one of my happiest childhood memories explaining for her the subtle differences between q's and g's or between b's and l's."

At Saint Augustine's, Annie took classes in Latin, algebra, and geometry. She met her future husband, the Reverend George Cooper, in Greek class. Both Coopers stayed on to teach at the school after graduation, but the energetic young minister died in 1879, leaving young Anna Cooper bereaved, but also free to pursue her growing ambitions. In 1881 she applied to Oberlin, a co-ed Christian college in Ohio that had served as a busy stop on the Underground Railroad. Cooper would have been aware of Oberlin's abolitionist reputation, as well as the fact that it was one of the few white liberal arts colleges in the United States that accepted black women. Her thirst for further education—a drive that would later lead her to become one of the first African American women to earn a PhD—shines through in her application letter to Oberlin president James Fairchild, as does her displeasure at the low wages (about $30 per month) she then earned as a teacher:

> I have for a long time *earnestly* desired to take an advanced classical course in some superior Northern college, but could not see my way to it for lack of means. . . . I am now teaching a two months' summer school in Haywood; Southern schools pay *very meanly,* but I expect to have money enough to keep me one or two years at your College, provided I can secure the favor . . . of free tuition and incidentals.

Cooper was accepted and granted lodging with the family of a professor. To pay her way through a bachelor's degree and then a master's, she taught French, German, and classics during the summers at Wilberforce University, a black college in Ohio, and at Saint Augustine's, her Raleigh alma mater. She became an active member of the North Carolina Teacher's Association, which advocated more funding for colored schools and equal pay for black teachers. For a time, North Carolina was the only southern state with roughly equal-per-pupil spending regardless of race, and where the average black teacher's salary was roughly commensurate with the average white teacher's: $204 to $207 annually, about $5,028 in today's dollars. (In the North, public school teachers of either race could earn five times more.) But North Carolina's support for black teachers and schools depended on the political influence of new black voters enfranchised during Reconstruction. In 1900 the state legislature effectively disenfranchised more than half of these black voters, through poll taxes, literacy tests, and a "grandfather" clause that required prospective voters to prove a direct ancestor had been registered to vote in 1867. As in other southern states, white resentment toward public spending on black schools was so high that it was only after North Carolina disenfranchised blacks that the state amended its constitution to provide for the ongoing direct levying of school taxes, in a fashion that would guarantee disproportionate funding for white schools. By the time Du Bois conducted a survey of southern black public schools in 1908, he found black teachers in North Carolina earning only 60 percent as much as white teachers. Black children made up 32 percent of the school-age population, but received only 17 percent of the state's education funding.

Cooper, like many other better-educated African Americans, chose to leave the former Confederacy as black political capital there declined after Reconstruction. In 1887, through Oberlin connections, she was hired as a Latin teacher at the most prestigious black public school in the United States: M Street High School in Washington, D.C. It was an attractive job for many reasons, not least of which was the relatively high pay, equal to that of almost any white public school teacher anywhere in the country. Charlotte Forten had taught at M Street after returning from the Sea Islands. The school sent graduates on to Ivy League universities each year, and alumni pursued white-collar careers in government, education, the law, and medicine. In 1899, M Street students scored higher on a district-wide exam than the students at any white public high school in Washington. The school's faculty held more advanced degrees among them than the teachers at any white D.C. public school; some went on to become university presidents and judges.

M Street served the children of the city's rapidly expanding black middle class in a grand Romanesque-style redbrick building in Washington's Northwest quarter. Cooper excelled there as a Latin teacher and became principal in 1901 while continuing to teach— part of an early wave of women ascending beyond the classroom to leadership roles in schools. When the French priest and educator Félix Klein visited Cooper's classroom in 1904, he found her leading a group of sixteen girls in a close reading of the *Aeneid*. The students eagerly translated Latin words and discussed with their teacher the relationship between history and mythology in Virgil's epic poem. Klein had never before seen black children engaged in such feats of intellectualism, and he reported in his subsequent book that Cooper was one of the most skilled teachers he had ever met. He was also impressed with her strict disciplinary strategies. She required M Street's 530 students to walk the hallways in military silence (a common practice at today's "no excuses" charter schools). Each school day began with a recitation of the Lord's Prayer.

Even while teaching full-time, Cooper built a national reputation as a public speaker and essayist. In lectures at the 1893 Chicago World's Fair and in front of a convention of black Episcopal clergy, she sketched a vision for "the colored woman's office," claiming a special place for black women within the same missionary teacher ideology that Catharine Beecher had applied to an earlier generation of white female teachers. "The earnest well trained Christian young woman, as a teacher, as a home-maker, as wife, mother, or silent influence even, is as potent a missionary agency among our people as is the theologian," Cooper said in an 1890 speech, "and I claim that at the present stage of our development in the South she is ever more important and necessary."

Cooper's 1892 book, *A Voice from the South by a Black Woman of the South,* was a groundbreaking articulation of black feminist thought. That same year, Elizabeth Cady Stanton delivered a valedictory lecture titled "The Solitude of Self." In the speech, seventy-six-year-old Stanton advised every woman to get an education and work outside the home in order to take "personal responsibility of her own individual life." Cooper, then thirty-four, argued for a more communitarian type of feminism. She expected black women to fight for gender equity not only to enrich their own lives, but also so they could better "uplift the race" as teachers, volunteers, or within their families. " '*I am my Sister's keeper!*' should be the hearty response of every man and woman of the race," she wrote, "and this conviction should purify and exalt the narrow, selfish and petty personal aims of life into a noble and sacred purpose." There could be "no shirking, no skulking" in the face of the "Race Problem," Cooper wrote. Stanton's white feminism looked down upon low-paid teachers. But Cooper's black feminism idealized teachers as leaders in the fight for racial and social equality.

Cooper lived out these ideals. In addition to teaching, she helped establish a settlement house in the mode of Jane Addams's Hull House in Chicago. The house, located in Southwest Washington, included a day nursery and kindergarten for young children, as well as a "milk station" that fed sixty babies per day. Volunteers visited poor young mothers at home to instruct them on good parenting methods, and provided adults with a "savings club," library, music lessons, and arts and crafts classes. Like the contemporary education reformers, such as Harlem Children's Zone visionary Geoffrey Canada, who advocate for "wraparound" social services as an integral complement to effective schools, Cooper saw direct anti-poverty work as part of her teaching mission. She used the term "sympathetic methods" to describe her practice of researching each of her students' home lives in order to better understand and address potential limitations on their academic success, such as unemployed parents, inadequate housing, or sick siblings.

Even so, Cooper's major goal as principal of M Street was strictly achievement oriented: the admission of students into elite colleges. During Cooper's tenure as principal, M Street graduates were accepted to Oberlin, Harvard, Brown, and Yale, and several alumni received Ivy League doctorates.

This display of black intellectualism provoked a moral panic in white Washington and among some black advocates for vocational education who were allied with Booker T. Washington. The coalition Du Bois dubbed the "Tuskegee machine" challenged M Street early in Cooper's principalship, when she successfully fought off an attempt by the city's white director of high schools to replace the school's classical curriculum with more vocationally oriented classes. In 1901 Washington personally intervened—perhaps with President Teddy Roosevelt himself—to prevent Du Bois from being appointed assistant superintendent in charge of the city's black schools. By 1906 the battle between the Washington and Du Bois camps had become openly hostile. Members of the D.C. school board launched a campaign of character assassination against Cooper, whom they likely perceived as aligned with the Du Bois "talented tenth" agenda. They first accused her of managerial incompetence. When those trumped-up charges didn't stick, white school board members claimed—probably erroneously—that she was having an affair with her young adult foster son. The *Washington Post* covered the scandal. Cooper was dismissed.

After nineteen years at M Street, this setback was emotionally and professionally devastating. Cooper was eventually rehired as a teacher at the school, but she never again enjoyed the full support of her supervisors. She went on to earn a PhD from the Sorbonne in Paris, at the age of sixty-six. Her groundbreaking dissertation was on attitudes toward slavery during the Haitian and French Revolutions.

Over the next half century, vocationalism remained the ascendant education reform ideology among philanthropists and politicians, not just for black students, but for the children of white immigrants from eastern and southern Europe as well. In the North, white female teachers began to organize in opposition to this agenda. Their protests sparked one of the United States' most powerful and controversial labor movements: the unionization of public school teachers.

Chapter Four

"School Ma'ams as Lobbyists"

THE BIRTH OF TEACHERS UNIONS AND THE BATTLE BETWEEN PROGRESSIVE PEDAGOGY AND SCHOOL EFFICIENCY

One evening in the 1870s, in the prairie town of Morris, Illinois, Michael Haley led his three teenage daughters to the first row of the town's auditorium. They were there to hear a lecture by a famous phrenologist. Maggie, Jenny, and Eliza Haley did not know quite what to expect, only that phrenology was an exciting modern science, and that it had something to do with deducing people's inner qualities by examining the bumps on their heads.

Their father had been working since he was ten years old, when he was hired as a "jigger carrier" to deliver whiskey to thousands of fellow Irish laborers as they dug the muddy Illinois and Michigan Canal. Since then, Michael Haley had survived a malaria epidemic, learned the skill of stonecutting, and gone on strike for higher wages. Now Haley had a successful cement-manufacturing business, but he hoped for a different life for his six children. They would go to school. Their labor would be easier than his had been.

As a proud Irish American republican, Michael Haley believed in the promise of utopian socialism and equality before the law. So when the phrenologist that night launched into a reactionary attack on the women's suffrage leader Susan B. Anthony, Haley did something that shocked and embarrassed his daughters. He marched them out of the theater, in full sight of the lecturer and audience. Just outside, he lined the three girls up and addressed them solemnly. "I don't know Susan B. Anthony and I suppose I never shall," he said, "but she's a woman who is working for a cause, a just cause, and I will not allow my children to listen to any half-baked nincompoop who sneers at her."

In three decades' time, Susan B. Anthony would refer to Haley's oldest daughter, Maggie, as a "dear friend" and would publicly hail her for continuing the fight Anthony had begun in the 1850s: the feminist organization of women schoolteachers. As the most prominent leader of the nation's first teachers-only union, the Chicago Teachers Federation, Margaret Haley succeeded where Anthony had failed. She won higher pay and significant political power for female teachers, in large part because of her canny ability to forge alliances with male unions, just as organized labor exploded in power at the turn of the twentieth century. Seven years after Anthony's death, in 1913, Haley even played a crucial role in winning Illinois women the right to vote.

But first, Maggie Haley was a teacher. At sixteen she graduated from a Catholic girls' boarding school, then taught in the countryside for several years. Frustrated that she earned only $35 per month (she thought she deserved $40) and eager to improve her teaching practice, she enrolled at the famed Cook County Normal School, where she studied with Francis Wayland Parker, the pedagogue John Dewey would celebrate as the "father" of progressive education. Parker, a Civil War veteran, believed that instead of reading aloud listlessly from textbooks, teachers should create their own teaching units and lesson plans, and that students should take classes in art, music, and drama. Haley left behind few written recollections of her teaching years, but she did express pride in belonging to the intellectual community gathered around Parker, which later included other educational leaders she admired, such as Dewey and the progressive Chicago schools administrator Ella Flagg Young.

In 1884 Haley was hired to teach sixth grade at the Hendricks School in the foul-smelling Packingtown neighborhood of Chicago's South Side, the area immortalized by Upton Sinclair in his muckraking novel about slaughterhouses, *The Jungle*. There she finally earned $40 per month, but like many Chicago teachers, she began to feel she was vastly underpaid. Chicago was a prosperous, expanding city; between 1890 and 1904 it would gain 830,000 residents. After the economic crash of 1893, business boomed again. The city was home to a thriving reform scene, driven by innovative thinking in the social sciences and progressive politics, much of it coming from the newly established University of Chicago. Yet you would not have known any of this from looking at the city's schools. Haley's students—between forty and sixty cramped in a classroom, sometimes with too few chairs and desks to go around—were the children of Irish- and German-born butchers; some spoke little English, and, in the absence of child labor laws, most would leave school permanently at the age of eleven or twelve to go to work. Each subsequent year brought a more challenging student population into Chicago public schools, from Italy, Russia, and Bohemia. Yet annual pay for entry-level elementary school teachers, 97 percent of whom were women, had been frozen for twenty years at $500 (about $13,300 in today's dollars). The school system's budget was so strapped that teachers were sometimes paid not in wages, but in "warrants" promising future pay, which teachers had to cajole grocers and landlords to accept in lieu of cash. Education policy was set by a school board appointed by the mayor, and board members were lobbied aggressively by Chicago's business and media elite, who resisted taxes that paid for "fads and frills" like foreign language classes. The *Chicago Tribune* editorialized against the preposterous idea of preparing "the children of working men" for college, and called summer school courses for poor students "alluring luxuries." The situation in Chicago was similar to that in other American cities at the turn of the century. Prominent education reformers across the country, such as Columbia University philosophy professor Nicholas Murray Butler, the founder of the school that would later be known as Teachers College, lobbied to replace teachers' and politicians' judgments on curriculum with education policies set by college-educated bureaucrats. These administrative progressives forged an alliance with business leaders, who liked the idea of top-down, expert management of schools, yet deplored paying higher taxes to fund public education.*

---

* There has been a century of debate over how to define "progressive" education. The reformers who sought to constrain the influence of female teachers in cit-

In Chicago the most prominent reformer was William Rainey Harper, president of the University of Chicago. Harper chaired a mayoral commission tasked with centralizing the curriculum, pedagogy, and administrative structure of the public schools. Like Charles William Eliot, the Harvard president, Harper believed Horace Mann's feminization of teaching had been a major misstep. His commission hoped to freeze a planned $50 annual raise for female teachers, saying the city should instead prioritize hiring and promoting male educators. When a group of female teachers complained to him, Harper responded that they should be happy they earned as much as his wife's maid.

These were the events that motivated, in 1897, the founding of the Chicago Teachers Federation, the precursor to today's American Federation of Teachers. The National Education Association, in which Susan B. Anthony had organized New York's female teachers, dated back to 1857 and included teachers, administrators, and even college professors and presidents. The NEA was genteel. It conducted research on education and advocated politely for school funding. From the start, the Federation intended to be a totally different animal: a militant organization modeled after the male labor unions to which the fathers and brothers of Chicago teachers belonged.

The purpose of the Federation was to aggressively advocate for higher teacher pay and for teachers' freedom on lesson planning and student discipline; the organization sought to counter the influence of school reformers who believed non-college-educated women were unqualified to make autonomous choices within their classrooms. The Federation held its first meeting on March 16, 1897, and by June had attracted over 2,500 members, about half of the elementary school teaching force. Two years later, after a pains-

---

ies like Chicago and New York thought of themselves as "progressives," for they believed they were applying modern, efficient business methods to the management of sprawling, inefficient school systems. Their administrative progressivism can be clearly contrasted, however, with the pedagogical progressivism espoused by Francis Wayland Parker and John Dewey. These schools of thought are well defined in *The Struggle for the American Curriculum,* by Herbert Kliebard.

taking organizing campaign throughout Chicago neighborhoods, Margaret Haley presented the Illinois state legislature in Springfield with a fifty-thousand-signature petition against William Rainey Harper's school reform bill. The legislation would have given the school superintendent the exclusive right to hire and fire teachers for neighborhood schools, while keeping teacher salaries frozen and assigning every Chicago child to either the vocational or academic track, which would have been segregated from one another. The bill was defeated. Teacher unionism had arrived as a potent force in American civic life.

At her 1899 inauguration, the Federation's longtime president, Catherine Goggin, sketched a vision of a political, not just an educational, organization:

> The Federation should have a broader outlook. It should consider all which properly comes with the scope of intelligent citizenship. Its endorsement should be a powerful aid, its disapproval equally mighty. It should so educate public sentiment that a newspaper which attempted to lower the teachers of the city in the estimation of the public should immediately feel the result of the attempts in its decreased circulation and depleted advertising columns.

Goggin's explicit threat to the city's moneyed interests—that they should support teachers or be made to pay—captured the spirit of early teacher unionism. While the stunted pre–Civil War efforts to empower female teachers had been led by women like Anthony who were born into relatively privileged and well-educated families, the Irish Catholic–dominated Federation had a more innate feel for working-class politics. Haley, in her job as the Federation's business representative, was known as the union's heavy, a five-foot-tall "lady labor slugger" with penetrating blue eyes, unafraid of knocking heads at city hall or in the state capitol. At the turn of the century, before women could even vote, it was shocking to see female schoolteachers organize into a fighting force for higher wages. The *Chicago Chronicle* editorial board typified the reaction of the popular press, calling the Federation "impertinent" in its demands for better pay, and complaining that "school ma'ams as lobbyists left an unfavorable impression." Observing the Federation from afar, the *Atlanta Constitution* wondered, "Does Unionism Make Girls Masculine?"

Haley seemed to delight in such criticism. She identified as a proud "fighting Irish" and a feminist, too: "To win rudimentary justice, women had to battle with brain, with wit, and sometimes even with force," she wrote in *Battleground*, her autobiography. "If you happened to be born wanting freedom for yourself, for your group, for people at large, you had to fight for it—and you had to fight hard."

Haley's combative posture would not always serve the long-term interests of the teachers union movement well. But at the birth of the Chicago Teachers Federation, she stage-managed several spectacular political victories. In 1900, at the age of thirty-eight, she took what would become a permanent leave of absence from the classroom in order to investigate why, at the height of the late-1890s economic boom, the city of Chicago claimed it had too little money to unfreeze teachers' wages and secure their newly established pension system. After immersing herself in the details of Illinois tax, corporate, and real estate law, Haley discovered two startling facts. First, land granted to the common schools system under the Northwest Ordinance of 1787 had been rented by the Chicago school board to some of the city's major corporations for far below market rates, on ninety-nine-year leases with few opportunities for reassessments of the properties' real values. The *Chicago Tribune,* for example, was paying the school board about half the market value for its headquarters in the desirable Loop district. The *Chicago Daily News* enjoyed a similar sweetheart deal. The underpayments became a scandal when the Federation publicized the fact that the president of the school board was also the *Tribune*'s attorney. All in all, if the downtown square mile owned by the Chicago Public Schools had been competently managed, each year it would have brought in $200 million in rent, which could have been used not only to pay teachers more, but to improve every aspect of Chicago public education. While the Federation did not succeed in raising the suspect rents, its campaign on the issue helped attract early support from the city's influential good-government reformers, like Jane Addams, the settlement house crusader, and Carl Sandburg, the socialist journalist.

Haley's second major finding had even greater implications for the Chicago public sector and won her the admiration of populist progressives across the United States. She discovered that the state of Illinois was not enforcing its own laws on corporate taxation. Seven for-profit public utilities, including streetcar, gas, electricity, and telephone companies, paid no taxes at all on their corporate franchises, costing the city millions in lost revenue. On October 29, 1900, the Teachers Federation hosted a dramatic mass meeting to publicize the lawsuit it had filed to compel the state to collect these taxes. Hundreds of teachers and other interested citizens crowded into the Central Music Hall downtown. The tone of the meeting was indignant. Female activists accused male businessmen of knowingly dodging their taxes over the course of decades, as politicians looked the other way. After Haley gave an exhaustive report on thirty years of Illinois tax history, the stately Jane Addams rose to frame the fight in more visceral, sentimental terms. Additional tax revenue could pay not only for higher teacher salaries, she said, but also for better public sanitation, to protect poor children's health. When businessmen evade taxes, "property . . . loses its moral value," Addams said, and she called on the entire community to unite to "bring [businessmen] back to a sense of moral obligation, in order to make it seem righteous to pay taxes—because I imagine that to many men, it seems righteous to evade taxes if you can do it in the interests of the stockholder."

Chicago's cultural leaders took their political cues from Addams, and they expressed wild enthusiasm about the Federation's tax fight. Eliza A. Starr, a prominent author and lecturer on Renaissance art, congratulated Haley on her "heroic efforts to stem the tide of plutocracy rushing over our land." Lucy Fitch Perkins, the children's book author, told Haley and Goggin, "You make me think of Moses and Aaron, and I firmly believe you will make your way through this Red Sea and bring the children of Israel through with you." The Chicago Symphony Orchestra headlined a January 1901 concert to raise Federation legal fees. Teacher unionism had become, at least momentarily, trendy.

On October 1, 1901, the Illinois Supreme Court ruled that Chicago public utility companies must pay back taxes, later assessed at $2.3 million. A federal court reduced the payments to a total of $600,000 annually, of which nearly a quarter-million dollars would be paid to the Chicago Board of Education. Teachers earned back pay. It was a major win for Haley and the early teacher unionization movement. She was soon traveling the country urging classroom teachers to organize everywhere. When the Wisconsin Teachers Association booked her for a lecture, they advertised Haley as "the plucky little woman who led the Chicago teachers in their successful struggle against the tax-dodging corporations of Illinois. She is a remarkably brilliant speaker, and every teacher in Wisconsin ought to hear her address." The journalist William Hard worked for the *Chicago Tribune* but disagreed with his employer's hostile stance toward teacher unionization. Hard took to the pages of the *Times Magazine,* in a freelance article, to celebrate "Margaret Haley, Rebel." Of two million Chicagoans, "there was just one human being, a female human being, who determined to set a great wrong right," he wrote of the tax fight. "I don't care what else Miss Haley has done. In that moment she achieved greatness."

When, in 1904, Harriet Taylor Upton, a leader in the women's suffrage movement, asked Haley to help reach out to newly organized teachers across the country to engage them in the fight for the vote, Haley happily did so. Her activism had convinced her that without suffrage, female teachers would always enter political negotiations at a severe disadvantage, since they couldn't back their policy preferences with votes. But rather than wait for suffrage to be won, in 1902 Haley had made an incredibly controversial decision: Through an introduction from the crusading attorney Clarence Darrow, who admired the Federation and had represented labor leaders like Eugene Debs, Haley led her organization for female teachers into an affiliation with the working-class male Chicago Federation of Labor, whose votes and lobbying prowess would help amplify teachers' policy preferences. The Chicago Teachers Federation also applied for a charter from the American Federation of Labor, led by the astute Samuel Gompers, who was building deep ties to the national Democratic Party.

When Susan B. Anthony suggested in 1869 that print shops respond to a typesetters' strike by training female replacement workers, she sowed distrust between the women's movement and organized labor. Thirty-three years later, female teachers, though often strident feminists, were less threatening to male craftsmen; male unionists were unqualified for and uninterested in elementary school teaching jobs, and allying with teachers gave the AFL an inroad into urban education policy making, which affected union members' children. But while female teacher unionists and male labor leaders saw affiliation as mutually advantageous, their partnership was deeply discomfiting to the Chicago establishment. Could unionized teachers simultaneously fight for their own interests as workers and for the educational interests of the city's children? Or were those two priorities at odds?

In the fall of 1902, just as the Teachers Federation and Chicago Federation of Labor were joining forces, Chicago children launched an extraordinary protest movement, one that seemed to take its cues from union politics. As part of his campaign to centralize and professionalize Chicago's school system, Superintendent Edwin Cooley had replaced two female principals with men and had transferred several popular women teachers away from schools in which they had long worked, because they had supposedly become too close with students and parents who shared their own ethnicity, often Irish or Czech. Instead of rewarding teachers only for time on the job, already the status quo policy in urban school districts, Cooley, like other reformers, wanted to tie teachers' promotions and raises to their scores on a written exam, as well as on "efficiency" evaluations conducted by principals. He was also sweeping the city's streets for truant children, bringing dozens of new students into already overcrowded working-class elementary schools, who were unaccustomed to the routines of the classroom.

Jane McKeon, an active member of the Federation, was a veteran teacher at the Andrew Jackson School, with personal ties to its surrounding, predominantly Irish West Side neighborhood. On Halloween, she booted a formerly truant student from her class of fifty-five children as a punishment for using profanity. When the new male principal sent the offender back to the classroom and McKeon refused to let him enter, she was suspended without pay for thirty days and told she would be transferred to another school.

A week later, Andrew Jackson students walked out of school to demonstrate solidarity with McKeon. The students said they would not return to class unless their teacher was permanently reinstated. A large photograph on page three of the *Chicago Tribune* showed a mass of cherub-faced demonstrators assembled at the entrance of their school. "We want Miss McKeon . . . and no one else," a girl with a large bow in her hair told the *Tribune*. One boy in a newsboy cap said, "We won't go back until we get her." McKeon secured a lawyer, who said his client had been targeted in retaliation for her union membership. In an editorial, the outraged *Tribune* ignored unmanageable class sizes and blamed the unrest on lax West Side parents, some of whom were supporting "the dismal burlesque presented down at the Andrew Jackson school," a "petticoated" place that would benefit from "a little starch"—presumably in the form of more male teachers who could impose proper discipline. The paper urged the school board to stand firm in its suspension of McKeon, writing, "Employment means work, not argumentation. The school system is not a debating society." Teachers who question administrators "carry little children with them into rebellion . . . What we need in Chicago is a set of teachers who will either work in harmony with the board of education or else get on the outside and stay there. Insurrectionists are not exactly fit guides for the young." In the end, the student protestors returned to class, but Jane McKeon refused her new assignment and resigned from the school system.

Union teachers triggered another moral panic among the media establishment in 1905, when Federation members marched in solidarity with thirty-five thousand Teamsters picketing for the right to "closed shops," where employment is available only to union members. The Teamsters strike targeted high-profile department stores like Marshall Field, Sears, and Montgomery Ward. It lasted an incredible 105 days, during which 415 people were injured and 21 killed. Teamsters took control of city streets in order to block the passage of replacement truckers carting merchandise to and from downtown businesses. Some of these replacements were black, and a few were savagely beaten. Liberal magazines like *Harper's Weekly* and *The Nation* compared the strike to the "Terror of Revolutionary France" and the Teamsters to a mob.

For the upper middle class, even those with liberal politics, it was utterly confounding that lady teachers would want to affiliate with such a movement. The *Tribune* worried that in their alliance with sometimes violent Teamsters, Federation members were teaching 240,000 Chicago schoolchildren "sedition, revolt against constitutional authority, disrespect for the law, and subversion of private and public rights." A more even-keeled (and prescient) critique of early teacher union activism came from Chicago writer David Swing Wicker. In a report for *Educational Review,* a national reform journal, Wicker argued that by opposing Superintendent Cooley's plan to evaluate teachers on their performance, Federationists were denying the fact that "teachers are not born, they are made" by high-quality training and supervision. The editors of *Scribner's Magazine* agreed. They believed teachers who affiliated with labor were shortsighted, because of "the cardinal principle of unionism, its most pernicious principle . . . that of subordinating individual development to the capacity of the average. To that principle, essentially hostile to independence or advance in education or professional life, do these Chicago teachers stand committed by their act in becoming 'unionists'?"

Indeed, teaching was not like many other unionized jobs. In education, poor job performance put children's well-being immediately at stake. Yet Haley and the Federation organized against Cooley's teacher evaluation plan without suggesting any alternative for judging teachers' professional merit and distinguishing good from bad performers. Cooley had proposed tests and merit pay for teachers not only as a way to reward the best practitioners, they believed, but also as a maneuver to avoid raising teacher salaries across the board. Wary of budget cutting, the Federation argued that teachers should be paid primarily for time on the job.* Haley and her orga-

---

* Merit pay and budget cutting often did go hand in hand. When Atlanta instituted teacher merit pay in 1915, overall teacher pay in the district declined by $15,000.

nization actually agreed with Cooley and his ally at the University of Chicago, William Rainey Harper, about many priorities for the school system, such as more art and music courses and the construction of playgrounds. But given the men's many sexist assumptions about female teachers—that they should never become principals and should be paid less than male teachers—rather than collaborate in these areas, the Federation developed a stance of across-the-board animosity.

In 1909 a Chicago factory inspector named Helen Todd conducted an informal survey of 500 child laborers who had dropped out of public schools. When she asked the children if, financial necessity aside, they would rather work in a factory or attend school, 412 chose work. They described school as a joyless place of ethnic bigotry, corporal punishment, and mind-numbing rote memorization.* The typical poor urban child experienced school as "sheer cruelty" and a "humiliation," Todd concluded—no wonder they dropped out in droves, sometimes turning to honest labor, but sometimes to crime.

Todd's study was not scientific, and considering that thirty thousand turn-of-the-century Chicago children never enrolled in school at all, one wonders if child workers could have been reliable judges of classroom practices. Yet during a tumultuous era for the nation's cities, muckraking reports like Todd's renewed the quintessentially American conviction that public education was the proper salve for the wounds of poverty; that if only schools and teachers did a better job, problems like child labor and juvenile delinquency could be solved. The writer and photographer Jacob Riis became famous for his stark depiction of New York slum life in *How the Other Half Lives,* first published in 1890. He interviewed boys who had never attended school and spent their days spying on neighborhood prostitutes or toiling in sweatshops. Most immigrant children, Riis wrote,

---

* Catharine Beecher had predicted the end of corporal punishment if female teachers replaced male teachers. This did not occur.

were so rooted in their ethnic ghettoes that they had never visited Central Park or gazed upon the architectural marvel of the Brooklyn Bridge, just a five-minute walk from their homes. Riis acknowledged the systemic constraints on immigrant children's lives. The United States lacked strong restrictions on child labor and relied mostly on overextended local charities, many with a proselytizing religious mission, to provide the poor with health care and job training. There were no housing sanitation laws, and far too few truant officers, who were supposed to encourage child workers to enroll in school. Nevertheless, like many of today's reformers, Riis considered teachers the determining factor in whether a child escaped poverty. In his 1892 book *The Children of the Poor,* he wrote that schools are "our chief defense against the tenement and the flood of ignorance with which it would swamp us . . . it is the personal influence of the teacher that counts for most in dealing with the child. It follows it into the home, and often through life to the second and third generation, smoothing the way of sorrow and hardship with counsel and aid in a hundred ways."

Despite sensationalism, many muckraking critiques of public education contained more than a kernel of truth. Classroom overcrowding meant schools did turn a blind eye to truancy, sometimes even counseling poorly behaved students as young as seven years old to quit school and get a job. A child who dropped out of the primary grades, or who never enrolled at all, would most likely end up on a factory floor working with massive, dangerous machinery, or selling newspapers or other goods on the street, exposed to harsh weather, typhoid-infected water hydrants, and speeding streetcars.

When Jane Addams was appointed to the city school board in 1905 by Chicago's new progressive mayor, Edward Dunne, she earnestly hoped to awaken the school system to these larger social challenges, especially truancy. Federation teachers like Jane McKeon, though, had long held a more pragmatic view: If problem children were allowed to remain in classrooms, they would threaten the learning of their well-behaved peers. Addams agreed with the Federation that teachers ought to have more influence over which textbooks were purchased and how to structure the curriculum. But she also believed there ought to be more formal tests of teachers' com-

petence; after all, some teachers had only a primary school education. "[T]here was a constant danger in a great public school system
that teachers lose pliancy and the open mind," she wrote, "and that
many of them had obviously grown mechanical and indifferent."
When Haley realized Addams would not support the entirety of the
Federation's agenda, she began to refer to the social reformer deri-
sively as "Gentle Jane."

Though Addams was entirely well intentioned, her support for
Superintendent Cooley's teacher evaluation plan may well have been
misplaced. Cooley attempted to keep teachers' evaluation reports
secret from them, which meant the system was useless as a tool for
improving classroom practice. Subsequent school board investigations of the secret evaluations found that some teachers with very
high scores—in the ninety-fifth percentile or above—had been
denied raises and promotions, while less highly rated teachers had
been rewarded for loyalty to administrators. Jane Addams found
the Board of Education entirely frustrating. She could broker no
consensus on how to improve the quality of teaching or lower class
sizes to better serve troubled children. Education in Chicago seemed
hopelessly politicized, with efforts at reform cyclically stymied by
either inept administration or the resistant teachers union.

In 1909 the Chicago Board of Education, now filled with Mayor
Dunne's more progressive appointees, hired a superintendent they
hoped could break through these divides—Ella Flagg Young, an
expert on teacher training.

By the time she became the nation's first female leader of a major
school system, Young had already built an extraordinary reputation.
She was a dainty, utterly serious, and fiercely intellectual woman,
whose much older husband had died when Young was still in her
twenties. After several years' teaching, she ran the normal division
of the city's first high school. There she attempted to turn girls as
young as thirteen into competent teachers by sending them for six
months to train in one of the city's poorest elementary schools. But
many of the normalites had received poor grammar school educations and were ill prepared to teach struggling immigrant children.

When Young attempted to toss incompetents out of the training program, she found city aldermen were protecting them, often because their parents were politically connected.

Young went on to serve for thirty years as a celebrated elementary school principal and then as a district-level assistant superintendent. A number of her ideas were startlingly ahead of their time. She discouraged her teachers from assigning homework, on the grounds that more privileged children would get help from their parents, while children from less-educated families would be left further and further behind, contributing to the problem we today call the "achievement gap." When she noticed some poor children arrived at school dirty, she established school baths, and she lowered as many class sizes as she could from seventy to fifty-four students. She opposed the use of the term "melting pot" to describe Chicago schools full of immigrants, because she believed the phrase obscured children's individuality and disrespected their various cultures. At the same time, she saw the teaching of proper English as perhaps the school system's most vitally important responsibility and was appalled by many teachers' lack of good grammar and writing skills.

Political opponents would later paint Young and other progressive educators across the nation as toadies of teachers unions. But throughout her long career Young was a frequent critic of the quality of the teacher corps. In an 1887 address on "How to Teach Parents to Discriminate Between Good and Bad Teaching," she pointed out that political debates about education reform were frustrating because journalists and the public had very little reliable information about what went on in schools. Instead of allowing sensationalistic muckrakers to sketch only the most appalling classrooms, administrators should observe every teacher's classroom regularly, and classroom doors should always be open to parents, too. The education profession had too much of a "thin skin," Young lamented, and ought to strive more deliberately toward improvement and transparency. This suggestion, an incursion on teachers' privacy in the classroom, was the sort of thing that usually enraged Margaret Haley, but the Federation leader was always willing to listen to Young's thoughts, because Young was "endowed with the keenest intellect

I have ever met in man or in woman," Haley wrote. What's more, Young's critiques were accompanied by real respect for teachers. She had hosted a teachers' book club at her own home every other week; the women, some of whom had little more than a seventh-grade education, read and discussed Shakespeare and Dante. Young arranged for educational theorists to speak to teachers about the latest research on child development. The academics who participated, including John Dewey and the Harvard philosopher William James, were excited by the opportunity to test their ideas on real-world practitioners, and for the female teachers it was thrilling to be taken seriously by leading thinkers.

Working with Dewey at the University of Chicago, in 1900 Young completed a PhD dissertation in pedagogy, called "Isolation in the School." It was as much a critique of ineffective management in any field as an essay on education issues in particular. For employees to feel respected and want to work hard, Young wrote, there must be "an interplay of thought between the members of each part" of a large organization, in which teachers, principals, and administrators all learned from the expertise of their colleagues, both those below and those above them in the professional hierarchy. Teachers should not be made to feel like mere "automatons," mechanically reproducing the favored textbook-based lessons of school administrators, many of whom had only limited teaching experience themselves. When school systems were organized more democratically, Young believed, children would better understand, through direct observation, the key rights and responsibilities of citizenship.

These ideas were tested at the University of Chicago Laboratory School, which Dewey founded in 1896, and where Young served for a time as the director of instruction. About 140 students attended the school; most were the children of professors or other professionals associated with the university. Dewey often expressed horror at what he called the "medieval" techniques of traditional public schools, in which children read textbooks, memorized their contents, and studied each subject, such as history or biology, in isolation from the others, hunched over a desk. In an 1894 letter to his wife, Alice, he wrote, "When you think of the thousands and thousands of young ones who are practically ruined . . . in the Chicago schools every year, it is enough to make you go out and howl on the street corners like the Salvation Army." By contrast, the Lab School's curriculum was based on an observation from child psychology, one that Dewey had also noticed as a young father: Children's games, from cops and robbers to playing house, often imitated the professional and domestic occupations of the adults around them. Instead of approaching learning through books and memorization, Dewey hoped to craft a "new education" based on "scientific" observations of how children actually learned—through playful experimentation in which they sought to understand the workings of the grown-up world.

Although Dewey talked about centering the school experience more on children's natural curiosity and less on adult-led lessons from books, he did not advocate a passive role for teachers. Educators should "direct the child's activities" by presenting her with interesting questions and the tools she would need to answer them, Dewey wrote. In one Lab School project, students were asked to consider the role of the textile industry in shaping human history. They examined raw flax, cotton plants, and wool, running each material through a spinning wheel. Through this practice, they learned cotton fiber is more difficult to separate from its plant than flax fiber is, which explains why linen and wool clothing predated cotton, why American cotton producers relied so heavily on slave labor, and also why the invention of the cotton mill was such a boon to the economy of the antebellum United States, making slavery less politically viable.

With lessons like these, Dewey hoped students would learn to respect and understand both the abstract and physical worlds. He often recalled his own childhood in Burlington, Vermont, where his grandparents manufactured candles and soap at home from materials produced on their farm. Dewey worried that turn-of-the-century urban children had no exposure to the process of how labor transformed the products of nature into the products of industry. He hoped students at the Lab School would come to understand that every item one ate, wore, or used carried a history of human ingenuity.

nds of
owudge

Dewey's approach hardly acknowledged the ways in which the population of the Lab School differed from the population of Chicago public schools. Lab School students were fluent in English, well fed, and well clothed. Few, if any, faced the prospect of leaving school at age twelve in order to help support their families. On the other hand, many Chicago public school students had parents who turned raw materials into industrial goods every single day, whether they worked as carpenters or butchers. Unlike more affluent children, they were not at all disconnected from the means of production.

In later decades, new types of experimental schools would demonstrate that progressive pedagogy could produce excellent results for disadvantaged students, too. Ella Flagg Young, however, had a very difficult time implementing in Chicago public schools the ideas she and Dewey had pioneered at the University of Chicago. As superintendent, she did experience some significant successes: She increased teacher pay and pension contributions, established afterschool and summer programs for struggling students, hired the first speech pathology specialists and female physical education instructors, and convened "teacher councils" that met twice per year to share ideas with top administrators. She decreased high school dropout rates by adding vocational electives in architecture, accounting, shorthand, mechanical drawing, and other skills.

The teachers union backed her. But the city's business elite did not.

In 1915 Chicago's new Republican mayor, William "Big Bill" Thompson, appointed Jacob Loeb and a number of other tax cutters to the Board of Education. Loeb was the founder of a Chicago insurance company and was elected the board president. His first agenda item was a 7.5 percent budget cut; he also opposed the very concept of female principals or administrators. Loeb led a coordinated effort to push Young from her job and essentially kill the Teachers Federation. The school board passed the "Loeb Rule," which forbade "membership by teachers in organizations affiliated with a trade union." Unionization, the board claimed, was "hostile to discipline, prejudicial to the efficiency of the teaching force, and detrimental to the welfare of schools."

At the Auditorium Building on September 8, the labor movement hosted a rally to organize against the Loeb Rule. Samuel Gompers of the American Federation of Labor told the crowd that businessmen were engaged in a campaign "to eliminate men of brain and heart and sympathy and character" from the teaching force. U.S. Assistant Secretary of Labor Louis Post, a former member of Mayor Dunne's progressive school board, spoke about the threat the Teachers Federation had long posed to corporate interests more interested in lowering their own taxes than in improving the education of other people's children. "All over this country, in one form or another, it is a fight between what has been called the Interests, the special interests, and the interests of the public, the interests of the common people. That is the fight."

After a long legal and political battle, the Teachers Federation agreed to disaffiliate from the AFL, possibly in a deal with Loeb to reinstate teachers who had been fired because of their union activism. Yet during the same period, the Federation won three longer-lasting victories for unionized teachers. First, in 1913, Haley and other Illinois suffragists successfully lobbied the state legislature in favor of women's right to vote. Federation members were finally empowered at the ballot box.

Second, in 1916, the Chicago Teachers Federation founded the American Federation of Teachers, which launched with locals in Chicago; New York City; Gary, Indiana; Atlanta; St. Paul, Minnesota; and Washington, D.C. The AFT organized an additional 174 affiliates over the next four years.

Last, Loeb's virulent attack on the Federation, including his attempted firing of popular and effective classroom teachers in retaliation for their opposition to his policies, raised the ire of liberal good-government reformers. Together with the Federation and the Chicago City Council, they lobbied the state legislature to pass a bill in 1917 granting teachers tenure protection after a three-year probationary period. Previously, teachers' contracts were year to year and could be terminated at any time. After the Otis Bill passed, to dismiss a tenured teacher the school board would have to hold hearings in which teachers had the right to legal representation.

The first American teachers to win tenure rights were those in New Jersey, in 1909. Tenure is by far the most controversial aspect of contemporary teacher unionism, but in the period before World War I, there was relative consensus among union leaders, school reformers, and intellectuals in favor of tenure. It had long been a feature of the celebrated Prussian education system, which had helped convince Harvard president Charles William Eliot and New York City's reformist superintendent William Maxwell to support stronger job security protections for teachers. In New York, the new three-year probationary period followed by tenure was seen as a clean government reform after decades of politically influenced teacher appointments, in which schools were part of the patronage machine. Tenure was also popular among leaders of the National Education Association, although the NEA was hostile to classroom teachers affiliating with blue-collar organized labor.

Fed up with Chicago politics, Ella Flagg Young made plans to retire and move to California. When she stepped down from the Chicago superintendency on January 1, 1916, she released a statement to the press that could still define progressive pedagogy today, with its view of the teacher as a creative and independent intellectual guide for children:

> I believe that every child should be happy in school. So we have tried to substitute recreation for drill. . . . We have tried to recognize types of minds as a mother does among her own children. We were losing the majority of children at the fifth grade. By letting them do things with their hands we have saved many of them. In order that teachers may delight in awakening the spirits of children, they must themselves be awake. We have tried to free the teachers. Some day the system will be such that the child and teacher will go to school with ecstatic joy. At home in the evening, the child will talk about the things done during the day and will talk with pride. I want to make the schools the great instrument of democracy.

Margaret Haley and the Teachers Federation would have liked to believe that in Young's absence, they carried on her legacy. At times they did, but amid increasing political and business pressure on schools during the interwar years, teachers unions in Chicago and beyond often found themselves making unsavory alliances, and engaging in rough-and-tumble politics far afield from education itself.

Chicago mayor William Dever was a good-government reformist Democrat. Voters elected him in 1923 to clean up the mess left behind by "Big Bill" Thompson, whose Board of Education, it was discovered, embezzled $8 million in school funds. Dever appointed William McAndrew as schools superintendent. A thoroughly modern bicycle enthusiast, McAndrew had risen to national prominence as an administrator in the Brooklyn public schools, where his ideas were shaped by Frederick Winslow Taylor, the founder of the "scientific management" movement. Taylor, an engineer, believed every aspect of the manufacturing process should be measured, such as how many hems an individual worker could sew in an hour, or how much money a company lost due to worker error, such as errant stitches. This would help companies improve job training, and make it easier to assign laborers to specific repetitive tasks they could complete quickly, in what Taylor termed the "One Best Way." To encourage good performance, he believed workers should receive small pay bonuses for crafting good products.

Though Taylor intended his theories to be applied to factory work, they soon became a fad among public school administrators, who were eager, during the bullish 1920s, to embrace innovative business practices. Prominent journals such as *Educational Review* published intricate tables for judging teachers' output. Teachers would be measured by evidence of their students' learning, which could be demonstrated through test scores or examples of children's essays, penmanship, and drawings. A study by education researcher William Lancelot explained how administrators could record a "pupil change" score for every teacher, by testing how much the teacher's students knew on a given subject at the beginning and then the end of a term. (Today this calculation is called a teacher's "value-added" score.) Lancelot applied his pupil change method to math instructors at Iowa State College and found that, indeed, some teachers were more effective than others. Yet gains for students who studied with the best teachers were modest: an average of less than three additional points on a hundred-point grading scale. Why? According to peer reviewer Helen Walker—as well as many of today's critics of value added—the pupil change measurement ultimately had a "low relationship" to true teacher quality, since so many factors beyond a teacher's control could affect a student's test score, from class size to family involvement in education.

Student achievement was not the only factor measured in the new efficiency rubrics. Evaluation systems called for teachers to be judged on their personal characteristics and given numeric ratings in largely subjective categories, such as "obedience," "honesty of work," "dress," "voice," and "force of character." A teacher's command of classroom discipline would also be assessed, by counting the number of students who were late or unruly, and even by measuring the number of seconds and minutes it took for a teacher to distribute or collect worksheets. Principals would painstakingly record all this data on spreadsheets—then handwritten, of course—and higher-level administrators could subsequently grade principals by looking at the performance of an entire school.

McAndrew, the Chicago schools superintendent, believed fervently in these new, supposedly rationalized teacher rating systems. In his 1916 book, *The Public and Its Schools,* he wrote that evaluating teachers based on their students' test scores was far superior to the traditional method: a principal "walking through the rooms once a day." His zeal for rooting out and firing inefficient teachers who could not improve is more than a little reminiscent of Michelle Rhee, the recent Washington, D.C., schools chancellor who seemed to take delight in mass layoffs. McAndrew wrote:

> If a principal is unable with a reasonable share of his time from other duties to show a teacher how to acquire teaching ability, he must take steps to secure for the teacher freedom to enter other employment. To permit the waste of the lives of

children and of the community's money through poor teaching is not only the worst of management, but a negligent dishonesty that is scandalous. There has grown up here a fallacy that the schools should be run to give employment to us and in case of doubt the benefit should be given us, the employees. No private school, no public service, runs on that basis. It is an absurdity.

When he arrived in Chicago, McAndrew immediately took two steps that earned him the ire of Margaret Haley and the rest of organized labor. First, he moved to disband the beloved teacher councils Young had founded. Like most Taylorites, McAndrew believed in the principle of a rational, expertise-driven manager presiding decisively over employees. If administrators had access to the knowledge and data necessary to improve the school system, they would not need to meet regularly with teachers to hear their ideas. He then proposed that junior high students be assigned, based on IQ scores, to either vocational or academic-track schools. The Chicago school board supported McAndrew's proposal, releasing a 1924 "research bulletin" claiming that IQ tests given to World War I army recruits had proven there were five levels of supposedly innate intelligence, each corresponding with an occupational class: "Professional and business," "clerical," "skilled trades," "semi-skilled trades," and "unskilled labor."

The Federation, like Ella Flagg Young, preferred a Deweyite "single track" approach to the curriculum: that schools should help all children become facile with their hands, but ought not to direct students toward specific jobs, nor neglect academics. Alongside the teachers union, male organized labor in Chicago helped lead the opposition to vocational determinism. The leader of the Illinois State Federation of Labor, John Walker, believed dual-track schools would make public education "a training place for cheap labor, beasts of burden, at the expense of the development of the children as broad-minded, big-hearted, intelligent, fine types of citizenship." The AFL published a pamphlet warning that IQ tests could be used to sear the children of working-class parents with "the brand of inferiority."

The unions were right to push back against high-stakes IQ testing. By 1922—two years *before* McAndrew came to Chicago— respected researchers had begun to decry the wartime intelligence studies as bunk science that failed to account for the differences in recruits' previous schooling. A study of over 100,000 New York City fifth graders found socioeconomic factors such as family income and access to health care outweighed IQ as predictors of academic success. What's more, IQ appeared to be changeable over time, not a measure of innate talent. *Harper's* published a study showing that after living in the North for several years, southern-born blacks were able to score higher on IQ tests.

Nevertheless, under the sway of efficiency reformers who hoped to match children to jobs, schools rushed to buy and administer standardized IQ exams. A 1932 survey of 150 school districts found three-quarters used intelligence tests to assign students to different academic tracks. IQ testing had replaced phrenology as school reform's favored "science" for sorting and classifying children.

As Haley fought against tracking and McAndrew's other efficiency policies—such as the requirement that teachers check in on a timesheet four times each day—she won support from the normally anti-union *Chicago Tribune,* which warned the superintendent against "antagonizing the bulk of the teaching force" through an overly top-down reform agenda. Yet in her passion for removing McAndrew from office, Haley teamed up with a shady character: "Big Bill" Thompson, the corrupt former mayor, who hoped to regain his office and run for president under the isolationist slogan "America First." In a March 30, 1927, ad in the *Tribune,* Thompson accused McAndrew and Mayor Dever of being "pro-British rats who are poisoning the wells of historical truth" by selecting history textbooks that called George Washington a "rebel" instead of a hero. Those allegations were false. In fact, McAndrew strongly supported American patriotism in the school curriculum. Yet with backing from the Teachers Federation, Thompson defeated Dever and then axed McAndrew, whose reform ideas were never fully implemented. Even after the "rat" McAndrew's departure, the Board of Education continued to hear testimony on so-called anti-American "propaganda" in schools.

During the first three decades of teacher unionism, the path-breaking Chicago Teachers Federation boasted achievements of high idealism: bringing tax-dodging corporations to heel, resisting IQ determinism on behalf of poor children, and helping women earn the right to vote. Yet the teachers union movement was (and remains today) a pragmatic, even sometimes cynical, lobbying effort, and one that protected some poorly performing teachers. By partnering with nativist political forces to target McAndrew as insufficiently patriotic, Margaret Haley and her "lady labor sluggers" had emboldened a movement—ideological litmus testing for professional educators—that was already wreaking havoc on American urban education.

Chapter Five

"An Orgy of Investigation"

WITCH HUNTS AND SOCIAL MOVEMENT UNIONISM
DURING THE WARS

In 1917, Mary McDowell taught Latin at Manual Training High School in the working-class neighborhood of Park Slope, Brooklyn. She was a square-jawed single woman in her early forties who lived with her widowed mother just south of Prospect Park. Befitting the caricature of an old-maid schoolmarm, McDowell was plain-looking and unglamorous, with thin, wire glasses framing her eyes in perfect circles. But while most of her female colleagues had only been to normal school, McDowell, a Quaker, had graduated from Swarthmore, studied at Oxford University in England, and then earned a master's degree at Columbia. Since the onset of the Great War she had been donating $35 per month, a fifth of her modest income, to the American Friends Service Committee, to be used for civilian relief efforts in France.

In a 1914 performance evaluation, Manual's principal noted McDowell "is a fine example for girls. I am impressed with her conscientiousness, her earnest desire to give the best. She is not of the 2:30 type"—meaning she did not rush out of school as soon as the final bell rang. But McDowell ran into trouble three years later, when a Yale-educated engineer named Horace Mann Snyder replaced her previous boss. Named by his superintendent father after the common schools visionary, Snyder arrived in Brooklyn filled to the brim with the popular education reform theories of the day and began implementing them with gusto. At the time, only 17 percent of Americans completed high school, where the classical, academic curriculum prevailed. Vocational tracking and sports programs were seen as a way to reduce dropouts by making school more engaging and relevant to teenagers. Snyder planned to introduce IQ testing to split Manual freshmen into three tracks, which would determine the courses they took for the next four years as well as the opportunities open to them after graduation. If only a third of Manual's students would be prepared for college, an old-fashioned, full-time Latin teacher like McDowell would almost certainly be considered superfluous—a dinosaur teaching a dead language to poor children ill equipped to use it.

The principal's second major enthusiasm was for "citizenship" training, a craze that swept the nation's schools during World War I. What Snyder had in mind was less a rigorous civics curriculum than a sort of suffusion of Manual High School with patriotic spirit. He required teachers to transcribe patriotic quotations on the blackboard each day and distribute leaflets encouraging students to buy war savings stamps. McDowell fulfilled these directives. But when Snyder asked her to spend an hour each week discussing the general merits of the United States above all other nations, McDowell demurred. She was there to teach Latin; diligent study, she believed, was the most patriotic way for her students to spend their time. Snyder retaliated via the teacher evaluation system.

During the late nineteenth century, New York City had a teacher evaluation system in which principals rated 99.5 percent of teachers as "good." When reformer William Maxwell became superintendent in 1898, he was frustrated by the lack of centralized information on teachers' performance. He instituted a new system, which required principals to grade teachers on a finer scale, from A to D. Within a few years, it was generally regarded, in the words of *The New York Times,* as "a joke"; principals resented the copious paperwork involved, and the vast majority of teachers, including McDowell, received a B+ each year, indicating better-than-average performance. But at Manual High School, Snyder was determined to punish McDowell for her resistance to his patriotism agenda. He decreased her rating to a B, threatening that "C or D more accurately reflects the present value of your services to the city and State." The animus between the two intensified just before Christmas break in

1917, when Snyder asked every member of his faculty to sign a so-called "loyalty pledge" then circulating throughout the New York City school system, at the behest of the mayor, the superintendent, and the Board of Education. There were several versions of the pledge, but the text of the one McDowell was asked to sign most likely looked something like this:

> We, the teachers of the public schools of the City of New York, do solemnly pledge our unqualified loyalty to the President and Congress of the United States in this war with the imperial governments of Germany and Austria.
>
> We pledge ourselves actively to inculcate in our pupils by word and deed love of flag and unquestioning loyalty to the military policy of the government and to the measures and principles proclaimed by the President and Congress.
>
> We declare ourselves to be in sympathy with the purposes of the government and its efforts to make the world safe for democracy, and believe that our highest duty at this moment is to uphold the hands of the President and Congress in this crisis.
>
> We believe that any teachers whose views prevent them from subscribing to such sentiments should not be permitted to teach the youth of our city.

Of New York City's twenty thousand teachers, hundreds initially expressed reluctance to recite these words or sign their name to them. But when they realized their jobs were at stake, all but thirty relented. McDowell was one of the holdouts. For a strict Quaker, this vow was impossible. She was a pacifist who opposed, in principle, all wars, no matter what their cause. After she expressed her views in a letter to Principal Snyder, she was suspended without pay. In May 1918 McDowell went on "trial" at the Upper East Side headquarters of the Department of Education. This was not an actual procedure of the city or state legal systems, but rather an internally conducted employment hearing to determine whether McDowell would lose her tenure protections and her job. The room overflowed with reporters, as well as teacher and Quaker supporters of McDowell. The "judge," called a trial examiner, noted that as a thirteen-year veteran of the New York City schools, McDowell had a "flawless" teaching record. There was no evidence she had ever indoctrinated her students into her own pacifist or Quaker beliefs. At issue, then, were her private convictions. New York City schools superintendent William Ettinger pressed McDowell, who was on the witness stand, to state whether she would personally take up arms to resist a military invasion. McDowell said she was sure most Americans, including her own students, would do so, but that she could not; there were "many ways of resisting" hostility other than with violence. Her attorneys noted that Quakers had been instrumental in building New York State's public school system, and an 1830 declaration by the state board of education had affirmed the right of schoolteachers not to be questioned on their religious beliefs.

It was no matter. A jingoistic climate had invaded the public schools, and teachers with dissident politics were being targeted for dismissal, regardless of their excellence in the classroom—and especially if they taught unpopular subjects that did not fit within the vocational framework, like the classics or foreign languages. McDowell was declared guilty of "conduct unbecoming a teacher" and fired.

For educators during World War I, the combination of dissident politics and opposition to IQ testing, strict vocational tracking, or new forms of teacher evaluation could prove especially professionally risky. Alexander Fichlander, a respected Brooklyn principal, was a pacifist who refused to sign the loyalty pledge. He also supported the AFT-affiliated New York City Teachers Union, which was founded in 1916 to emulate the success of Margaret Haley's organization in Chicago. Fichlander was well known as a critic of the city's A–D teacher rating system, which he thought imposed a bureaucratic burden on principals without actually improving instruction for students. In 1917 the Board of Education denied him a promotion he had already won from his Brooklyn district supervisor, to be the principal of a larger elementary school. John Greene, a member of the committee who made the decision, said the honor would only give Fichlander "a sphere for wider influence for his unpatriotic views. Here is a man who debased his citizenship and who refused to sign the declaration of loyalty to the United States."

There was broad public support for the witch hunts that ensnared Fichlander and McDowell. On November 18, 1917, the editorial board of *The New York Times* declared: "The Board of Education should root out all the disloyal or doubtful teachers. This little private war of these misguided or out-of-equilibrium persons on the United States must stop. They must be put out of the schools; and if they continue to profess sedition publicly, they must be locked up."

The moral panic about supposedly unpatriotic educators was driven by international war hysteria combined with agitation over the growing domestic political strength of teachers unions. In 1917 and 1918, Congress passed the Espionage and Sedition Acts, which sought to ban public speech and actions "disloyal" to the United States military and government, especially among socialists, communists, pacifists, immigrants, and other groups perceived as affiliated with European leftism. More than any other force, the American Legion, a veterans' organization, pushed this ethos of unquestioning patriotism onto the nation's public schools. The Legion was influential: 16 U.S. senators and 130 congressmen identified as members. It promoted the idea that the Communist Party in Moscow actively recruited American teachers in order to enlist them in brainwashing the nation's youth. The Legion saw all left-of-center political activity as unacceptably anti-American. In a directive to its local affiliates, the group asked its one million members to watch for "reds and pinks" working in public schools, asserting, "There is little difference between some kinds of so-called Socialism, liberalism, radicalism, and Communism."

In 1921 the Legion partnered with the National Education Association to counteract the growing influence of Margaret Haley's AFT, which both organizations were eager to paint as unprofessional, thuggish, and radical—a labor union in the mold of Bolshevism, which any decent teacher should shun. With the support of the NEA, the Legion introduced an annual "American Education Week" in November, during which teachers were asked to preach that "Revolutionists, Communists, and extreme pacifists are a menace" to "life, liberty, justice, security, and happiness." The curriculum suggested the following essay topic: "Patriotism, the Paramount Human Emotion."

The Legion also cultivated a relationship with newspaper magnate William Randolph Hearst, an opponent of the income tax and increased funding for teacher salaries and schools (all priorities of the AFT). In 1935 Hearst's papers ran a series of articles written by a Legion commander, attacking public school teachers who explained the Depression as a failure of free markets. Teachers who did not purchase Liberty Bonds, did not display the American flag in their classrooms, or did not salute the flag were depicted in Legion literature as a "fifth column" loyal to the Soviet Union. Principals, school boards, and mayors sympathetic to the Legion—or scared to buck the group—targeted such teachers for investigation and sometimes dismissal. In 1939, the Legion's advocacy helped prompt the House Un-American Activities Committee to investigate communist influence within the AFT.

Between 1917 and 1960, several waves of patriotic moral panic convulsed the nation's schools, in what the historian Howard K. Beale termed "an orgy of investigation" that targeted tens of thousands of teachers. Over the course of four decades, the American public was periodically riveted by the drama of teachers fired or put on trial for their leftist political beliefs—even "taking the Fifth" or "naming names" in front of congressional committees. Joining the American Legion's campaign of fear were conservative advocacy groups like the Veterans of Foreign Wars, the Daughters of the American Revolution, and the Christian Front, an anti-Semitic organization associated with the Catholic radio preacher Father Coughlin. At the local level, activists often targeted individual teachers for dismissal. The education historian and commentator Diane Ravitch remembers that in Houston in the early 1950s, at the height of McCarthyism, her public high school came under the sway of mothers who were members of the Minute Women of the USA, an anticommunist group that also opposed New Deal social programs and the formation of the United Nations. Under pressure, the school's librarian removed books about the Soviet Union from the shelves, and the school board forced Ravitch's favorite teacher, Nelda Davis, out of her job in retaliation for her liberal internationalist views. Davis had also opposed racial segregation.

Witch-hunted teachers were part of an unusual demographic moment in American public education. Because of Depression-era unemployment in the private sector, as well as racial, ethnic, and gender quotas in professions such as academia, medicine, and the law, the urban teacher corps of this period became particularly diverse and well educated, even to the point of being overqualified. From the 1930s through the 1950s, big-city school districts employed a growing number of teachers with master's degrees and doctorates. The male share of the teaching force increased from 17 to 30 percent between 1929 and 1960—higher than it is today. In New York City during the Depression, there was such an oversupply of college-educated teaching hopefuls that the Board of Education instituted a complex, multi-step process for earning a credential. Candidates took exams on pedagogy and content knowledge; a prospective high school English teacher, for example, would be asked to interpret a classic poem. Candidates had to pass a Standard English speech test (which was often used to discriminate against those who spoke with a working-class black or Jewish inflection), and then teach a sample lesson in a real classroom. Lastly, prospective teachers sat for a nerve-wracking interview with school officials, in which their appearance, dress, and manner were bluntly assessed.

Some of the young, educated teachers who passed these stringent tests had left-wing or radical politics, inculcated on university campuses. This did not change the fact that the vast majority of midcentury public school educators remained apolitical. When Beale, the historian, conducted a national survey of teachers during the 1930s, he found many were disturbingly ignorant of current affairs. But conservative activists were correct that a small yet politically significant segment of the urban teacher corps actively participated in left-wing movements seen during the interwar and Cold War years as a major threat to a stable American government. In a few shocking cases, communist educators were even involved in international espionage. Three female New York City teachers participated in an early-1940s plot to free the Stalinist assassins of Leon Trotsky, the Soviet dissident killed in Mexico.

Yet the vast majority of pacifist, socialist, and communist teachers were like Nelda Davis and Mary McDowell: local activists and intellectuals who were loyal to the United States yet critical of its wars and domestic inequalities. Sadly, those teachers who lost their jobs in witch hunts tended—exactly because of their social justice views—to be some of the most dedicated educators, and the most passionate about reaching disadvantaged students. As Beale noted, it was not the "average" teacher who was hurt by red-baiting, but "the exceptional teacher" who brought a strong sense of mission into the classroom.

This story played out most dramatically in New York City, where Communist activists gained control of the Teachers Union in 1935. They created a "social movement unionism" that went far beyond the bread-and-butter organizing Margaret Haley pioneered in Chicago. Though both mainstream and communist teacher unionists opposed IQ tracking and supported higher teacher pay and smaller class sizes, the far-left politics of some of the younger teachers during the interwar period split the still-nascent teacher union movement into two camps. One camp, affiliated with Haley and John Dewey, was the precursor to today's unions. Led by the moderate New York City Teachers Guild, it was social democratic and concerned with legislative maneuvering in support of school funding and teacher autonomy. The second camp, which has no real equivalent today, was affiliated with communism and the global anticolonialist ideology of W. E. B. Du Bois, who turned toward Marxism after World War I. This gadfly band of teachers fought aggressively for academic freedom and for schools to embrace a broad antiracist, antipoverty agenda—a platform that, despite its radicalism in its own time, anticipated many later-twentieth-century goals of education reform.

Irving Adler always said that his wife, Ruth, introduced him to communism. The two first crossed paths in the early 1930s at a meeting of pacifist student activists, flirting as they made posters for a demonstration. Irving, a City College math major, considered himself a socialist. But Ruth, the daughter of Jewish farmers who had emigrated from Minsk to upstate New York, was far more radical. She belonged to a branch of the Young Communist League, and even picketed her own Barnard graduation, in defense of medical students who had been expelled from Columbia because of their antiwar views. Because she did not participate in the ceremony, she did not find out until the next day that she had won the college's highest prize in mathematics. Later that week Ruth and Irving were married, and both began training to become New York City public school teachers.

Communist teachers tended to be highly educated Jews and often, like Adler, graduates of City College, known as Harvard-on-the-Hudson. Unlike Ivy League universities, City College did not discriminate against Jewish applicants, many of whom wished to study math, physics, and the emerging social sciences, such as political science and sociology. What drew these young intellectuals to teaching? When Jewish students graduated from City College, they entered a job market tightly limited by both the Great Depression and anti-Semitism. Irving Adler won high honors in math but quickly learned that few of New York's top insurance or accounting firms hired "out" Jews; even City College's own math department employed no Jewish faculty. Ruth Adler experienced even more virulent employment discrimination, due to both her ethnicity and her gender. Working in public education offered a respite from such blatant prejudice. The couple officially joined both the Communist Party and the New York City Teachers Union.

The New York union had launched in 1916 with social democratic politics, as Local 5 of the American Federation of Teachers. In 1927 it successfully lobbied the state legislature to increase teachers' wages. It was a major victory. But after the devastating economic crash of 1929, New York began to pursue austerity budget measures. The city hired new teachers, including Irving and Ruth Adler, as full-time "permanent substitutes"—a classification that allowed the district to pay them lower wages and deny them paid sick days. For the older teachers who dominated the Local 5 leadership, substitutes weren't a major issue; instead the union prioritized fighting proposed wage cuts for tenured teachers. Nor did Local 5 take a strong position on the dismal physical conditions in many overcrowded and unsanitary New York City school buildings, particularly those in poor black neighborhoods, where young Jewish subs were more likely to work. Irving Adler was assigned to Haaren High School in Harlem. He helped recruit sixty teachers there to join the union, and helped organize one of the city's first free lunch programs for poor children.

In the view of Adler and other younger teachers, the union's leaders had became too "cautious and conservative," unwilling to criticize the politicians with whom they had once negotiated to advance teacher pay legislation. An opposition caucus, the Rank and File, formed within the union and in 1935 gained control of the Local 5 executive committee. The union's new leaders were in their twenties and early thirties, and many were involved in antifascist organizing; a few even spent their summer vacations volunteering with the loyalist forces fighting Franco in Spain. Most of these activist teachers, including the Teachers Union's new president, Charles Hendley, and its most prominent black leader, Lucille Spence, were not Communist Party members. The union often advised its members to vote for candidates affiliated with the American Labor Party, a New York State socialist organization that endorsed Franklin D. Roosevelt. But several of the TU's most vocal organizers, including Adler, were card-carrying communists.

Local 5's new leadership relaunched the union's newsletter, *The New York Teacher News,* as a serious journal of education policy. In the magazine's first issue, Hendley articulated "The Union's Stand" in favor of "intellectual honesty" and against "deadening routine" and "lock-step methods" in the classroom. Though Dewey's "new education" was ascendant among intellectuals and in private schools, only a few of his progressive ideas—typically the less radical ones, like arranging elementary school children's desks in groups instead of rows—had penetrated urban public education. The vast majority of teachers continued to base their lessons on standardized textbooks selected by administrators, and to teach by reading aloud or lecturing in front of the class. In New York City, 41 percent of classes had over forty students. The new union leaders saw lowering class sizes, especially in low-income schools, as a prerequisite for more progressive, creative styles of teaching.

Local 5 embraced a mission beyond the classroom. Mary McDowell had kept her antiwar politics to herself, until she was provoked by the loyalty oath. But the Teachers Union and Hendley loudly swore to "take a stand against the militarists and the imperialists who promote war." They vowed to lobby for health insurance, Social Security, unemployment benefits, and child labor laws. On education policy, the union concerned itself largely with racial equality. With the Great Migration of southern blacks into northern cities, the educational challenges of racial diversity were ever clearer. Should northern schools, which were de facto, not de jure, segregated, be integrated? Given the rapid acceleration of white flight—the exodus of middle-class Irish, Italian, and Jewish families from neighborhoods like Harlem in Manhattan and Bedford-Stuyvesant in Brooklyn—was integration even a realistic goal across the city, or were there too few white children to spread around? The TU chose to pursue a three-pronged civil rights agenda: first, fighting for a rigorous curriculum at schools that served poor children; second, removing racist textbooks from schools and writing new curricula for black and Puerto Rican history; and third, partnering with community organizations to improve social conditions in poor neighborhoods.

In the 1940s and 1950s, one of the union's protests involved Yorkville High School on Manhattan's far East Side, where 95 percent of the student body was black or Puerto Rican. Many girls chose the school because it had a well-regarded pre-nursing program, yet when freshmen arrived, they were given a battery of IQ and aptitude tests that resulted in most of the nonwhite girls being directed instead to a three-year "annex" course that had nothing to do with nursing. Annex students took few English classes and no math. They spent the day learning "homemaking" skills, such as simple sewing, and left school with scant qualifications for either employment or further education. Meanwhile, several of the city's most academically rigorous schools, like Stuyvesant High in lower Manhattan and Science High in the Bronx, began using test scores to limit enrollment so that they could continue to serve an exclusively white population in a rapidly diversifying city. (Both of those schools remain today bastions of selectivity where admission is determined solely by standardized test scores and where the student bodies contain few black or Hispanic kids.)

Teachers Union leaders did not oppose vocationalism, since they felt job training was a crucial service for the majority of students who would never graduate from college. During the Depression, even Du Bois, champion of the "talented tenth," became an ardent supporter of high-quality vocational programs for black teenagers. But TU teachers like Irving Adler believed vocational high schools ought to continue offering courses in advanced math and foreign languages, instead of seeing those subjects as perks working-class children didn't need and that the school system couldn't afford. Like the Federation in Chicago, the New York union argued that students and their families should choose what courses to take, instead of being confined to a specific track, either vocational or academic, because of the results of an intelligence test.

Because so many black migrants from the South arrived in northern cities with few literacy skills, the TU believed black neighborhood schools should be guaranteed class sizes under thirty and given more funding for guidance counselors, hot lunches, and health clinics. In both Bed-Stuy and Harlem, union activists urged local police precincts to establish afterschool programs and sports leagues to prevent juvenile crime, instead of relying on harsh curfews and other punitive measures that treated every young black male as a potential criminal, leaving teenagers fearful and wary of authority.

Union pamphlets suggested that teachers of immigrant children learn basic Spanish and create units on Puerto Rican history. From the 1930s on, the union lobbied the New York City Board of Education to discontinue the use of curriculum materials that contained racial stereotypes. A 1950 union study of city textbooks found that in general, they ignored slave revolts, declared that most slave owners had treated their human chattel kindly, treated emancipation as a privilege for which blacks were unprepared, and depicted Reconstruction not as a time of expanded opportunity for freedmen and -women, but as a period of political chaos that practically justified the rise of the Ku Klux Klan and Jim Crow politics. Geography textbooks portrayed European colonialism as a benevolent force bringing culture to "backward" countries like Nicaragua and Guatemala, whose populations one textbook called "quarrelsome and therefore lacking in progress."

The commitments of civil rights leaders animated the TU's agenda on race. In 1952 W. E. B. Du Bois accepted the Teachers

Union annual award. But as historian Clarence Taylor demonstrates in his 2011 study of the Teachers Union, *Reds at the Blackboard,* the organization's commendable work on racial justice cannot obscure the deeply problematic nature of its relationship to the Communist Party.

Teachers Union publications were filled with rose-colored depictions of life behind the Iron Curtain. A 1943 TU pamphlet praised Soviet scouting programs for boys and farming education for girls. Three years later, an entire issue of the *New York Teacher* was devoted to celebrating the USSR. It suggested a civics lesson in which teachers would explain to students the difference between the American concept of "freedom from" government intervention and the Soviet concept of "freedom to," such as freedom to have a job and freedom to have enough to eat. Yes, the Soviet Union was a one-party state, the newspaper acknowledged, but that one party was the representative of the working class. Some prominent TU activists paid little heed to the gathering evidence of Soviet authoritarianism and human rights abuses.

Were communist teachers disloyal spies or patriotic American dissidents? From 1932 to 1945, during the TU's strongest years, Earl Browder led the American communist movement. Though he participated in Soviet espionage, Browder was a relative moderate. He had come to radical politics through his midwestern involvement in labor unionism and pacifism, and he believed communism could fit within the larger American democratic tradition. During World War II Browder sought to cool hostilities between communists and socialists. He advocated for progressives to present a unified front against fascism, and by the late 1930s he led American communists to support President Roosevelt's New Deal.

Browder's vision of the Communist Party as a cooperative partner within the broader American Left attracted many activist public school teachers. Though radical, the Teachers Union had six thousand members by 1940, making it by far the largest teachers organization in New York City. Some communist teachers worked diligently on FDR's reelection campaigns; they saw themselves as pragmatic idealists. Unionists, however, were a comparatively small segment of the teacher corps. During the interwar years, most public school teachers felt unionism carried a blue-collar stain, and they worried that joining with organized labor would decrease the public's respect for teaching as a profession. In December 1940, the American Federation of Teachers expelled the New York and Philadelphia locals, afraid their communist politics would taint the entire teacher unionism movement. In its place the AFT recognized the smaller New York Teachers Guild, a precursor to the United Federation of Teachers, the union that today represents New York City teachers. Yet even after its expulsion, the Teachers Union retained most of its former members. It affiliated with the Congress of Industrial Workers (CIO), an umbrella group of unions sympathetic to communism.

Within a few years, the more moderate communism typified by Browder and many TU members began to lose international support. In 1946, Communist Party radicals expelled Browder. His inner circle, including Bella Dodd, the TU's legislative director, were suddenly on the outs with their fellow travelers, and what had been an intimate social group of activist teachers was riven by infighting. Irving and Ruth Adler ran into Dodd at a protest and were dismayed to see many old friends and colleagues refusing to acknowledge her. Isolated and depressed, Dodd, a charismatic speaker well known in New York political circles, reconnected with her Catholic roots and began a new career as a defector media darling, speaking and writing about the evils of godless communism, and—like the American Legion—depicting public school teachers as brainwashers of America's youth. The "function of a Communist teacher is to create people willing to accept Communist government," she said. Teachers who did not toe the line in their classroom lectures were purged from the party, she claimed.

These dramatic events coincided with the dawn of the Cold War. The United States and Soviet Russia were no longer allies in the fight against Nazism, and American communists found themselves not only attacking one another, but once again in the crosshairs of jingoistic politicians. In 1949 the New York state legislature passed the Feinberg Law, which allowed school districts to dismiss teachers who belonged to any "subversive organization," including the Communist Party. Even the far-left wing of the labor movement rushed to distance itself from the red menace. In March 1950 the CIO expelled the Teachers Union and eleven other communist-sympathetic unions. What followed was a decade of anticommunist purges that ended the careers of 378 New York City public school teachers, most of them tenured and extraordinarily professionally distinguished. (An additional 1,000 teachers were investigated but were allowed to continue working.) A purge began when a teacher, typically a TU member, received a notice requesting that she report to the office of Superintendent William Jansen. Once the teacher arrived, Jansen would ask the notorious question: "Are you now or have you ever been a member of the Communist Party?" A reply of "yes" would lead to immediate dismissal; a refusal to answer could bring on an investigation of a teacher's political activities and personal life, followed by a school board trial, which would be breathlessly covered in the newspapers and on radio and television. At least a handful of teachers saved their own careers by "naming names" of supposedly communist colleagues; many others resigned immediately upon receiving a summons, unwilling to perjure themselves, endure a public trial, or inform on friends.

The most notorious trial took place in September and October 1950. Eight Jewish members of the Teachers Union had refused to answer the question about whether they were communists and were charged with "insubordination and conduct unbecoming a teacher." *Teacher News* editor Celia Zitron taught Latin and had created a Hebrew curriculum. Teachers Union president Abraham Lederman was a World War II veteran and a junior high school math teacher. Of the group of eight, Alice Citron was especially celebrated. As a nineteen-year veteran of Harlem public schools, she was well known for writing an African American history curriculum, inviting students to her home, and using her own money to buy needy children eyeglasses, books, shoes, and food. Fifteen Harlem parents attended the trial to speak on Citron's behalf. Pearl Messiah described the peeling paint, broken toilets, and "ugly, nasty books" in her children's schools, explaining that Citron "inspired us and showed us that we could get these things changed" through advocacy. "Everybody loves Alice," Messiah said. Another mother, Rose Scott Gallant, said, "She is everything to our neighborhood, to the community as a whole." Citron's boss, P.S. 185 principal Abraham Gold, testified that Citron did "splendid work" deserving of "nothing but the highest praise."

But the Board of Education had little interest in the classroom records of communist teachers; prosecutor John McGrath freely admitted he had no "proof of any specific classroom act" that had indoctrinated students with communist beliefs. New York's Feinberg Law, which was later upheld by the U.S. Supreme Court, concerned itself solely with teachers' private political ideas, and whether those "anti-American" views were incompatible with educating the state's children. A second justification for the McCarthy-era witch hunts was the supposedly unprofessional stance of "insubordination" that teachers displayed when they refused to answer the superintendent's questions about their political affiliations. Such insubordination, the Board argued, would teach children to question, instead of to heed, authority—the same charge the *Chicago Tribune* had once leveled against the nation's first teachers union.

In his ruling terminating the employment of all eight teachers, trial examiner Theodore Kiendl resurrected the rhetoric of the Mary McDowell trial of 1918. He found no distinction between a teacher who actively indoctrinated students and one who simply belonged to an organization with unpopular views. He ruled:

> . . . a teacher who consciously subscribes to any ideology that advocates the violent overthrow of our government and is prepared to carry it into effect when that seems possible, is utterly unfit to be entrusted with the education of our public school children. The dangers inherent in the continuance of such a teacher far outweigh all other considerations, and even otherwise perfect performance as a teacher cannot be invoked to preserve his tenure.

In 1952 the U.S. Senate Committee on Internal Security arrived in New York to investigate the TU. Bella Dodd testified that the union's neighborhood activism was merely a "sinister conspiracy" used to dupe bleeding-heart teachers into joining the Communist Party. "I love Joe McCarthy," she declared. Irving Adler invoked the Fifth Amendment regarding his Communist Party membership. He lost his job and went on to become a bestselling author of math and science books for children. (In 1956 he and his wife left the party in protest against the Soviet invasion of Hungary.) Many purged teachers led illustrious second careers. Alice Citron became the personal secretary to the writer and activist Shirley Graham Du Bois, the second wife of W. E. B. Du Bois. Citron arranged for former TU member Abel Meeropol and his wife, Anne, to adopt the young sons of Julius and Ethel Rosenberg, the communists who were executed for treason in 1953. (Abel Meeropol was the lyricist who wrote "Strange Fruit," the anti-lynching anthem sung by Billie Holiday.)

Not all teachers caught up in the witch hunts were actually communists. TU secretary Lucille Spence, the union's highest-ranking African American, never joined the party. But after an informant claimed Spence was a member, the FBI shadowed her for nine years. The Senate committee grilled Spence on her summer 1936 visit to the Soviet Union to observe schools there. When asked if she believed communists—or Nazis—should be able to teach public school, she responded, "I think a school teacher should be judged by the teacher's performance in the classroom, including a communist, a Negro, or Jew."

The last New York City teacher purges took place in 1960. Just a few years later, the fear and jingoism of the McCarthy era lifted. Several purged teachers were rehired and given back pay. In 1967, in a case brought by faculty members at the State University of New York, the Supreme Court reversed its earlier ruling on the Feinberg Law, declaring it unconstitutional. Ten years later the New York City Board of Education restored the pensions of Irving Adler and other teachers who were victims of the witch hunts.

The Teachers Union, however, never recovered. In 1960 a new union called the United Federation of Teachers burst onto the scene, an alliance between the social democratic Teachers Guild and secondary school teachers, mostly men, who believed they deserved higher pay than their female elementary school counterparts. The UFT brokered a compromise by supporting a new kind of salary schedule, one that rewarded teachers not only for time on the job, but also for advanced degrees. This system would be gender neutral but would guarantee higher pay for many male high school teachers, who were more likely to have college and graduate degrees. The UFT promised to address day-to-day frustrations like teachers' lack of lunch periods free from school duties. And it promised to jettison communist politics. The UFT's new leaders, men like David Selden, George Altomare, and Al Shanker, were the sons of blue-collar union members and, compared to the leaders of the Teachers Union, advanced a far less idealized vision of the teaching profession. "High school teachers are assembly line workers, they're piece workers," Altomare told historian Daniel Perlstein, recalling the UFT's early years. Since teachers worked with each individual student for only forty minutes per day, Altomare said, "You don't know the kids [well enough] to get any job satisfaction."

Though its political ideology was more moderate, the UFT embraced militant protest tactics, including strikes, which even the TU had considered off-limits for "professional" teachers. On November 7, 1960, the UFT led a one-day strike demanding higher teacher pay, collective bargaining, smaller class sizes, and lunch periods free from school duties. TU members crossed the picket lines and went to work. State law said the five thousand strikers could lose their jobs, but in reality, it was impossible to fire and replace 10 percent of the city's teaching force. Though the strike was not immediately effective in winning concessions on pay and working conditions, teachers throughout the city were impressed by the UFT's show of force, and in 1961 they voted overwhelmingly in favor of collective bargaining, with the UFT as sole bargaining agent. This meant that for the first time in American history, a major teachers union not only was an activist group, but was legally empowered to negotiate employment contracts on behalf of its members, across the table from administrators, the school board, and politicians. The next year, the UFT won a $995 annual raise for every teacher, then the largest in the city's history, as well as a grievance process for teachers to dispute the decisions of their supervisors. The TU, now irrelevant, disbanded in 1964, and by 1967, 97 percent of New York City teachers belonged to the UFT.

Had anything been lost? In Harlem, Bed-Stuy, and across the United States, far-left politics often made a teacher more, not less, effective in low-income classrooms. It is difficult to imagine TU activists like Irving Adler, Alice Citron, or Lucille Spence comparing teaching poor children to assembly-line work. In 1978 Harlem minister David Licorish lamented the purges that had pushed communist teachers out of his neighborhood's schools. Those teachers had been "much more dedicated to teaching black children the way out of the crucible of American life than the teachers we have now," Licorish told historian Mark Naison. "When they left, Harlem became a worse place. They stayed after school with the children and gave them extra curricular attention to bring them up to level. . . . These people were dedicated to their craft."

Though the number of teachers purged across the United States was small, witch hunts sent a powerful message to the teacher corps as a whole. Certain educators—those who lived outside the cultural and political mainstream—were not welcome in the classroom. The irony is that from racial integration to the culturally relevant curriculum to the need for higher academic expectations for poor students of color, many of the radical teachers' ideals would become mainstream school reform priorities over the coming decades.

Chapter Six

"The Only Valid Passport from Poverty"

THE GREAT EXPECTATIONS
OF GREAT SOCIETY TEACHERS

On May 17, 1954, a unanimous Supreme Court declared in its *Brown v. Board of Education* decision that de jure school segregation was unconstitutional. Though W. E. B. Du Bois was a lifelong defender of black schools led by black teachers, he was moved to elation by the symbolism of the event. "I have seen the impossible happen," he wrote. The novelist Ralph Ellison declared, "Another battle of the Civil War has been won."

It seemed the nine justices—all of them white men born during the nineteenth century—had overturned the very structure of American race relations. *Brown v. Board of Education* was nominally about the right of Linda Brown, the black daughter of missionaries, to attend a white Topeka elementary school just seven blocks from her family's home. But attorney Thurgood Marshall and his colleagues at the NAACP had pursued a bold legal strategy. Instead of arguing that segregated black schools were unconstitutional because they were of lower quality than white schools—less well funded, with older textbooks and fewer athletic facilities—they argued that segregation itself should be outlawed, under the Fourteenth Amendment's promise of equal protection under the law. In doing so they successfully challenged the fundamental Jim Crow legal principle of "separate but equal," first established by the Court fifty-eight years earlier in *Plessy v. Ferguson*. Chief Justice Earl Warren's *Brown* decision became one of the most quoted judicial opinions in American history:

Segregation of white and colored children in public schools has a detrimental effect upon the colored children. The impact is greater when it has the sanction of the law, for the policy of separating the races is usually interpreted as denoting the inferiority of the Negro group. . . . We conclude that, in the field of public education, the doctrine of "separate but equal" has no place. Separate educational facilities are inherently unequal.

Though segregated schools were the norm all over the country, including in the North, the *Brown* ruling applied only to the seventeen southern, western, and border states, as well as to the District of Columbia, where explicit laws prevented white and black children from attending the same schools. (In the North, school segregation could be attributed mostly to the neighborhood demographics that resulted from discriminatory housing policy, as well as to school districts' deliberate decisions to assign black children to predominantly black schools, even when they lived near white schools.) Forty percent of the nation's public school students, some 10.7 million children, would be affected by the ruling. But what about teachers? Even before *Brown* there had been concern in the black community that merging black and white schools could decimate the black middle class, which depended on jobs in segregated schools. Writing in *The Nation* in 1953, the black sociologist Oliver Cox wondered if Negro teachers would become "martyrs to integration . . . Freedom to work is at least as sacred as the right to non-discrimination in education." Any school desegregation program, Cox argued, must contain strong protections for black workers.

The text of the *Brown* decision mentioned teachers only once, noting that southern states had already taken steps to equalize teacher qualifications and pay across black and white schools. In fact, state legislators had done so with the hope of forestalling demands for integration. Now the court directed states to move with "deliberate speed" to integrate schools. But the justices did not define their terms, and in the absence of specific requirements white southerners turned to nakedly racist political tactics, collectively referred to as "massive resistance," that fought desegregation

in large part by attacking veteran black educators. Half the southern states passed laws revoking the teaching license of anyone who
joined an organization that supported school integration, including
the NAACP. In 1955 Alabama, Florida, Tennessee, South Carolina,
North Carolina, Kentucky, and Virginia all repealed teacher tenure,
with the goal of more easily terminating black teachers in the event
that they began to compete with whites for jobs in newly integrated
schools. Four southern states even modified their constitutions to
abolish the right to a public education. In the wake of *Brown,* many
white southern legislators behaved as if an integrated public school
system would be worse than having no public school system at all.

A few prominent black southerners, themselves proud alumni
of segregated schools, sized up white resistance to integration and
concluded it wasn't worth the trouble. When asked about *Brown v.
Board* in 1958, Anna Julia Cooper, the trailblazing feminist teacher
in Washington, D.C., told a newspaper reporter, "I'm against it."
She was one hundred years old, old enough to know, she said, that
in black schools led by black educators, children were more likely
to "take pride in themselves and the achievements" of their race.
The sixty-four-year-old writer Zora Neale Hurston, who grew up
in segregated central Florida, agreed. In a 1955 letter to the *Orlando
Sentinel,* she worried that committed black teachers and administrators would lose their jobs as all-black schools were shuttered and
their students dispersed. "The whole matter revolves around the
self-respect of my people," Hurston wrote. "How much satisfaction
can I get from a court order for somebody to associate with me who
does not wish me near them?"

In the mid-1950s and early 1960s, desegregation was moving so
slowly that no one could say for sure how *Brown* might ultimately
affect the education of black children, or the employment of black
teachers. A decade after the ruling, over 90 percent of southern
black students still attended all-black schools. Of the 333,000 black
children who had been integrated, 80 percent lived in border states,
not in Deep South strongholds of massive resistance. In Mississippi,
not a single black child had been allowed to enroll in a white school.

Why? Except in a few high-profile cases, such as President Eisenhower's use of federal troops to integrate Little Rock Central High School, neither the courts nor the executive branch stepped in when white schools turned away black students, when local banks denied credit to black parents who petitioned for their children to attend white schools, or when employers fired those black parents in retaliation.

All that changed in 1964. President Johnson's enormous popularity in the wake of the Kennedy assassination, as well as his peerless legislative maneuvering, allowed him to establish an unprecedented role for the federal government in local public education. Previous efforts to expand Washington's influence over local schools had brought limited results. The launch of the Soviet Union's Sputnik satellite in 1957 prompted Congress to pass the National Defense Education Act (NDEA), which provided several hundred million dollars to prepare high-achieving students for careers in the sciences, math, engineering, and foreign languages. The law did not address educational inequalities driven by race and class. John F. Kennedy ran for president in 1960 promising to pass a comprehensive federal education aid package, a liberal dream dating back to Reconstruction. But Kennedy's efforts were stymied when fights broke out on Capitol Hill between lobbyists representing Catholic bishops, who wanted funding for parochial schools, and those representing teachers unions, who opposed aid to religious schools and prioritized higher pay for teachers. Then, during the frustrated decade after *Brown*, desegregation was the law, but not the reality.

When Congress passed the Civil Rights Act of 1964, the Department of Justice could finally sue schools that resisted or delayed integration. The following year, the Voting Rights Act allowed many southern black parents to register to vote for the first time. That meant black citizens could threaten to unseat politicians and school board members who opposed integration. By 1972, less than 10 percent of black students in the South attended an all-black school. Though true school integration would prove relatively fleeting in many neighborhoods, it had, at least temporarily, been achieved.

The most lasting Great Society change for the nation's schools came through the Elementary and Secondary Education Act (ESEA), the precursor to the Bush-era No Child Left Behind. The 1965 law, initially funded at the massive level of $1.2 billion per year, united the Left and center around a new role for Washington as a standard setter for state education agencies and local schools. While the NDEA had targeted funding toward the best and brightest students, ESEA was all about "compensatory education" for the 19 percent of low-income public school students falling behind in poor, largely black and Hispanic schools. Federal aid would now be offered or withheld depending on whether local policy makers followed national directives, such as supplying low-income schools with up-to-date textbooks, establishing school libraries, and pulling at-risk students out of class for supplemental tutoring. States that offered their low-income students more state-level funding would be rewarded with more money from the federal government. Johnson portrayed this expansion of the federal bureaucracy in stirring, soaring rhetoric. He signed ESEA in his hometown of Johnson City, Texas, with his own elementary school teacher at his side. "By passing this bill, we bridge the gap between helplessness and hope for more than 5 million educationally deprived children," he said. "And we rekindle the revolution—the revolution of the spirit against the tyranny of ignorance. As a son of a tenant farmer, I know that education is the only valid passport from poverty. As a former teacher—and, I hope, a future one—I have great expectations of what this law will mean for all of our young people." Those sky-high expectations placed on educators—as revolutionary foot soldiers in the War on Poverty—are still with us today.

To illustrate the transformative power of education, the president wove a careful political mythology around his own nine months working as a teacher in a low-income public elementary school. As a twenty-year-old college dropout in 1928, Johnson followed a girlfriend to south Texas, where the couple planned to earn a little money by teaching school. Johnson found work in the dusty cattle village of Cotulla, home to three thousand residents. He had attended subpar schools in central Texas Hill Country, but he was appalled by the even worse conditions at the segregated Welhausen

School, where he taught the children of Mexican American laborers. The school had no extracurricular activities, no lunchtime, and no athletic equipment. The students and their parents struggled with basic English and lived in homes without indoor plumbing or electricity. Johnson wrote to his mother to ask her to send 250 tubes of toothpaste. Because he was male, he was quickly appointed principal. He instituted an "English only" rule on school grounds, founded a debate team that competed against nearby schools, assigned classic poems for students to recite from memory, and required teachers to stay after school to tutor children who needed extra help. His students would remember him as a strict disciplinarian who spanked children who spoke Spanish or talked back to their teachers. But by most reports, Johnson was an inspiring educator nonetheless. He began each school day by telling the story of "the little baby in the cradle"—a poor Mexican American child who sometimes grew up to be a teacher, sometimes a doctor, and sometimes even the president of the United States.

Johnson has been accused, in the words of historian Irwin Unger, of viewing education as "a magic cure for social failure and economic inequality." But Johnson's political messages about the children he knew in Cotulla were in fact quite complex. Rather than paint schools and teachers as saviors who could overcome the challenges of poverty (to borrow the phrasing of so many contemporary school reformers), Johnson described his teaching years with considerable humility. He recalled students who came to school hungry and who wordlessly understood that they were despised by whites for their brown skin and foreignness. In a March 1965 speech to Congress on "the American promise," he portrayed himself as a young teacher walking home from work exhausted and lost in thought, simply "wishing there was more I could do":

> But all I knew was to teach them the little that I knew, hoping that it might help them against the hardships that lay ahead. Somehow you never forget what poverty and hatred can do when you see its scars on the hopeful face of a young child. I never thought then, in 1928, that I would be standing here in 1965. It never even occurred to me in my fondest dreams that I

might have the chance to help the sons and daughters of those students and to help people like them all over this country.

As a mere classroom teacher, Johnson implied, he could not fully address the social challenges his students faced. To do more for them he would need to advance not only an education program, but also a broad agenda to negate the disadvantages of poverty and racism. There would be expanded access to food stamps, affordable housing, and afterschool and summer programs. There would be a federally funded preschool program for the poorest children, called Head Start. Johnson framed this agenda in nearly religious terms. "I want to be the president who helped to end hatred among his fellow men and who promoted love among the people of all races and all regions and all parties," he told Congress. "I want to be the president who helped to end war among the brothers of this earth." While there remains a consensus that income and educational opportunity are deeply linked, never again would a national school reform agenda be accompanied by so aggressive an antipoverty push.

Yet Great Society education programs were often badly implemented, with results that were difficult to quantify. A 1971 report to the federal government on ESEA-funded summer programs in Bedford-Stuyvesant, a poor Brooklyn neighborhood, illustrates the problem. The evaluation found that a 510-child preschool program was "significantly effective." The children were immunized and received medical, dental, and eye exams. In the classroom, they reviewed letters and numbers, learned table manners, and made flowerpots out of juice cans. But another program, for disabled children, met in dirty classrooms. Tests that were supposed to diagnose the students' academic needs were never delivered, and many teachers were chronically absent. In an African American culture program, the dance teacher claimed it was too hot to dance, and she let the children hang out while she played one record of African music over and over again. A teacher in a program on Hispanic culture seemed to know little about Latin America except that Christopher Columbus had once landed on Puerto Rico. Test scores showed that a few of these programs increased children's reading comprehension and spelling skills, but the results were generally uneven, and some programs were not assessed at all.

Anecdotes like these quickly led to political hostility to Johnson's broad—and expensive—conception of school improvement. In the short term, however, the president's policy incentives worked very effectively to advance at least one of his education priorities: the integration of southern public school students. In September 1966 white administrators across the South reviewed Johnson administration regulations and reluctantly concluded that they would miss the chance for federal funding, or get sued, if they did not integrate schools. In Tuscaloosa, Alabama, the school board began cautiously, not by reassigning students, but by transferring two black teachers to white schools. White parents panicked. Dozens of them flooded a school board meeting, where superintendent W. W. Elliott told them that although integration "upset our stomach," the district had no choice given Washington's insistence. Alabama governor George Wallace—the man who had bellowed, "Segregation now, segregation tomorrow, segregation forever!"—disagreed. He announced he would use police power to remove black teachers from white public schools. The threat of violence worked, at least temporarily; the two black teachers were too scared to return to work. But by 1970, even white supremacists like Wallace begrudgingly accepted at least token school desegregation in exchange for significant federal education funding.

In schools where integration was implemented thoughtfully, teachers of both races described a new sort of idealism about the power of education. At West Charlotte High School in North Carolina, black and white teachers attended workshops to learn from each other's experiences. "We got bonded," remembered Eunice Pharr, a black teacher at the school. "As the students came in, I noticed the faculty helped the students to bond. I get chills just thinking about the situation. It was so exciting to me." At newly integrated Woodlawn High in Birmingham, Alabama, teacher Cleopatra Goree, who was black, styled herself after Angela Davis, wearing an Afro and a fringed leather vest. She created a history curriculum built around the African American experience, with lessons on the Middle Passage, black soldiers during the Revolutionary War, and Reconstruction and the birth of the Ku Klux Klan. Both her black and white students enjoyed it, she thought—even though the parents of a few of her white students actually belonged to the Klan. "I learned to love the students," Goree said, the white ones too. "I learned them just like I did my black students, and we became endeared to each other."

Desegregation could improve schools surprisingly quickly. In the 1960s, the all-black First Ward Elementary School in Charlotte had a playground littered with glass shards and an outdated library. When white children began to attend the school in 1970, political pressure to improve the school increased. The school board soon renovated the playground, built a fence to keep children from running into the street, and purchased new classroom supplies. A PTA made up of both black and white parents established curricular partnerships with a local science museum and an African American cultural center.

But all too often, school desegregation was accompanied by a number of the troubling complications predicted by *Brown*'s black critics. Where integration led to staff redundancies and school closings, black schools were disproportionately closed and black teachers were disproportionately dismissed or demoted, regardless of their seniority, qualifications, or success in the classroom. Across the South, there was a sense, especially among whites, that black teachers were acceptable only for black children. Many white parents assumed black teachers were less qualified than white teachers, though black and white teachers held college degrees at nearly equal rates. And fears of miscegenation may have made white parents anxious about sending their teenage daughters to schools in which young black men worked.

White school boards used a number of strategies to obscure the role racism played in decisions to terminate black educators. During the integration process, black teachers were more likely than white teachers to be reassigned to subjects or grade levels in which they did not have expertise; then they were given poor evaluations and fired for incompetence. New black teachers were also being hired at a slower rate than new white teachers. Many southern school districts began to require teacher candidates to take a controversial standardized test, the National Teacher Examination, known for producing higher scores among whites. By the 1960s, both the AFT and the NEA supported integration and, from their Washington headquarters, decried racially motivated dismissals. But the post-*Brown* merging of black and white union affiliates in most states meant black teachers no longer had dedicated organizations to turn to with grievances. The federal Department of Health, Education, and Welfare estimated that between 1954 and 1971, the nation lost 31,584 black teaching positions and 2,235 black principalships, even as the total number of jobs in public education grew.

For black teachers, a transfer to an integrated school was considered a vote of confidence; for white teachers, it was considered a demotion. Willie Mae Crews taught English at Hayes High School in Birmingham, once known as the "Little University" for the city's black community. In 1970 Crews, who was black, joined the Hayes integration committee and was dismayed by the white students—mostly those with disciplinary problems—and white teachers the city Board of Education assigned to the school. Some of the new white faculty members assumed they would have to lower their academic standards to teach poor black children—pretty ironic, Hayes thought, since it appeared to her that black teachers, many of them with graduate degrees and few options for employment outside of education, had been teaching at a higher level than their white counterparts who had attended only low-quality normal schools.

Meanwhile, administrators handpicked guidance counselor Helen Heath, also black, to leave Hayes and desegregate a white school in Birmingham, Glenn High. Heath recalled that the white principal at Glenn was racist. He encouraged white students to avoid Heath and visit the white counselor instead. But she valued the opportunity to help high-performing black students in a newly integrated setting realize that they, too, were "college material." It is impossible to know what role merit played in reassigning Heath and other competent black educators away from historically black schools, since the process was so corrupted by obvious discrimination. But

Heath believed historically black schools like Hayes had been "stripped of their excellent teachers, and they were substituted by unprepared white teachers." Education researcher Clifton Claye observed in 1970 that "senile" white teachers were being assigned en masse to formerly black schools.

Several surveys of southern teachers during desegregation revealed that whites often expected little of their black students. White teachers were more likely than black teachers to report discipline problems with black children, and white teachers complained that black parents had "different values"—that they were less supportive of education or of good behavior generally. In 1965, thirteen-year-old Gloria Register integrated the formerly all-white Guy B. Phillips Junior High School in Chapel Hill, North Carolina. She and other black students were told by white teachers to wash their faces and brush their teeth each morning. "It's not as though we were monkeys from the zoo," she remembered, "but that is how we were treated. And I was angry."

The mainstream social science of the day may have buttressed such attitudes among white educators. In his 1965 essay "The Negro Family: The Case for National Action," Assistant Secretary of Labor and future New York senator Daniel Patrick Moynihan warned that "the tangle of pathology is tightening" over the black community, with increasing numbers of children born out of wedlock and raised in segregated neighborhoods far removed from the social norms of middle-class white America. Black children with absentee fathers, he wrote, demonstrated low scores on IQ tests, not because they were genetically inferior, but because they had less parental stability and support. The following year, sociologist James Coleman submitted to Congress his report on "Equality of Educational Opportunity," which attributed about two-thirds of the academic achievement gap between black and white children to family poverty and segregation. The two reports dovetailed in their suggestion that parents and neighborhoods were far more influential on children than teachers and schools. But they did not claim that education did not matter. The Coleman Report, in particular, continues to be misconstrued by both its supporters and its critics, who take it to assert that teachers are helpless in the face of poverty. What

Coleman's research really revealed was that compared to white students, the average black child was enrolled in a poorly funded school with less qualified teachers and fewer science and foreign language classes. Those black students who attended integrated, well-resourced schools, however, tended to earn higher test scores than black students in segregated schools, and reported feeling a greater sense of control over their lives. "Just as a loaf of bread means more to a starving man than to a sated one," Coleman wrote, "so one very fine textbook or, better, one very able teacher, may mean far more to a deprived child than to one who already has several of both." Coleman's message was that although family income might be the biggest factor in student achievement, teachers and schools also mattered, especially for poor kids. Yet by calling attention to disparities like the relative lack of books in black homes—and by ignoring identical deficiencies among poor whites—the Moynihan and Coleman reports may have led some teachers to conclude there was little they could do in the classroom to help black students succeed. As research would begin to show definitively by the end of the decade, such low expectations for children could be self-fulfilling.

But prejudice and low expectations were not the only explanations for why too many schools failed to effectively educate black and low-income children. Many teachers lacked relevant experience or training in working with poor students of any race, and too many of them were ignorant of the strategies developed by African American educators, ever since the Civil War, to reach a student population simultaneously fighting racism, poverty, and political disempowerment. The education theorists Lisa Delpit and Gloria Ladson-Billings have articulated some of the tactics black teachers (like Charlotte Forten and Anna Julia Cooper) used throughout history to successfully educate black students. Strict discipline was employed less as a means of control and more as a way of demonstrating love for the child: *I help you understand the consequences of your actions*, teachers tell their students, *because I am personally invested in your success.* Effective black teachers sought close ties to their students' parents, often socializing with them outside school and engaging them in conversations about their children's education. Black teachers introduced black children to heroic figures from

African American history, to build racial pride. And because many poor black children did not speak standard English at home, their teachers spent extra time on phonics and vocabulary building.

As early as 1965, the Johnson administration acknowledged the growing problem of black students, especially in the South, being taught by too few black teachers. U.S. Commissioner of Education Francis Keppel worried that without black role models at school, black children would be forced to face the upheavals of school integration alone. "We must not deceive ourselves that the exclusion of Negro teachers is not noticed by children," he said. Even President Johnson, in a speech to the National Education Association, said he was concerned about dismissals. Yet neither the executive branch nor the courts held school districts accountable for more than token faculty integration. In 1965, after the New York City school board hired five hundred southern black teachers displaced by integration, NAACP lawyer Jack Greenberg wrote a letter to *The New York Times* complaining that it wasn't enough. Policy makers must protect black teaching jobs in the South, he wrote, since black educators held a "uniquely important place in Southern society." The Health, Education, and Welfare Department "has, with reluctance, adopted the formal position that teacher integration is necessary . . . We have, however, seen no enforcement from the department." Indeed, the following year the embattled Tuscaloosa school board received a letter from HEW suggesting that in a majority-white school, one black teacher would suffice.

This painful episode in American education history has generally gone unacknowledged by today's accountability reformers, as they pursue policies, such as neighborhood school closings and school "reconstitutions" as charter or magnet schools, that lead disproportionately to the loss of teaching jobs held by African Americans. According to a federal lawsuit filed by the Chicago Teachers Union, 40 percent of the city's teachers were black in 2000, but only 30 percent were black in 2010. When the district reconstituted ten schools in 2012, 51 percent of the teachers dismissed were black, although black teachers make up only 28 percent of teachers citywide. In New Orleans between 2007 and 2009, the proportion of black teachers fell from 73 percent to 57 percent, a net loss of a hundred jobs, as fast-track teacher training programs with comparitively low minority representation expanded their presence in the city's schools. Unlike in the past, today's layoffs are less a function of explicit racial animus than an outgrowth of the fact that black teachers are more likely to work in underperforming, segregated black schools targeted for closure or layoffs. And like other baby boomer teachers, they are beginning to retire in large numbers. But these figures are worrisome all the same, given a half century of research demonstrating that teachers of color are more likely to hold high expectations for students of color and are more likely to work in high-poverty schools over the long term—and both factors are correlated with higher student achievement and college-going rates among students of color. Competitive programs that offer alternative pathways into the teaching profession, like Teach for America, have made a concerted effort to recruit nonwhite teachers, and have had considerable success in attracting them—more success, in many cases, than traditional teachers colleges. Yet overall the number of teachers of color nationwide has not grown in many years, and has declined in many high-poverty, minority-majority cities that have been undergoing massive school turnaround efforts. Only about 17 percent of American teachers are nonwhite, compared to 40 percent of American public school students.

Even as President Johnson declined to take regulatory steps to protect veteran black teachers, he aggressively pursued a strategy personally familiar to him from his year in Cotulla, Texas, and one that has been resurrected today by the growing organization Teach for America: recruiting elite young college students to teach for a short time in poor children's classrooms. One of Johnson's favorite Great Society programs, for which he mustered considerable political energy to pass through Congress and then reauthorize, was the National Teacher Corps, established in 1965 as part of the Higher Education Act. It was based in part on a program founded two years earlier by a Washington, D.C., schoolteacher named Joan Wofford.

In 1962 Wofford, a graduate of Bryn Mawr and Yale, was teaching at Newton High School in the Boston suburbs, one of the nation's most affluent and progressive public schools. Inspired by President Kennedy's call to public service, she became determined to find work in an inner-city neighborhood. When her husband won a judicial clerkship, the young couple moved to Washington, D.C., and Wofford was hired as the second-ever white teacher at Cardozo High School, in the working-class black neighborhood of Columbia Heights. The school's principal, Bennetta Washington, was married to the city's future mayor, Walter Washington, and was a politically connected reformer willing to take a chance on a young white woman.

At Cardozo, Wofford taught honors English, and she adored her students. But she was horrified by the pedagogical and disciplinary practices she witnessed at the school. An assistant principal spent most of his day running through the hallways, prodding boys to take off their hats. When Wofford sat down with a math teacher to select photos of classroom scenes for the yearbook, the math teacher refused to consider one in which students had exploded with great energy, every hand up in the air. "There was this idea of 'keep the lid on, be well behaved,'" Wofford told me. "That was not my thing. I wanted enthusiasm, excitement! I wanted people turned on, not sitting with their hands folded."

Wofford admits that at the time she was arrogant, even "blind." When she studied organizational development later in her career, she realized that if you want to change an institutional culture, you can't ignore the managers and employees who are enforcing the rules— you have to cooperate with them and get their feedback. If she had done so at Cardozo, she might have heard that for generations, strict discipline had been considered a hallmark of high-quality teaching in the black community, in order to prepare children for a prejudiced world in which they would rarely enjoy the benefit of the doubt. Yet Wofford's brashness effectively shifted the national debate about public school teaching.

National surveys showed that half of all teachers working in low-income schools hoped to transfer to middle-class settings. What if, Wofford wondered, inner-city teaching could become a coveted, glamorous job, even for the most privileged young adults? This idea had come to Wofford as she read a letter from her brother-in-law

Harris Wofford, a Kennedy adviser who was then working for the Peace Corps in Africa. Many Peace Corps members were assigned to teach in African schools and had developed a passion for the work, Harris wrote. Yet they wouldn't be able to continue teaching when they returned to the States, because they had not studied at education schools or earned teacher certifications, as state laws required.

Wofford rushed to write back to her brother-in-law. On lightweight blue airmail paper she sketched a plan for how much good Peace Corps veterans could do at schools like Cardozo. She never mailed the letter, which became, instead, a program proposal. She envisioned a special group of young teachers recruited from the Peace Corps or competitive colleges. They would be mentored by "master teachers"—people like Wofford, who also came from elite backgrounds but had already demonstrated success in the classroom. In their first year at Cardozo, the "intern" teachers would lead only two lessons per day. They would spend the rest of their time observing the master teacher, observing one another, and sharing feedback with colleagues within the program. After school, interns would take a class in urban sociology to learn about the challenges poor children faced, and they would work to develop new, culturally relevant curriculum materials that would renew children's excitement about learning. Through a partnership with Howard University, the recruits would earn a master's degree in teaching, thus circumventing the traditional role of education schools and their "Mickey Mouse courses," in Wofford's words. This vision echoed that of former Harvard president James Bryant Conant, who published the widely discussed *The Education of American Teachers* that same year, 1963. Conant warned that the nation's growing ranks of high school dropouts would become "social dynamite," unemployed and prone to crime. He saw higher-quality teaching as the best way to keep low-income kids in school, and he called for deemphasizing undergraduate education courses for future teachers in favor of classes in the liberal arts coupled with "practice teaching" in real classrooms.

Harris Wofford helped his sister-in-law arrange a meeting with Sargent Shriver, the Kennedy cousin and founder of the Peace Corps. Shriver signed on as a behind-the-scenes supporter of the idea. Within a few months, Bobby Kennedy invited Wofford to his office. He handed over a check from the President's Committee on Juvenile Delinquency and Youth Crime, and the Cardozo Project in Urban Teaching launched in the fall of 1963, with ten intern teachers. The media loved the idea. The *Washington Post* women's section profiled "Michigan farm-bred" Judith Crindler, a Peace Corps veteran teaching ninth-grade English at Cardozo. She had assigned her students *Antigone* and Thoreau as part of a unit on civil disobedience. A reporter from *The New Yorker* shadowed Wofford and her team for two weeks. "As a youngster, I was sort of the toast of the town," Wofford remembered with a self-effacing laugh. "We got so much good publicity, I even had white parents saying, 'Can we send our kids to Cardozo?'"

But right away, resentments bubbled up between interns and veteran teachers, who had few opportunities for formal interaction. The Cardozo Project received federal funding, which meant the interns had their own mimeograph machine and other school supplies veterans often lacked. Interns were young, inexperienced, and mostly white, while Cardozo's veterans were generally middle-aged and black. Some of the biggest clashes were over the curriculum. In the Peace Corps, Roberta Kaplan had taught African American literature at a private school in Sierra Leone. But when she tried to bring some of the same material to Cardozo, including *Black Boy, Invisible Man,* and the poems of Langston Hughes, she heard pushback from long-standing members of the English department, who saw a young white teacher assigning black students a second-rate reading list—these works were not yet highly regarded. "They wanted to make sure the kids were exposed to the same classic literature white kids were," Kaplan told me, works like *My Antonia,* Willa Cather's novel about white pioneers in Nebraska. "Even *To Kill a Mockingbird* was not considered a classic then!"

Wofford left the program after two years, frustrated that the school district banned her from teaching while she was pregnant—a common practice across the country, soon after abolished. But her work had taken root: In 1965, Senate Democrats Ted Kennedy and Gaylord Nelson began drafting legislation based on replicating the Cardozo Project and another similar effort, the Milwaukee Intern

Program, nationally. They envisioned a National Teacher Corps that would give elite young people an opportunity to enter and then transform the teaching profession, without having to proceed through teachers colleges or education degrees, which were seen in the media and on Capitol Hill as intellectually stagnant. As the historian Bethany Rogers has noted, this vision of recruiting "better people" into teaching explicitly denigrated the wisdom of those teachers already working in high-poverty schools. The assumption was that the existing teachers, many of whom were older black women, could offer little insight into how to educate poor children.

In later years the Cardozo Project, then led by teacher and theorist Larry Cuban, made better use of the collective experience of Cardozo's veteran teachers, hiring some of them as mentors to new interns. Jane David, a twenty-two-year-old white Oklahoman, began teaching at Cardozo in 1966. In those days, newspapers had separate sections for men's and women's job listings, and as an ambitious Antioch graduate, David had been frustrated by the menial "gal Friday" ads she saw. She figured she would try teaching, and though initially ambivalent about the job, David quickly fell in love with it. From her mentor, a veteran black teacher named Bess Howard, she learned to use "manipulatives" in her math lessons— physical objects, like blocks, that could help students grasp mathematical concepts. Equally powerful for David was earning Howard's trust. The older woman told the younger one she was a natural in the classroom, which David attributed to having grown up with a college professor and professional dancer as parents. "Teaching is one part performance," she told me, "and I had some performance genes in my blood. Unlike some newbies, I didn't have any trouble with classroom control."

One unusual aspect of the Cardozo Project and the Teacher Corps was the expectation that interns live in the neighborhoods in which they worked. In 1970 Larry Cuban explained the rationale:

> [T]eachers [must] get out of their fortresses and into the neighborhoods. They must work with students in non-authoritarian settings. They must get to know people in the community. These things must be done, if for no other rea-

son . . . than to improve the quality of instruction. Simply stated, effective teaching is intimately related to how well a teacher knows who his charges are and the nature of their surroundings. If he doesn't, his perceptions will continue to be shaped by TV, newspaper, social science formulas, and fear—not by first-hand experience. And by experience I don't mean bus tours through the slums, hurried walks up and down streets, or unannounced welfare-like visits. No instant urban sociology. I mean the tough business of getting to know people who live in the area. Let the community teach the teacher.

For middle-class white recruits like David, who lived just a few blocks from Cardozo High, the experience offered a powerful education in American inequality. The high school was perched on a hill, which offered students a breathtaking view of the U.S. Capitol Building, three miles south. David was shocked to learn most neighborhood kids had never been there—just as Jacob Riis, sixty years earlier, had lamented the Lower East Side ragamuffins who never visited Central Park.

The community where David lived taught the teacher in Technicolor on Friday, April 5, 1968, the day after Martin Luther King's assassination. As grieving students and teachers anxiously gathered in Cardozo's hallways, a voice called out: "Fourteenth Street is on fire!" It was the beginning of riots that engulfed the city for four days. Cardozo's basketball coach offered David a ride home in his car. As he inched through the clogged intersections, rioters rocked the vehicle back and forth. David crouched on the floor and hid her face. "The coach was scared," she recalled. "He didn't want to be caught with this white chick in the car. . . . We were both praying no one saw me." When school reopened the following week, David led her students in a discussion of what had taken place. "There was a moral dilemma, to loot or not to loot? Half the kids justified it. One said, 'You know, it was the first time in my life I had a suit for Easter.' And the other would argue, 'No, it's stealing.' . . . It was just fascinating listening to them argue among themselves about what was right and wrong. And I thought there were strong arguments on both sides."

Cardozo and Teacher Corps interns were also expected to participate in community service outside the classroom. Evaluations of Teacher Corps sites around the country showed that because teaching itself was so time-consuming, many interns ended up giving their community responsibilities short shrift. Some interns, however, took the community service element of the program quite seriously. Beverly Glenn, a black Cardozo Project recruit who had grown up middle-class in Baltimore, joined the Concerned Citizens of Central Cardozo, a group working to improve conditions inside housing projects. With a few other intern teachers, Glenn organized a summer program for preschool children living in one particularly blighted development, Clifton Terrace.

Glenn and her roommate, another intern teacher, even volunteered to take custody of a student who was being sexually abused by her stepfather. Glenn was just twenty-one years old at the time, four years older than her foster daughter. Those years at Cardozo were "emotionally exhausting and physically exhausting," Glenn said. But despite her dramatic experiences outside school, what she valued most about the program was the pedagogical training she received. She would recall it often later in her career, as a teacher in Boston, a graduate student at Harvard, and then a nationally recognized education policy expert and dean of the School of Education at Howard University. "We had a lot of adventures in Teacher Corps, but mainly we learned how to teach," Glenn said. "We learned a lot about child development and psychology, about curriculum development and what it means to write a lesson plan, about what it means to individualize for students and how you do evaluation to know what kids have learned." Those practical matters were not always part of the curriculum at traditional teachers colleges, which tended to emphasize theory over practice, and—until recently—paid little attention to how to measure children's learning outcomes.

In its first year, the National Teacher Corps office in Washington, D.C., selected all the recruits for Corps sites across the country. But in Congress, Representative Edith Green, a Democrat and former union teacher from Oregon, sought to subject the program to more local control. Like today's critics of Teach for America, Green and the NEA believed shortcuts into the classroom were unfair to career teachers who had taken the time to earn education degrees, and that these kinds of programs would deprofessionalize teaching in the long term. She forged an alliance between labor-affiliated northerners and states' rights southerners that resulted in legislation to revamp the program. By 1967 the National Teacher Corps was just the Teacher Corps, a tiny, decentralized program in which local sites had the power to hire interns and supervise their work. This change was remarkably successful in bringing more black, Hispanic, and Native American teachers into the classroom; during the Corps' first three cycles, between 10 percent and 30 percent of interns came from minority groups, but in later years, more than half did. The requirements for community service and mentor-intern relationships remained, as did the partnerships between the Corps and local colleges, which provided recruits with afterschool academic courses. *The New York Times* editorial board nevertheless expressed disappointment that the federal government no longer fully controlled the program—particularly the quality and demographics of incoming interns, not to mention how they were trained. "Far from being a threat, the 'outsider' [teacher] tends to be a bearer of new ideas," the *Times* board wrote. "There is nothing the urban and rural slum schools need more than escape from the inbred rigidity of local and state education systems."

It is difficult to judge the Teacher Corps' success in today's terms; during the 1960s and 1970s, standardized achievement tests were not in wide use as measures of student learning or teacher effectiveness. Sociologist Ronald Corwin published the definitive evaluation of the program in 1973. Teacher Corps sites had hired three thousand interns who worked in twenty-seven states and Puerto Rico, including in cities like New York, Chicago, and Los Angeles; in the rural Black Belt; and on Indian reservations. Fifty-five percent of recruits came from upper-middle-class homes, compared to only about a quarter of experienced teachers. Corwin found that recruits did bring the high expectations for students that reformers like Joan Wofford had hoped for. Corps interns were more likely than veteran teachers to believe poor students could graduate from high school, and less likely to indicate that "poor home backgrounds" prevented children from learning. Interns cited education as the most effective antipoverty tool, while veterans believed job training, a guaranteed income, and marketable skills were more valuable. The vast majority of Corps recruits did not become career teachers, but many did pursue jobs in educational administration or policy.

Teacher Corps interns reported that they helped poor children complete college applications and launched parent-teacher associations where none before existed. In the rural South, interns sometimes were the only white people black children had ever gotten to know or trust. Some program sites, however, went bust. Many Corps members disdained their coursework at the cooperating universities, which were less elite than the undergraduate colleges they had attended. In the South, angry parents accused several interns of teaching about evolution or communism, and in a few cases, interracial relationships among interns aroused local gossip and hostility. Some principals resented the presence of Teacher Corps teams at their schools and attempted to isolate them from the regular faculty. Overall, Corwin concluded, the program had failed in its goal of pressuring the educational establishment to embrace new pedagogical ideas and make it easier for high-status young people to enter teaching without traditional certification. This relatively small federal intervention had aroused widespread "status threat" within college education departments and among K–12 administrators and veteran teachers, many of whom felt disrespected by "hippie" Teacher Corps members. According to the National Education Association, which had always been skeptical of the Corps, "the greater the difference between interns and teachers in social attitudes or in status, the less change took place."

Except for the hippie insinuation, much of the controversy regarding the Teacher Corps sounds a lot like the debate about today's Teach for America, which was founded, like the Cardozo Project, by an idealist who sought to provide a shortcut into the profession. Teach for America's mission is to help lead "an educational revolution" in America's poor communities. President Johnson— who revered educators and understood their work perhaps better than any other president in the nation's history—had much the same aim. His Great Society agenda, from the Teacher Corps to Title I to Head Start, did make a mark. Federal funds flowed like never before to high-poverty schools. Ambitious young people were encouraged to teach in low-income schools, via the missionary teacher model first promoted by Catharine Beecher.

But true to Anna Julia Cooper's and Zora Neale Hurston's warnings, the Johnson administration's aggressive push toward school integration in the South often came at the expense of veteran black teachers. And due to the complicity of the courts and Department of Justice, de facto segregated schooling endured in most northern cities. By 1968 the limits of the Great Society education agenda were clear. Parents and activists who were committed to educational equality for poor children were disappointed and sometimes angry. The world of urban public education would soon explode in racial animus, much of it targeted toward teachers and their unions.

Chapter Seven

"We Both Got Militant"

UNION TEACHERS VERSUS BLACK POWER
DURING THE ERA OF COMMUNITY CONTROL

Al Shanker is the bridge who links today's teacher union politics, driven by promises of reform and accountability, to the democratic socialism of the early twentieth century, from which the modern teachers unions emerged. Shanker spoke no English on his first day of kindergarten in 1927. At home in Queens with his father, who sold newspapers from a pushcart, and his mother, a sweatshop seamstress, Yiddish was the tongue and labor politics— just as much as Judaism—the religion. His mother's pay improved when she joined the Amalgamated Clothing Workers of America; the union, Shanker later remembered, was practically a god to his family. He was hardly a passionate student, but he loved to read. As a teenager, he walked from Queens over the Fifty-ninth Street Bridge to buy copies of *Commentary* and *Partisan Review* from the newsstands outside the New York Public Library on Fifth Avenue. He excelled on the debate team at Stuyvesant High School, and his father expected him to become a lawyer. Later, in college at the University of Illinois at Champaign-Urbana, Shanker joined CORE— the Congress for Racial Equality—and chaired the Socialist Study Club. When socialist presidential candidate Norman Thomas visited campus in 1948, Shanker organized a huge rally, bigger than the ones for Harry Truman and Thomas Dewey.

Shanker graduated and returned to New York to enroll in Columbia's PhD program in philosophy. There he studied with John

Dewey and took copious notes for a dissertation. But he seemed to lack the discipline to simply sit down and write. Dejected and short on cash, he dropped out in 1952 at the age of twenty-four. It was the peak of the baby boom, and there was a shortage of public school teachers. A college graduate could quickly earn a New York City teaching credential by passing a written exam and speech test. After initially failing because of his working-class Jewish accent, Shanker practiced his diction—rehearsing the phrase "Look at the lovely yellow lilies"—and earned a certification. He began teaching, first in a Harlem elementary school and then at a junior high in Queens.

In Shanker's mind, it turned out to be demeaning, infantilizing work—nothing like the career he had imagined for himself in academia. During his lunch break, Shanker had to patrol the schoolyard to break up snowball fights and trail students into a local A&P to prevent shoplifting. To take a sick day, a teacher needed a note from his doctor. Even worse, Shanker realized he didn't know how to teach, and he hoped for some guidance. But when an administrator finally visited Shanker's classroom, his only feedback was to complain that there were three pieces of paper on the floor. Faculty meetings could last more than three hours, during which principals would complain about broken clocks, noisy classrooms, and other matters that had little to do with instruction. The average teacher earned $66 per week, less than an experienced car washer.

So Shanker became an organizer with the Teachers Guild, the small anticommunist alternative to the old Teachers Union. He was a key player in the Guild's transformation into the United Federation of Teachers, America's largest teachers union, which claimed 28,000 members in its early years. The UFT was the standard-bearer of a new national movement organized around the rallying cry of "teacher power," calling for collective bargaining, higher pay, and an end to "non-professional chores" like the ones Shanker had resented. By the mid-1970s, public school teaching became the most unionized profession in America, with 90 percent of teachers joining either the American Federation of Teachers or the National Education Association, and more than 70 percent working in districts whose unions gained collective bargaining rights, meaning union leaders could represent teachers' interests and demands at the negotiating table with districts.* Between 1960 and 1980 there were over a thousand teacher strikes across the United States. Despite laws in many states that made strikes by public employees illegal, union leaders were increasingly willing to face jail time in the hopes of improving conditions similar to the ones Shanker had experienced. The aggressive organizing worked. Teachers with collective bargaining rights earned, on average, 10 percent more than their colleagues without collective bargaining. Teacher power could mean significant advantages for students, too. In New York City in 1962, UFT co-founder George Altomare's high school economics classes had as many as fifty-two students each. The following year, after a disruptive 20,000-teacher strike, contract negotiations between the union and school board reduced the maximum high school class size to forty-nine, and soon the union pushed the number lower, to thirty-four.

Militant teacher unionists were inspired to protest and strike by the civil rights movement. In 1963 Shanker marched alongside Dr. King in Washington and from Selma to Montgomery. When Shanker was elected UFT president the following year, he committed the union to Freedom Summer. UFT members volunteered to teach in southern Freedom Schools to train civil rights activists, and the union provided buses to transport black voters to the polls. Sandra Feldman, a young UFT administrator and later on Shanker's successor as president, was arrested for attempting to dine with an interracial group of CORE activists at a segregated Howard Johnson's restaurant in Maryland. The UFT was considered a trusted ally within the civil rights movement.

Within several years, however, CORE and a litany of other civil rights groups would turn against the UFT and teacher unionism more broadly. Al Shanker, a leftist intellectual with working-class activist roots, was cast as a villain in the debate over educational

---

* In 1961, under pressure from the AFT, the NEA reversed itself and reluctantly embraced collective bargaining for teachers. In 1967 it approved of teacher strikes in special circumstances, and by 1970 administrators were no longer active within the organization.

equality, seen as a defender of teachers' interests at the expense of poor children of color and their parents. That characterization of teachers unions remains politically potent today—although, as we shall see, it is not a wholly fair assessment. How did union teachers and inner-city parent activists, who agreed on issues like smaller class sizes, school integration, and more school funding, end up on different sides of the school reform debate in the late 1960s? And why did the rise of teacher power coincide with the decline of the public's confidence in teachers and their unions?

In the late 1960s, unions gained unprecedented political influence over education just as the public—and especially black parents and activists—was growing increasingly cynical about schools. It was becoming clear that desegregation, which the national unions supported, would not be the cure-all for educational inequality that so many liberals had hoped for. The Coleman Report had demonstrated that racial achievement gaps remained stubbornly persistent even where desegregation was enforced most aggressively, in the former states of the Confederacy. In the North, meanwhile, most black and Hispanic communities were still waiting for integration to take root. White parent activists in cities like Boston and New York were organizing, sometimes violently and often successfully, to oppose school busing programs. And the courts were doing little to intervene in places where school segregation had been caused by housing patterns or even the discriminatory drawing of school district lines (as opposed to the legally mandated "dual systems" for white and black children that existed in the South). These northern forms of segregation, though deliberately created by white policy makers, were considered de facto, not de jure.

School segregation actually deepened in the North. In 1960, 40 percent of black and Puerto Rican children in New York City attended schools with no white children; by 1967 more than half did. Students in majority-white middle-class public schools scored two years ahead of grade level on achievement tests, while students in inner-city schools tended to be at least two years behind.

Worsening segregation led activists and researchers to shift their focus to teacher quality. Were teachers in segregated schools doing a good enough job at educating poor nonwhite children? Surveys had already shown that white teachers often held low opinions of their black students' intellects, but the effect of those views on children's learning had been unclear. Then in 1968 an academic paper appeared that became one of those touchstone studies, cited ad nauseam by the media, politicians, and activists for years to come. The paper was called "Pygmalion in the Classroom," by Harvard professor Robert Rosenthal and elementary school principal Lenore Jacobson. Rosenthal and Jacobson told San Francisco public school teachers the names of several of their students who had performed well on the Harvard Test of Inflected Acquisition and thus were expected to "bloom" academically. In fact, the Harvard test did not exist. Twenty percent of students, of varying IQ scores and races, were selected at random to belong to this "high expectations" group. At the end of the school year, those students demonstrated bigger gains on both IQ and achievement tests than did their peers in the same classrooms. The researchers concluded that teachers' lower expectations had damned the control group students—a finding that had disturbing implications for children from groups that had been historically discriminated against, who teachers might assume could not learn at a high level. Now it seemed clear that when teachers held low expectations, student achievement was actually hindered.

In New York City in 1967, the UFT went on strike again, in part for the right to evict unruly students from the classroom. Newly unionized Chicago teachers had demanded that same right back in 1902, arguing that the majority of children could not learn when a few disrupted class. Sixty-five years later, critics saw a racially explosive subtext: White teachers—90 percent of the New York City workforce—seemed to be claiming the right to determine exactly which children of color were capable of learning. Rhody McCoy, a crusading black principal who emerged as a union nemesis, believed that if parents of color got involved in their children's schools, they would be able to show teachers how to "set a tone so you didn't have any such thing as 'disruptive children.'" Luther Seabrook, another prominent black educator, had a more scarring critique of supposedly racist white teachers: "Even liberal educators view the Black child as a freak of nurture, if not of nature. . . . They speak of the Black child as 'culturally deprived'; or, as their racism becomes more subtle, 'culturally different.' Despite these euphemisms, the child knows that he is being called 'nigger.'"

These arguments penetrated the white mainstream. Bestselling books and hit movies about heroic educators, like *Up the Down Staircase, To Sir with Love,* and *Death at an Early Age* advanced the idea that most inner-city children were being denied energetic teaching and a challenging curriculum. African American culture, too, reflected a jaundiced view of urban schools and the teachers who worked within them. The black writer LeRoi Jones, a member of the Beat movement, grew up in Newark, New Jersey, the son of a social worker and postal worker. At the integrated Barringer High, Jones worked on the school newspaper, eventually earning a scholarship to Howard University. In his fiction, however, he focused not on the opportunities integration provided, but on the ways in which majority-white schools could alienate black children, both academically and psychologically. His autobiographical short story "Uncle Tom's Cabin: Alternative Ending" features Mrs. Orbach, a bigoted spinster white teacher who resents and discourages the efforts of her brightest student, a black boy named Eddie McGhee. Finally the child's loving college-educated mother visits the principal to complain. That sort of parent activism would become the hallmark of the community control movement, in which urban activist parents, some with ties to the Black Power movement, demanded greater say over who taught in their children's schools, and how. Community control never coalesced around a single set of demands, but a few features defined the national movement. Activists wanted teachers who embraced a sort of Teacher Corps ideology—who would visit children at home, stay after school to offer extra help, and even live in the ghetto communities in which they worked. They believed parents and neighborhood school boards, not citywide boards or superintendents, should have control over budgeting and the hiring and firing of teachers at local schools. Many community control advocates, though not all, thought an Afrocentric curriculum would reengage black children in school and learning.

The two major organizational backers of community control, CORE and the Ford Foundation, made strange bedfellows. CORE was increasingly leftist, flirting with black separatism. The president of the Ford Foundation was McGeorge Bundy, the former White House national security advisor under Presidents Kennedy and Johnson, and a key architect of the Vietnam War. Bundy was deeply influenced by Mario Fantini, the Ford Foundation's program officer for education. Fantini's scholarly work argued on behalf of multiculturalism in schools, such as lessons in African music and history. He convinced Bundy that if black parents and teachers worked together to set a more engaging Afrocentric curriculum for their children's schools, the liberal integrationist dream of *Brown v. Board of Education* would become a reality; inner-city schools would improve so drastically that white parents would be eager to enroll their own children in them. In retrospect, this theory of change seems willfully naïve. There was no evidence at all that significant numbers of white parents were willing to send their children to Afrocentric schools. Yet in 1967 community control appealed to activists and politicians who were eager to move away from wars over whether to bus black children to white schools. New York City mayor John Lindsay, a progressive Republican, appointed Bundy to lead a city commission on improving schools. The resulting Bundy report argued for abolishing the city school board and turning over teacher hiring, tenure, firing, and matters of curriculum to between thirty and sixty neighborhood community boards partly elected by parents and partly appointed by the mayor.

This community control agenda was soon under consideration in Detroit, Newark, Washington, D.C., and other cities across the country. It aroused bitter opposition within teachers unions. Having just won collective bargaining rights, unions reacted harshly against the potential erosion of their power that could result from being forced to negotiate with dozens of locally controlled school boards instead of one central administration in each major city. Union leaders also feared the rise of an empowered grassroots Left, funded by deep-pocketed philanthropists like the Ford Foundation, which could impose an ideological litmus test—Afrocentrism—on teachers. Most fundamentally, unions resented the community control movement's assertion that bad, racist teachers were to blame for poor children's low academic achievement, and what would emerge as the movement's frontal attack on the due process rights that made it difficult for principals to remove tenured teachers from classrooms.

There have always been tensions between teachers unions and other progressives committed to public education. Jane Addams thought Margaret Haley was wrong to resist tougher evaluations of teachers. President Johnson created the Teacher Corps over the objections of the National Education Association. But during the urban teacher strikes of the late 1960s and early 1970s, when unions opposed black and Hispanic community control in favor of job security for predominantly white teachers, the unions became downright villains not only to antilabor conservatives, but, for the first time, to large segments of the American Left as well.

In the push for community control, we see an antecedent to so many of today's school reform battles. Just as the Ford Foundation in the late 1960s funded parent activists in Brooklyn who eventually took over their school district and tried to fire tenured teachers, today Bill Gates donates to "parent trigger" efforts in California and other states, in which school reformers go to low-income communities and help parents organize petition drives in favor of overhauling the management and staffing of their children's schools, sometimes turning them into nonunionized charter schools.* Both then and now, reformers who describe themselves as progressives believe unions impede quality schools. Howard Kalodner, an NYU law professor and member of the Bundy commission, spoke for many in 1967 when he professed the desire "to destroy the professional educational bureaucracy. Seventy-five to 80 percent of the educators do not believe that black and Puerto Rican children can learn. You can't have a professional educational system like that." Today's reformers have coined the term "the Blob" to refer to the

---

* The parent trigger movement is portrayed in the 2012 movie *Won't Back Down*, starring Maggie Gyllenhaal and Viola Davis. The film was funded by philanthropists with a history of conservative, antilabor activism, such as Phil Anschutz, owner of *The Weekly Standard*.

same tangle of bureaucracies—teachers unions, school boards, and teacher education programs—that Kalodner denounced, and they too equate loyalty to these institutions with a belief that minority students do not have intellectual potential.

This vilification of union teachers misses a much more complex reality. Even as unions argued—often in a tone-deaf way—for job security protections that few parents could support, organized teachers were (and remain) potent advocates for many of the education policies that most benefit disadvantaged children, from tuition-free pre-K to better training for teachers. Regardless, as hopes for President Johnson's vision of an integrated Great Society curdled in the late 1960s, the community control and Black Power movements loomed with a powerful critique of union teachers—a critique that was eagerly adopted by the liberal elite within philanthropy and government, and that remains salient today.

As Richard Kahlenberg points out in his indispensable biography of Al Shanker, *Tough Liberal,* the idea of community control of urban schools originated in Queens in 1964, among white opponents of school desegregation who believed parents should band together to prevent busing. Within two years, however, the Left adopted the concept. In 1966, twenty-five-year-old Stokely Carmichael, a proponent of black separatism, burst onto the national political stage when he defeated the moderate John Lewis to become head of the Student Nonviolent Coordinating Committee (SNCC), the vanguard of the civil rights movement. Carmichael's election represented the ascendance of Black Power. His lanky good looks and conservative outfits—slim-cut suits and ties—were paired with revolutionary politics inspired by his anticolonialist philosophical studies at Howard. Carmichael was deeply concerned with education policy. He had attended integrated public schools as a child, including New York's elite Bronx High School of Science, but had come to believe that far too much time had been wasted on futile school integration efforts. In 1966 Carmichael delivered his most famous speech, in front of an audience of ten thousand largely white left-wing students at Berkeley. He talked about Vietnam and civil rights legislation, but also about public schools. "We cannot afford to be concerned with the 6 percent of black children in this country whom you allow to enter white schools," he said. "We are going to be concerned with the 94 percent" who attend majority-black schools—which he believed should be staffed entirely by black teachers and principals. "We cannot have white people working in the black community—on psychological grounds. . . . [B]lack people must be in positions of power, doing and articulating for themselves." The white crowd cheered. In front of black audiences, he was harsher. At a birthday party for Black Panther defense minister Huey Newton, Carmichael declared that black youth "are more intelligent than all those honkies on those school boards . . . We have to understand that until we control an educational system that will teach us how to change our community, there's no need to send anybody to school."

Martin Luther King called this philosophy "nihilistic" and said it made more sense to advocate for poor people overall, not just blacks. "In a multiracial society," he wrote, "no group can make it alone." But black separatism quickly gained momentum in inner cities, mostly because of broken promises about the integration of housing and schools. In Ocean Hill–Brownsville, an economically depressed neighborhood in central Brooklyn, the city had recently opened Junior High School 271. The low-slung redbrick and blue-tile building was like dozens of others constructed across New York City in the early and mid-1960s to accommodate a surging student population and, the Board of Education hoped, to stem the exodus of working-class white families from inner-city neighborhoods. That hadn't worked. Over the previous decade, almost all of the remaining white families in Ocean Hill–Brownsville had fled, lured by cheap mortgages in the suburbs of Long Island and New Jersey. Apartments that had housed three- or four-person, mostly Jewish families were now packed with eight or ten people each, immigrants from Puerto Rico and black migrants from the South. Across nearby Rockaway Avenue, practically a highway, stood a number of massive public housing developments, clustered together, as the city was wont to do, in a neighborhood and school district already filled with poor residents, and with no grocery stores, movie theaters, or other basic amenities. JHS 271 and other nearby schools became 98 or 99 percent black and Hispanic.

Though life in Ocean Hill–Brownsville could be difficult, the neighborhood had a well-established community services sector, anchored by churches and social welfare organizations. After *Brown v. Board of Education*, these groups had hoped to address the problem of overcrowded, underperforming schools by busing children out of the neighborhood. Father John Powis, a white Catholic priest, helped arrange for seventeen hundred Ocean Hill–Brownsville elementary school students to enroll in majority-white schools in other Brooklyn neighborhoods. The aftermath, he said, was "very sad." Neighborhoods and schools that received children of color rarely made the children feel welcome, nor were teachers in those schools prepared to work with students who were several years behind academically. Back in Ocean Hill–Brownsville, parents like Dolores Torres were dismayed by what they saw at their children's schools. Teachers were essentially babysitting, Torres remembered. The curriculum included little writing. Parents pressed for a longer day and more help for their children, yet when the afternoon bell rang, Torres said, "Teachers were out of there before the kids were. . . . We felt we couldn't put up with it anymore." Even the United Federation of Teachers agreed that neighborhood students were not being taught well. In 1967 the union assigned one of its most effective organizers, Sandy Feldman, to work with teachers in the area. "You'd walk in, and the kids were out of control," she said. "The hallways were wild. They were dirty." Teachers seemed to react to the poor conditions by closing themselves off in their individual classrooms.

Powis, Torres, and other Ocean Hill–Brownsville activists began to wonder if the solution to these malfunctioning schools was not to bus children to hostile neighborhoods, but to do what Stokely Carmichael had suggested: cut white bureaucracies entirely out of the equation when it came to determining what happened to poor students of color. If parents in affluent suburban New York towns like Chappaqua or Scarsdale could directly elect school boards to set policy for just a few thousand students, why couldn't parents in teeming Ocean Hill–Brownsville, with nine thousand children?

The union's solution was different: It believed the neighborhood should be part of a program called More Effective Schools, which the UFT had designed and convinced the city to adopt. The MES program provided select schools in poor neighborhoods with extra funding for smaller classes, pre-K, and more support staff, such as social workers and reading specialists. The directors of the program, like many progressive educators, also aimed to end tracking by training teachers in how to work with "heterogeneous groups"— classrooms in which students had diverse family backgrounds and academic ability. (Today this strategy is often called "differentiation." It is a lot easier to do with smaller class sizes.)

But the MES program wasn't given a chance in the neighborhood. In the spring of 1967 New York City mayor John Lindsay granted community control to Ocean Hill–Brownsville and two other majority-black and Hispanic neighborhoods, Harlem and the Lower East Side. Even though More Effective Schools and community control were in no way contradictory to one another and could have been implemented simultaneously, the city denied the three "demonstration" districts MES funding, saying that if community control were to prove itself an effective school governance strategy, it would need to do so operating under regular budgetary constraints. Barbara Carter, a journalist who published an early book about the Ocean Hill–Brownsville upheaval, wrote that in keeping the districts out of the MES program, "school officials deprived the community of one of the few points . . . around which teachers and parents, growing ever further apart, might have rallied." This was even more tragic considering the MES program's impressive track record. Over a year, students enrolled at MES schools gained 2.5 to 4.5 months more in their reading comprehension than did peers who did not participate in the program. Test scores went up in math, speech, and oral communication.

Yet at the city level, support for community control didn't have much to do with teaching and learning. It was about money, political alliances, and power. Mayor Lindsay, who had presidential ambitions, was eager to avoid busing controversies and to ally with black civil rights leaders, who were abandoning the *Brown v. Board of Educaton* consensus. The nation's most prominent civil rights organizations—the NAACP and Urban League in the former integrationist camp, and SNCC and CORE on the Black Power Left—supported community control. Lastly, the language of school decentralization anticipated a shifting tone in national politics. When Richard Nixon took office in 1969, he proposed a "New Federalism," turning policy-making power over to state and municipal governments where possible.

Under the initial experiment in community control, voters in each of the three demonstration districts won the right to elect a neighborhood school board, which was established with funding from the Ford Foundation and organizational assistance from CORE. In Ocean Hill–Brownsville, the board selected Rhody McCoy, the critic of the union's positions on student discipline, to oversee the entire project. He was a forty-six-year-old black principal with experience in the city's "600 schools," which served children with social and emotional problems. As a young teacher he had experienced trouble, like many black candidates, in passing exams to become an administrator and join the white-dominated principals union. So he came to the community control experiment with long-standing frustration toward union-negotiated work rules. He spoke movingly about what black and Hispanic families could contribute to their own children's education. "It was a joy to go to board meetings" when parents were in charge, he recalled in 1988. "It was always on a positive note: How do we help the youngsters? . . . We were able to get an enthusiasm. The entire community came together around the schools."

McCoy had close ties to the city's activist Left, despite his seemingly moderate lifestyle as a father of eight in suburban Long Island. He hired Herman Ferguson, a Black Panther and former assistant principal in Queens, as a paid educational consultant, even though Ferguson had recently been charged with conspiring to murder Roy Wilkins of the NAACP and Whitney Young of the Urban League, supposedly in retaliation for their moderate "Uncle Tom" politics. At a February 1968 memorial rally for Malcolm X, held at a Harlem public school, Ferguson delivered a frightening speech. He likened American inner cities to the battlefields of Vietnam, advising the crowd of adults and teenagers, "To die takes only a split second, and you don't feel anything. But if you can't do anything at all, take someone with you. Make yourselves gun fanciers. Get a gun and keep it out of sight. Use it at the appropriate time."* In the audience that day was Les Campbell, a tall, dashiki-clad black teacher in the Bedford-Stuyvesant neighborhood of Brooklyn, who taught history from an Afrocentric perspective. Campbell had defied his supervisors by bringing middle school students to the rally, and within a few weeks, lost his job.

He wasn't out of work for long. On Ferguson's recommendation, McCoy hired Campbell to work in Ocean Hill–Brownsville. Campbell became a charismatic and infamous presence at JHS 271, where some of his most committed Black Studies pupils began rejecting their "slave names" and referring to themselves with new names borrowed from black Muslim cultures. (Theresa Jordan, for example, became Karima Jordan, a name she used into adulthood.) Campbell's politics were so extreme that even some black parents in the neighborhood were uncomfortable with his teaching. One of them was Elaine Rooke, the school's PTA president and a harsh critic of the UFT. She told her son to avoid Campbell, whom she considered a troublemaker. Not every community control supporter was a separatist radical, but the presence of figures like Ferguson and Campbell in Ocean Hill–Brownsville's public schools enraged Al Shanker, and the district kept supplying the union leader with fuel for outrage, with which he was able to build opposition to community control. The morning after Martin Luther King's assassination, an assembly was called at JHS 271. As Rhody McCoy stood by, cries of "Black Power!" and "Kill whitey!" rang out, and then white teachers were encouraged to leave the room. Campbell delivered a speech to the students that some interpreted as an incitement to riot. "If whitey taps you on the shoulder, send him to the graveyard," he said.

---

* In June 1968, Ferguson was convicted of conspiracy to murder and sentenced to up to seven years in prison. He fled the United States for Guyana, but returned in 1989 and served his sentence. In 1996, New York Supreme Court justice Bruce Wright granted Ferguson parole and cast doubt on the charges against him, noting that in the late 1960s, "all Black nationalist activists were targets, not only of local police, but of the FBI as well."

An oil portrait of Catharine Beecher, c. 1830, when she was already—in her early thirties—America's first media-darling school reformer. American teaching had been a largely male profession, but as Beecher recruited well-bred young East Coast women to become pioneer teachers in the West, she helped transform teaching into acceptable work for middle-class ladies. She attacked male teachers as "intemperate . . . coarse, hard, unfeeling men, too lazy or stupid" to educate America's children.
(Harriet Beecher Stowe Center, Hartford, Connecticut)

A daguerreotype of Horace Mann, c. 1844, when he was the nation's first state secretary of education, in Massachusetts. Mann realized employing female teachers would save taxpayers millions of dollars due to women's lower wages. He idealized female educators not as academics but as "celestial" public servants motivated by Christian faith and moral purity.
(Massachusetts Historical Society)

An 1848 portrait of Susan B. Anthony, when she was a twenty-eight-year-old teacher at the Canajoharie Academy in upstate New York. She proudly wrote home about this plaid dress, wondering if her sisters, who did not earn their own wages, did not "feel rather sad because they are married and can not have nice clothes." Anthony would soon travel across New York State organizing female teachers to demand equal pay. *(Department of Rare Books and Special Collections, University of Rochester)*

Elizabeth Cady Stanton in 1856 with her daughter Harriot. Stanton was a wealthy woman who educated her seven children at home. She disdained the teaching profession as "a pool of intellectual stagnation" and hoped young women would soon be able to pursue more prestigious careers in law, medicine, and the clergy. *(Library of Congress)*

Charlotte Forten in 1860 at the age of twenty-three. An affluent black woman born free in Philadelphia, Forten volunteered to teach in a one-room schoolhouse for emancipated slaves in the South Carolina Sea Islands. She helped inaugurate a tradition of privileged, highly educated African Americans serving the race through teaching. Forten called her time on St. Helena Island "a strange, wild dream"— one that challenged many of her pious preconceptions about lifting her people out of dependence and poverty. *(Getty Images)*

Emancipated slaves working with cotton at Port Royal in the South Carolina Sea Islands, 1862. As part of the Port Royal Experiment, the Union initially offered the freedmen communal ownership of their former owners' land. But President Andrew Johnson ended the project in 1866, allowing former slave owners to return and reclaim their property. Many of the students Charlotte Forten taught became sharecroppers. *(Library of Congress)*

W. E. B. Du Bois, the pioneering theorist and historian of African American education, who taught for one summer in a rural, black public school. He believed black teachers should be part of the college-going "talented tenth," writing that teachers must "be broad-minded, cultured men and women, to scatter civilization among a people whose ignorance was not simply of letters, but of life itself." In 1901 his critique of Booker T. Washington and strict vocational tracking for black children cost Du Bois an appointment to lead the colored public school system in Washington, D.C. *(Library of Congress)*

Margaret Haley, leader of the nation's first teachers-only union, the Chicago Teachers Federation, founded in 1897. Called a "lady labor slugger" and accused of leading teachers and children into "sedition" and "revolt," Haley understood that through an alliance with male, blue-collar organized labor, female teachers could better advocate for equal pay, the vote, and increased school funding. *(Chicago History Museum)*

Ella Flagg Young, c. 1810–1815, when she was the superintendent of the Chicago public schools—the first woman in the United States to lead an urban education system. Young began her career as a teacher and fought vocational tracking based on IQ scores. Inspired by her mentor John Dewey, she argued, "In order that teachers may delight in awakening the spirits of children, they must themselves be awake"—meaning intellectually engaged and empowered by their work. *(Library of Congress)*

New York City Teachers Union members lobby for substitutes' rights and multicultural education, 1945. This gadfly band of young teachers, many of them communists, fought aggressively for academic freedom and for schools to embrace a broad antiracist, antipoverty agenda—a platform that anticipated many later-twentieth-century goals of education reform.

(November 3, 1945, issue of the New York Teacher News, *Collection of the Tamiment Library, New York University)*

(ABOVE) In 1940 the American Federation of Teachers expelled the New York City Teachers Union (TU), afraid its communist politics would taint the still-nascent teacher unionism movement. The TU then affiliated with the Congress of Industrial Workers (CIO). In this promotional image from a 1945 issue of the *New York Teacher News*, a white-collar teacher forges a partnership with a blue-collar worker.

(October 13, 1945, issue of the New York Teacher News, *Collection of the Tamiment Library, New York University)*

Alongside his own elementary school teacher, "Miss Kate" Deadrich Loney, President Lyndon B. Johnson signs the Elementary and Secondary Education Act, 1965. As a young man Johnson taught in a segregated, Mexican American public school in rural south Texas. He later portrayed teachers as revolutionary foot soldiers in the War on Poverty. Federal funding for poor children's schools would "bridge the gap between helplessness and hope for more than 5 million educationally deprived children," he said. *(Francis Miller, the LIFE Picture Collection, Getty)*

Al Shanker in 1965, as president of the United Federation of Teachers in New York City. The UFT was the nation's first major teachers union to earn collective bargaining rights. With a series of daring strikes, Shanker and his union raised teacher pay and empowered teachers in the education policy debate. Though he advanced many ideas for school improvement, from racial integration to pre-K to tests of teachers' subject-matter knowledge, Shanker was infamous as a defender of teachers even when students got in the way. He once said, "Listen, I don't represent children. I represent the teachers." *(Library of Congress)*

(ABOVE) By a show of hands, members of the United Federation of Teachers vote over-whelmingly for a strike on the first day of school, September 9, 1968. Al Shanker is at the podium. "This is a strike that will protect black teachers against white racists and white teachers against black racists," he said. But some UFT members were motivated more by fear of activists and parents of color making demands on urban teachers and schools. *(Bettmann/Corbis)*

(RIGHT) Rhody McCoy, administrator of the community control experiment in Ocean Hill–Brownsville, Brooklyn. In 1968, McCoy attempted to remove nineteen tenured teachers and administrators from the neighborhood's public schools, all of them white. The action provoked a sixty-thousand-teacher strike led by Al Shanker. McCoy believed that if black and Hispanic parents got involved in their children's schools, they would be able to show white teachers how to "set a tone so you didn't have any such thing as 'disruptive children.'" *(Bettmann/Corbis)*

Secretary of Education Terrel Bell and President Ronald Reagan meeting at the White House in 1983, the year *A Nation at Risk* was published to widespread acclaim. The federal report, Bell's brainchild, depicted a "rising tide of mediocrity" in American public education, and blamed dullard teachers drawn from the bottom quarter of high school and college graduating classes. While promoting merit pay and alternative certification for teachers, Bell and Reagan ended the federal government's commitment to school desegregation. *(Corbis)*

A Teach for America corps member works in her third-grade classroom in Washington, D.C., 2008. Her white board references the priorities of the standards and accountability school reform movement: high standardized test scores on the DC-CAS exam and other forms of measurable learning growth. *(Brendan Hoffman/AP/Corbis)*

All in all, the first school year of community control, 1967–1968, was a struggle. McCoy and the community board moved quickly to hire black and Puerto Rican administrators for each of the district's eight schools, and in doing so ousted several popular principals. Teachers were restive. Students still often left class and roamed the hallways. McCoy and his deputies were determined to get the situation under control. Sometime in early May 1968—the exact date is lost, for the school kept few records—a hall monitor named Cecil Bowen observed Richard Douglass's art class at JHS 271. Bowen later reported that when he stepped inside the classroom, he saw students shouting and flinging paint at one another as Douglass stood by helplessly. Bowen broke up the fight. Several days later, McCoy and the Ocean Hill–Brownsville community board dismissed Douglass and eighteen other white teachers and administrators. Some of the shocked teachers were called out of their classrooms to receive the dismissals in the form of a telegram. The dismissals were not terminations—they simply asked the selected teachers to report to city school board headquarters for new assignments. But McCoy clearly intended to send a message—that black parents and administrators deserved veto power over the employment of white teachers. "Not one of these teachers will be allowed to teach anywhere in this city," he predicted of the group he dismissed. "The black community will see to that."

Long before collective bargaining, it had been difficult to oust an experienced teacher. Teacher tenure, after all, had existed in New York since 1917, and in other cities since 1909. Only in rare cases (or during moral panics, like the Red Scare) would districts pursue an expensive and time-consuming trial to terminate the employment of a tenured teacher. This "due process" was the bedrock principle of teacher unionism, the protection that could help prevent teachers from being fired because of their political leanings, gender, race, religious beliefs, pregnancy, or opposition to administrative policies.

But what could be done about teachers who were just plain bad at their jobs? Working around tenure rules, administrators and the UFT had established an informal, backstage process for removing—or, more accurately, juggling—ineffective tenured teachers: A principal would put in a request with the Board of Education that a teacher be transferred to another school, and as long as the principal removed no more than one or two teachers per year, the union would not typically raise objections. In this way, bad teachers hopped from school to school, often ending up at the schools in the poorest neighborhoods with the least political clout.*

The history of American public education had shown that teachers needed some sort of protection; female, black, gay, and radical teachers had experienced wave after wave of ideologically motivated dismissals, unrelated to professional competence. But by the late 1960s, education reformers feared the pendulum had swung too far in the opposite direction. One of the most cited statistics by supporters of community control was that over a five-year period in the mid-1960s only 12 out of 55,000 teachers in New York City were fired for cause. Everyone, even the union, agreed there were more than 12 bad tenured teachers. Shanker and the UFT argued that the low termination rate obscured the fact that many others were urged to leave the profession through private conversations. In Ocean Hill–Brownsville, McCoy had willfully ignored this tacitly accepted, slow-moving way of doing business, telling the media that time was of the essence. "We've got to make them learn," he said of his district's disadvantaged students. "They've been so deprived so long that they've tuned out."

Could neighborhood schools hire and fire based on community instructional and even political preferences? The union argued they could not, and it sent several of the dismissed Ocean Hill–Brownsville teachers back to work, where they were met by activists, some affiliated with black separatist groups, who physically prevented the teachers from entering school buildings. Two weeks later when 350 UFT teachers walked out of the Ocean Hill–Brownsville schools in solidarity with their dismissed colleagues, the community board attempted to terminate all their contracts, too. Mayor Lindsay hadn't approved McCoy's plans and did not

* The catchphrase "dance of the lemons" was coined by education reformers in the late 1990s to describe how union protections allow ineffective teachers to be moved from school to school, instead of being forced out of the system.

know how to react. Did a neighborhood community board have the power to terminate teachers en masse?

This seemingly local event triggered not only the most infamous and largest teachers' strike in American history, but also a political and racial crisis of national proportions, which continues to reverberate in almost every debate about contemporary school reform. On one side, community control advocates argued that the education of poor black and brown children was too urgent a matter to bother with labor protections, bureaucratic protocol, or even basic politesse—much the same argument we hear from today's opponents of teacher tenure. On the other side, the United Federation of Teachers worried that allowing parents and non-educator activists to essentially fire teachers they did not approve of would devalue the professionalism of educators and return them to a climate of constant job insecurity. What's more, the unionists feared that a community control movement affiliated with Afrocentrism could potentially turn neighborhood schools into places of political indoctrination. The moderate wing of organized labor had succeeded in vanquishing a strong challenge from radical communists in the old Teachers Union. Now the UFT worried that Black Power, funded by the powerful Ford Foundation, posed a similar threat. A May 22, 1968, union ad in *The New York Times,* responding to the Ocean Hill–Brownsville dismissals, summed up the UFT's fears:

> Teachers have been physically threatened. . . . School buildings have been taken over by extremist groups using public property and tax money to teach children to hate. . . . Teachers and children have been kept out of school by outsiders— not parents and community groups. With over 15,000 parents in the district, less than a dozen participated in the action. The Legislature's Decentralization Plan Will Mean More of the Same. Don't let our school system be taken over by local extremists.

In reality, the Ocean Hill–Brownsville dismissals were as much about competence as about ideology. Art teacher Richard Douglass, for example, had been transferred to JHS 271 from another middle school, whose principal had also complained he lacked classroom management skills. Like most teachers in Ocean Hill–Brownsville and low-income schools across the country, Douglass had received no special training in how to work with poor children, children with behavioral problems, or non-native English speakers. In fact, Douglass was an adherent of A. S. Neill, the British education theorist whose 1960 bestseller, *Summerhill,* described the radical "free" pedagogy of the boarding school he had founded in England, which served children from mostly affluent families. Summerhill students lived "free from adult authority," allowed to play or learn in whatever proportion they saw fit. Children voted on rules and punishments, and parents were encouraged to take a hands-off approach, only getting involved at school with their children's permission. The art room at Summerhill was an unstructured place where students could pursue whatever projects they liked. These practices, though attractive to many liberal educators during the 1960s, were a bad fit in Ocean Hill–Brownsville, a neighborhood where parents had been organizing in favor of a more traditional approach: structured lessons, stricter discipline, and a longer school day. Douglass knew he was in over his head, but he seemed to blame his students more than his own poor training or ill-suited philosophy. Maybe, he told a *New York Post* reporter, the problem was that a liberal arts curriculum was irrelevant to these particular kids. "The children are not motivated to learn," he complained. Instead of art, the school should "stress reading in the mornings and electives in the afternoon, like inviting an electrician or maybe a plumber, because realistically all the kids wouldn't be going to college."

Douglass was plainly an ineffective teacher. So were some (though not all) of the other teachers dismissed alongside him, who admitted later that they had trouble managing student behavior. The summer following the dismissals, the city Board of Education conducted hearings to determine the fates of ten of the original thirteen dismissed teachers who wished to return to their jobs in Ocean Hill–Brownsville. (The others had resigned or accepted positions at other schools.) A widely respected African American judge, Francis Rivers, served as trial examiner. He threw out the cases of four of the dismissed teachers, saying they had been targeted not because of problems in the classroom, but simply because they had voiced skepticism of community control. Of this group, Daniel Goldberg, a UFT rep, was considered an especially gifted social studies teacher. His supposed offense had been sniping about the district's administrative practices to a colleague at a Christmas party. In the cases of Douglass and five other teachers, Rivers concluded that the district's accusations of classroom management problems, lateness, and even corporal punishment were nearly impossible to substantiate, since McCoy's administration kept no records of observations or other personnel matters. Rivers did not deny adults were remiss in the classrooms of Ocean Hill–Brownsville. But the dismissals seemed arbitrary to him, since testimony indicated that more than a quarter of the teachers in the district were similarly weak. What's more, some of the dismissed teachers had repeatedly asked for instructional help from their supervisors but were ignored.

On August 26, 1968, Rivers ordered McCoy to reinstate all ten teachers, along with the 350 who had struck in solidarity the previous May. When UFT teachers arrived at JHS 271 on the first day of school that fall, however, it was clear many would not be allowed to work. Administrators "paired" returning union loyalists with teachers considered friendly to community control, and several union-affiliated teachers reported that when they began to teach, their partner teacher either led students out of the classroom or directed children to disrupt the lesson. It was chaos, an all-out factional war. Shanker had to determine how to respond. He believed McCoy and the community control movement were bullying union teachers who were skeptical of Afrocentrism, and that if this behavior was allowed to stand, black teachers could be bullied because of their race, too. At a UFT meeting he advocated a citywide walkout, arguing, "This is a strike that will protect black teachers against white racists and white teachers against black racists." The union's delegate assembly voted in favor of the strike, and 93 percent of New York City teachers chose to honor the picket line, compared to just 77 percent during the 1967 strike and 12 percent during the UFT's first walkout in 1960.

The 1968 strikes of sixty thousand teachers, the largest ever, were particularly disruptive because they were staggered in intervals of several days and weeks between September and November. In total, a fifth of the school year's instructional time was lost, and nearly one million children were affected. Shanker presided over giant City Hall rallies of up to forty thousand union teachers chanting in favor of due process. "You're a racist, Mr. Shanker!" shouted community control supporters in response. Anti-union demonstrators trailed the UFT leader everywhere he went, even to his family's split-level home in suburban Putnam County, where they issued Shanker a "report card" with a grade of F for "works and plays well with others" and A for "racism."

In Ocean Hill–Brownsville, 60 percent of students continued to show up at school during the strikes. The district attempted to function with replacement teachers, who were culled from several groups that were critical of union leadership: the African-American Teachers Association, a black separatist group; white liberal supporters of community control, some of them the sons and daughters of communist Teachers Union members; and young New Left activist teachers who judged that the staunchly anticommunist Shanker was insufficiently opposed to the Vietnam War. Teacher interviews were held in a gymnasium, where McCoy, community board members, and parents all questioned the applicants. Dolores Torres remembered that she and other parents sought teachers who were enthusiastic about working with nonwhite children and who were pedagogically flexible. "What did they feel about coming to work in a neighborhood that was predominantly black and Hispanic? Did they feel that our children could learn as well as anybody else's children, in, say, a white neighborhood, an affluent neighborhood? . . . A lot of the teachers were agreeable. They felt that if you couldn't teach a child one way, then try something else—but that all children could be taught."

In an essay for *The New York Times Magazine,* replacement teacher Charles Isaacs, a white, freshly minted graduate of the University of Chicago Law School, described instruction during the strike in idealized terms. Students at JHS 271 were reading Langston Hughes, studying African history, and calling teachers by their first names, Isaacs wrote. They took a weekend field trip to hike at Bear Mountain, chaperoned by "younger, better educated" teachers like himself, who were "having too good a time" to ask for overtime pay. But students realized their education was being compromised by the upheaval. They had to enter school through police barricades erected to separate picketing teachers from community control activists, some of them armed Black Panthers. More police were stationed on the school's rooftop, wearing helmets and riot gear and carrying nightsticks. Helicopters buzzed overhead, and there were so many reporters and cameras that "it was like someone was filming a movie or something," remembered Karima Jordan, who was in ninth grade. "You couldn't believe this was happening."

Television news footage of the picket line showed a solemn circle of middle-aged white men and women trudging along with UFT-produced signs hung around their necks: "CIVIL RIGHTS FOR TEACHERS." "CONTRACTS MUST BE HONORED." "STOP TEACHING RACE HATRED." The scene was punctuated by moments of ugliness. Children witnessed blatant racism, from name-calling to physical confrontations. Peter Goodman, a strike leader, was married to a black teacher who supported the strikes. He considered himself a civil rights activist who opposed community control on pedagogical grounds. But he admits that some of his white colleagues had baser motivations. "Lots of teachers were pretty racist," he told me. "They saw the strike as white versus black, there's no question in my mind about that." Those fears were fanned by the violent rhetoric swirling around the community control movement. During the strikes, an anonymous anti-Semitic flyer was placed in the mailboxes of some Ocean Hill–Brownsville teachers. It read:

> If African-American History and Culture is to be taught to our Black Children it Must be Done by African-Americans Who Identify With And Who Understand The Problem. It is Impossible For the Middle East Murderers of Colored People to Possibly Bring to This Important Task The Insight, The Concern, The Exposing of the Truth that is a Must If The Years of Brainwashing and Self-Hatred That Has Been Taught to Our Black Children By These Blood-sucking Exploiters and Murderers Is To Be Overcome.

Rhody McCoy and the community board denounced the leaflet's message. There was no reason to believe anti-Semitism was a core value of the community control movement, which included many prominent Jews. Seventy percent of the replacement teachers McCoy hired were white, and half of them were Jewish—almost identical demographics to the teachers he fired or who went on strike in response to his policies. But McCoy's embrace of radicals like Ferguson and Campbell left him vulnerable. Al Shanker was eager to portray community control as bigoted, in order to build public support for his union and its disruptive strike.* He circulated five thousand copies of the anti-Semitic flyer with the statement, "Is that what you want for your children? The UFT says NO!"

The labor impasse finally ended in late November, when the New York State Board of Regents placed Ocean Hill–Brownsville and the city's two other demonstration districts under state management, essentially ending the experiment in community control. The strike had exhausted the public and politicians, whose support for school decentralization had been predicated mostly on the hope of ending battles over school desegregation, and less on what community control advocates were really demanding: the empowerment of low-income, minority, sometimes radical parents and activists to control the budgets and agendas of local schools. Yet the racial inflammation continued unabated, making national news. On the day after Christmas, Black Studies teacher Les Campbell was a guest on the WBAI radio show of Julius Lester, a black musician and activist. At Lester's suggestion, Campbell recited a poem written by one of his students, a fifteen-year-old girl named Sia Berhan. It was titled "To Albert Shanker: Anti-Semitism":

Hey Jew boy with that yarmulke on your head
You pale faced Jew boy I wish you were dead . . .

---

* In his 1973 movie *Sleeper,* Woody Allen captured the intelligentsia's fear that Al Shanker would stop at nothing to defend union teachers. The film's protagonist is cryogenically unfrozen two hundred years in the future and learns civilization had been destroyed because "a man by the name of Al Shanker got hold of a nuclear warhead."

Jew boy you took my religion and adopted it for you
But you know that black people were the original Hebrews
When the UN made Israel a free, independent state
Little four and five-year-old boys threw hand grenades
They hated the black Arabs with all their might
And you, Jew boy, said it was alright
And then you came to America the land of the free
Took over the school system to perpetuate white supremacy
Cause you know, Jew boy, there's only one reason you made it
*You had a clean white face colorless and faded.**

The disturbing piece of writing distilled, from a teenager's immature perspective—one obviously heavily influenced by her teacher—some of the real racial resentments underlying demands for community control. It did seem, to many people of color, that the white, two-thirds Jewish UFT had taken over the city's school system. The old communist Teachers Union had essentially been a civil rights organization, working alongside parents. But the old union never had collective bargaining rights; its ability to shape teachers' working conditions was sharply limited, so it focused on other issues. The UFT was a different animal. One of the key insights of historian Marjorie Murphy's groundbreaking study of teacher unionism, *Blackboard Unions,* is that collective bargaining actually allied teachers to the central administration of urban school districts—the exact constituency Margaret Haley had founded teacher unionism to counteract. Under collective bargaining, it was easier for unions to negotiate with one strong administrative body, such as a city superintendent, board of education, or mayor, than with a plethora of neighborhood school boards or principals, each with their own set of demands. In New York, this meant that the UFT, though a supporter of school integration, worked closely and cooperatively with the Board of Education, which (as black communities knew all too well) had repeatedly stymied desegregation

---

* Despite his role in this infamous incident, radio host Julius Lester later converted to Judaism and taught Judaic Studies at the University of Massachusetts Amherst.

efforts. With their increased influence, teachers unions like the UFT were able to quickly raise teacher salaries, which could generate resentment among black and Puerto Rican public school parents, who tended to earn much less than college-educated teachers, and who had not benefited from the rise of largely white organized labor.

Yet union leaders were in utter disbelief that *they* had been accused of racism. After all, hadn't the UFT protested Jim Crow in the South and supported desegregation in the North? Hadn't Martin Luther King in 1964 proudly accepted the UFT's highest honor, the John Dewey Award? Al Shanker saw black separatism as a radical, illiberal ideology. "To me, the Civil Rights Movement was a movement for integration," he said. "In a sense, [community control] represented a kind of backward step."

Union members boasted of the fact that after King's death in 1968—right in the midst of the community control debate—several labor-oriented members of King's inner circle, like Bayard Rustin and A. Philip Randolph, continued to side with the UFT. Randolph led the Brotherhood of Sleeping Car Porters, the most prominent majority-black union. Rustin was the brilliant Quaker who played a key role in introducing King to notions of nonviolence. He had participated, alongside Shanker, in the socialist, anti-Soviet workshops organized by Max Shachtman, a former confidant of Leon Trotsky himself. During the strike, Rustin enthralled majority-white crowds at teachers union rallies in New York City, sometimes leading them in singing black spirituals. He urged unionists to pay more attention to improving children's educational outcomes but believed community control provided few answers. "The proposal seems concerned more with political self-determination in education than with quality," he said.

Fundamentally, however, Rustin and Randolph saw a lack of good jobs—not bad schools or teachers union work rules—as the primary barrier to enlarging the black middle class. Unionists eagerly subscribed to this interpretation of events. Early UFT leaders, like Shanker, George Altomare, and Peter Goodman, had a lifelong respect and affection for unions because their parents had belonged to them. Altomare's mother, like Shanker's, was a member of the Amalgamated Clothing Workers, while Goodman's father was a union furrier. Yet labor politics had changed since the 1930s. Those older unions represented private, not public, employees. When seamstresses won higher wages, it was ownership who saw reduced profits. Teachers, on the other hand, were paid with tax dollars. By the late 1960s both community control activists and the mainstream media portrayed union-won raises for teachers as a drain on school budgets, sucking up money that could go toward much-needed new school buildings, textbooks, and other educational resources. A 1967 profile of Shanker in *The New York Times Magazine* summarized both elite and activist opinion that the union chief "gets the most he can for his teachers, even if it means sacrificing the needs of the school system." Shanker boosted this perception when, in the midst of the Ocean Hill–Brownsville controversy, he gave a lecture at Oberlin College. When an audience member asked him if he worried about how strikes affect children educationally, Shanker replied, "Listen, I don't represent children. I represent the teachers." It remains among his most-quoted statements, often used to denigrate the teachers union movement as a whole. Yet the needs of teachers and children were not always so diametrically opposed. That was one of the lessons of the More Effective Schools program, which improved academic outcomes in part by hiring more teachers for poor children. Judge Rivers had concluded that teachers in Ocean Hill–Brownsville had sought professional help in order to better serve their students, and that they had been ignored by administrators. Union positions were not always to blame for disappointing student outcomes.

Had the short experiment in community control worked as an educational program? After the strike ended in November 1968, Rhody McCoy told the media, "I'm going to produce! Come back a year from now and I promise you I will have done it." He even claimed to have already raised student achievement by 30 percent, though he refused to release the district's standardized test scores to prove it—rather ironic, considering that low test scores had been a prime motivator in the movement toward community control. When the media unearthed the data, it showed that the years from 1967 to 1969 had been educationally disastrous for the district's students. Third graders fell from four months behind before community control to twelve months behind after. Students' reading skills barely budged from the end of eighth grade to the end of ninth grade, even though they had gained the equivalent of fifteen months in reading skills over the course of their eighth-grade year under the previous administration. Though McCoy had instituted some promising programs, like bilingual education, Montessori-style elementary classrooms, and improved school libraries, critics believed his reforms had been long on political verve but short on instructional details. In attempting to explain these disappointing results, McCoy stated, poignantly, "Everyone else has failed. We want the right to fail for ourselves."

In 1969 the state legislature split the New York City schools into thirty-three districts. Each new district could elect a school board, but these bodies were a far cry from the community control ideal: They lacked the power to certify, hire, offer tenure to, or fire teachers—all rights that remained centralized under the superintendent and Board of Education. The eight experimental Ocean Hill–Brownsville schools were absorbed into the city's new District 23. Rhody McCoy left the school system, as did Les Campbell, who opened up a night school that taught Swahili and African martial arts.

The city canceled the UFT's treasured—and genuinely effective—More Effective Schools program, amid complaints that it favored some schools over others. Of course, that had been exactly the point: to provide extra resources to the neediest children. Canceling MES, getting rid of the community districts, and decentralizing the school system did little to improve educational outcomes in New York's poorest neighborhoods and did not change the lack of accountability throughout the system. In the spring of 1971, adults at three schools in Ocean Hill–Brownsville were accused of showing standardized test questions to students before the testing date and coaching them on the correct answers. When confronted by *The New York Times* with evidence of this illegal behavior, the reading coordinator at one elementary school claimed her cheating was a sort of protest tactic, to call attention to how "unfair" standardized tests were to disadvantaged students. Her principal backed her.

In 2008, New York City mayor Michael Bloomberg and his

hard-charging schools chancellor, Joel Klein, shut down Ocean Hill–Brownsville's JHS 271, citing persistently low test scores. Physically, the building remains largely unchanged since the time when it was the UFT strike staging ground. But today it houses the Eagle Academy for Young Men, a school that has proven very popular with Ocean Hill–Brownsville parents: In 2011, sixteen hundred students applied for eighty-six seats. Why do thousands of families finally appear enthusiastic about a school in Ocean Hill–Brownsville? As if in response to parents' requests during the 1960s, the Eagle Academy, though a unionized school, emphasizes a longer school day and strict discipline, with required uniforms and even military-style routines. As at many other "no excuses" schools, teachers refer to Eagle Academy students as "scholars" to emphasize high academic expectations. The school is supported by a foundation whose board of directors is dominated by executives from companies like News Corp and Credit Suisse. A separate advisory board includes two community members alongside a number of education professionals, from organizations like Teach for America and Scholastic, the publishing house. Though the rhetoric of black separatist politics has all but disappeared, in many ways today's "no excuses" school reform movement has inherited the mantle of community control by aligning low-income parents with elite school reformers and philanthropists from outside their neighborhoods.

Yet for all that support, the Eagle Academy at Ocean Hill–Brownsville is not much more successful, in measurable ways, than JHS 271 once was. The tide of gentrification and school improvement that has swept other Brooklyn neighborhoods has not reached Ocean Hill–Brownsville. The Eagle Academy is deeply segregated (less than 2 percent white), a quarter of its students receive special-education services, and 76 percent live in poverty. Only 13 percent of Eagle Academy middle school students are reading at grade level, and 6 percent are proficient in math. Student achievement there remains an unsolved puzzle.

Across the Hudson River in 1970, Newark, New Jersey, became the site of the longest and most violent teachers' strike in American history—one that is little known compared to the explosion in New York two years before.

On the afternoon of November 17, 1970, eight-year-old Matilda Gouacide, a black third grader at Newark's South 8th Street School, was hit by a car as she left school grounds. A few weeks earlier, a teacher would have met Matilda just outside the school building and shepherded her and dozens of other children safely across a tree-lined road of clapboard attached houses. But the previous spring the Newark Teachers Union had negotiated the furthest-reaching contract in the history of American public education, one that freed all classroom teachers of "nonprofessional chores" such as cafeteria duty, hall duty, and dismissal-time supervision.

Unlike in New York City, where the teaching force was overwhelmingly white, nearly four out of ten Newark teachers were African American, and the Newark Teachers Union was led by a black woman, Carole Graves. Even so, parent activists in Newark, led by the writer LeRoi Jones, who had become a black nationalist and changed his name to Amiri Baraka, seized upon Matilda's accident as proof of unionized teachers' self-interest and disrespect for poor black children. The Newark union, like its New York counterpart, found itself enmeshed in a nasty confrontation with community activists demanding changes to teachers' work rules. The resulting fourteen-week, 2,500-person strike left one teacher dead and led to the conviction and imprisonment of 185 more. As reported by the historian Steve Golin, dozens of people on both sides of the strike—teachers and their allies, as well as Black Power activists—were the perpetrators and victims of shootings, physical assaults, and vandalism. Carole Graves, the union head, was at home when bullets shattered her windows, injuring her infant niece. Avant Lowther was a young black teacher and union member whose father had also taught in the Newark public schools. Though Lowther had supported previous teacher strikes, in 1971 he crossed the picket line to express solidarity with black community control—and ended up in a knife fight with a white colleague who called him a scab. The union encouraged teachers to arm themselves.

What ties these two strikes together—the nationally prominent, white-versus-black strike in New York City and the far more violent, racially mixed strike in Newark—is that the unions generally won. In the subsequent decades, teachers across the United States saw unprecedented gains in salaries and benefits. They retained lengthy, strict contracts limiting their working hours and responsibilities outside the classroom and successfully negotiated even more detailed grievance procedures, which allowed teachers to protest poor working conditions—like outdated textbooks or terminations based on political bias—but sharply limited administrators' ability to rid schools of ineffective teachers. Nationally, teachers unions wielded extraordinary political influence by becoming among the largest donors to both state and federal elections. At Democratic Party national conventions, teachers union activists typically made up about 10 percent of the delegates.

Additionally, in the years just after the strikes, teachers unions across the country, including in New York and Newark, successfully organized teachers' aides to join their union. This greatly increased the ranks of nonwhite members. It did not, however, neutralize critiques of the unions as perpetrators of the racial and educational status quo. Shanker's biographer Kahlenberg notes that the great paradox of teacher unionism is that as the movement increased in power, it declined in popularity.

Perhaps that is because union-won gains for educators coincided with a steady rightward shift in the nation's larger political life, with severe shortages of living-wage jobs and affordable child care, housing, and health care—many of the social supports, other than schools, that have the potential to improve poor children's lives. Urban teachers, who were making strides in income and benefits, appeared to be riding high compared to the families they served, even though teachers remained underpaid compared to their college-educated counterparts in the broader economy.

In the wake of the 1960s and 1970s teacher strikes, a few visionary educators resolved to bring teachers unions and parent activists back together, for the good of children. In 1974 Shanker became president of the national AFT. Though he never explicitly apologized for any of the union's actions in 1968, he subsequently introduced a number of innovative ideas aimed at improving instruction and raising student achievement, from charter schools to teacher peer review. Meanwhile, a small movement of teacher-led, community-driven schools gained steam.* In 1974 New York City teacher Deborah Meier founded the Central Park East School in Harlem, which quickly attracted national attention for offering a Deweyite, progressive curriculum to poor students of color—while raising test scores. Meier considered herself a supporter of both teachers unions and parent empowerment. As a teacher during the New York City strikes, she had organized "freedom schools" in her home and at local churches, where striking teachers could continue to work with their students without breaking the picket line. But even community-oriented Central Park East would, in its third year, lose a number of students whose parents wanted "more say about the curriculum than we were prepared to cede," Meier recalled. "Teachers felt very vulnerable because [in the typical public school] they weren't free to make decisions. And here were parents coming to say, 'We want to make decisions!' So we both got militant at the same moment. We were fighting each other for a piece of the pie."

It is striking that in interviews even forty-five years later, union teachers who took to the picket lines to protect due process tend to portray community control as a faux grassroots movement, one led less by parents and civil rights groups than by elite economic conservatives who wished to cleave blacks from the labor movement, thus weakening unions and their claim to the moral high ground. It is true that Mayor Lindsay was no great friend to organized labor. Union activists also point the finger at Ford Foundation president McGeorge Bundy, who came from a wealthy Republican family. UFT co-founder George Altomare, a lead organizer of the 1968 strike, told me, "There was really no leadership [on community control] in the community itself."

That interpretation, however, gives too little weight to strains from within black culture and politics in favor of community control and teacher accountability; even the NAACP, which argued *Brown*

---

* Eventually, many of these union-parent allies would unite under the banner of Ted Sizer, the Brown University education theorist who founded the Coalition of Essential Schools in 1984 to advocate for teacher-led, community-supported schools.

v. Board of Education, turned around to support community control in the most stubbornly segregated schools. It downplays the leadership of parents, like Dolores Torres in Ocean Hill–Brownsville, who demanded a better education for their children. And it ignores long-standing evidence from social science that suggested that white teachers often did have low expectations for their nonwhite students, and that those views negatively impacted academic achievement. Philanthropists like the Ford Foundation were responding to a real groundswell of frustration with white teachers from within communities of color.

In the 1980s and 1990s, critics of teachers unions became far more politically sophisticated in exploiting the clash between unions' visions of themselves as fighters for underdog workers and the public's view of unions as defenders of peculiar privileges, like tenure. The Reagan Revolution brought a new American school reform movement, "standards and accountability," to national prominence. It adopted and sanitized the radical Left critique of teachers and unions that had developed in the inner-city neighborhoods of Brooklyn and Newark. These new centrist critics rejected Black Power, but, more powerfully than ever before, they promoted a view of career public school teachers as professionally incompetent and insufficiently committed to closing racial and socioeconomic achievement gaps.

Chapter Eight

"Very Disillusioned"

HOW TEACHER ACCOUNTABILITY
DISPLACED DESEGREGATION AND LOCAL CONTROL

R onald Reagan was an unlikely president to preside over a new era of Washington-driven school reform. The B-list actor-cum-Goldwater-Republican launched his 1980 presidential bid in Philadelphia, Mississippi, the town in which three civil rights workers were murdered in 1964. Reagan's message there: "I believe in states' rights." He promised to end the federal government's expensive interventions on behalf of disadvantaged minority groups, including schoolchildren, and to shutter the one-year-old cabinet-level Department of Education, which he referred to as "President Carter's new bureaucratic boondoggle." Reagan favored classroom prayer and tax credits for parents who enrolled their children in parochial schools, and named judges who gradually ended the era of school desegregation.

So it was somewhat of a surprise that Reagan appointed Terrel Bell secretary of education. Ted Bell, as he was called, was an outlier in the cabinet in every way: a Mormon as the Christian Right was gaining influence, a supporter of Medicaid and Head Start among virulent budget cutters, and the shortest cabinet member, too, with a shock of white hair and a smiling, avuncular manner that led critics to underestimate him. He was a former public school chemistry teacher who held a PhD in education and had worked in public university administration. Bell hailed from a world Ronald Reagan loathed, dating back to Reagan's confrontations, as governor of California in the late 1960s, with a restive teachers union and activist faculty at the University of California.

But Reagan chose Bell because the Washington establishment trusted him. Bell had served as education commissioner for Presidents Nixon and Ford, and had testified to Congress in support of creating the Department of Education. Reagan's advisers hoped Bell had earned the credibility to argue that cutting school funding and turning the DOE into a lower-level agency wouldn't hurt kids. Bell was willing to accept this cynical assignment, which he privately opposed, if it helped him advance his own ideas for school reform within the Republican Party. President Reagan "may be using me," Bell realized, "but I am doing all I can to use him for my cause and take advantage of his great popularity."

Bell did so brilliantly, despite the fact that he was hired to preside over his own demotion, and was ousted in Reagan's second term in favor of the family-values conservative Bill Bennett. He deployed cagey bureaucratic maneuvering to produce *A Nation at Risk,* one of the most influential federal documents ever published. The report, a battle cry against the country's supposed educational mediocrity, harshly critiqued America's working teachers and secured a Washington toehold for the national standards and accountability education movement, which had begun percolating in state capitols after the Ocean Hill–Brownsville strike. Like the community control radicals before them, the accountability crowd complained bitterly about teachers and their unions. But the new reformers relied on data—not racial ideology—as their weapon.

This reform wave eventually produced organizations like Teach for America and the "no excuses" charter school movement. Its agenda recalled the school efficiency progressivism of the early twentieth century: standardized testing, numbers-driven evaluation of teachers, and merit pay. And although it was committed to closing the test score gap between white children and black and Latino children, it explicitly rejected many of the other civil rights–oriented goals of the previous two decades of American education reform, from school integration to a culturally relevant curriculum to empowering parents of color to manage their neighborhood schools.

Lastly, by promoting the idea that schools and teachers are the primary levers for improving the nation's—and individual students'—standard of living, many accountability reformers accepted as inevitable the retrenchment of the welfare state in the realms of job creation, vocational training, housing, and child care. *A Nation at Risk* set the terms of a debate we are still having today.

The particular obsessions of accountability school reform are neatly summed up in Ted Bell's life story. There is a passionate belief in the power of public education—yes—but also a profound desire to test, to quantify, and to rationalize.

Bell grew up in rural Lava Hot Springs, Idaho, in a house with eight siblings, a single mother, and no indoor plumbing. Like Lyndon Johnson, Bell attended public school and enrolled in a state teachers college, Albion State Normal School, because it was the only higher education he could afford; he paid his tuition, $11.50 per term, with wages from a part-time job with the National Youth Administration, a New Deal program. At Albion, Bell was fascinated by a course he took on educational tests and measurements, which focused on IQ. This interest had gotten him into trouble: In the Marine Corps, Bell mouthed off that a commanding officer would rate as a "moron" on an IQ test. Bell's head was shaved, he was stripped down to his underwear, and he spent three days in solitary confinement, subsisting on bread and water. Yet his interest in testing proved lifelong. As superintendent of the Weber County, Utah, public schools in the early 1960s, he instituted a merit pay plan in which teachers were offered the option to be paid based on how well they scored on the National Teacher Examination, as well as on how their students performed on standardized tests.* The program attracted virulent resistance from the Utah Education Association, which successfully lobbied the state legislature

---

* The National Teacher Exam, published by ETS, was the same test southern states used post-*Brown* to effectively pay black teachers less or deny them credentials entirely.

to withdraw its funding for the plan. Voters then rejected a ballot initiative to raise taxes to fund the program. Though merit pay had failed to gain political traction in Utah, the episode cemented Bell's reputation as a reformer with free-market leanings—credibility he was able to exploit as Ronald Reagan's secretary of education.

Because of his time working in the Nixon and Ford administrations, Bell understood Washington and knew from the get-go that the Democratic-controlled Congress would never eliminate the Department of Education or its major civil rights program, Title I, which provided federal funding to schools with large numbers of poor, minority, and handicapped students. What's more, he personally supported those programs. So instead of wasting much effort on the quixotic campaign to close his own department, Bell began, in the spring of 1981, to circumvent Reagan's inner circle and go straight to the media with messages about school improvement. He created an infamous wall chart inside the Department of Education, on which he ranked states according to their SAT scores, high school graduation rates, teacher salaries, and school funding levels. It was the first time—but by no means the last—Washington set states in educational competition with one another.* A press conference revealing the chart was packed to overflowing, though the results were predictable: States with little poverty and strong social supports, like Vermont and New Hampshire, ranked well. The Deep South scored poorly.

Bell's numbers-driven, get-tough approach brought to Washington a new flavor of centrist school reform that had emerged in state capitols during the 1970s. The violent confrontations over busing, collective bargaining, and community control had darkened the public's view of teachers and schools, with polls showing that by 1980 only about a third of Americans felt confident in the nation's education system, down from 59 percent in 1966, at the height of

---

* The spirit of the data wall continues with President Obama's Race to the Top program, in which states compete to enact school reform agendas built according to the administration's specifications. For teachers, this now means evaluation and pay tied to student test scores and other measures of academic achievement.

the Great Society. If everyone from the Black Power Left to the seg-regationist Right believed schools were failing, state policy makers, especially Democrats who supported greater school funding, knew they would have to justify education spending in terms of tough reform and results.

The school reform efforts of the 1960s had not called for new standardized tests; instead the focus had been on teachers' racial attitudes and classroom skills. That began to change. By the mid-1970s, thirty-three states had instituted testing programs to eval-uate student achievement, often in an effort to help the public understand why education was a wise investment. If scores were low, school funding could be depicted as an emergency necessity. If scores improved, politicians could claim that their investments were working.

The idea of linking students' test scores to specific teachers was not yet in vogue. Instead, under the new reforms, teachers were sub-ject to "competency based" evaluation. During the early 1970s, Cal-ifornia, Texas, and New York passed laws requiring that all teacher education programs be organized around specific teaching "compe-tencies," and that working teachers be evaluated according to their skill in the classroom. The impact ranged from minimal to disas-trous. In 1975 the National Institute of Education, a federal agency, hired Teacher Corps alumnus and future education journalist John Merrow to write a report on the competency movement. Merrow concluded it had little substance. Popular teacher competencies, such as the ability to ask students "higher-order questions," were ill defined, vague to the point of meaninglessness. To appease lawmak-ers, many college education departments simply renamed traditional courses to feature competency lingo, while nothing changed in the curriculum. And in a time of antitax sentiment, competency laws were often unfunded mandates, with little or no money provided to actually implement new ways of training and evaluating teach-ers. California essentially prohibited the undergraduate education major in 1970. Prospective elementary school teachers there could choose any major and then spend a post-baccalaureate year student teaching while taking a few education classes. According to research from the National Council on Teacher Quality, a single year turned out not to be enough time to train teachers in the pedagogical skills needed for the broad range of subjects elementary teachers, especially, must tackle. Early-grades math instruction in particular was shortchanged in California, and students paid the price.

Teachers' reputations continued to suffer, with much of the new moral panic focused on teachers' own test scores. In 1980, "Why Teachers Can't Teach," a piece in the *Texas Monthly*, won the prestigious National Magazine Award for Public Service.* The exposé, by Gene Lyons, revealed that public school teachers in urban Houston and Dallas scored lower on standardized tests than did the average suburban sixteen-year-old. Lyons visited President Johnson's alma mater, Southwest Texas State University at San Marcos, and reported that students enrolled in teacher education classes there were functionally illiterate. Teacher credentialing was "a hoax and an educational disgrace," he concluded, blaming the misapplication of John Dewey's ideas: an overemphasis on student-centered pedagogy at the expense of subject matter training in history, literature, math, and science. As an aside, Lyons mentioned that teachers' low pay might be preventing more academically talented students from pursuing the profession in the first place.

As secretary of education, Ted Bell sought to amplify the Lyons critique. In 1982 he appointed an eighteen-member National Commission on Excellence in Education, which included college presidents, scholars, business leaders, school board members, a retired governor, several principals, and one public school teacher. Bell hoped the commission would produce a sort of Marshall Plan for school reform—an inspirational call that would unite the media and public behind efforts to improve education, forcing President Reagan to embrace a more centrist agenda. Bell was not disappointed. The commission ignored the president's directions for them— "Bring God back into the classroom," Reagan told the members at one meeting, and "leave the primary responsibility for education to

---

* Nine years later, Wendy Kopp would cite "Why Teachers Can't Teach" in her Princeton senior thesis, laying out a plan for the organization that would become Teach for America.

parents"—and instead produced the succinct and readable *A Nation at Risk*. The report's unforgettable introduction artfully deployed the militant language of the Cold War in service of school reform:

> If an unfriendly foreign power had attempted to impose on America the mediocre educational performance that exists today, we might well have viewed it as an act of war. As it stands, we have allowed this to happen to ourselves. . . . We have, in effect, been committing an act of unthinking, unilateral educational disarmament.

The report went on to depict a "rising tide of mediocrity": a twenty-year decline in SAT scores, electives like cooking and drivers ed considered acceptable substitutes for physics and calculus (at the so-called "shopping mall high school"), and Japanese and German public school graduates who were able to engineer more desirable cars and better machine tools, kneecapping the U.S. economy. American teachers were dullards drawn from the "bottom quarter" of high school and college graduating classes, and they were especially deficient in math and science.

To improve teacher quality, the commission recommended higher base salaries, merit pay to reward effective teachers, and stricter teacher evaluation systems that made it more difficult to earn and keep tenure. Most of the European and Asian nations that built high-prestige teaching professions after World War II required prospective teachers to spend several years training for the classroom. *A Nation at Risk* made a different suggestion, in line with the American tradition of missionary teaching: to allow career changers and young college grads who had not studied education to quickly obtain "alternative" teaching credentials.

Better teachers were just one of four priorities the commission identified. The others were raising expectations for students and adding rigor to the high school curriculum, lengthening the school day by one hour and the school year by forty days, and encouraging the federal government to play a larger role in setting the national education agenda and funding it. But the report was released into a political climate of budget-cutting fervor—federal aid for poor children's education was cut by 16 percent in Reagan's first term—and a culture war. There was little enthusiasm in Congress for providing the massive influx of funding needed to extend learning time, the costliest proposal in *A Nation at Risk*. The idea of more rigorous, universal curriculum standards was also a nonstarter; the American Right had long demonstrated an overactive paranoia about supposedly liberal national attempts to influence the curriculum of local schools—a paranoia Reagan fully shared as a former anticommunist activist. Consequently, despite *A Nation at Risk*'s broad set of recommendations, policy makers focused increasingly on teachers alone: their training, demographic traits, and how they were evaluated and paid.

The teaching establishment—unions and teachers colleges—was divided in its response to the report. At the American Federation of Teachers, most high-level staffers were reluctant to support any initiative of a presidential administration that wanted to cut school funding and provide vouchers to parochial schools. But Al Shanker, who had become AFT president in 1974, bucked his advisers—and his counterpart at the National Education Association—to embrace the core message of *A Nation at Risk,* that American schools were failing. "I like the phrase 'a nation at risk' because those words put education on the same par as national defense," he told his members. This was a bold position, in stark contrast to how most unionists felt about the report; in the words of Dennis Van Roekel of the NEA, who at the time led the state teachers union in Arizona and later served as NEA president, "I took it as a personal insult."

Even Shanker didn't like the commission's policy prescriptions—especially merit pay for select teachers or the idea of a longer school day. On pay, unions believed that if they resisted differentiation based on competence, grade level, or subject taught, the higher salaries needed to attract and retain better teachers would be paid to all teachers. Shanker didn't support extended work hours, but rather the opposite: His union had called for a four-day teaching week, with aides taking over on Fridays in grades one through eight and high school students using the time to work on research projects. (Teachers would use the fifth day to plan lessons and grade papers.) Nevertheless, Shanker's credibility as a militant labor leader, one who had gone to jail for leading strikes, allowed him, throughout the 1980s, to promote a number of innovative policy solutions to the problems outlined in *A Nation at Risk*—proposals that earned him growing credibility with accountability reformers and reversed the impression that the AFT was the intransigent union while the NEA was the "professional" one.

Peer review was one Shanker-endorsed innovation. In 1981 the AFT local in Toledo, Ohio, negotiated a contract that called for skilled veteran teachers to observe the classrooms of novices and underperforming tenured teachers, and then to either coach them to improve or approve their terminations. At the time, national surveys of teachers showed that the majority hated the idea and saw it as undermining solidarity. But Shanker thought it was an important step toward making teaching more like medicine or law, professions that regulated and policed themselves. What's more, peer review addressed the American teaching profession's key deficiency: Teachers never watched one another work. For most teachers, many of whom had never student-taught, the only time they witnessed teaching practice firsthand was when they were students themselves, many years in the past.

Another new idea Shanker promoted was the "charter school," a concept he borrowed from Germany. Shanker envisioned charters as unionized, teacher-run schools freed from state or district mandates in order to experiment with new ideas. Some Republican education reformers initially hated the concept, which they saw as a union attempt to exempt certain teachers and schools from state standards. Their perspective changed quickly, however, once reformers from across party lines realized that charter school laws could be crafted in ways that made it possible to open nonunion public schools, or even allow public schools to be managed by for-profit companies. The first charters opened in Minnesota in 1992, and just a year later Shanker was calling charter schools an anti-union "gimmick" and worrying that "hucksters" would use the charter movement to divert public funding away from students and teachers and toward private profit.

While Shanker selectively embraced *A Nation at Risk,* professors of education turned out to be the report's harshest critics. Their perspective is summed up in David Berliner and Bruce Biddle's 1995 call to arms, *The Manufactured Crisis,* which argued that American education was in fine shape, contrary to the report's core assumptions, and that where it was weak, it was the fault of regressive policies, such as those that produced gaps in teacher pay between rich and poor school districts. The authors pointed out that SAT scores had declined in large part because a more diverse group of students was taking the exam, including poor children, who never would have dreamt of applying to college in the years before World War II. They acknowledged that American teachers were less academically distinguished than their counterparts abroad. But that was not because of deficiencies in the teacher certification process, they wrote, but because American teachers were paid less than other white-collar workers. In Japan the average teacher earned as much as the average engineer; in the United States, teachers earned only 60 percent as much as engineers.

Jay Sommer had his own critiques of the new reform push. Sommer was a national "teacher of the year" who taught foreign languages at New Rochelle High School in New York, and the only working teacher on the commission that produced *A Nation at Risk.* He believed the main problem with teaching in America was that school districts invested almost nothing in improving their employees' skills. "Basically, no teacher wants to fail," Sommer told Fred Hechinger, the eminent education columnist at *The New York Times.* "If they are failing, it's because they get no supervision, no direction, no leadership."

In the long term, *A Nation at Risk* prevailed over its critics. The report, quite smartly, differed from other national drives for school reform in that it focused on raising standards for all children, not just poor children. That helped it appeal to business leaders and middle-class parents, who were attracted to the dramatic portrait of educational complacency in the face of unrelenting international competition. Magazines aped the report's style and assumptions. "It's like Pearl Harbor," *Fortune* declared. "The Japanese have invaded and the U.S. has been caught short. Not on guns and tanks and battleships—those are yesterday's weapons—but on mental might. In a high-tech age where nations increasingly compete on brainpower, American schools are producing an army of illiterates."

State policy makers, especially a new generation of "education governors" such as Lamar Alexander in Tennessee, Bill Clinton in Arkansas, and, later, George W. Bush in Texas and his brother Jeb in Florida, were eager to claim they had followed the advice of *A Nation at Risk*. Two-thirds of the states launched new student testing programs, and thirty began requiring teachers to pass pre-service exams. Twenty states created fast-track alternative pathways into the classroom, which allowed college graduates who hadn't studied education to quickly become teachers. Twenty-four states claimed to have implemented some sort of "career ladder" rewarding teachers with merit pay, but by the end of the decade, almost all of those ladders had collapsed, weighed down by low budgets and lack of teacher buy-in. Since the rhetoric and policy prescriptions of *A Nation at Risk* have proven so enduring—the very same assumptions and ideals underlie No Child Left Behind, Race to the Top, the Common Core, and almost every other contemporary reform effort to improve teaching—it is crucial to look at why, exactly, the first generation of accountability-driven national teacher reform failed.

By 1988, just five years after *A Nation at Risk* debuted, *The New York Times* declared: "Merit pay for teachers is beginning to look like a flawed idea whose time has gone. . . . In retrospect, the rise and fall of merit pay were probably inevitable."

Indeed. Even at the time *A Nation at Risk* was published there was already compelling evidence that merit pay plans across the country had been overhyped—evidence ignored by reformers, like Ted Bell, who were eager to propose low-cost solutions to educational underperformance. Several nationwide studies of merit pay programs instituted between the 1930s and 1970s found that the majority failed within six years and faced similar barriers to effectiveness: excessive administrative paperwork, low funding, disagreements about how to judge good teaching, and strong opposition from teachers themselves.

Kalamazoo, Michigan, provides a powerful example of the hype-disillusionment cycle characteristic of teacher merit pay plans. In 1974, the *American School Board Journal* published a rapturous series of articles about the district's new superintendent, William Coats, who had never before worked in public school administration (he had been a college professor). Coats had proposed a merit pay system in which every teacher would be graded according to her students' standardized test scores. Her classroom practice would be observed by five to fifteen peer teachers, by her principal, and by pupils, all of whom would produce written reports on her performance. The teacher would also write a self-assessment. Administrators, too, would be evaluated by their colleagues, by the teachers who reported to them, and by students and parents.

Just a year after implementation, the *Journal* reported that this system had transformed the Kalamazoo public schools. "Student achievement is up—significantly so. Racial violence, which for years has plagued Kalamazoo's schools, has almost disappeared. Board members smile more pleasantly and more frequently, they report, confident for the first time in years that most taxpayer dollars are not wasted in city schools."

In reality, superintendent Coats and his merit system lasted less than three years in Kalamazoo. The plan attracted immediate backlash from every corner, including from administrators exhausted by the overwhelming number of employee reports they had to write. Although test scores improved—in reality, only modestly—parents did not celebrate and instead complained about classroom time spent prepping for multiple-choice tests now that teachers were being graded according to their students' scores. As for the decrease in racial violence, it had little or nothing to do with merit pay. In 1971 the courts had ordered Kalamazoo to desegregate its schools, which put black and white children into contact with one another at the elementary school level, so that by the time they entered the city's two high schools, racial tensions were less extreme. The district renovated classrooms in formerly all-black schools, hired more black teachers, and actively recruited black children into advanced courses. Coats had been hired by a majority-white school board that opposed the court desegregation order. He claimed his mechanistic teacher evaluation scheme had produced the district's student achievement gains. But principals disagreed. "Now the schools are free to focus on performance and academics, since desegregation has eliminated the racial conflicts and the cost of controlling those conflicts," a Kalamazoo junior high school principal told the U.S. Commission on Civil Rights. "In my school we need fewer crisis staff and it is now a quiet school."

All over the country, heavy paperwork burdens turned principals into skeptics of politically imposed merit pay plans—much as the dissident principal Alexander Fichlander had complained, in New York City in 1920, that the city's complex A–D evaluation scheme sucked up time while doing little to help teachers improve. In Texas, a 1984 guidebook advising principals on how to hold teachers accountable suggested an evaluation rubric with sixty-three categories, each requiring a rating on a scale of one to five. Some of the items contradicted one another. Were teachers ignoring "attention-grabbing" behavior from students? That was a good thing. Yet another category called for teachers to quickly "negatively reinforce" bad behavior.

There were several merit pay plans that were popular with teachers, and they had one major feature in common: Bonuses were available to every high-performing teacher in a school district, regardless of the grade level or subject they taught. That was rarely the design of merit pay programs launched in the wake of *A Nation at Risk,* which tended to be funded at such low levels that bonuses were available only to teachers of some subjects and grades: just 15 percent of teachers in Tennessee under Governor Lamar Alexander's widely celebrated plan, and 10 percent of teachers in Florida. When so few teachers could benefit from merit pay, the bonuses were seen as divisive, undercutting morale.

Gera Summerford, today the president of the Tennessee Education Association, the state teachers union, was a first-year middle school math teacher in Nashville when the merit pay program rolled out in 1982. "I was very idealistic," she recalled. "I felt like it was an opportunity for me to demonstrate that I was a more effective teacher than maybe some of the ones who had been teaching for a long time. But when I went through the process, I was very disillusioned."

Summerford was supposed to be evaluated by three people, including a peer with experience in her subject area. But the district sent a business teacher, not a math teacher, to observe her classroom, and she found this unhelpful. The system applied to both teachers and administrators, and it created three levels of recognition, with bonuses between $1,000 and $7,000. Teachers soon noticed that almost every principal who applied for the extra pay was quickly bumped up through all three levels, while just 13 percent of teachers achieved Level 2 or 3. That created resentment. The most popular part of the system was overtime pay offered to teachers who supervised afterschool programs or provided extra tutoring. "That really did help kids," Summerford said. But ultimately the relatively small bonuses tied to capricious classroom observations seemed almost absurd, "an insultingly small amount of money" distributed through a labor-intensive process yet in an unpredictable way. Within a decade, the system was phased out, in part because of continued NEA opposition, and in part because it had been financed by an unpopular increase in the state sales tax.

All this foment around merit pay occurred at a time when the average American teacher earned just $23,500 per year ($47,400 in today's dollars), less than a mail carrier and half that of the average lawyer or accountant. An alternative corner of the education reform movement tried to send the message that raising base salaries—by 25 percent, the Carnegie Foundation recommended, or to an average of $50,000, according to RAND—would do much more to increase the profession's prestige.

But influential business leaders were eager proponents of numbers-driven merit pay for teachers. Ross Perot, for example, pushed Dallas to implement a plan to use test scores alone to evaluate teachers and distribute pay increases. So it was ironic that private industry had, by the 1980s, mostly turned away from efforts to pay white-collar workers according to strict productivity measures, finding that such formal evaluation programs were too expensive and time-consuming to create and implement. Research showed that companies with merit pay schemes did not perform better financially than did organizations without it, nor were their employees happier. Instead, management gurus recommended that workers be judged primarily by the holistic standards of individual supervisors.

It is important to note that in public education, teachers unions have had a long history of fighting attempts to institute subjective evaluation systems; at the most basic level, New York City teachers had gone on their massive strike in 1968 to deny an administrator, Rhody McCoy, the right to evaluate his teachers and staff his schools as he saw fit. In the 1980s both the AFT and the NEA responded to calls for merit pay by saying they would support it only when it was based on "objective" measurements, such as teachers' scores on tests of subject matter knowledge. Al Shanker said, "I always was and still am against any merit pay notion that would be based on the idea that some principal walks into your room and gives a judgment as to who is a better teacher." Some accountability reformers actually shared Shanker's skepticism. Chester Finn, a longtime moderate Republican education reform guru who advised Lamar Alexander on teacher career ladders, described to me the grim status quo in classroom observation: "The principals were often former gym teachers, and had almost never been trained to be sophisticated overseers of teacher quality or performance. In the absence of quantitative data, a principal would be a perfunctory and ill-trained observer, and either liked or didn't like what he saw. It was awfully easy for the principal to then make decisions based on 'Who do I like? Who's my cousin? Who's my girlfriend?' or a variety of other factors that don't have to do with classroom effectiveness."

When unions brought this suspicion of principals to the negotiation table, the results in some instances were even more complex and expensive evaluation systems, like Tennessee's, in which principals' ratings were cross-checked and sometimes overruled by teams of observers from outside each school, a plan Shanker approved. In the end, nearly all the merit pay and career ladder plans of the *Nation at Risk* era—underfunded, unpopular, and overly bureaucratic—were defunct by the end of the 1980s. Supposedly more objective measures of teachers based on student test scores would emerge in the national conversation in the late 1990s, in large part because both union leaders and some reformers had for so long refused to trust principals to evaluate their staffs.

While merit pay failed in the 1980s, in another respect the Reagan administration achieved its education goals by displacing the previous era's commitment to school desegregation.

On October 8, 1984, in the thick of his reelection campaign, President Reagan appeared in front of a majority-white audience in Charlotte, North Carolina. He claimed the city's storied busing program "takes innocent children out of the neighborhood school and makes them pawns in a social experiment that nobody wants. And we've found out that it failed." To Reagan's surprise, he was greeted with stony silence, not cheers.

In response to a 1971 Supreme Court ruling, the Charlotte-Mecklenburg school district had developed a desegregation plan that paired kindergarten through third-grade schools in majority-white neighborhoods with fourth-grade through sixth-grade schools in majority-black neighborhoods. Each cohort of children was bused for half of their elementary school career, and no school in the district could be more than 50 percent black. What Reagan's speechwriters did not realize was that the plan was popular and academically effective. Students of all races demonstrated steady test score gains in Charlotte after desegregation. A greater proportion of the district's financial resources and experienced teachers moved to schools in low-income neighborhoods, which gained powerful advocates in the parents of middle-class and white children bused in from more affluent areas. The day after Reagan's comments, the *Charlotte Observer* editorialized that the district's integration program was, in fact, the region's "proudest achievement."

It was an achievement the Reagan administration actively worked to undermine. Early leaders in the teacher accountability movement were often simultaneously engaged in efforts to defund and delegitimize desegregation. In 1980, under President Carter, the Department of Justice filed twenty-two school desegregation suits. The following year, under President Reagan, it pursued just ten desegregation cases. In 1984 Secretary Bell spent $1 million of his discretionary budget to seed fifty-one new teacher merit pay plans across the country, even as the Reagan administration denied tens of millions of dollars of previously promised funding to school districts, such as Chicago's, which were struggling to implement desegregation orders. Bell was even on the record in support of a federal law or constitutional amendment to forbid busing as an integration strategy.

In 1981 Reagan had appointed Robert Potter, a onetime antibusing activist, to the U.S. District Court in western North Carolina. In September 1999, Potter ruled in favor of a Charlotte father who sued the school district to end busing, arguing that it discriminated against his biracial daughter, who was white and Latina. What happened next was tragic. According to research from the labor economist C. Kirabo Jackson, as Charlotte schools reverted to the demographics of their surrounding neighborhoods between 2002 and 2005, schools that became predominantly black suffered a loss of high-quality teachers as measured by growth in students' test scores, teachers' years of experience, and scores on teacher certification tests. Though black teachers were more likely than white teachers to remain in majority-black schools, those black teachers who left had been more effective than those who remained—especially at increasing the achievement of black students. Jackson estimated that this shift in the distribution of effective teachers could explain up to 7.5 percent of the achievement gap between black and white children in Charlotte. The movement of experienced teachers away from high-poverty schools has often been cited as proof of white teachers' racist attitudes. And while discrimination certainly accounts for some of the movement, the fact is that many effective nonwhite teachers, too, seem to prefer working in integrated or middle-class settings. Part of the explanation is that high-poverty, minority-majority schools are more likely to experience administrative turnover and inept management, which erode teacher job satisfaction over the long term.

There is a wealth of other evidence that integration can boost student achievement. A second study of Charlotte, from economists Stephen Billings, David Deming, and Jonah Rockoff, found that between 2002, when schools resegregated, and 2011 the math achievement gap between the races widened. Young minority males assigned to Charlotte schools that experienced an influx of non-white students were more likely to be arrested and imprisoned than their demographically identical neighbors who remained in more integrated schools. In a separate paper, Byron Lutz of the Federal Reserve demonstrated that the end of court-ordered busing in northern school districts led to an increase in black high school dropout rates. (Interestingly, dropout rates did not change in southern districts that were released from busing orders. This could be because northern districts interpreted desegregation orders more faithfully than southern ones did, so the impact of lifting the court orders was more severe. Or it could be because some southern cities, like Nashville and Charlotte, pledged to accompany desegregation by increased investment in majority-black schools.)

One of the most compelling studies of the relationship between school integration and student achievement was conducted by Heather Schwartz of the Century Foundation. She examined Montgomery County, Maryland, where a lottery determines in which public housing development a low-income family lives. The children of families living in public housing within integrated school zones—where poor, typically nonwhite children were less than half of the student body at their schools—experienced an additional 8 points of math gains and 4 points of reading gains on 100-point tests, compared to demographically identical peers placed by lottery in schools where the vast majority of students were poor. In 1980 American school integration reached its height, with 37 percent of black children nationwide attending majority-white schools. After Reagan's intervention, that progress eroded. By 2000, just 28 percent of black children were in majority-white schools, and 40 percent of black and Latino students attended deeply segregated schools, where 90 to 100 percent of the student body was poor and nonwhite.

The teacher accountability agenda that has emerged over the last two decades—stricter evaluation systems, merit pay, the weakening of teacher tenure, and the creation of alternative pathways into the classroom, like Teach for America—is often talked about as a sort of next step in school reform, because integration failed. In her 2011 book *A Chance to Make History,* TFA founder Wendy Kopp wrote, "In the sixties and seventies we committed to desegregate schools in order to ensure that all of our nation's children have access to an equal education. Unfortunately, though, poor and minority students continued to lag academically."* The conclusion that desegregation did not work is not fair, though—because the United States did not, in fact, commit to integration. In 1974 the Supreme Court ruled in *Milliken v. Bradley* that majority-white northern school districts had no responsibility to cooperate with inner-city schools toward the goal of integration, even in regions where affluent all-white school districts were just a few minutes away from urban neighborhoods ravaged by poverty. Desegregation was never widely implemented outside the South, and where it was implemented, as in Charlotte or Montgomery County, it often succeeded in raising student achievement to a similar or greater degree than did later teacher accountability reforms. Today there is still a demand for integrated schools. In cities like Boston and Hartford, tens of thousands of parents have their children on waitlists to be bused to higher-quality suburban schools. From Brooklyn to Atlanta to Los Angeles, a small group of socioeconomically diverse charter schools has proven enormously popular with families. So it is unfortunate that these two strains of American education reform, integration and teacher accountability, rarely work in tandem.

Since 1980 the federal government has done almost nothing to encourage local school districts to create racially and socioeconomically mixed schools, even as billions of dollars are sent to states and districts that agree to tie teacher pay and evaluation to student test scores and to open new charter schools, most of which are as racially and socioeconomically homogeneous as the schools the civil rights crusaders fought to reform.

When "education governor" Bill Clinton became president, he sought to push the standards and accountability movement further and faster. Through two pieces of 1994 legislation, the Improving

---

* In July 2013 Teach for America invited me to its alumni conference to moderate a panel on school integration. By then, Kopp had stepped down as CEO.

America's Schools Act and Goals 2000, Washington required states to adopt new curriculum standards and tests in order to receive Title I money. Clinton hoped to address one of Title I's long-standing flaws: that states and school districts lacked the expertise to create high-quality curricular materials. He tried to establish a National Education Standards and Improvement Council where researchers would use best practices to develop standards, textbooks, and tests that states and local schools could choose to adopt. But in 1995 the GOP-controlled Congress withdrew support for the program, and it never launched. By the late 1990s, education reformers who had applauded *A Nation at Risk* were hugely frustrated at the continued lack of oversight of failing schools. States had new tests, but if scores remained low year after year, there were no consequences.

One of those frustrated reformers was Kati Haycock. She began her career in the 1970s, managing affirmative action programs and student outreach for the University of California system. That experience led her to conclude that college was too late to close achievement gaps between white and minority children, and that the real work was in K–12 school reform. In 1990 Haycock quit her job as executive vice president of the Children's Defense Fund, a civil rights organization whose motto was "Leave no child behind." Her new project, the Education Trust, became a totally new kind of progressive advocacy group, one that unapologetically used test scores— long considered suspicious on the Left—to argue that education, especially better teachers, could effectively fight poverty.

The Education Trust distributed massive data books ranking states on many indicators of educational quality, to spread the word to the media that public schools were in dire trouble: In many districts half of all black and Latino kids were dropping out of high school, and throughout the nation the achievement gap between black and white children was growing. What was the Education Trust's theory as to why? In later years Haycock would talk more explicitly about removing bad tenured teachers from the classroom. But in the 1990s her focus was on many of the factors that accountability hawks today downplay: inequalities in funding, pre-service teacher qualifications (like scores on certification exams), and years of teaching experience. In 1990 the average middle-class, predominantly white school spent nearly $1,400 more per pupil than the typical low-income school. In New York City's high-poverty public schools at the time, a third of all teachers had failed their licensing exam at least once, compared to one in twenty teachers in the rest of the state. Eighty-six percent of science teachers in majority-white schools were certified to teach science, compared to 54 percent in majority-minority schools. Poor children were twice as likely "to serve as training fodder for inexperienced teachers," the Education Trust reported. Another issue was the teachers unions' treasured class-size laws, which in states like California and Florida led to a burst in the hiring of underqualified teachers, without lowering class sizes to the very low number—sixteen students—that research showed actually benefits young children.

Haycock, who is white, often painted a grim picture of incompetent urban teachers with woefully low expectations for students, such as one who told eleventh graders to "color a poster" about *To Kill a Mockingbird* instead of writing an essay. In 1992 she characterized teacher's assistants paid through Title 1, the Great Society program, as "semiliterate aides who repeatedly mispronounce words," thus miseducating poor students of color.

Haycock warned fellow liberals that if they did not begin holding teachers and schools accountable, the public education system would be decimated by demands for private school vouchers. "The polls among black folk around vouchers versus public education are an indication that you cannot continue screwing a whole bunch of people and have them not catch you at it and decide that the game is so rigged that they may not continue to play," she said in 1998. She was equally harsh on the legacy of the community control movement, the last major left-of-center effort to insist on better teachers for poor children's schools. "Twenty or 30 years ago, people really did believe that black or Hispanic kids needed something different—voodoo education, multicultural, whatever. What I think is so clear now is that what they need is the same thing white kids need, the same thing suburban kids need. It's high-quality education with high expectations from teachers who know their stuff. There's no mystery about this and there's no reason we can't supply it to all our kids."

Haycock often cited Texas as a state that was making positive

strides. After *A Nation at Risk,* Texas created a statewide accountability system in which schools that failed to raise test scores could
be denied funding. Sure enough, test scores rose, improvement her-
alded as the "Texas Miracle." When George W. Bush spoke during
his presidential campaign about using a similar approach to allo-
cate Title I funding nationwide, Haycock was enthusiastic, telling
reporter Joan Walsh of *Salon* in 1999 that the Clinton White House
and Democrats in general had become too timid on school reform,
scared to focus on the needs of poor children over middle-class children. "Bush's message on education gives me more hope that something might happen for poor kids than what I'm hearing elsewhere,"
Haycock said.

When Bush entered the White House after a divisive election, he
knew bipartisan support would be key to passing a school accountability bill—and that the Education Trust could help provide a progressive imprimatur. His administration riffed off the slogan of the
Children's Defense Fund, Haycock's old employer, in naming its signature education proposal: No Child Left Behind. Bush introduced
the law in 2001 with the beautiful promise of freeing poor nonwhite
children from "the soft bigotry of low expectations"—the problem
Kati Haycock had been talking about for over a decade. In a fit of
irrational optimism, Congress declared that by 2014, 100 percent of
American children—including poor children and those who were
not native English speakers—would be "proficient" in reading and
math, as measured by new state standardized tests to be given every
year in grades 3 through 8, and at least once in high school.

No Child Left Behind's sanctions were focused not on individual teachers, but on schools. Those that did not bring all students
up to proficiency would be publicly declared failing, and could lose
Title I funding or get taken over by their states. Based in part on
the Education Trust's recommendation that more teachers of poor
children should have majors in the subjects they taught, the law also
told states that all teachers, including those in low-income schools,
must be "highly qualified" and certified. Crucially, states could choose
their own standards and tests for kids and decide what constituted
passing them, as well as what rendered a teacher highly qualified
and certified.

The political scientists David Cohen and Susan Moffitt argue that most federal attempts to improve local schools fail because in our constitutionally decentralized education system there are few policy "bridging instruments"—like high-quality tests or national school inspectors—to provide states and districts with the expertise they would need to fulfill federal mandates. That was certainly the case with No Child Left Behind. State education departments had neither the will nor the way to take over the management of hundreds of underperforming schools. As a result, many states followed the letter but not the spirit of the law and made their new tests absurdly easy for kids to pass. In Texas a student who scored 13 percent was declared proficient. In 2009 Alabama reported that 86 percent of its fourth graders were proficient in reading, even though according to the gold standard National Assessment of Educational Progress, only 28 percent of Alabama children were proficient readers. While some states, like Massachusetts, chose on their own to adopt rigorous academic standards and high-quality tests, the top-down shaming and threats associated with NCLB, combined with lax federal oversight, discouraged states from reaching for rigorous academic goals. Parents whose children were far behind international norms for grade-level performance were told their kids were proficient. And the law did next to nothing to change the distribution of effective teachers. Perhaps the most lasting outcome of the "highly qualified teacher" provision was that Teach for America, in an early flexing of its political muscle, successfully lobbied for a loophole that defined uncertified alternative-route teachers as high-quality, as long as they were enrolled in a program that provided professional development.

In the years after NCLB became law, more schools adopted scripted or so-called teacher proof curricula, like Success for All, which standardize lesson plans and materials across all the classrooms in a school and provide prescriptive day-to-day, even minute-to-minute schedules for teachers to follow. But most teachers noticed NCLB primarily through its annual testing mandate, the first of its kind in American history, which required that all fifty states adopt testing schemes for grades three through eight. In elementary and middle school classrooms, test questions sometimes became the de facto curriculum, especially in the low-income schools that were under the most pressure to raise scores and had the least rigorous curricula to begin with. The education journalist Linda Perlstein described this phenomenon in *Tested*, her book about a third-grade teacher working diligently to bring her low-income students up to "proficiency" on the Maryland State Assessment. The teacher knew from past exams that students would likely be asked to identify the "features of a poem," such as rhyme, stanzas, and rhythm. On more than thirty occasions the students copied some variation of the following from an overhead projector: "I know this is a poem because it has stanzas and rhyme. I know the text has stanzas and not paragraphs because they didn't indent. . . ." The class wrote actual poems three times—one haiku and two acrostics—and did almost no lessons from the science curriculum because science tests were not yet required by NCLB.

Research confirmed Perlstein's anecdotal evidence that the curriculum had narrowed. A survey of administrators found that 65 percent of all districts, and 75 percent of those with at least one school in danger of "failing," increased instructional time for reading and math while decreasing time for social studies, science, art, music, physical education, and even recess. There were signs of other perverse incentives, too: Schools transferred some of their best teachers out of the earliest grades, kindergarten through second, and into the tested grades, third through eighth, despite evidence that good instruction in those early years has the most profound impact on children's long-term reading ability. Teachers showered attention on so-called "bubble kids," those right beneath the proficiency threshold, while ignoring the needs of high-ability students who would pass the tests no matter what, or low-ability ones who had little chance of rising to the proficiency bar. And there was cheating. In Florida, schools were more likely to suspend struggling students in advance of test days so they wouldn't bring down school averages. In 2003 it turned out that the "Texas Miracle" of higher standards and swiftly rising test scores for minority children had been a sham: Schools fudged dropout rates and gave struggling students special education designations just so that their test scores would not affect accountability ratings. Other students were told to stay home on test days.

By 2005 the NEA's national survey of teachers showed that 60 percent identified "testing demands/teaching to the test" as the single biggest hindrance to public education. In a 2009 valedictory speech reflecting on his education legacy, President Bush addressed NCLB's anti-testing critics. "The key to measuring is to test," he said. "And by the way, I've heard every excuse in the book why we should not test: *Oh, there's too many tests; you teach the test; testing is intrusive; testing is not the role of government.* How can you possibly determine whether a child can read at grade level if you don't test? And for those who claim we're teaching the test, uh-uh. We're teaching a child to read so he or she can pass the test. Testing is important to solve problems. You can't solve them unless you diagnose the problem in the first place."

Bush had not acknowledged the law's true shortcoming: that it tied high stakes to low-quality academic standards. That said, the greatest legacy of No Child Left Behind was making the problem of the achievement gap visible on a national scale for the first time. The law required that states collect comprehensive achievement data and break down the results by race, class, English-language status, and disability status. Weaknesses among certain groups of students could no longer be masked by a school's overall good test scores.

Four decades of presidential leadership on education had raised the public's expectations about what schools could do to close inequality gaps, and had finally resulted in a national treasure trove of student achievement data. Policy ideas like desegregation, parent leadership, and the multicultural curriculum were out. Standardized testing was in. Meanwhile, outside Washington a network of renegade education researchers was beginning to use student test scores in a whole new way—to measure the success not only of schools, but also of individual teachers.

Chapter Nine

"Big, Measurable Goals"

A DATA-DRIVEN VISION FOR MILLENNIAL TEACHING

Though she would later write that she felt like an outsider at Princeton—she never joined one of the college's storied eating clubs—Wendy Kopp was well known on campus. A petite blonde from Texas with a Princess Diana haircut, she was the publisher and editor in chief of *Business Today,* a nationally distributed magazine for college students, founded in 1968 by Steve Forbes and two other Princeton undergrads. Each year *Business Today* ran a national essay competition for college students interested in corporate careers. The winners attended a conference in New York, where they networked with executives. In an early example of her fund-raising prowess, Kopp grew the publication's annual budget from $300,000 to $1.4 million. Her secret was asking the CEOs she interviewed for articles to buy ads in the magazine, instead of having her salespeople get in touch later with lower-level staff. Going straight to the top worked.

During her senior year Kopp joined her classmates in applying for jobs on Wall Street and with consulting firms. Then at *Business Today*'s fall 1988 conference she attended a session on the national teacher shortage. As Kopp and the other conference-goers learned about the crisis in teaching—12 percent of first-year teachers across the country were uncertified, clustered in urban and rural areas— they started to discuss whether *they* should teach. Most said they'd be open to the idea, as long as they didn't have to major in education. (Princeton had a teacher certification program, but Kopp hadn't heard much about it.) Though their cohort of college students had been parodied as the Me Generation, motivated by money above all else, they were also enthusiastic about community service. Kopp called it "the new idealism," a "yuppie volunteering spirit" that inspired even New York City bankers to staff soup kitchens. But what if elite young college graduates could be convinced to do more—to teach in low-income public schools, even for a short period of time?

That conversation turned Kopp into a public policy entrepreneur, one who would come to dominate the long-running debate over teaching in America. Skipping classes, she withdrew from the world to produce an extraordinarily ambitious senior thesis, "An Argument and Plan for the Creation of the Teacher Corps." The paper's rhetoric was filled with moral panic borrowed from *A Nation at Risk*: Compared to Japan, the United States was suffering from a dilapidated school system. Companies like Motorola and Xerox had trouble finding workers with decent literacy skills. Poor teaching was to blame, she wrote, since education majors had low SAT scores and grades.

Kopp crafted her thesis to suit a small-government era. Unlike the national Teacher Corps, which had existed from 1966 to 1981, the teacher corps she imagined would not be federally funded, but would instead be supported by foundations and corporate donors— just as in the nineteenth century, Catharine Beecher raised money from wealthy individuals to send East Coast girls to teach in western frontier schools. Nineteen-sixties postcollege antipoverty programs, like the old Teacher Corps and the Peace Corps, had taken on a "politicized nature," Kopp critiqued, and had asked recruits to live among the poor. Her teacher corps would not be radical but pragmatic. While the old Teacher Corps had aimed to bring innovative ideas, like the culturally relevant reading list, into schools, Kopp's corps would be simply a straightforward effort to prepare "the brightest minds" to do "the best possible job during the two years they would be teaching," using established methods conveyed during a summer training institute. Under the terms of the Higher Education Act, recruits would be able to defer repayment of their college loans, an arrangement that would be especially attractive to graduates from low-income and minority backgrounds.

Kopp thought it would be wonderful if corps members chose teaching as a long-term career. Some surely would. But for most, the program would provide a "break" from "fast-paced lives to serve the nation," she wrote. Later in life, as lawyers or business leaders, former corps members would be able to speak with passion and authority about the importance of public education, and this would seed a nationwide, elite-driven movement for school improvement.* What's more, the media attention sure to fix on an effort to place Ivy Leaguers in poor kids' classrooms would "send the signal that [teaching] is fulfilling and meaningful, that it is challenging, that it is important and respectable."

Kopp's thesis relied on a comparison between teaching and volunteer work. Since the nineteenth century, this conception has worked against efforts to pay teachers more and attract more men and more ambitious women to the profession. It was all well and good to assert that teaching deserved higher prestige. But if recruits to Kopp's program entered the classroom as if on a missionary vacation and left after only a few years, wouldn't the opposite seem true—that for the smartest, most ambitious people, teaching was not prestigious but a pit stop on the way to a real job?

While researching her thesis, Kopp reached out to the NEA, and Sharon Robinson, the national union's director of instruction, sent her a cautious letter in response. Although the concept of a new teacher corps was "an interesting one," Robinson wrote, it would be effective only if it attracted "career educators" to the classroom. "Even a suggestion that acceptable levels of expertise could develop in short termers simply doesn't mesh with what those of us in the business know it takes to do the job—much less with what our young people need and deserve." Kopp took note and made clear in her thesis that union cooperation would be crucial. The new teacher corps was merely "an emergency response to a shortage of experienced, qualified teachers" in high-needs schools, she wrote, "and would

* Note how different this top-down theory of change is from that of the community control movement, in which parents at the grassroots level were conceived of as the vanguard of school reform.

therefore not be telling the nation that its inexperienced members were preferable to, or as qualified as, experienced teachers."

After turning in her thesis, Kopp revised it into a thirty-page proposal for grant funding and began applying her *Business Today* skills to the task of bringing Teach for America, as she later named it, to life. She remembered that Ross Perot had been a leader in Dallas education reform (chiefly in the area of merit pay), and she made sure he got a copy. Union Carbide, the chemicals manufacturer, donated office space in Manhattan, and Mobil offered Teach for America its first grant, for $26,000. With that money Kopp was able to support herself in New York after graduation, where she shared an apartment in an Upper West Side brownstone with two other young women. She paid $500 per month in rent but was rarely home; along with her growing staff, she routinely stayed at the office until two or three a.m. Her first hire was Whitney Tilson, a friend of her brother's who had graduated from the exclusive Northfield Mount Hermon boarding school and then Harvard. Tilson's parents had been Peace Corps volunteers. Daniel Oscar, a Princeton alum who had taught in China, also came on board. The group's relentlessness, fueled by Kopp's charisma and *Business Today* connections, paid off. Perot eventually donated a $500,000 challenge grant, which helped TFA raise an additional $1.5 million. The organization's early backers included Merck, Chrysler, Morgan Stanley, Hertz, and the Carnegie and Kellogg foundations.

In November 1989, 160 college students were trained at Princeton as recruiters and dispatched to search a hundred campuses for potential Teach for America members. Many seniors first heard about TFA from flyers like this one, which had the intriguing title "Something to Think About," and promised recruits a feel-good interlude of sorts:

> Do you have the least bit of indecision about your plans after graduation? Would you consider devoting two years to teach for America, in either elementary or high school grades, to make her a continuously competitive nation, one capable of continued sustenance of her democratic institutions, with equal opportunity for all? Math and science majors—remember

that America has been steadily sliding in her technical and scientific capability. People of color, recall that perhaps the single greatest key to achieving full equality lies in achieving high levels of education. Liberal arts majors, remember that America is headed toward dangerously low levels of literacy, at precisely the time that they need to be high. Yalies, remember the great privilege we've been given, and please consider, before embarking on your ambitious careers, to devote two years toward bolstering the general strength and well being of our nation.

At Brown University in Providence, Rhode Island, Alex Pearl's roommate saw a similar flyer and told him about it. Pearl was a campus activist who had served on a student committee that supported university cafeteria and maintenance workers when they were demanding higher wages. He had volunteered as a Big Brother to a local public school student and traveled to El Salvador to protest the Reagan administration's support for that nation's right-wing authoritarian government. But he wasn't sure what he wanted to do after graduation. So along with 2,500 other seniors from across the country, he applied to join TFA's inaugural class. Pearl wrote an essay, taught a five-minute sample lesson, and was interviewed for an hour. He and nearly five hundred others were selected. They would begin teaching in the fall of 1990, after an eight-week training institute, including one week of teaching in Los Angeles summer schools.

It was during "Institute" that the tensions between TFA's straight-laced founders and activist recruits like Alex Pearl first exploded. The corps members were living in the dorms at the University of Southern California. After sessions listening to anecdotal lectures from teachers and education experts, a party atmosphere took hold in the evenings. Within a few days, TFA's few dozen non-white recruits mounted a protest: They felt the group discussions about low-income teaching were uninformed by real-world experience. How could this group of mostly young white upper-class college graduates hope to truly understand poor black and brown children and their neighborhoods? The implied question—should teachers be selected from within their students' communities?—was age-old in American education, but it had not been the focus of Kopp's research. She was terrified and holed up in her room to escape the onslaught of negativity.

It would only continue. Deborah Appleman, a Carleton College education professor who sat in on the Institute's training sessions, wasn't impressed. On August 8, 1990, she wrote a *Christian Science Monitor* op-ed titled "Teach for America: Is Idealism Enough?" Appleman called the idea of an eight-week teaching crash course "ludicrous," noting that TFA was doing little to train recruits in how to plan lessons or tailor their instruction to reach bilingual or special-education students. Alex Pearl agreed. Within a few hours of stepping into his third-grade classroom at Anderson Elementary School in Compton, he realized he was woefully unprepared to teach. He had no concrete strategy to manage a classroom or impart knowledge to students. If it hadn't been for the veteran black teacher in the classroom next door, Cleopatra Duncan, who shared her lesson plans with Pearl and taught him how to control a classroom—by expressing a firm sort of love—he might have quit.

Of the first class of TFA recruits, 80 percent fulfilled their two-year commitment, and 42 percent stayed in teaching beyond that (including, as we shall see, Alex Pearl). It was a higher attrition rate than the national average, but lower than the turnover in many of the chaotic low-income schools where TFA recruits were hired. Michael Shapiro, a journalist who wrote an early book on TFA, noted that although the program's training was inadequate, so were many traditional teacher certification programs. Like TFA in its early years, college education departments were often too theoretical and unspecific about pedagogy and lesson planning. And as with TFA, the student teaching stints required by traditional certification programs were too short. "What Teach for America had accomplished in its first summer of teacher training was to condense into eight weeks the same shortcomings that traditional education schools stretched out over four years," Shapiro wrote.

Despite such early criticism, over the next decade TFA became one of the most coveted postgraduation placements for young Americans. Philanthropic support continued to grow, and the program attracted overwhelming media attention. Teach for America teachers became some of the most scrutinized workers in the nation, with researchers tracking their career trajectories, their attitudes about politics and society, and their students' test scores. The debate TFA opened up about teacher preparation and quality teaching, while often rancorous, has been deeper and more evidence based than any the nation has had since the inception of common schooling in the nineteenth century. In part, this is because so many TFA alumni have written frankly about their experiences and have had the connections to amplify their critiques and defenses of the program through magazine articles, books, and op-eds.

Jonathan Schorr was one early critic from within the TFA family. After sixteen years of private schooling, including college at Yale, Schorr sailed through his TFA summer institute student teaching, in which he was responsible for a group of only four students. He entered his classroom at Pasadena High School with naïve enthusiasm. But as the newest teacher, Schorr was assigned the toughest students, and he found himself trying, and often failing, to reach a group of kids who included teen parents and students with severe disabilities, behavior problems, and legal troubles. "Giving the least experienced teachers the toughest classes to teach is a stupid plan, even for the most eager of teachers," Schorr concluded in a widely cited 1993 *Phi Delta Kappan* article. "Though I would not have admitted it at the time, I—perhaps like most TFAers—harbored dreams of liberating my students from public school mediocrity and offering them as good an education as I had received. But I was not ready." He recommended that, as in the Cardozo Project and the National Teacher Corps, all first-year teachers teach only half a day and spend the rest of their work time observing classroom veterans and reflecting on their practice. Kopp dismissed this suggestion. She felt the most ambitious college graduates, the type of people she wanted to participate in TFA, would want to be in charge of a classroom right from the start.

TFA's most persistent adversary was Linda Darling-Hammond, a respected researcher then at Columbia University's Teachers College. In a 1994 essay she excoriated TFA for being "a frankly missionary program" that elevated the résumé building of its recruits over the educational needs of poor children. She pushed back against the reflexive disdain for education majors. Indeed, studies of teachers' impact on student achievement found that certain types of education classes, especially methods courses in specific disciplines, like the teaching of math or the teaching of science, were helpful. Lots of education programs were subpar, Darling-Hammond admitted. But some, such as the graduate-level teacher preparation programs at Teachers College, Harvard, Vanderbilt, and the University of Michigan, were competitive and highly respected. Even at the undergrad level, 10 percent of entering teacher-ed students nationwide had SAT scores in the top fifth of the distribution. All this suggested that public education *already* had a small but significant group of highly intelligent, mission-driven teachers. With all the attention paid to TFA, those professionals could feel invisible, as if all traditionally trained educators were lazy and ineffectual, their schools waiting passively for the booster shot of enthusiasm provided by Wendy Kopp and her small army of saviors.

All too often the public discussion of school reform has pitted TFA recruits against veteran teachers, in a competition for legitimacy that relies on gross generalizations about what this or that kind of teacher is like. "We need an entirely new teaching workforce," Dave Levin, an early TFA corps member who co-founded the KIPP charter school network, said in the late 1990s. "There are some great teachers out there, but they've been mixed among a bad element for too long." Years later Joel Klein, the chancellor of the New York City public schools under Mayor Mike Bloomberg, said, "Generally, the TFA teachers are much less excuse-bound and more entrepreneurial and creative." The organization's critics have been equally harsh. "TFA members do not work in service of public education," wrote Catherine Michna, an apostate TFA alumna who in 2013 announced that as a professor of education, she refuses to write recommendation letters for students who want to enter the corps. "They work in service of a corporate reform agenda that rids communities of veteran teachers, privatizes public schools, and forces a corporatized, data-driven culture upon unique low-income communities with unique dynamics and unique challenges." If Teach for America and its allies have sometimes promoted a moral panic about career educators, this relatively small organization has also provoked a virulent moral panic among its critics.

In my experience as an education reporter, Teach for America recruits are neither the saviors nor the banes of public education. Rather, like other novice educators I've observed and interviewed, they run the gamut from talented and passionate to lackluster and burned out. What corps members share is the experience of being introduced to teaching through a truncated training process that stresses strict discipline and quantifiable results.

Samantha Arpino is a petite native Brooklynite with an eyebrow ring, a nose ring, and long, dark curls. She graduated in 2013 from the State University at Albany, majoring in women's studies and communications. Alongside her sorority sisters she helped organize her college's SlutWalk, part of an international protest movement against rape. She marched with a megaphone wearing a crop top, with the words NOT "ASKING FOR IT" painted on her belly.

A few months later Arpino was teaching summer school kindergarten in the South Bronx, at the Hyde Leadership Charter School. For the five weeks of Teach for America's summer training institute—its twenty-third, now held in eleven cities, preparing more than six thousand corps members—Arpino lived with six hundred other recruits in college dorms in Queens. Each day she and seventy others were bused to Hyde, arriving by seven a.m. They supervised the kids' breakfast, then spent the morning teaching under the watchful eyes of mentors—generally young TFA alumni with just two or three years of classroom experience. The mentors flooded the newbies with advice: Speak louder. Move around the room. Stick to your lesson plan. In the afternoons Arpino and the other corps members attended workshops on topics such as how to teach students who are learning English (use a lot of hand gestures, they were told). Then they went back to the dorm and planned the next day's lessons.

The schedule was grueling. At one afternoon workshop, several corps members nodded off in the back of the room. But looking at Arpino as she taught, you'd have never known she was tired. She knelt on the floor in a floral-print dress, in front of five cross-legged black and Latino first graders, all clad in the Hyde uniform of khaki pants and navy polo shirts. Arpino speaks with the nasal, drawn-out vowels of a working-class New Yorker; she was the first in her family to attend college, and she is determined that her students will be the first in their families, too. The goal of the day's lesson was to help children understand that every story has a beginning, a middle, and an end. To do that, Arpino read the kids *Beanie and the Missing Bear,* a story constructed to help young children understand basic literary concepts: setting (a house), character (Beanie and her sister), and timeline (Beanie loses her teddy bear and finds it again). Every time Arpino introduced a new idea, she repeated herself several times in a singsong voice, answering her own question. "I'm thinking," she said, tapping her temple with her index finger, "that this happens in the middle of the story. In what part of the story does this happen? The middle, the middle, the middle."

It was almost lunchtime, and the kids were yawning and fidgety. Arpino stopped every few minutes to enforce rules on how to sit. "I'm waiting for all my scholars to sit in criss-cross-applesauce!" she demanded. "With their hands folded and back straight. We have to grow our brains for first grade! Because why? Why do we grow our brains?"

"For second grade!" said Melvin.

"Yeah, but what's the *big* goal?" she asked.

"College!" cried a little girl named Chanel.

"Yes, college," Arpino repeated. "And then we can change the world."

Later on I visited the fourth-grade math class of Tarik Walmsley, a lanky University of Washington graduate who was home-schooled at his students' age. Walmsley's lesson was on the idea that multiplication and division are inverse operations: that $8 \times 2 = 16$ and $16 \div 2 = 8$. He passed out small plastic blocks and had the kids arrange them in various groupings: four groups of four blocks each, two groups of eight blocks each. Student behavior had been a challenge, Walmsley told me. One girl sometimes got up from her seat to dance across the classroom. A boy with a special-ed diagnosis could answer problems on paper but had trouble speaking up in front of his classmates. On a quiz, he wrote Walmsley a note: "Teacher, you think I'm stupid, but I'm not."

On the wall was a chart showing a ladder, each level representing one behavioral demerit. Step 1 is a warning. At Step 3, a child is sent to the "icebox," an isolated chair at the back of the classroom. By Step 5, a parent is notified, and the child is removed from the classroom. Each student's name was written on a wooden clothespin, and as he or she accrued demerits, the pin moved up the ladder. Like Arpino with her kindergarteners, Walmsley spent an extraordinary amount of time policing how his fourth graders sat. Were their eyes "tracking" the teacher? Were pencils resting in the pencil groove of the desk? He didn't hesitate to give demerits for small infractions. "Remember how I was talking about chocolate milk? How milk and chocolate are our *products*?" he asked the students, referencing the previous day's multiplication lesson. When a boy named Anthony answered, "Yes!" he earned a demerit for speaking out of turn. By the end of the period, Anthony's clothespin had moved up the ladder, and Anthony was sitting in the icebox, scowling.

After class Walmsley said, "Being stern is not what I grew up with. But it feels useful and fair." He acknowledged he was still learning how to teach. His TFA mentor had said he was performing like only a "typical" teacher; his students were not yet demonstrating the "dramatic" or "path-breaking" levels of achievement TFA expects, and which the program literature told recruits would eventually close the national achievement gap between affluent and poor children.

While TFA was once criticized for producing teachers with little idea of how to manage a classroom or create a lesson plan, today TFA offers its corps members a prescriptive set of directions on how to teach, and even how to *think* about teaching. It is called Teaching as Leadership. Teach for America is often lauded as an alternative to hidebound graduate schools of education, but the central idea of Teaching as Leadership is borrowed from two theorists,

Jay McTighe and Grant Wiggins, whose ideas are popular at some traditional teachers colleges, too. McTighe and Wiggins call their concept "backward design," and TFA calls it "backward planning." According to the *Teaching as Leadership* sourcebook, the first step in backward planning, whether one is teaching public school or running a company, is for the visionary leader to come up with "a big measurable goal." For a CEO, that goal might be to sell one million gadgets. For teachers, TFA recommends goals like "All my first graders will advance two reading levels within one school year," or "I will put my sixth-grade students on a path to get accepted into competitive high schools in our city." Citing "Pygmalion in the Classroom," the 1968 study showing that children earn higher test scores when their teachers have high expectations, the *Teaching as Leadership* book tells recruits not to worry if the goal seems too ambitious—even "crazy"—for a classroom full of students who are far behind grade level. Thinking big is the point. And it warns teachers against perhaps worthwhile but unquantifiable goals like "I will turn my English students into lifelong readers" or "I will develop my history students' sense of citizenship."

The next step is to determine what data can be collected to prove the big goal has been achieved. The data will almost always be test scores, from either a state standardized test, a district test, or a test the teacher finds or creates on her own. A sixth-grade teacher might know that students need at least an 85 on the state's end-of-year English test to be considered for competitive high schools. So she will pore over exam questions from previous years and will target every lesson plan, homework assignment, and student assessment toward building the skills that will enable her students to do well on that test. If she has to, she will host evening tutoring sessions at McDonald's, tempting her students with free food. She will write a weekly class newsletter with celebratory "shout-outs" to students who perform well on quizzes. When she calls or visits a student's home, she will seek to "invest" parents in the big goal.

During the recruitment and selection process, TFA seeks corps members who are likely to embrace this backward-planning, data-driven mind-set. The organization constantly tracks which recruits produce the largest test score gains for their students, reviews those teachers' characteristics, then looks for new candidates who display similar achievements and behaviors during the interview process.

Teach for America was founded during an era of teacher shortages and promoted on the basis that it was filling a great need. Today, with teacher layoffs and high unemployment, the organization cannot justify itself on the same grounds and instead explicitly advertises its corps members as more effective than veteran teachers. The research consensus on TFA suggests that corps members are about equally effective at raising students' test scores as teachers from all other pathways, though better in math than in reading and writing. A September 2013 study from Mathematica Policy Research found that TFA middle and high school math teachers outperform other math teachers in their schools, though only by the equivalent of students gaining 3 points on a 100-point test. The researchers could not discern exactly why. Like other research on teacher credentials, the study found that regardless of the pathway into the classroom, teachers who majored in math or who had attended selective colleges did not seem to significantly outperform other teachers with less impressive résumés.* So if the "best and brightest" theory isn't true—if traditional meritocratic credentials aren't the reason that TFA teachers are good at their jobs—then what accounts for many corps members' success?

The work of John Hattie provides some clues. He is an education researcher from New Zealand who has reviewed eight hundred meta-analyses that summarize the results of over fifty thousand education studies. Hattie has found that completely separate from a teacher's demographic traits, a few specific teacher behaviors—including some emphasized by TFA—powerfully influence student achievement. A wealth of research indicates that one of the best

---

* In *Visible Learning,* John Hattie notes that while researchers generally have trouble locating the effects of teachers' content knowledge on student outcomes, there is other evidence suggesting that teachers' general intellectual ability, particularly vocabulary and verbal facility, are positively associated with student achievement gains. These skills, however, may have very little to do with the competitiveness of a teacher's college or graduate school, or the content of the classes he or she took there.

things a teacher can do for her students is to set high, individualized expectations for each one of them, regardless of a child's past performance or whether he comes to class with a label such as low-income, special education, or learning disabled. Effective teachers believe all children can learn—a fundament of the TFA philosophy too—and reject the idea of intelligence as an inborn trait, instead seeing it as something a teacher can develop in every student. In general, academically ineffective teachers are those who set the bar too low; some evidence suggests that half of what is taught in most classes is already known by most students. That brings us to another teacher behavior Hattie identifies as potentially transformative, and which TFA promotes: formative assessment. To avoid teaching children what they have previously learned, teachers should assess students at the beginning of the school year and at the beginning of new units, to identify their strengths and weaknesses. Students should be quizzed again when units end, to determine if concepts and skills have been successfully taught. A cache of studies from cognitive scientists confirms that students score higher on end-of-course standardized tests when they have been periodically quizzed along the way.

Although education research seems to confirm some of TFA's practices and mind-sets, it calls others into question, particularly those having to do with student discipline. When teachers provide constant, controlling behavioral feedback, as Arpino and Walmsley were being taught to do, they waste precious time they could be spending giving feedback related to the academic content of the lesson, which is far more powerful in terms of raising student achievement. One of the challenges of training a new teacher, Hattie writes, is convincing her that "developing a strong desire to control student behavior can be inconsistent with implementing many conceptual approaches to teaching."

There has been little convincing research done on those "no excuses" teaching strategies: incentive systems (pizza for good behavior and high test scores); the focus on children's posture and eye contact as teachers read or lecture; and the school uniforms and silent hallways. Yet this type of teaching has exploded in prominence since the mid-1990s, driven in large part by the strategies and rhetoric used at the KIPP charter schools and adopted by TFA and many of the other charters at which its corps members and alumni increasingly work.*

The KIPP schools (pronounced "kip") are the most celebrated in America. They were founded in 1994 by two TFA alums, Dave Levin and Mike Feinberg, who, as struggling first-year teachers in Houston, became entranced by the classroom strategies of Harriet Ball. A magnetic, six-foot-one African American woman, Ball seemed to work miracles with her African American fourth graders. Her students exuberantly sang songs—mnemonics about what they were learning, as well as exhortations of *why* they were learning (*'cause knowledge is power, and power is money, and I want it!*)—but when Ball snapped her fingers, they went dead silent. If children acted up or didn't do their homework, she threatened to transfer them to another teacher's classroom. They were lucky, she told them, to have her as a teacher, and they better not waste the opportunity.

Ball emphasized education as a privilege and literacy as the pathway to personal financial empowerment—an ideology with a long, proud history in the African American community, traceable to Booker T. Washington. Her high expectations for her students echoed the promise of Rhody McCoy, the superintendent in Ocean Hill–Brownsville, that children would learn if teachers set the right tone. In the 1990s a multiracial group of Generation X education reformers began to adopt and translate these strategies. Levin and Feinberg named their schools KIPP—the Knowledge Is Power Program—after the refrain in Ball's song. Her "no excuses" methods supposedly proved, as Wendy Kopp has written, that "education can trump poverty," as long as a teacher accepts her responsibility as the "key variable" driving student outcomes. "We"—not parents,

---

* In 2007 TFA sent 13 percent of corps members to charter schools. In 2013, as recession budget cuts slowed district hiring, one-third of corps members were hired by charter schools and about half of alumni still teaching were working in charters. Not all charters are "no excuses" schools. Some, like Global Community in Harlem and Community Roots in Brooklyn, emphasize project-based learning and other progressive pedagogies.

not neighborhoods, not school funding or health care or racism or stable housing—"control our students' success and failure," states *Teaching as Leadership.*

This ideal of the all-powerful individual teacher, solely responsible for raising student achievement in measurable ways, soon transcended start-ups like Teach for America and KIPP to become the foundation of national education policy making during the Obama years. It received a big boost from a new way of evaluating teachers and schools, called value-added measurement.

On May 20, 2003, Kati Haycock of the Education Trust appeared in front of Congress to share her opinion on how No Child Left Behind could be improved. Haycock had been instrumental in pushing for NCLB. Now she had a new message for lawmakers: It was clear that individual teachers, even more than standards or schools themselves, were "the number one ingredient of high achievement" for kids. She cited a body of research from a University of Tennessee statistician named William Sanders. Using a technique called value-added measurement, Haycock said, Sanders had proved that a child with a sequence of good teachers could demonstrate up to 50 points of gain on a 100-point standardized test, "the difference between entry into a selective college and a lifetime working at McDonald's." Teachers should be evaluated, she said, on whether they "produce student learning gains."

Sanders's claims were stunning. The most important education research of the 1950s and 1960s had been conducted not by testing experts, but by psychologists and sociologists. Kenneth Clark and James Coleman had looked at a broad range of factors that influenced children's school performance and overall well-being: how many books their parents owned, what toys they played with, whether schools had science laboratories or libraries. When the older generation of researchers tried to pinpoint what made a teacher successful, they often looked for particular personality traits like warmth, extroversion, and conscientiousness. But the explosion of state testing programs since the 1970s provided researchers like Sanders with an unprecedented data trove. Statisticians and economists have used this achievement data to ask a much narrower question: Which teachers raise or lower a child's test scores?

Value-added measurement is the method researchers developed to find an answer. In its relatively crude, early form, value-added simply used a student's score on an end-of-year standardized test to predict her score on the following year's exam. Teachers who presided over larger-than-expected jumps in scores earned above-average value-added ratings. (For example: Sarah scored an 89 in third-grade math. The typical child who scores 89 gets a 91 next year, but Sarah scored a 93 in fourth grade. Those 2 points of unpredicted achievement gain are attributed to her fourth-grade teacher and are computed into the teacher's value-added rating.)

A more sensitive early value-added formula was developed in Dallas in the mid-1990s, where statisticians recognized the fact that disadvantaged students tend to experience slower academic growth than their middle-class peers, no matter how good their teachers. That's because poor children are more likely to experience out-of-school disruptions, such as poor nutrition, a move, or homelessness, which can affect learning. The Dallas research team created a value-added equation that included controls for children's demographic traits, such as parental income and proficiency in English, essentially giving teachers who worked with disadvantaged kids bonus points. This technique found smaller, yet still significant, teacher effects on kids' test scores.

Value-added measurement changed pretty much everything in our national conversation about student achievement. To assess a school's improvement or decline, No Child Left Behind compared the "snapshot" score of one group of third graders on an end-of-year math test to the scores of the children who were in third grade the previous year. These snapshots made the teachers and schools that serve poor children look especially bad, because those schools earned low scores year after year. Snapshots obscured whether any individual student was doing better or worse over time. Growth measures that track one group of children over the course of several years, like value-added, present a more nuanced picture. But in 2001, when NCLB was designed, most policy makers in Washington hadn't heard about value-added. While the law's real-world consequences were playing out in schools across the country, value-added research grew much more sophisticated. Economists created experiments that randomly assigned students within one school to various teachers, and then measured differences in test score growth. That method eliminated the bias caused by principals clustering the most challenging or most able students in particular classrooms. Researchers also identified more sensitive controls for the factors that influence a child's test score but are not related to his classroom teacher's performance. A value-added model developed by the University of Wisconsin for New York City included controls not only for family income and English proficiency, but also for a student's race, gender, disability status, how often he was absent from class, whether he had been enrolled in summer school, and whether he had recently moved, been suspended, or repeated a grade. The New York City value-added model also compared teachers only to other teachers who taught similar-sized classes, and who had the same number of years of experience.

Using these methods, labor economists produced a massive body of research. It suggested that a teacher's pathway into the classroom—whether through a traditional teachers college, a graduate-level program in teaching, or an alternative program like Teach for America—hardly mattered with regard to how well they raised student test scores, nor did their college major. There was more value-added variation between teachers within a school than across all the schools in a district—a hopeful finding proving what many urban teachers had long argued: that even "failing" schools employ some excellent educators. First-year teachers were not very good, but they made major leaps in effectiveness by the end of their second year on the job, and they continued improving steadily for five to ten years, after which their measurable performance generally flatlined.

The results of these experiments remain "noisy," as social scientists say. When value-added is calculated for a teacher using just a single year's worth of test score data, the error rate is 35 percent—meaning more than one in three teachers who are average will be misclassified as excellent or ineffective, and one in three teachers who excel or are terrible will be called average. Even with three years of data, one in four teachers will be misclassified. It is difficult, if not impossible, to compute an accurate value-added score for teachers who work in teams within a single classroom—a method rapidly growing in popularity—or for the two-thirds of teachers who teach grades or classes not subject to standardized tests.

Some advocates of value-added downplayed these problems and made huge claims based on the technique. The Stanford economist Eric Hanushek, a fellow at the conservative Hoover Institution and proponent of cutting school funding, advanced the hypothesis that if poor children were assigned five "good teachers in a row"—those with value-added scores in the top 15 percent—it would completely close the academic achievement gap between the poor and the middle class. In a 2006 paper for the Brookings Institution, three economists, Robert Gordon, Thomas Kane, and Douglas Staiger, used similar logic to estimate that firing the bottom 25 percent of first-year teachers annually, as determined by a single year's worth of value-added data, could create $200 billion to $500 billion in economic growth for the country, by enabling poor children to earn higher test scores and go on to obtain better jobs.

The most important thing to realize about these claims, which appear frequently in the media, is that they are untested. According to Tulane University economist Doug Harris, another leading value-added scholar, no experiment has ever been conducted in which poor children are randomly assigned to multiple high value-added teachers in a row, to test if the achievement gap totally closes. "It's still purely hypothetical," he told me, "and it would be an incredibly tough experiment to pull off." Even if such an experiment did take place, Harris guesses that it would fail to confirm the hypothesis that teachers alone can close achievement gaps. Here's why: The Hanushek theory is that five teachers who each add 10 points to a child's test score will move that child from the fortieth to the ninetieth achievement percentile over the course of five years. But in real-world conditions, value-added gains tend to fade out over time; next year the average child will lose 50 percent of the test score gains she made this year, and by three years from now she will have lost 75 percent of this year's gains. According to Harris, that means the academic and economic effects of having multiple above-average teachers in a row have been inflated by more than half. Effective teachers can narrow, but not close, achievement and employment gaps that reflect broader income, wealth, and racial inequalities in American society.

This reality was demonstrated by the most celebrated value-added study ever conducted. Economists Raj Chetty, John Friedman, and Jonah Rockoff tried to figure out if teachers who were good at raising test scores were also good at improving their students' long-term life outcomes—in other words, if value-added was a good proxy for some of the other goals, aside from raising test scores, that we want teachers to fulfill. Using tax returns and school district records from an unnamed large city, they examined twenty years of data from more than one million children and their teachers, tracking the students from third grade through young adulthood. One finding was that the current achievement gap is driven much more by out-of-school factors than by in-school factors; differences in teacher quality account for perhaps 7 percent of the gap. But it turned out that the group of students who had been assigned to just one top value-added teacher—a teacher one standard deviation more effective than the norm—experienced small, yet observable, differences in life outcomes. These students earned, on average, 1.3 percent more per year, the difference between a salary of $25,000 and $25,325. They were 2.2 percent more likely to be enrolled in college at age twenty, and were 4.6 percent less likely to become teen mothers.

The researchers posited that if there were a way to systematically move the top value-added teachers to the lowest-performing schools, perhaps 73 percent of the test score achievement gap could be closed. That, however, is a gargantuan policy challenge: When a separate Department of Education/Mathematica trial offered more than one thousand high value-added teachers $20,000 to transfer to a low-income school, less than a quarter chose to apply for the jobs. (Those who did transfer produced test score gains among elementary school kids, but not among middle schoolers.) There was another major caveat, which Chetty, Friedman, and Rockoff acknowledged: Like almost every other major value-added study ever conducted, this one took place in a low-stakes setting, meaning that teachers were not being evaluated or paid according to their students' test scores. It was possible, the three economists noted, that in a higher-stakes setting, test scores would lose their predictive power, for instance in cases where they reflected not students' true learning but rather teaching to the test or cheating.

Value-added measurement had proven to be a useful research tool. Now the question was whether it could actually be used as a policy instrument—to select, promote, train, reward, and terminate teachers. Education history (and some economists) urged caution. No Child Left Behind had provoked states to lower standards and the scores that would qualify as proficient. It had narrowed the curriculum and increased teaching to the test. These trends proved the wisdom of "Campbell's law," the oft-quoted social scientific rule named for the educational psychologist Donald Campbell: "The more any quantitative social indicator is used for social decision-making, the more subject it will be to corruption pressures and the more apt it will be to distort and corrupt the social processes it is intended to monitor."

Yet by the time Chetty, Friedman, and Rockoff published their study with its caution about using value-added measurement in high-stakes settings, the tool had already made the giant leap from research into practice. Congress never did get around to updating NCLB. But Bill Gates stepped in. The technology titan's early philanthropic efforts in education had focused on placing computers in schools, and then on breaking up large high schools into smaller ones. He'd been frustrated by the mixed record of those reforms; they might have helped raise high school graduation rates, but they did not produce the test score jumps he was looking for. In 2007 Gates met value-added scholars Thomas Kane and Robert Gordon, who had already talked to New York City schools chancellor Joel Klein about using value-added to compare some teachers, like those from the Teaching Fellows alternative certification program, to others. Gates, too, liked the idea, and within a year he was making grants of up to $100 million to school districts that agreed to use value-added measures to evaluate teachers. Gates loved data and believed in the importance of employee evaluation and incentives. As CEO of Microsoft, he had implemented a system known as stack ranking, in which every manager ranked his direct reports from worst to best in two stacks: one on performance this year, and one on potential to improve over time. The system was used to distribute cash bonuses and stock options, and sometimes to lay off low performers.

Gates's successor at Microsoft, Steve Ballmer, made the so-called "rank and yank" system much more rigid, using just one pile to rate employees on every factor of their performance. An August 2012 *Vanity Fair* article on Microsoft's corporate troubles called attention to some of the downsides of this plan, namely that by ranking workers from top to bottom, it focused employees on competing against the other members of their teams, instead of working together to share best practices. Elsewhere in the corporate world, companies spent the 1990s adopting a Japanese management tool, used at Toyota and Sony, called continuous quality improvement. Under that system, managers and teams of workers looked at performance data together, not to rank individuals, but to identify group weaknesses and work cooperatively to address them. Even Japanese schools are set up this way; through a practice called lesson study, teachers collaborate to plan lessons, observe one another delivering them, and then share feedback.

Many education leaders worried that high-stakes evaluation tying individual students to individual teachers had the potential to introduce the Microsoft problem of competition into a profession that almost every expert agreed was far too lacking in collaboration. American schools were finally moving toward group lesson planning and paired or team teaching. With those setups it could seem counterproductive to focus so much on the test score link between one teacher and one student. *Many* different teachers were now impacting each child's learning, even in the elementary grades.

"I am actually really intrigued by value-added systems done right," said Randi Weingarten in 2005, then the president of the United Federation of Teachers in New York City. She agreed to an experiment in which teachers at two hundred New York City schools could win up to $3,000 in bonuses if value-added evaluation showed test scores had improved. It was a collective, not an individual, value-added scheme: If scores went up, every teacher would get the same amount of money, no matter how little or how much she had contributed to the effort. This was in line with what Al Shanker, shortly before his death, had laid out as the correct union position on performance pay tied to student learning outcomes: in favor of it, but only if achievement was measured collectively across classrooms, to encourage collaboration. Citing the high error rates and noise in value-added calculations, Weingarten resisted account- ability plans that linked a teacher to the test scores of students in his or her individual classroom. But she was about to lose that battle in the biggest way possible—with the president of the United States as her adversary.

One of the hottest tickets at the 2008 Democratic National Con- vention was to a panel discussion on education reform hosted by a coalition of foundations, nonprofits, and businesses that supported charter schools and teacher evaluation based on value-added. The event was held at the glittering postmodern Denver Art Museum, and the featured speakers were two young African American may- ors thought to have the ear of Barack Obama, the party's nominee: Adrian Fenty of Washington, D.C., and Cory Booker of Newark. Fenty praised his schools chancellor, Michelle Rhee, a Teach for America alum who was pushing a plan, funded by philanthropists, to weaken teachers' tenure protections in exchange for bonuses tied to value-added data and tougher classroom observations. A small number of top D.C. teachers would supposedly be able to earn the eye-popping salary of $130,000 per year. "The American Federa- tion of Teachers, which I don't think does anything for the people of the District of Columbia, is weighing in against it," Fenty said at the event, "and the only thing I can think of is that the heads of the union, they want to keep their jobs." Booker added, "Ten years ago when I talked about school choice, I was literally tarred and feath- ered. I was literally brought into a broom closet by a union and told I would never win office if I kept talking about charters."

Never before had prominent Democrats critiqued teachers unions so brazenly at a convention in which 10 percent of the par- ty's delegates were union teachers. The Denver event represented a new way of talking about the unions, one that melded the righteous outrage of the old Black Power critics, like Stokely Carmichael and Amiri Baraka, to the moderate technocratic politics of the post-Reagan Democratic Party. Younger African American politicians, like Booker, Fenty, and, the most prominent of all, Barack Obama, personified this shift.

As an Illinois state senator Obama passed legislation that brought accountability reformers, the Chicago Teachers Union, and the Chicago school board together to expand the number of non-unionized charter schools in the city. In 2005, during his first term in the U.S. Senate, he spoke at the launch party of Democrats for Education Reform (DFER), a political action committee founded by charter school philanthropists who work in the financial sector, and who are often harshly critical of teachers unions. One of them was Whitney Tilson, the hedge fund entrepreneur who had been TFA employee number one. At dinner before the event, Obama impressed the DFER founders by telling them about a visit he had made to a successful Chicago public school, where a teacher complained to him that too many of her colleagues at "traditional" schools had the attitude that "these kids"—poor kids—"can't learn." Later on, he elicited cheers from the DFER crowd by saying, "If someone can tell me where the Democratic Party stands on education reform, please let me know. Because I can't figure it out. Our party has got to wake up on this!" When Obama was running in the Democratic Party presidential primary two years later, he was booed at an NEA event after he praised performance pay for teachers. The two big teachers unions endorsed Hillary Clinton. Then, during a televised debate with John McCain, Obama referred to Michelle Rhee as Washington's "wonderful new superintendent," seemingly impervious to the fact that she had become enemy number one to much of organized labor. (A few weeks after the debate, Rhee appeared on the cover of *Time* magazine, standing in a classroom holding a broom. The implication was that she would take on the unions and sweep incompetent tenured teachers out of D.C.)

When it came time for President Obama to appoint a secretary of education, he passed over Linda Darling-Hammond, the TFA critic, union ally, and teacher training expert who had been an adviser to his campaign. Instead he took DFER's advice and nominated Arne Duncan, who as superintendent in Chicago had shut down underperforming schools, opened new charter schools, and experimented with teacher performance pay tied, in part, to value-added measurement. Despite warnings from nonpartisan experts to move cautiously on using value-added for teacher accountability— "the current research base is insufficient to support the use of VAM for high-stakes decisions," RAND wrote—value-added became a cornerstone principle of the Obama administration's signature education program, Race to the Top. On the day he announced the Race, the president emphasized that one of its goals was firing bad teachers. "Let me be clear," he said to the Hispanic Chamber of Commerce. "If a teacher is given a chance or two chances or three chances but still does not improve, there's no excuse for that person to continue teaching. I reject a system that rewards failure and protects a person from its consequences."

Originally passed through Congress as part of the 2009 economic stimulus alongside funds for less controversial school improvements, like saving teaching jobs and renovating school buildings, Race provided over $4 billion to states and school districts that agreed to implement a reform agenda focused, for the first time, on individual teachers. To win a grant, states would have to evaluate, pay, and grant tenure according to how effectively a teacher grew student achievement in measurable ways. The administration's guidelines did not include the term "value-added." But the Department of Education defined "student achievement" as "a student's score on the state's assessments . . . end-of-course tests . . . and other measures that are rigorous and comparable across classrooms." It defined "student growth" as "the change in student achievement . . . between two or more points in time." That was value-added. Race to the Top also asked states to require principals to evaluate every teacher every single year—a huge new responsibility for administrators, many of whom had been accustomed to giving cursory checklist evaluations to each employee only once every three or five years, in which teachers were rated on simplistic factors like appropriate dress, punctuality, and neat and quiet classrooms. And the law expected states to find a way to legally remove teachers, even tenured teachers, whose performance did not improve. Race to the Top "turnaround schools," those with the very lowest test scores, would have the option of removing over half of their teachers, including those with tenure.

In a nod to the unions, especially to the powerful new president of the AFT, Randi Weingarten, states would lose points in the competition if their own teachers unions opposed their plans. (Weingarten was a sophisticated New York politico who, although untrammeled in negotiations with Mike Bloomberg and Michelle Rhee, signaled more openness toward teacher accountability than any union leader since Al Shanker.) States could win points, however, for doing something the unions resisted bitterly: hiring more teachers from alternative certification programs, like Teach for America. There were some important non-teacher-related priorities in Race to the Top, too. States that wanted grants would have to shut down or restructure failing schools, open more high-quality charter schools, and sign on to high-quality curriculum standards. The Common Core State Standards in English and math, an effort driven by governors, philanthropists, and the teachers unions, became the first politically viable nationwide curricular reform in American history.

In the midst of the worst economic downturn since the Great Depression, Race to the Top had an ingenious design. It held out an irresistible carrot—federal funding—and directed financially starving states to compete against one another to grasp it. Other Department of Education grant programs adopted similar priorities on teacher accountability, so the entire federal reform agenda was tightly aligned. Politically, it worked. Though only nineteen states won Race to the Top grants, two-thirds of the states changed their laws on public school teachers in order to compete, half of the states declared that student test scores would be included in teacher evaluations, and eighteen weakened tenure protections. In Colorado a young, charismatic state senator and TFA alum named Mike Johnston crafted legislation decreeing that student achievement data would account for 51 percent of a teacher's evaluation score, more than evidence from classroom observations. If a Colorado teacher earned two bad ratings in a row, she would lose tenure protections.*

In New York, student achievement growth would now count for 40 percent of a teacher evaluation score. Eleven states moved to end "last in, first out," the policy that requires districts to lay off inexperienced teachers before tenured teachers, regardless of performance—an increasingly relevant issue around the country as budget cuts forced many districts to consider staff reductions. Florida and North Carolina ended tenure altogether. Wisconsin, Michigan, and Indiana limited the scope of issues teachers unions can address through collective bargaining; so did deep blue Massachusetts, though only for teachers in low-performing schools.

Teachers unions that had been involved in tense standoffs with accountability reformers found themselves weakened. In Central Falls, Rhode Island, a tiny bankrupt town that had lost its manufacturing economy, the local high school, which had a dropout rate of more than 50 percent, became a Race to the Top "turnaround" school. In March 2010, when the AFT local there resisted a proposal to require teachers to work a longer day without much extra pay, superintendent Frances Gallo attempted to fire the school's entire teaching staff, eliciting praise straight from the White House. "There's got to be a sense of accountability," President Obama said.

In June 2010, the most acrimonious labor negotiation in the nation, between Weingarten and Rhee, ended with 80 percent of D.C. teachers voting to accept a contract that offered an across-the-board 20 percent raise, a faster process for tenured teachers who wished to file an appeal of a termination, and the option for any individual teacher to forgo tenure entirely and work to earn bonuses of between $3,000 and $25,000. The bonuses would be paid for

---

* Johnston's enthusiasm for test-score-based accountability was a sign of changing times. Less than a decade earlier he had published a poignant memoir about his time as a TFA corps member in the Mississippi Delta, in which he complained about "innumerable state testing sessions" and "the furor to try to improve test scores."

through $64.5 million in philanthropic donations and distributed according to a new evaluation system based on value-added scores and classroom observations.

Several of the same donors helped fund *Waiting for "Superman,"* a 2010 documentary film that told the story of five charming kids hoping to gain admission to oversubscribed charter schools. Oprah Winfrey interviewed the film's director, Davis Guggenheim, and Thomas Friedman wrote a *New York Times* column praising it. The cover of *New York* magazine asked, "Can one little movie save America's schools?" The film portrayed all urban neighborhood public schools as blighted places packed with incompetent tenured teachers, while presenting nonunionized charters as the solution. It failed to depict any unionized charter schools, like the highly regarded Green Dot Schools, or any low-performing charter schools—about a quarter of the sector—or any successful traditional schools in high-poverty neighborhoods. Ominous music played when Randi Weingarten appeared on-screen; there was no indication of the fact that even while defending unpopular policies, like "last in, first out," the AFT had already signed on to a number of groundbreaking new teacher evaluation plans that considered student performance and weakened tenure.

Weingarten was realistic about why her union was under attack. Teacher tenure provided a level of job security inconceivable to most American workers, many of whom were barely hanging on during a recession with a nearly 10 percent unemployment rate. "Only 7 percent of American workers are in unions," she told me. "America looks at us as islands of privilege."

But all the attention paid to teacher tenure as The Big Problem in American education, and to value-added evaluation and firings as The Big Solution, had a way of eliding how these major policy changes were affecting kids in real-world classrooms. One of the biggest impacts of Race to the Top was the explosion in the number and types of tests and assessments students take in order to collect the data used to evaluate their teachers. A 2013 AFT study of two major urban school districts found that in one, students spent the equivalent of thirty days taking practice tests and learning test-taking strategies, and about two full weeks sitting for exams. In another, students spent sixteen days practicing and three days taking tests. In one district I visited, Harrison District 2 in Colorado Springs, the typical child experienced at least twenty-five testing days each school year, which cut down on time for instruction, field trips, group projects, and any other classroom activity not associated with collecting student growth data.

Under the new guidelines, even art teachers would be evaluated by student growth measures. Thus, on exam day in Sabina Trombetta's first-grade art class at Chamberlin Elementary School in Colorado Springs, the six-year-olds were shown a slide of Picasso's *The Weeping Woman,* a 1937 cubist portrait of the artist's lover, with tears streaming down her face. It is painted in vibrant greens, bluish purples, and yellows. Explaining the painting, Picasso once said, "Women are suffering machines."

The test asked the first graders to look at *The Weeping Woman* and "write three colors Picasso used to show feeling or emotion." Another question asked, "In each box below, draw three different shapes that Picasso used to show feeling or emotion." A separate section of the exam asked students to write a full paragraph about a Matisse painting.

In its Race to the Top guidelines, the Department of Education hadn't specified exactly how to collect student growth data for the two-thirds of teachers nationwide who taught a non-tested grade or subject, ranging from art to kindergarten to social studies to theater. After all, NCLB had required testing only in math, reading, and science, and only for kids in the third grade or higher. That caused a gaping hole between policy and practice that states and districts rushed to fill. In Harrison District 2, a largely low-income Latino district in Colorado Springs, superintendent Mike Miles was considered a national trailblazer on one possible solution: Give children paper tests in every single subject, at every grade level.

In order to assess Trombetta, thirty-eight, a ten-year teaching veteran and winner of teaching awards from both her school district and her county, the district required her first graders to sit for seven pencil-and-paper tests in art that school year. To prepare them for those exams, Trombetta lectured her students on art elements such as color, line, and shape—bullet points on Colorado's fine-arts curriculum standards. Something similar was happening in the district's gym classes, where a test asked second graders, "Draw a picture of how your hands look while they are catching a ball that is thrown above your head."

When I visited Trombetta's cheery, colorful classroom on a November afternoon in 2010, she really wanted to talk. As she ate a TV dinner for lunch, she said she liked the idea of exposing her young students, many of whom had never visited a museum, to great works of art. But, she complained, preparing the children for the exam meant teaching them reductive half-truths—that dark colors signify sadness and bright colors happiness, for example. "To bombard these kids with words and concepts instead of the experience of art? I really struggle with that," she said. "It's kind of hard when they come to me and say, 'What are we going to make today?' and I have to say, 'Well, we're going to write about art.'" She confided that she wasn't sure if she wanted to continue working in the district. And sure enough, at the end of that school year Trombetta quit her job and moved to Vienna, Austria, where she now teaches at the American International School. There her students are assessed only on the art projects they create.

Douglas Harris, the value-added economist, warns in his book, "There might be good reason to extend testing, but doing it solely for measuring educator performance could be a grave error. Decisions about standardized testing should be driven by the testability of particular subjects and with an eye toward ensuring that they don't distort teaching in unproductive ways." In the absence of guidelines from Washington, states and districts have forged ahead on their own to create new tests. Harrison District 2 now supplements its paper exams with what testing experts call "performance-based assessments": In elementary grades, phys-ed students must show they can dribble a basketball; high school music students perform three songs; art students must demonstrate the difference between a one- and two-point perspective drawing. South Carolina's fourth-grade music exam, administered via computer, asks: "When singing a melody together with a friend, what dynamic level should you

sing? A) Louder than your friend B) Not too loud and not too soft
C) Softer than your friend or D) the same as your friend." (The correct answer is D.) Students are then shown a measure of sheet music
and asked to identify which of four electronic recordings matches
the notation. Florida plans to create new tests for every grade and
subject level that is currently untested, a plan that Bill Gates, in a
2013 interview with me, called rushed and "crazy."

Can creativity be quantified? The upside to high-stakes assessment programs like these is that they signal to teachers, students,
and parents that the arts matter. A downside is the ever-increasing
amount of paperwork for teachers and principals, and the increased
testing time for kids. And high-quality performance assessments are
more difficult to administer and grade than are traditional tests. So
some districts and states are finding easier and cheaper ways to measure achievement. In New York City, teachers of non-tested grades
and subjects, like kindergarten or music, are often graded according
to school-wide test score gains in core subjects. This could conceiv-
ably encourage all teachers in a school to focus on worthy goals;
it's easy to imagine how a social studies teacher might include more
essay writing in his course, which would help kids do better on an
English test. But in September 2013 the Web site Chalkbeat New
York reported on how some New York principals were gaming this
system by choosing their school's strongest tested area—for example, fourth-grade math—as the means by which to evaluate gym
and theater teachers with no math expertise. In Florida, Tennessee, and other states, kindergarten, first-, and second-grade teachers
are held accountable for third-grade test scores, even the scores of
students they never taught. That's what happened to Kim Cook, a
second-year first-grade teacher at Irby Elementary in Alachua, Florida, a K–2 school. She received a perfect score on her lesson study
and 88 points out of a possible 100 on an appraisal from her principal. She was even voted "teacher of the year" by her colleagues. But
she received an unsatisfactory evaluation because third graders at a
school down the street performed poorly on exams. If she receives
another "unsatisfactory" next year, she can be dismissed. The NEA
has sued the Florida Board of Education on behalf of Cook and six
other teachers, to protect teachers from a practice that defies com-

mon sense: being rated based on the test scores of students they have never even met.

Some union critics hope today's young teachers will shift the profession away from its strong identification with organized labor. In 2010 Educators 4 Excellence launched in New York City to give a voice to teachers who support accountability reforms and sometimes oppose traditional union protections. It quickly attracted funding from the Gates Foundation and expanded to Los Angeles, Connecticut, and Minnesota. A 2012 survey of ten thousand American teachers showed their opinions *have* shifted during the era of accountability reform. Respondents believed tenure should be granted after 5.4 years on the job, an increase from the current national average of 3.1 years. Other polls show almost half of teachers younger than age thirty-five support charter schools, compared to less than a third of teachers over the age of fifty. But overall, American educators remain strongly committed to their unions. Over 80 percent of teachers support collective bargaining, and the majority believe they should have the right to go on strike.

President Obama's accountability agenda took on the teachers unions. But was the public as hostile to unions as the political elite was? In late 2010 D.C. mayor Adrian Fenty lost his reelection bid. Polls showed Washington's black middle class had turned against Fenty's education reform agenda, frustrated by Michelle Rhee's brash management style, her closure of underperforming schools in black neighborhoods, and her layoffs not only of teachers, but of 121 staffers in the district's central office. Student test scores had increased incrementally under Rhee, but it turned out D.C. voters saw their public schools—which had been some of the first in the nation for African Americans—as more than just achievement factories: They were neighborhood meeting places, sources of treasured civil service jobs, and repositories of community history and racial pride.

Teachers unions got another unexpected boost in public support in February 2011, when Wisconsin governor Scott Walker introduced a plan to roll back public sector collective bargaining and cut pensions. Teachers helped lead massive protests at the state capital in Madison, and shortly afterward a poll found 70 percent of Wisconsinites had a favorable opinion of public school teachers. A national poll from Gallup and *USA Today* found 61 percent of Americans opposed laws, like Walker's, limiting teachers' rights to collective bargaining. (In the weeks before the protests, the Wisconsin state teachers union had actually agreed to a number of reforms: value-added teacher evaluation, weakened tenure, and higher employee contributions to health care and pension plans. None of it swayed Republican lawmakers, who approved Walker's plan.)

Even more surprising was public opinion in the wake of a teachers' strike in Chicago in September 2012. The city's students missed seven days of school, throwing parents' work and child care plans into turmoil. But polls showed the majority of parents—and even higher proportions of black and Latino parents—supporting union teachers, who, two years earlier, had rejected the relatively moderate, reform-oriented politics of Randi Weingarten and her local allies and elected the far more confrontational Karen Lewis as president of the Chicago Teachers Union (CTU). Lewis called Mayor Rahm Emanuel's reform agenda—especially his policy of using low test scores to select fifty schools for closure in poor neighborhoods, sometimes replacing them with nonunionized charter schools—"a corporate attack on public education . . . This is warfare now."*

Accountability reformers, including Emanuel and the organization Stand for Children, had worked with the Illinois state legislature to pass a law making it harder for teachers to strike, by requiring 75 percent of union members, an increase from 51 percent, to vote in favor of any walkout. Nevertheless, nearly 90 percent of CTU members authorized the 2012 strike. The result was a compromise contract. It provided a 3 percent raise and more funding for support

---

* School closings have emerged as one of the most controversial issues in education reform. Closings are sold as a way to get kids into better schools. But according to the Consortium on Chicago School Research, only 6 percent of Chicago students whose schools were shut down ended up enrolled in a school within the top achievement quartile, and 40 percent of students from closed schools ended up at schools that were on academic probation.

services, such as social workers and guidance counselors, especially in high-poverty schools, in exchange for a longer school day. The contract continued to tie teacher salaries and bonuses to years in the classroom and advanced degrees earned. But the CTU agreed, at least in theory, to professional evaluations that include evidence of student learning (which usually means test scores). In the event of layoffs, only high-performing teachers would be protected.

The following spring the Chicago Public Schools did indeed lay off 1,000 teachers, citing a budget shortfall. Another 161 teachers in the city, all with good evaluation scores, were left without assignments because their schools were being shut down. Teach for America emerged as a flash point, since it expected to place 500 corps members in Chicago public and charter schools despite the crisis, at a cost of $1.6 million to the struggling district.* At TFA's July 2013 conference in Detroit, which I attended, some Chicago-based alumni reported a job market so tight that veteran, traditionally trained teachers were applying to TFA in the hopes of using the organization's connections to secure coveted jobs in charter schools, which are not affected by the district's hiring freeze and tend to favor TFA-affiliated candidates.

A vocal group of TFA alumni believe sending corps members into districts experiencing staff reductions, or into functional charter schools with already high test scores, betrays Kopp's original mission, to send the youngest and least experienced teachers only to schools experiencing shortages of qualified teachers. One of the alumni critics is Steve Zimmer, a member of the Los Angeles school board who had tried to carve a middle path between accountability reformers and the teachers union—only to find, after he was endorsed by the union, that reform philanthropists began heavily funding his challenger, whom he nonetheless defeated in 2013. "There are still places in the United States where it is difficult or

---

* Districts and charters pay TFA $2,000 to $5,000 per corps member, which helps cover the costs of the summer institute and the support TFA provides to its teachers during the school year.

impossible to staff schools," Zimmer said, mentioning rural areas. "And that's where TFA should be. It shouldn't be in charter schools."

Robert Schwartz agrees. He taught for seven years at Stevenson Middle School in East L.A., where TFA placed him in 1994. He then jumped over to the charter school sector, where he eventually became the chief academic officer of the Inner City Education Foundation (ICEF), a fifteen-school network. At ICEF, he often hired TFA alumni as teachers. They had taught for two years in the toughest schools in the city, then decided to stay in teaching beyond their initial commitments. That was impressive. They also knew how to analyze student performance data, a priority at ICEF. But he preferred to avoid first-year teachers who were learning on the job and were unlikely to commit to his schools long term, including TFA corps members, and he says that new teachers with only five weeks of training should be working only at schools that lack better options.

Teach for America alumni are popping up in another unexpected place: charter school unionization campaigns. Rob Timberlake, a member of Teach for America's 2010 corps, was one of several TFA alumni leaders of the union drive at Detroit's four César Chávez charter schools, part of the larger Leona Group, a for-profit network active in five states. At the end of each school year, Timberlake says, his principal would lay off "at least one or two teachers, and those were unexpected." Some of his colleagues had received evaluation reports when no administrator had visited their classroom for an observation, and it was unclear to teachers how they might earn a raise or promotion. "One of the interests I and other teachers had in organizing was to make sure there was a process for teachers to work on improving their practice, rather than a process for merely getting rid of lower performers," Timberlake said. "Before I came to Detroit, I thought the conversation was 'unions vs. TFA.' But it's not as clear-cut as that. People are attracted to the social justice aspects of TFA's mission, and union organizing follows in line with that. It's about trying to correct what teachers in the community see as problems with the school system."

Twelve percent of charter schools are now unionized, but that number may grow quickly. New York, Detroit, Los Angeles, and

Philadelphia have all experienced bursts in charter organizing. In Chicago, where the teacher wars have been the nastiest in recent years, a quarter of charters are now represented by the AFT. The "no excuses" ideology of many of these schools—they expect teachers to work twelve hours a day, hold weekend test-prep sessions, and be available at all times by e-mail or phone—motivates some teachers, especially those who intend to teach for more than just a few years, to seek representation. "There's a problem when we're creating a job you can't do if you have kids," Dennis Van Roekel, former president of the National Education Association, told me. "There are a lot of us who spend too much time working. But ultimately, you need time for family, time for community, time for church."

According to a union executive who has negotiated charter school contracts across the country, at many schools teachers are expected to eat lunch with their students, and have no prep period to plan lessons. At others, when a teacher calls in sick, the school will not hire a substitute, but will instead require other teachers to fill in during their prep periods. At one Chicago charter school, teachers complained that they had so little free time during the day that they could not visit the bathroom. Some of the most prominent charter school and TFA funders were interested in these models in part because of their potential to weaken teachers unions' sway over education policy.* By making their schools particularly difficult— even unpleasant—environments in which to work, some charter school outfits are opening the door for a new generation of educators to seek protection in teachers unions.

By 2011 results of value-added reform efforts began to trickle in. Research from the National Center on Performance Incentives at Vanderbilt University found that where teachers had been eligible for bonuses according to value-added ratings, whether $3,000 per

---

* The foundation run by the Walton family, the descendants of the Walmart founders, is a key TFA funder, and has also contributed to the National Right to Work Legal Defense Foundation, an anti-union group.

teacher in New York City or $15,000 per teacher in Nashville, student outcomes did not seem to improve. In Austin, where teachers could earn up to $3,000, only a third of teachers reported changing their practice in response to the incentives. As in previous experiments in merit pay, the assumption underlying these policies was simply incorrect. Underperforming teachers were not hiding some sort of amazing skill set they failed to use either because they were too lazy or were disgruntled about low pay; they were already trying as hard as they could to improve student learning, but they did not have the skills to do so. This seemed to suggest that, absent serious professional development efforts, merit pay was a nonstarter in terms of raising student achievement.

The push to change how teachers were evaluated did, however, impact teachers' working lives. Principals were spending more time than ever before in classrooms, and more time filling out paperwork describing what they had seen there. In New York City in 2012, under pressure from the Bloomberg administration, nearly half of all teachers who applied for tenure were denied; 3 percent of those were fired, and the rest were kept on probation. Just five years earlier 97 percent of teachers who applied for tenure had been approved.

In Washington, D.C., by 2012 10 percent of the teacher corps had been laid off based on performance evaluations. It's worth looking more deeply at Washington, in part because Michelle Rhee's agenda for teachers anticipated, by several years, many of the policy trends that Race to the Top spread nationwide. Despite the wave of research suggesting that merit pay was ineffective at raising student achievement, the District of Columbia stuck with its plan. Each year, six hundred to seven hundred teachers were offered annual bonuses, typically of $15,000 or less, though 20 to 30 percent of them were turning the money down because they were unwilling to lose their tenure protections in exchange. The city's average teacher salary rose to $77,512, higher than in the surrounding suburbs or in the region's charter schools. But only one or two teachers per year, out of four thousand, earned the city's top bonus of $25,000. Perhaps the biggest question is whether D.C. will be able to afford this generous pay moving forward: The program's philanthropic funding has run out, and it now costs the district $6 million annually.

Was teaching improving in D.C.? A 2013 study reported hopeful results. It found a significant number of low-rated teachers were choosing on their own to leave the district, while those low-rated teachers who stayed produced higher student test scores the following year. A separate report from The New Teacher Project presented more mixed evidence. It found 88 percent of the city's highest-rated teachers chose to stay, yet highly rated teachers who left were more likely than teachers in other districts to cite the evaluation system itself as one of the reasons they were unhappy. Historically, teachers have gotten little feedback on what they need to do better, much less how. New systems were meant to offer improvements, but often they failed to. Indeed, professional development in D.C. remained patchy, with only one-third of low-performing teachers and one-quarter of high-performing teachers reporting that they had received constructive feedback on their practice. Even more problematically, the data revealed that inexperienced and low-performing teachers were increasingly clustered in the city's poorest neighborhoods, east of the Anacostia River. It was unclear why this was the case: because it was easier to score well if one worked in a middle-class school, or because many effective teachers in D.C. were avoiding high-poverty schools.

To address these problems, in 2012 Michelle Rhee's successor, Kaya Henderson, accelerated the pace at which teachers in high-poverty schools could qualify for financial bonuses tied to student performance, hoping to make working in those schools more attractive. She also decreased the amount of teachers' evaluation scores tied to value-added, from 50 to 35 percent in tested subjects and grades, and she added a new evaluation category to reward teachers for "commitment to school community."

Those shifts to a more holistic system of teacher evaluation were overshadowed by a series of exposés, published by Jack Gillum and Marisol Bello of USA Today, demonstrating that during Rhee's chancellorship, the test-maker CTB/McGraw-Hill flagged hundreds of D.C. classrooms for statistically improbable answer sheet erasure rates on state tests, possible evidence that adults had corrected students' mistakes. The average child erases zero, one, or two answers on a multiple-choice test; typical answer sheets at one

D.C. school, the Noyes Education Campus, contained between five and twelve erasures, depending on the classroom. The school's principal, Wayne Ryan, resigned in disgrace, but only after collecting $20,000 in bonuses attached to test score increases.

Noyes was not an isolated case. Increasingly, there was evidence that a significant number of unscrupulous administrators and teachers nationwide had responded to the higher stakes attached to state-level standardized tests—evaluations, bonus pay, and public release of data—by cheating. The same *USA Today* team that revealed the D.C. irregularities studied six other states and found over sixteen hundred examples of probable test score manipulation between 2002 and 2010. (The newspaper would have almost certainly found even more cheating had it not zeroed in on only the most suspicious test score leaps: those that statisticians said were about as likely to be legitimate as a Powerball ticket was to be a winner. For example: At one Gainesville, Florida, elementary school, math proficiency rates jumped from 5 percent to 91 percent in three years.) A subsequent investigation by the *Atlanta Journal-Constitution* discovered 196 school districts across the country with suspicious test score gains.

Atlanta itself was the site of the nation's most infamous recent cheating scandal. On March 29, 2013, thirty-five Atlanta teachers and administrators, including the city's former superintendent, Beverly Hall, were indicted. The grand jury report revealed a shockingly sick culture of adult cheating, in which Hall, who had been the 2009 national "superintendent of the year," fired whistle-blowers and protected the jobs of employees who purposefully sat struggling kids next to high-performing ones to encourage cheating on tests, and who gathered at afterschool "erasure parties" to correct multiple-choice answer sheets before submitting them to be graded. Teachers and principals in Atlanta could earn thousands of dollars in bonuses for raising scores; Hall's bonuses totaled $580,000.

In the wake of this appalling ethical lapse, which resulted in thousands of Atlanta children—largely poor and black—being told they had acquired crucial academic skills they actually lacked, accountability reformers rushed to defend high-stakes testing policies. "The existence of cheating says nothing about the merits of testing," Arne Duncan argued in the *Washington Post*. Bill Gates said that cheating represented just a "tiny" rounding error in the landscape of standardized testing. They all advocated blaming the adult cheaters while absolving the policies that provided incentives to cheat.

Even where no systemic cheating was alleged, there were disappointments with the new teacher evaluation schemes. When New York City released value-added data for individual teachers in 2012—and the *Times* and other news organizations made them searchable by teachers' names—the margin of error was a staggering 53 points out of 100 for English teachers and 35 points out of 100 for math teachers. Numbers like that forced even strong supporters of data-driven accountability, including Bill Gates, Wendy Kopp, and Doug Harris, to speak out against the public release of such data. Kati Haycock began to worry that reformers, including many of her allies, had run "roughshod over those who were anxious about whether value-added was strong enough to support all of this . . . There are voices who said, 'Do it anyway! This is the moment!' Those people may still be right, but I count myself among a group of folks who are saying, as mad as I was about how slow we went before Race to the Top, I think I might be almost more upset now about the decision to go faster than these systems can handle."

Chester Finn, the moderate Republican reformer and former assistant secretary of education in the Reagan administration, agrees. "We'll probably discover ten years from now you can't do truly quantitative achievement-based evaluation of teachers with any great reliability," he told me. This is the typical hype-disillusionment cycle in American education reform, driven by moral panic about bad teaching.

Already there is some evidence that the new Race to the Top evaluation systems are failing to meaningfully distinguish between teachers, in much the same way that past evaluation systems failed. In Michigan and Tennessee in 2012, 98 percent of teachers were rated effective or better; in Florida, 95 percent; and in Georgia, 94 percent—numbers hardly different from those under the old systems.

It is unclear exactly why this is happening, but we can wager a few guesses. It could be that, as in the past, principals are not taking the time to thoroughly evaluate each teacher on the classroom observation components of these systems, either because of the large administrative burden this imposes—Florida's observation system requires ratings in sixty categories for each teacher—or because they lack the training in how to do so.

Teachers union leaders have suggested the low ineffective rates prove that only a tiny fraction of teachers, after all, are bad at their jobs. Before you dismiss this response as self-serving, consider this: Even tough reformers like Colorado state senator Mike Johnston say they'd like to see only the bottom 5 to 10 percent of teachers fired each year. Economist Eric Hanushek has even written, "The majority of [American] teachers are effective. They are able to compete with teachers virtually anywhere else in the world." If only a small minority of teachers are truly terrible, then evaluation systems that flag 2 to 6 percent of a state's teachers as problematic, produce layoffs of 10 percent of teachers in D.C., and deny or defer 50 percent of teachers tenure in New York City represent a huge step forward toward a more accountable profession. In New Haven, a new union contract eliminated tenure protections for just the 2 percent of teachers declared "ineffective" annually. Superintendent Garth Harries, an accountability reformer, is satisfied. "I think the 2 percent represents a real and significant number of teachers," he told me. "In the end, it's not a huge number, but the fact that these teachers are, in fact, leaving for reasons directly rated to performance has a fairly profound impact on the rest of the force. Folks saying, 'Thank God!' and folks saying, 'They're serious. I have to make sure I get my act together!' If we're truly going to have a professional construct for teaching, I don't think there's a set number of teachers we remove and then we're done. I don't think I'd want it to be below 2 percent [annually]. But I'd be perfectly happy with 2 percent in perpetuity."

Jonah Rockoff, a coauthor of the landmark value-added study linking test score growth to later income, says that because of concerns over teaching to the test, the next frontier for research will be to measure a teacher's impact in new ways. That could be done by looking at how teachers influence student behavior, attendance, or GPA. "We all know test scores are limited not just in their power and accuracy, but in the scope of what we want teachers and schools to be teaching our kids," Rockoff said. "If we had a more holistic view of teaching, that would be great. But I don't mean touchy-feely, 'you can teach however you want.' It's the idea that there's not just one thing we care about our kids learning. We're going to measure how kids do on socio-cognitive outcomes and reward teachers on that, too."

But as Arne Duncan has acknowledged, states can't simply use value-added to "fire their way to the top." Even if test scores were a flawless reflection of student learning and teacher quality, there is no evidence that the new teachers who replace the bad teachers will be any better—it is practically impossible to predict, via demographic traits, test scores, grades, or pathway into the profession, who will become an effective teacher.

Research and experience demonstrate that it makes good sense to tie teacher tenure and job security more closely to performance, and less to seniority. The contract provisions of the 1960s and 1970s make less sense now that we know so much more about how teachers' mind-sets and practices impact children's learning. But the history of American public education shows that teachers are uniquely vulnerable to political pressures and moral panics that have nothing to do with the quality of their work. Even Michelle Rhee says she believes in due process, as long as the process of grieving a termination is conducted quickly. "I'd seen too many examples of good teachers who had been railroaded by ineffective administrators," she wrote in her memoir. "Those teachers had to have a structure through which they could appeal evaluations when appropriate."

If the key to systemwide improvement is not through mass firings or union-busting, then what remains is to turn the existing average teacher into an expert practitioner, what Rockoff calls "moving the big middle" of the teaching profession. That effort will require a lot more than data—it will require a shared vision of what excellent teaching looks like, and the mentorship and training to get teachers there.

Chapter Ten

"Let Me Use What I Know"

REFORMING EDUCATION BY EMPOWERING TEACHERS

To many American teachers, the last decade of value-added school reform has felt like something imposed on them from outside and from above—by politicians with little expertise in teaching and learning, by corporate philanthropists who long to remake education in the mold of the business world, and by economists who see teaching as less of an art than a science. According to a 2013 poll conducted by Scholastic and the Gates Foundation, the majority of American teachers feel alienated from education policy making, with only a third reporting that their opinions are valued at the district level, 5 percent reporting they are valued at the state level, and just 2 percent reporting they are valued at the national level. Those frustrations have begun to break into the public debate. Dissident teachers and their unions are winning support from parent activists who are protesting the increased number of standardized tests, the time spent on test prep, and the lack of instructional time for projects, field trips, art, and music. Testing is a part of any functional education system, but in recent years it has often seemed like the horse of school improvement has been driven by the cart of collecting student data to be used in teacher evaluation. Meanwhile, more and more accountability reformers acknowledge that new teacher evaluation systems are not a panacea. They identify only a small number of teachers as ineffective, and do nothing, on their own, to guarantee that teachers' skills will actually improve over time. The hope that collecting more test scores will raise student achievement is like the hope that buying a scale will result in losing weight. We now have a lot of numbers to back up our inkling that something is wrong. But if we don't start improving instruction in the classroom, those numbers simply will not change.

"No excuses" strategies are not the only promising avenue for instructional reform. In the long term, reform programs that combine high-stakes standardized tests with scripted lesson plans and a limited arsenal of pedagogical strategies may make teaching a less attractive job for exactly the sort of ambitious, creative, high-achieving people we most want to attract. Polls of teachers who leave the profession show many did so because they received no constructive feedback on their practice, they had too little time to think creatively and collaborate with colleagues, and they had no opportunity to take on additional responsibilities and grow as professionals. So the next step in American education reform may be to focus less on top-down efforts to ferret out the worst teachers or turn them into automatons, and more on classroom-up interventions that replicate the practices of the best. Today reformers across the country are experimenting with empowering teachers to coach their peers, to remake teacher education, to design creative curriculum materials, and to lead school turnaround efforts. These practices conceive of veteran teachers as assets, not liabilities. As history has taught us, that is a pragmatic stance crucial to sustaining any reform program, which teachers must carry out on the ground.

Race to the Top focused attention on the teacher evaluation process, particularly on how student test scores are used to judge teachers. But in every state, a large, if not dominant, part of a teacher's evaluation score is still tied to classroom observations.

Observation is a challenging endeavor, in large part because it can be so subjective. Remember William Maxwell? He was the superintendent in turn-of-the-century New York City who complained that 99.5 percent of teachers were being evaluated as "good." He created a complex new A–D system based on principal observations and ratings, in which, it turned out, the vast majority of principals rushed through the motions and gave all their teachers a

B+. For over a century, classroom observation has failed to successfully differentiate between teachers. So how can that change? How can observation capture what everyone knows—that some teachers are better than others—and what everyone doesn't yet know: What exactly makes them that way?

The importance of looking beyond value-added measurement to carefully watch how teachers work with children is underscored by new research on what actually occurs in many classrooms, especially those populated by low-income students. In 2009 economist Thomas Kane and the Bill and Melinda Gates Foundation began a massive study on teacher effectiveness, known as the MET (Measures of Effective Teaching) project. MET collected videos of 1,333 teachers at work and gave them to highly trained evaluators to analyze. The experts found that only a third of the classrooms showed evidence of teachers promoting intellectual growth beyond rote learning.

That aligns with past research. A 2011 observation of elementary school classrooms in Baltimore showed that the majority of teachers failed to use challenging vocabulary words, failed to ask questions that probed for conceptual understanding (as opposed to simply correct answers), and rarely led their classes in whole-group discussions. In the weeks before state standardized tests, the Baltimore teachers engaged in those desirable activities even less frequently than usual and also decreased their personal interactions with students, who were "spending a good deal of their time on paper and pencil skill-based worksheets that did not require critical thinking or collaboration," the researchers reported. A 2009 review of the research literature on teacher practices, including several studies of thousands of elementary school classrooms across the country, found that low-income children are likely to spend their school days drilling in low-level skills, like spelling, and watching teachers deal with poorly behaved students.

Maybe none of that matters, if multiple-choice worksheets help children learn. But research shows that when teachers promote more interactions among students and focus their lessons on concepts that are broader and more challenging than those represented on multiple-choice tests, children's scores on higher-level assessments—

like those that require writing—actually go up. Rigorous, interactive classrooms promote higher student achievement.

When I visited Harrison District 2, the Colorado school system that created standardized tests for every subject and grade level, I accompanied crusading superintendent Mike Miles on a round of classroom observations at Fox Meadows Middle School.* There is no collective bargaining in Harrison, so Miles had incredible autonomy in shaping teachers' working conditions. Teachers had to keep their classroom doors open at all times. They were told to expect up to sixteen surprise observations each semester from administrators, instructional coaches, or outside consultants. Teachers told me they felt constantly watched. A TFA corps member who generally supported Miles's accountability efforts described Harrison as "a high-anxiety district to work in."

This all seemed a little extreme. And since I hadn't been impressed with the quality of the district's paper tests in art or physical education, I was prepared to find the classroom observations less than compelling. But I was wrong. In spot observations of about ten or fifteen minutes each, Miles was able to make a series of insightful critiques of teachers' performance. He traveled through the school's hallways with a six-person team of administrators and consultants, some of whom were being trained in these new observation methods. When the group stepped into the classroom of a science teacher in her early twenties, the young woman began to tremble ever so slightly. She was conducting a lesson on "hypotheses, graphs, and data." But the activity she had assigned the seventh graders, reading a graph and answering questions about the values on it, had nothing to do with hypotheses, which Miles thought was the most important concept in the lesson. Out in the hallway, he discussed with his team what they had observed. "Did she get to the idea of using data to construct a hypothesis?" he asked. "No." He also noted that while the students worked in small groups, the teacher could have

---

* Miles has since left Harrison for a higher-profile job as the superintendent of the Dallas public schools.

been moving around the classroom more actively, making sure each child was participating.

In a social studies class, Miles was unimpressed with the teacher's assignment for students: "Using geographic facts, which Western European country most resembles Colorado?" It was vague, kind of boring, and far too easy. Plus, there was no map displayed of Europe, making it hard for the students, most of whom had never left Colorado, to visualize what they were learning about.

For a math teacher working with students on circumference, the superintendent suggested that instead of simply writing equations on the whiteboard, the teacher could have demonstrated the concept using a physical object, like a basketball. A second math teacher spent ten minutes—far too long—explaining that the word "denominator" referred to the bottom part of a fraction. "She's not a superstar," Miles said. He knew of an exemplary math teacher whose classroom this teacher should observe.

Before he left Fox Meadows that day, Miles took some time to evaluate the evaluators. Leafing through the notes the administrators and consultants had taken on each teacher, he said, "I'm not seeing enough validating comments. Every room I went into, I saw positive things." Later on he told me he thought the school had two to three "distinguished teachers," the district's highest designation, and perhaps four who would be dismissed at the end of the year, one of whom had tenure. In a school of thirty teachers, that was a roughly 14 percent ineffective rate.

There is nothing new about the idea of an administrator taking a detailed look at a teacher's classroom practice. Progressive Era reformers promoted "efficiency" observations, in which supervisors used lengthy rubrics to rate teachers according to measures like how many children were late to class or how many seconds it took to hand out worksheets. After World War II, a "supervisory visit" to a teacher's classroom might have entailed a principal judging whether sufficiently "democratic ideals" were being promoted in the lesson. By 1980 many school administrators used a "clinical" model to observe classrooms, a system based on medical rounds, popularized by Robert Goldhammer of Harvard's graduate-level teaching program. Principals would conduct pre-observation and post-observation conferences with teachers to reflect on their practice, areas for improvement, and long-term goals. But because Goldhammer had not defined specific characteristics of effective instruction, principals who used his model often failed to provide concrete, helpful feedback to teachers.

Later, Madeline Hunter's more prescriptive "lesson design" system became popular. Principals looked for whether a teacher's lesson included several key components, such as a lesson objective written on the board, a "model" of successful performance, and an opportunity for students to practice new concepts. Mike Miles was clearly influenced by the Hunter system—a combination of direct instruction and student group work, similar to how Teach for America expects its corps members to work. A criticism of Hunter is that she focused too much on teacher-directed behavior, and not enough on whether the teacher helped students become self-directed learners. Today there are other, potentially more sensitive classroom observation tools, and because of Race to the Top's emphasis on improving teacher evaluation, these methods are now being adopted in thousands of classrooms nationwide. The Classroom Assessment Scoring System, CLASS, was developed at the University of Virginia. It gives teachers numeric ratings based on whether they exhibit behaviors associated with achievement gains, such as "expanding on student talk"—repeating a child's speech back to her, using corrected grammar and more sophisticated vocabulary.

Another popular and detailed classroom observation model is embedded within Charlotte Danielson's Framework for Teaching, first developed in 1996. Danielson was a former Washington, D.C., public school teacher who went on to become an education researcher at Educational Testing Service, the test-maker. She knew that during the "competency" craze of the 1970s there had been a lot of vague talk about asking students "higher-order questions." Danielson wanted to watch teachers work, look at their students' performance, and figure out exactly what effective, higher-order instruction looked like. According to her findings, an effective classroom discussion question has more than one correct answer. (Not "When did Hitler come to power?" but "What social, political, and economic factors led to the Nazi Party gaining power in Germany? Which factors do you think were most crucial? Why?") Danielson found that an excellent teacher asks students to explain concepts to one another, instead of repeating herself ad nauseam. She highlights connections between disciplines—for example, by giving students background information on Elizabethan England before assigning a Shakespeare play. She chooses books and works of art from a broad range of cultures, including the cultures from which her students hail. She allows students to debate one another in class, and requires them to cite evidence to support their claims. If the teacher is really skilled, the students can talk among themselves for many minutes about the topic at hand without her interrupting. She assesses her students throughout a unit, not just at the beginning and end, through pointed questioning and the use of tricks like "exit slips"—quick problems students must solve, on paper, before they leave the classroom.

In New York City, principals must now use the Danielson framework to observe each teacher's classroom at least four times per school year, and to conference with each teacher for professional development. If there is a downside to systems like these it is that most research-driven observation rubrics require administrators to rate teachers on many, many different competencies—twenty-two in the Danielson framework. Historically, evaluation systems with heavy time and paperwork burdens have not been viable in the long term, because principals either go through the motions without making meaningful distinctions among teachers, or they find ways to use the great number of subjective variables in these rubrics—for example, "compliance with standards of conduct," in Danielson's framework—as a way to target disfavored teachers for dismissal, regardless of more objective measures of performance.

One of the most frequent complaints I heard from teachers about classroom observation in Harrison District 2 (and many of the other school systems I've visited) was that consultants and other non-teacher observers had a poor understanding of curricular content and so failed to provide relevant feedback. Bringing respected teachers into these observation processes as peer coaches and evaluators can not only lighten administrators' workloads, but also greatly increase teacher buy-in. To do that, accountability reformers and teachers unions are taking a second look at teacher peer review, the practice first developed in Toledo in 1981.

Bob Lowe, a thin, short man in his fifties, was a little jittery when he arrived at a drab suburban conference room at the headquarters of the Montgomery County Education Association, his union, on a rainy morning in June. He was there to fight for the continuation of a thirty-three-year teaching career.*

Lowe had to make his case to a panel of eight teachers and eight principals who had been selected by their unions and the county school district as expert practitioners. The panel had already heard from Lowe's boss, the principal of a large, diverse suburban high school. She had tried everything to help Lowe improve as a teacher, she said, even assigning one of her deputies to spend 60 percent of her day in his classroom. But he was disorganized—he turned his grades in late and lost student work. In class he lectured in front of the room, sharing anecdotes from history that often amused students. But he offered little sense of the lesson's objectives or what students would have to do to perform well on an essay or test. The teenagers lost focus and wandered around the room. Even his honors kids did poorly on final exams.

It wasn't easy for the principal to recommend Lowe's dismissal. He was a big part of the school community. Every year he hosted a cultural exchange with a Russian high school, whose students visited Maryland. "He is an extremely good person, a good man," the principal said. "Students generally like him. He has a passion and deep knowledge of his content area. But he can't *teach* this to his students."

The panel had also heard a report from Lowe's "consulting teacher" (CT), part of a fleet of peer coaches, one of whom Mont-

* The names and several identifying characteristics of Bob Lowe and the other teachers called before the Montgomery County Peer Assistance and Review board have been changed to protect their privacy.

gomery County assigns to every novice teacher and to veteran teachers flagged by a principal for underperformance. Consulting teachers work full-time as coaches and evaluators for three years, earning a $5,000 bonus above their regular teaching salary, and then return to classroom positions. The report from Lowe's CT included an actual script from several of Lowe's lessons, and it didn't sound good. Lowe's directions to students were so vague that he had to re-explain one assignment three times. During a five-minute warm-up activity, he demanded the students' attention seven times. He spent nine minutes having kids rearrange their desks to transition to a new activity, and he allowed struggling students to evade participation in class discussions. At his coaching sessions, Lowe had attempted to explain away his poor performance by recounting family tragedies and medical problems.

By the time Lowe appeared to plead his case, the outlook was grim. He spoke about his love for the county's public education system, which he had attended as a student and where his own children went to school. "I never wanted to be anything other than a teacher," he said. "I'm a third-generation teacher. My sisters are teachers. I don't know what I'd do if I weren't a teacher." But it was clear that expectations had risen at his school and he hadn't kept up. Tracking student data had not been a demand earlier in his career, nor had aligning lesson plans to specific curriculum standards. His lectures were, in his own words, "ad hoc." Yes, he admitted, more of his students were failing this year than at any time in the past six years. He seemed to blame the kids. "Am I unclear, or are they deer in the headlights?" he pondered. "Some kids are like that most of the time." He demonstrated the terrified deer, stiffening his entire body and staring wide-eyed into the distance. In the end, he simply pleaded for mercy. "I just hope that I can end my career with some dignity."

After Lowe's presentation he left the room. Since his principal was actually a member of the peer-review panel, she recused herself, as did another member, a teacher who had taught Lowe's daughter. There were fourteen judges left, solemnly perusing huge binders full of information on Lowe and his students, including grades, test scores, e-mails from parents, and photographs the principal had taken of his messy classroom. How many of his students were classified as special education, the panel discussed? Had that made his job tougher? Lowe had been in peer review once before, five years ago. Had anything improved since then?

One young teacher on the panel seemed to have made up her mind. "I don't believe more support would help him," she said. "He's not leading the students strongly enough. I see no strategies or methodologies for improvement." A principal agreed. "He rambled on. If he teaches like this, how can there be clarity for students?"

In the end, the panel voted unanimously for dismissal. Union vice president Christopher Lloyd, a lanky middle school teacher, went upstairs to tell Lowe his career in Montgomery County was over. When Lloyd returned to the conference room, his face was drawn. But he gave the peer-review panel a pep talk. In Toledo teachers can remain in the peer-review system indefinitely, as long as they show some small amount of improvement. "That's not the philosophy of our system," Lloyd said. Struggling teachers are owed at least one year of intensive coaching on lesson planning, the use of student data, and classroom management. But ultimately, "teachers need to be able to support themselves on their own. . . . We own this process, and it's something very important to us as an association. We have to be about protecting the profession, not just about protecting anything that breathes."

Peer review has sometimes been portrayed as a sort of union front; a faux accountability plan labor leaders use to distract policy makers from demands to end tenure and use test scores to evaluate teachers. It is true that in Montgomery County, a district of more than nine thousand teachers, only forty-one were dismissed or pressured to resign in 2013 through the peer-review process. At least eight of those were tenured teachers, including Lowe. These low numbers are typical of many of the older peer-review systems across the country. Journalist John Merrow ran the numbers in Toledo in 2010 and found that the nation's first and most prominent peer-review system terminated 8 percent of first-year teachers annually, but only an average of two-tenths of 1 percent of tenured teachers, likely a much smaller figure than the true number of ineffective veteran teachers in the district.

In 2004 Montgomery County commissioned an outside report on peer review, which included a survey of principals. One of the questions the district wanted to answer was why so few tenured teachers per year were being put through the process. A number of principals replied that they were overburdened by paperwork and had missed deadlines for referring teachers. Others seemed emotionally reluctant to punish ineffective teaching, telling researcher Julia Koppich, "It's gut-wrenching. These [teachers] are not strangers. You know their stories. They're not evil people."

Koppich is not the only researcher to mention that principals seem reluctant to fire teachers. Economist Brian Jacob found that in the years after the Chicago Public Schools significantly reduced the paperwork burden for dismissing nontenured teachers, 30 to 40 percent of principals chose not to dismiss a single staffer. Why? It may be that principals fear replacement teachers will be just as bad as ineffective ones who are laid off. Kati Haycock, the president of the Education Trust, has heard another theory: "Maybe the problem is that your best principals don't give up on a single kid, and they don't give up on a teacher, either."

Supporters of peer review say it is a mistake to judge these systems solely on how many teachers they dismiss; rather, the ideal outcome of the process is helping a struggling teacher develop into an effective one. "The worst thing you can do is fire someone," says Dennis Van Roekel, the former NEA president. "It means you've lost all of your investment in recruiting and training."

Peer review is also criticized as too little concerned with student achievement outcomes. Montgomery County was initially denied Race to the Top funding because it refused to give value-added scores a fixed weight in its teacher evaluation process. But "data" was one of the most frequently spoken words in that June day of peer-review deliberations. In one case, a tenured pre-K teacher had adjusted special-ed students' learning plans without presenting supporting data to parents—a big problem. The panel voted to enroll her in peer review for the following year, to help her develop student assessment skills. If she did not improve, she could be dismissed.

The next case was of a nontenured teacher in a fourth-grade language immersion program. She was a native Spanish speaker in her midthirties who had moved to Montgomery County after teaching in another Maryland district. Her principal reported that the teacher had increased the reading skills of her gifted and talented students by only 1.84 book levels—less than he thought was reasonable—and in math, test scores showed 26 percent of her gifted students had made no progress at all. In that case, after interviewing the teacher and looking closely at the principal's supporting documents, the panel chose to return her to the regular teaching pool. It turned out the teacher had been assigned an especially large class of twenty-nine fifth graders, including all of the grade level's special-education students, some of whose parents had requested her. She had worked successfully with one boy with selective mutism, a condition in which a child will not speak in social situations. That boy now participated in class discussions. "I'm really happy about that," the teacher said. But she left the room knowing she had serious work to do on differentiation—making sure that her class is as challenging as possible for both special-education and gifted kids. She would have the opportunity to apply for tenure in the future, though there was no guarantee she would earn it.

Given the massive changes in expectations for teachers over the past decade—the requirement that they become technicians of measurable student achievement—it makes sense that many veterans need additional training. And the truth is that few principals can offer struggling teachers the level of support peer-review systems are designed to provide. Historically, principals served as building and personnel managers while teachers made instructional decisions mostly on their own. At teachers colleges, "autonomy" in the individual classroom has been promoted as a key ethos of the profession. But when taken too literally, autonomy can create a situation in which classrooms are so-called "black boxes," places impenetrable to outside observation or constructive critique. Now principals are expected to do their old managerial jobs and oversee instruction, too—what and how students are learning. That growing bucket of responsibilities is often an untenable load, given that the average American principal or assistant principal oversees twenty to forty teachers, compared to an eight- to ten-employee "span of control" in most other professions. Consulting teachers in Montgomery

County, Toledo, Rochester, and other districts that use peer review have caseloads of ten to twenty teachers per year—still a lot of work, but, unlike principals, they are focused 100 percent on improving instruction.

Peer review also offers districts the opportunity to reward the best teachers with mentor roles. And it can save money: Replacing a teacher costs a district, on average, $10,000 in recruitment and training fees, while peer review costs just $4,000 to $7,000 per teacher served. Newer peer-review systems tend to be much more aggressive than the one in Montgomery County. In Newark, a new teacher evaluation process based partially on value-added has declared 20 percent of the city's teachers either "ineffective" or only "partially effective." All low-rated teachers receive peer assistance and review and lose their right to raises for years of service. In Baltimore a landmark contract ended seniority raises for all teachers and instead moves teachers through a series of steps related to job performance, called standard, professional, mentor, and lead. Peer evaluators, who observe videotapes of lessons, grant teachers some of the points that move them forward in the progression. Other points are distributed by administrators to reward teachers for taking on extra responsibilities, like leading afterschool tutoring sessions.

In Saint Louis, tenured teachers flagged for poor performance have the choice to either keep or waive their tenure rights. If a teacher keeps tenure, she has only eighteen weeks to demonstrate progress in the classroom, after which the district can pursue a termination hearing. If a teacher waives tenure, she has a full year to work with a peer coach; if she improves, she re-earns tenure, and if she does not she can be dismissed by a panel of teachers and principals. All first-year teachers in Saint Louis participate in peer mentorship and review, with the goal of convincing more of them to stay on for that critical second year, when research shows teacher effectiveness takes a huge leap. Between 2011 and 2013, 7 percent of Saint Louis teachers were terminated under this system. Yet Randi Weingarten has said "the powers that be in this country" should celebrate the Saint Louis Plan as a model of union-management cooperation.

Accountability reformers who once saw peer review as too soft on teachers have become more sympathetic to the idea, in part because embracing the practice has allowed districts like Saint Louis, Newark, and Baltimore to negotiate huge concessions from unions on seniority. And the Gates Foundation MET study found that when teachers are observed by both principals and peers, observation scores are more likely to match value-added ratings than when principals alone do the observing. The MET project's concluding report had a peculiar circular logic, in which all teacher evaluation methods were judged according to how strongly they correlated with value-added scores. Given the Gates Foundation's longtime orientation toward measurable student achievement gains, that is no surprise. Yet another interpretation of the study's results is that classroom observations and value-added scores actually measure different elements of successful teaching, and thus should be used side by side even—perhaps especially—when they do turn up different results.

An obvious benefit of taking classroom observation seriously is that once a supervisor or peer coach has identified the strategies of the most effective teachers, he or she can teach them to other teachers. "If all you do is judge teachers by test results, it doesn't tell you what you should do differently," says Charlotte Danielson, the observation pioneer.

Watching a great teacher at work can feel like watching a magic show.

Lenore Furman's seventeen kindergarteners at Abington Avenue, a high-poverty, largely Latino public elementary school in Newark, were rapt as they sang along with Furman's guitar in English and Spanish, then settled into a circle for story time. Furman had selected *Time to Sleep,* by Denise Fleming. The lushly illustrated book is about how animals experience the transition from fall to winter, a perfect topic for a chilly November day. As Furman read, she stopped to review some difficult vocabulary words related to animal hibernation: "burrow," "perch," "trudge," and "slither." "The turtle trudged up the hill," she said. "That means he kind of walked slowly. It was hard for him. Turtles have little legs. He trudged." On another page, she called attention to the difference between "worm" and "worms." The children practiced the two different pronunciations as Furman pointed at the words. In the middle of the book she paused for a "turn and talk," in which each student discussed with a partner what had happened in the story so far, and what he predicted might happen next.

After story time Furman asked who would like to tell the class a personal story. Hands shot up. There were five weekly vocabulary words, all very simple, that the kids were supposed to practice using in spoken and written sentences: *mom, dad, me, go,* and *this.* One little girl said she banged her foot and her dad put a Band-Aid on it. The class then worked independently to write two full sentences each as Furman and a teacher's aide circulated, working with students one-on-one.

It is rare for a kindergarten classroom to feature such a strategic balance between teacher-led instruction, peer dialogue, and individual work. And it was magical how Furman seemed to be simultaneously teaching at two levels—an advanced level, with the hibernation vocabulary, and a basic one, with the emphasis on learning one-syllable words. Her expertise displayed just how complex good teaching is. But her practice is not magic, nor does it rely solely on some innate talent for teaching. What I saw was a set of research-based early childhood reading strategies developed by the Children's Literacy Initiative, a Philadelphia nonprofit. The underlying methods are simple: Children need to encounter a new word three times before they learn it. Not only are singing and chanting fun; they are also proven to help kids remember vocabulary. The "turn and talk" is meant to take advantage of what researchers call "peer effects," the fact that discussing a new idea with a peer is often a more effective learning strategy than hearing a teacher repeat it over and over. Content-related vocabulary—words that describe concepts in social studies and science, like hibernation or metamorphosis—are the ones that most grow a child's academic potential. While teaching is often characterized as a field in which there are few broadly agreed-upon best practices, early childhood reading is an exception. "Teaching reading is a science," says Caryn Henning, who directs CLI's work in Newark. "You need specialized training."

The Children's Literacy Initiative used a $26 million grant from the Obama administration to provide teachers in fourteen of Newark's forty-nine elementary schools with three years of training in how to teach kindergarteners through third graders, including English-language learners, to read. At each school, one expert teacher, like Lenore Furman, was identified as a "model" whose classroom door would always be open for observations, and whom other teachers could go to for coaching. Furman has taught at Abington Avenue for thirty years, and has been playing that role informally for a very long time. She stays current on teaching strategies by visiting high-achieving classrooms in other districts, a practice CLI supports.

The organization's theory of change—teachers teaching teachers, outside formal evaluation systems—works. An initial study of the program released in 2014 found kindergarteners in schools with CLI model classrooms in Newark, Philadelphia, Camden, and Chicago outperformed their peers in reading. A 2010 randomized trial showed that over the course of the kindergarten year, students in Philadelphia schools with CLI model classrooms gained an average of 8.3 percentage points more on reading assessments than did demographically similar students in schools without model classrooms. These are large gains. Most of the education research cited in the news is based on test scores in math. In part, that's because it is easier for schools and teachers to increase math achievement than it is for them to increase reading achievement, since most children learn math only at school, while reading ability is closely tied to the books and vocabulary children are exposed to at home. The problem with basing so much education policy making on math test scores is that reading skill is more closely tied to life outcomes than math skill is. The Raj Chetty, Jonah Rockoff, and John Friedman study confirmed that—by showing that teachers with high value-added scores in reading had more of an impact on their students' future well-being than teachers with high value-added scores in math. That backs up what education researchers have known for a long time: that a child who ends third grade below level in reading will likely never catch up to his peers, and has a disproportionate chance of dropping out of high school. Reading is the foundation for almost every other type of learning a child or adult will do, from word problems in math, to learning tough new scientific vocabulary, to comprehending a history textbook or even a medical consent form.

One of the frustrating things about programs like CLI, which focus on empowering teachers to share effective instructional practices, is that so few people have heard of them. I visited Furman's classroom in October 2010, just a few weeks after Facebook founder Mark Zuckerberg announced on *The Oprah Winfrey Show* that he was making a $100 million donation to the Newark public schools.* Zuckerberg's donation, alongside matching funds from other philanthropists, has supported mostly familiar policies. About half the money was spent on a three-year merit pay plan to reward teachers rated "highly effective." The money also went toward building a student data tracking system, opening new charter schools, and hiring more TFA teachers. A relatively small grant—$100,000—was used to develop a new "early literacy initiative" through BRICK, a school turnaround group. But none of the millions went to expand the nationally recognized early literacy program that was already operating successfully in fourteen Newark schools.

It is difficult to achieve policy or instructional coherence in a school reform climate in which priorities are constantly changing with each new governor, superintendent, or big donor. Evidence-backed programs, like CLI, are rarely replicated so they can reach every school in a district. "Too much school reform is about blowing up systems," says Jen Weikert, CLI's director of communications and giving. "What we know is that no matter how many systems you blow up, you can't charter-ize everything. We feel like by helping teachers in the classroom, particularly within the public school system, we serve a major need. Unfortunately, we haven't gone to scale in any district that we're in."

---

* A year after I visited the Abington Avenue School in Newark, it was investigated by the state for possible adult cheating on standardized tests, and its principal was removed. The investigation was of grades three through eight, not kindergarten, and there is no suggestion the class or teacher portrayed here was involved.

During President Obama's second term, standards and account-ability reformers like Kati Haycock of Education Trust began focus-ing the kind of sustained attention on teachers colleges that they had once devoted to overhauling teacher evaluation and tenure. They urged Congress to pull federal funding—essentially, to shut down—teacher preparation programs whose students have SAT or ACT scores in the bottom third of the national distribution and who go on to have low value-added scores in the classroom, or who can't find jobs at all because they are underprepared. The concern about teachers colleges is not unwarranted. The nineteenth-century com-mon schoolers, the founders of the Teacher Corps in the 1960s, and the authors of *A Nation at Risk* had all acknowledged major prob-lems with teacher education in America. Today only half of teacher candidates undergo supervised student teaching in a real classroom, and most teacher education programs have no mechanism for mak-ing sure mentor teachers are themselves successful or trained in how to coach an adult peer. Undergraduate education majors often take few college-level courses in the subjects they will actually teach—an especially big problem for the elementary grades, which tend to attract prospective teachers who are personally hesitant about math and science, yet who are not required by their colleges to beef up their skills. Education classes for trainee teachers are often taught by PhD academics, who may or may not have firsthand experience in K–12 classrooms. These courses can focus more on theories of child development or multicultural education than on practical ways to deal with student discipline problems or offer feedback on kids' writing. And teachers colleges are overproducing elementary, English, and social studies teachers, while underproducing those ready to teach underserved students, like those who are learning English or are autistic.

Of course, the vast majority of teachers working today—including a majority of celebrated, excellent teachers—are alumni of teachers colleges or graduate programs in teaching. Yet a widely cited 2013 report from the National Council on Teacher Quality carried a damning conclusion: that the ideology of teacher "autonomy" in the classroom had diverted traditional teacher education programs from the hands-on skills teachers must build to help students learn. "Many in the field do not believe that training will arm novice teachers with skills that might make them more effective, as specific surgical methods are taught to medical students," the NCTQ researchers wrote. "Instead, the belief is that training only creates automatons, so it is better to instill in new teachers the 'professional mindset' that theoretically allows them to approach each new class thoughtfully and without any preconceived notions, much like a blank page that's been carefully bleached of any prejudices."

Teach for America offers one model for challenging the status quo in teacher education, by quickly providing its corps members with an intensely practical and prescriptive set of classroom strategies. But there are other alternative pathways into the teaching profession, too.

One of those models is the urban teacher residency. In 2010 Marcus Clark was a twenty-seven-year-old IT manager in Houston, working at a small business that made software for oil companies. His job was to manage computer hardware, including every employee's PC. "But I felt kind of frustrated, because I was living two lives," he said. "My professional life had nothing to do with what I was doing at church."

On weekends and after work, Clark, who is black, was leading a youth ministry at the Friendship Community Bible Church, work he loved. In the summer he volunteered to take students from the program to Kids Across America, an evangelical Christian camp in Missouri for urban youth of color. That's where he heard a presentation about the Memphis Teacher Residency (MTR), which recruits career changers into high-poverty classrooms. Unusual among programs attached to public schools, MTR specifically looks for people of faith. Its mission is not to proselytize to public school students, but to support teachers "in a Christian context," according to the group's Web site. "Teaching is a vocational response to the Gospel and an active participation in the work of the Church to glorify God by bringing justice to the poor and oppressed."

The Memphis Teacher Residency is about as competitive as Teach for America. Each year, only 13 to 18 percent of applicants are accepted. It allows aspiring teachers to enter the classroom before they have a teaching degree. And, like TFA, MTR is driven by the belief that high academic expectations can transform poor children's lives. But MTR and the eighteen other urban teacher residencies across the country (most of which have no faith component) differ from TFA in their conception of what makes an excellent teacher. First, residency programs favor candidates who are eager to commit to a longer career in public education, and who understand the community in which they are applying to work. Second, instead of giving recruits just five weeks of summer training, residency programs require them to spend one school year working full-time in a mentor teacher's classroom, while studying education at a local graduate school. They are paid a modest stipend ($12,000 in Memphis). Most first-year teachers say classroom discipline is their biggest challenge. Residents get to watch how a veteran teacher establishes discipline from the first moments of the first day of school. They then build their skills slowly, learning how to plan a lesson and deliver it effectively, while their mentor teacher and outside coaches critique their practice. In Memphis, residents wait until January of their first school year to do a three-week "lead teach," in which they take over full responsibility for the classroom. Residents' graduate classes and a weekly seminar they attend are designed to link theory and teaching strategies with their classroom experiences in real time.

Residents who complete the year successfully can be hired as full-time teachers and earn a regular salary. In Memphis, recruits are required to commit to teach in a high-poverty school for at least three years after their residency year, and if they back out, the consequences are serious: They are on the line to pay $10,000 to MTR for every year they fail to complete. Ninety percent of MTR's recruits are still working as teachers four years later. Nationwide, urban teacher residencies have an 87 percent retention rate at four years, compared to the loss of nearly half of all new urban teachers over a similar period of time, and two-thirds of Teach for America teachers.

In education, teacher retention matters. An eight-year study of 850,000 New York City fourth and fifth graders found that in schools with high teacher turnover, students lost significant amounts of learning in both reading and math compared to socioeconomically similar peers at schools with low teacher turnover—even if their own classroom teacher was not new, and even if overall teacher quality at the school remained constant. The negative effects of turnover were even higher in schools with many low-achieving or black students.

These results are common sense. At high-turnover schools, administrators spend more time recruiting, interviewing, and hiring, when they could be focused on improving instruction. When many teachers resign each year, institutional memory is lost, and ties to the community weaken. There are fewer veterans around to show newbies the tricks of the trade.

That is why the urban teacher residency model is so exciting. Teach for America cracked an important code in American education: With its 14 percent acceptance rate, it made teaching in high-poverty schools elite. When Thomas Kane, Douglas Staiger, and Robert Gordon studied 150,000 Los Angeles elementary school students, they found no large student achievement differences related to how a child's teacher entered the classroom: through a traditional college of education, TFA, or some other alternative route. But the study did find that, across the board, first-year teachers struggled and their students generally earned lower test scores than they had the year before. This is an important consideration for superintendents and principals as programs like Teach for America grow each year, and as veteran teachers are laid off. Some reformers, like Eric Hanushek, believe teacher churn is fine, as long as the new teachers coming in are high quality. But the latest research shows schools simply do not have an unlimited capacity to absorb and train first-year teachers, and that students suffer when they are assigned to a string of novice teachers in grade after grade. Where schools do need to hire newcomers, they'd be better off hiring ones who will stay.

Of course, every teacher must have a first year in the classroom, and there is a real lack of evidence that teachers colleges are especially good at selecting the best potential educators. Many teacher residencies use what's called the "star teacher" criteria to recruit and select nontraditional candidates. This is a system developed by Martin Haberman, a psychologist who died in 2012. Haberman studied the characteristics of teachers in high-poverty schools in several cities. His "stars" were those who were rated highly by principals and who stayed in their jobs for many years. It turned out the stars were more likely than unsuccessful teachers to be thirty or older, to have extensive work experience in fields other than education, to be parents, and to have a working-class black, Latino, or white background. Though they demonstrated deep content knowledge, many had graduated from non-elite colleges, and had often begun at community colleges. They had grown up in the city, not the suburbs, and already had experience spending time with low-income children, often as volunteers. Many hailed from church communities or families in which teaching was considered a high-status profession, not a fallback or an unusual choice for a well-educated person. They had already lived, or they wanted to live, long term in the city in which they would teach. And they were coachable—they responded quickly and well to critical feedback from mentors. In short, they were a lot like Marcus Clark, who was accepted into MTR. "God was really changing my heart to work with kids," he said.

By casting a wide net, urban teacher residencies have recruited an unusually diverse group of teachers. Forty percent are people of color (compared to 17 percent of teachers nationwide), 48 percent have been out of college for three years or more, and 39 percent have the content knowledge to teach the underserved STEM subjects: science, technology, engineering, and math.

The yearlong residency in a mentor's classroom—a requirement in high-achieving places like Finland and Shanghai—allows residency programs to screen out residents who, even with the intense coaching they receive, aren't able to develop into good teachers, typically 15 to 20 percent of residents per year. That level of rigor is attractive to ambitious people who want to be part of a select group of highly qualified professionals (and to principals looking to hire them). And unlike the typical student teaching program run by a college education department, urban teacher residencies have a selective process for identifying mentor teachers, who must show proof that they can raise student achievement, and who undergo training on how to provide other adults with helpful feedback.

Research from Urban Teacher Residency United, a national network of nineteen programs, shows that principals consistently rate urban teacher residency grads as more effective than other first-year teachers. In Memphis, residency grads produce higher student test score gains in fourth- and eighth-grade math, and they perform similarly to other teachers in reading, science, and social studies. A small, initial evaluation of the Boston Teacher Residency (BTR), one of the more established programs, found a mixed record on student achievement. In their first few years, Boston Teacher Residency teachers were no different from other teachers in English language arts, and they were less effective in math. But BTR graduates also improved much more rapidly than other teachers, and by year four they were outperforming both novices and veterans from other pathways. On retention, BTR was clearly superior, with 75 percent of teachers remaining through year five, compared to just 50 percent throughout the district. BTR graduates were also much more likely to be people of color (48 percent compared to 32 percent of the other teachers in the district) and were more likely to be qualified to teach math and science.

The fact that BTR graduates seem to struggle in their first year as teachers of record, despite the residency year, is disappointing. Like other research, this seems to suggest that the only way to truly learn how to manage one's own classroom is to actually do the job. Yet the researchers concluded that the big financial investment Boston is making in the teacher residency program is paid back over the course of residents' more stable careers, suggesting that over the long term, increasing the number of BTR teachers in the district could lead to overall student achievement gains.

The growing body of evidence on the importance of teacher retention has even changed the culture within Teach for America. In 2012 New York City's top TFA official, Jeff Li, announced he was stepping down to return to classroom teaching. He launched a campaign inside TFA called Teach Beyond 2, an effort to spread the message about how a longer classroom career could positively impact students. Two years later TFA's new co-CEOs, Elisa Villanueva Beard and Matt Kramer, announced two pilot programs: one to provide preselected college seniors with a full year of teacher training before they enter the classroom and one to provide up to five years of professional development support for corps alumni who continue to teach. "Teaching beyond two years cannot be a backup plan—it has to be the main plan," Kramer said in a March 2014 speech.

There is some evidence that today, more TFA corps members than in previous years are staying in the classroom beyond their two-year commitment. (The tough recession job market could be one reason why.) A 2010 independent study found 60 percent of TFA corps members still teaching after three years, a retention rate comparable to national averages in urban schools, though only 36 percent were still teaching after four years, fewer than average. About 85 percent of TFA teachers who stay in the profession, however, leave their initial placements to work at more desirable schools, a level of turnover that the researchers described as "very problematic" for those schools most struggling with low achievement.

At a July 2013 "listening session" I attended with corps members and alumni in Detroit, the co-CEOs acknowledged that over one-third of principals who work with TFA recruits have asked for a longer commitment. "Are we destabilizing communities?" Villanueva Beard asked. "That is one question we've got to take and really critically examine." She and Kramer have also promised to be more cautious about sending TFA recruits into regions with low demand for new teachers.

One telling difference between TFA and urban teacher residencies is that TFA has always embraced its outsider status. It uses its own, typically very young alumni to train corps members, and boasts about the achievements of famous TFAers, like Mike Johnston, Michelle Rhee, Dave Levin, and Mike Feinberg, who have challenged the educational establishment by opening nonunionized charter schools and pushing for weaker tenure laws and value-added evaluation of teachers. In that sense, TFA has always been as much a political movement as an organization focused on classroom instruction.* Urban teacher residencies are agnostic on the issue of traditional versus charter schools—they exist in both—but in

---

* In addition to TFA's partnerships with corporations like Google and Bain and Company, which allow recruits to defer employment while they serve as TFA corps

terms of day-to-day practice, they embrace the opportunity to work closely with teachers and unions already entrenched in the public school system.

"A lot of UTRs are working to really engage their local union in the design and development of these programs," says Christine Brennan Davis, the curriculum director at Urban Teacher Residency United. "Our model resonates with unions in the sense of the role of the mentor teacher. We value excellent veteran teachers and their role in preparing the next generation." Union partnerships have been helpful to UTRs politically, too. When the recession hit and teacher hiring freezes and layoffs became a reality, programs worked with unions to identify ways to keep bringing residents into the classroom, but only in the subjects and grade levels where they were truly needed.

At Kingsbury High School in Memphis, where Marcus Clark works, about a third of the school's teachers have participated in the Memphis Teacher Residency, as either residents or mentors. This degree of penetration, sometimes called the "teaching hospital" model, allows best practices tailored to a specific school to be passed from professional to professional. The close contact between veterans and trainees is a two-way street: Veterans may be great at classroom management, but trainee teachers may bring in new ideas from their courses about how to analyze student data. This model changes the typical direction of American school reform, from top down to bottom up. Instead of policy makers imposing a reform structure or pedagogical agenda on teachers, groups of teachers work together to improve a school. Though high-quality teacher residencies are currently producing only five hundred teachers per year, the exponential growth of Teach for America over the last two decades suggests that if philanthropists and policy makers were to recognize the value of this model, they might be able to scale it up relatively quickly—as long as effective classroom teachers were willing to participate as mentors.

---

members, TFA now sends some of its alumni directly into fellowships in congressional offices, where they advocate on education policy.

Alex Caputo-Pearl also believes that groups of teachers, working together, have the power to transform failing schools. After joining TFA's very first corps, back in 1990, Caputo-Pearl taught for four years in Compton, got married (and hyphenated his last name), then tried law school and urban planning classes. He spent two years organizing a campaign in support of L.A.'s public bus system. But he kept feeling tugged back to the classroom. He liked spending time with kids every day and meeting their parents. Teaching was so much more rooted in the real world than the social justice theory he'd studied in grad school. In 2001 he began teaching history at Crenshaw High School. He and his wife, Lisa, another TFA alum, moved to the surrounding neighborhood of Leimert Park, which is filled with low-slung, colorful bungalows, neatly kept, and ringed by car-clogged boulevards rife with empty storefronts. They were among the few white residents.

The school itself had a long, often proud history. Darryl Strawberry's 1979 Crenshaw Cougars baseball squad is remembered as one of the most talented high school teams ever. Crenshaw is also the school depicted in the 1991 movie *Boyz n the Hood,* the one where the gangs are a little less tough than those in Compton, and the most talented kids hope to escape and attend college. But by the time Caputo-Pearl arrived, the situation at Crenshaw was bleak. Charter schools, some of them in impressive new buildings paid for by private philanthropists, had siphoned off many of the school's working-class and lower-middle-class students, the ones whose parents had been most involved. Ninety-five percent of Crenshaw students were living in poverty, and 12 percent lived in homes where no English was spoken. A quarter lived somewhere without a parent, an unusual number of them in group homes or foster homes run by the state. Test scores were the lowest in the district.

Administrators were constantly arriving with new reform plans and then fleeing after a year. (In the last seven years Caputo-Pearl worked at Crenshaw, there were five principals and twenty-four assistant principals.) Because of missing paperwork, the school briefly lost its accreditation in 2005. Frustrated with constant mismanagement, Caputo-Pearl began organizing with parents to demand more basic resources for Crenshaw, including new computers. The group called itself the Crenshaw Cougar Coalition, and it eventually wrangled $2 million for Crenshaw from the district, and $1.5 million for ten other struggling L.A. high schools. Around the same time, Caputo-Pearl co-founded a dissident caucus within the United Teachers Los Angeles union, a group whom UTLA president A. J. Duffy referred to as "leftist crazies." Bottom line: Caputo-Pearl was stirring up a lot of trouble for a lot of different people. In 2006 the district transferred him, against his will, to an affluent middle school across town. After hundreds of parents, students, and teachers protested in front of district headquarters—and the protests were covered in the *Los Angeles Times*—he was reinstated.

In 2007, with a total lack of stable leadership at Crenshaw High, Caputo-Pearl and a few other veteran teachers pretty much took over. There are a small number of formally teacher-led public schools across the country, but this was an ad hoc setup. The group had its own idea of how to revitalize Crenshaw: not through management reforms, but by overhauling the curriculum. Poor children often hear that they need to do well in school in order to escape their communities. What if, instead, kids understood that doing well in school could help them become more effective advocates for their families and neighbors?

Working with education researchers and local nonprofits, the teachers created a novel plan called the Extended Learning Cultural Model, which won millions of dollars in funding from the Ford Foundation and then President Obama's school turnaround program. It eschewed most of the popular strategies in the accountability playbook, like mass staff layoffs or turning a neighborhood school into a charter school. Instead, taking a page from theorists like Ted Sizer, the plan broke Crenshaw up into teacher-led "small learning academies" with themes such as business and social justice. Within each academy, teachers worked together to create interdisciplinary units built around neighborhood problem solving. In the fall of 2011, the tenth-grade Social Justice and the Law Academy focused on school improvement across L.A. For their final project, students analyzed a data set that included test scores at various schools, neighborhood income levels, school truancy rates, and incarceration rates.

In math, students graphed the relationship between income and social opportunity in various south L.A. neighborhoods. In social studies, they read conservative and liberal proposals for school reform and practiced citing data in their own written arguments about how to improve education. In science, students designed experiments that could test policy hypotheses about how to improve schools. And in English class, they read *Our America,* a work of narrative nonfiction about life in the Ida B. Wells housing projects on the South Side of Chicago.

Working with researchers at UCLA and the University of Southern California, Crenshaw students conducted surveys on local food and health issues. Student volunteers grew produce in a community garden and sold it at local farmers' markets. One senior earned $1,000 per semester coordinating this work as an intern at Community Services Unlimited, a nonprofit that focuses on urban agriculture and food issues. Placing students in professional internships, some of them paid, was a key element of the Crenshaw reform plan. "Extended learning time" is a popular school reform strategy, but Crenshaw's teacher-reformers believed it shouldn't just take place in the classroom.

What was heartening about Crenshaw's plan was that it was rooted in solid research on the reasons why kids drop out of school: because they find it boring, they don't see how it connects to the world of work, and they would rather be earning money. The Crenshaw program provided teachers with intensive professional development and paid them bonuses for it. A big focus of the training was how to fit these creative, interdisciplinary units into the new Common Core shared standards. Every assignment had to be aimed at meeting the goal of "high literacy" for students—deep reading comprehension, critical thinking, and writing.

What was controversial about the Crenshaw reform agenda was that it was explicitly political. It asked students to question the social forces shaping their lives and to work actively to improve their low-income neighborhood. There was no doubt the school was a hotbed of feisty left-wing politics, and that this alternate approach to school reform differed from the technocratic, centrist character of the contemporary school accountability movement. When I visited the Crenshaw campus in 2011, several classrooms were plastered with posters declaring: "No more prisons!" At a faculty meeting, teachers debated the questions: "Is school oppressive? How can we make it less so?" The mood was a bit reminiscent of the old communist Teachers Union in mid-twentieth-century New York City. The TU had also united low-income parents with radical teachers in a quest to make the curriculum more relevant for black and Latino kids. And it had also alienated the powers that be.

Caputo-Pearl had begun his career through Teach for America, but seeing the group's increasingly close relationship with the charter school sector—and watching how charter schools left schools like Crenshaw depopulated and overwhelmed by the most challenging students—he had become a critic; he even wrote an anti-TFA column for the *New York Times* Web site. These sorts of opinions were bound to rub certain people the wrong way, especially the new L.A. superintendent appointed in 2011, John Deasy, a charter school fan whose signature reform was purchasing iPads for all 600,000 Los Angeles public school students. (Deasy had also been the first American school superintendent to embrace Charlotte Danielson's comprehensive classroom observation framework, when he worked in Coventry, Rhode Island, in the 1990s.)

In 2012 Deasy announced that Crenshaw would be "reconstituted" and the social justice academy would be shut down. Every teacher had to reapply for his or her job, and half would be removed from the school. These mass dismissals have become a common practice at underperforming large urban high schools. The policy, one of several school turnaround strategies suggested by Race to the Top, is based on a faulty premise: that veteran teachers are to blame when schools experience many years of low test scores. In fact, Donald Boyd's 2010 study of teacher transfer requests in New York City found that teachers who choose to leave underperforming, high-poverty schools tend to have been less effective, as measured by value-added, than teachers who stay in tough assignments over the long haul, like Caputo-Pearl. A number of other studies have found similar results at the district level—teachers who flee urban school systems are less effective than those who stay. It is the constant churn of first-year teachers and administrators that makes these schools and districts so unstable. Nevertheless, at Crenshaw, Caputo-Pearl was dismissed. So were union rep Cathy Garcia and the leader of the award-winning debate team. Most longtime observers of Los Angeles politics believed the school's activist educators were being targeted, regardless of classroom performance. Twenty-one of the thirty-three laid-off teachers were black, and twenty-seven had over ten years of experience.

Had Crenshaw's reform model worked for kids? Deasy said it hadn't, citing persistently low test scores. "It is a fundamental right to graduate, and it is not happening at Crenshaw," he said. "Students are not learning. Students are not graduating. Students are not able to read." He wanted more Advanced Placement and International Baccalaureate classes at Crenshaw, a potentially good idea that could have been pursued in tandem with the Extended Learning Cultural Model. What Deasy didn't say was that the achievement data at Crenshaw was trending upward, especially for African American and special-ed students. Since 2007, the graduation rate had increased by 23 percent, and there was a 19 percent reduction in student suspensions.

Turnarounds of comprehensive high schools are widely considered one of the toughest jobs in school reform. At Central Falls High School in Rhode Island, test scores remain abysmal three years after all the teachers were pink-slipped. But accountability reformers there are celebrated for raising graduation rates. What was different at Crenshaw was that teachers—and union activist teachers, at that—were driving the reform.

Ultimately, it's impossible to say if the Extended Learning Cultural Model could have revitalized Crenshaw, but it probably should have been given more of a chance to try. The plan was focused on the curriculum—what books kids read and what questions about the world they ask and answer—a crucial aspect of education that is usually neglected in debates over teacher evaluation and standardized testing. Developing new curricula is one of the most interesting, intellectually engaging aspects of schooling. It is a responsibility that, if granted to more teachers, could potentially help convince many well-educated, ambitious people to remain in the classroom. And Crenshaw's curriculum was rigorous and aligned with the Common Core, especially its focus on teaching kids to use evidence to back up persuasive arguments. The plan had attracted positive national attention from funders and the U.S. Department of Education. What had been the problem?

Caputo-Pearl, who is now president of the L.A. teachers union, believes he and his colleagues were targeted for challenging orthodoxies about what works and what doesn't in education reform. Deasy "crushed" the Crenshaw reforms despite community support, Caputo-Pearl told me, "because it competed with him philosophically."

When American policy makers require every public school to use the same strategies—typically without confirming if their favored approaches are actually effective for kids—they reduce the discretion of the most motivated teachers, like Alex Caputo-Pearl and Lenore Furman, whose contributions to the profession should be scaled up, not shut down or ignored. This is an age-old problem in American education reform. Our system is highly decentralized in terms of curriculum, organization, funding, and student demographics and needs, yet we have expected local schools to implement one-size-fits-all reform agendas imposed from above. Since political reality suggests we aren't likely to drastically centralize our education system anytime soon, perhaps it is time to look not just to nationally prominent politicians or philanthropists or social scientists to improve our schools, but also to teachers themselves.

When I visited Colorado in the midst of its divisive legislative battle over value-added measurement, I talked to Christina Jean, a social studies teacher who went on to work as an instructional coach in the Denver public schools. Like many smart young educators, she was cautiously optimistic—excited about the nation's renewed commitment to closing achievement gaps, but anxious that the imperative for meaningful collaboration to improve teachers' practice would be overlooked in the rush to impose new canned curricula and multiple-choice tests. "A lot of the discourse is about getting rid of bad teachers," she said. "Very rarely do I perceive teachers shown as anything other than cogs in a machine." To improve the profession's prestige over the long haul, she told me, it is crucial that the job feel not embattled but empowering and be "challenging and stimulating to adults. I am an intelligent person who has this love and passion for educating kids. So let me use what I know to create an experience for my students that reflects my expertise."

Epilogue

LESSONS FROM HISTORY
FOR IMPROVING TEACHING TODAY

Throughout this book I have tried to be more analytical than sharply opinionated. Nevertheless, my study of over two hundred years of the history of public school teaching has led me to draw some conclusions about the policy pitfalls that have dogged education reform, as well as the potential paths forward. Here are some ideas for improving both the teaching profession and, consequentially, the quality of our schools.

TEACHER PAY MATTERS

There is a mantra in education policy circles: "Money doesn't matter." Accountability reformers love to cite evidence that the United States spends more per student than many other nations, whose kids kick our kids' butts on international tests. It's true that there are many things American schools spend money on that don't improve academic achievement, like cheerleading uniforms and football equipment. But education finance expert Bruce Baker has demonstrated that one particular type of spending—higher teacher pay—is absolutely associated with better student outcomes. We must take this evidence seriously, because we are not paying teachers the upper-middle-class salary that would align with our sky-high expectations for their work.

In 2012 the median income of an American teacher was $54,000 per year, similar to the salary of a police officer or librarian, but significantly less than that of an accountant ($64,000), a registered nurse ($65,000), or a dental hygienist ($70,000), not to mention a lawyer ($114,000), a computer programmer ($74,000), or a college professor ($69,000).

While the incomes of American teachers do not look all that bad compared to teacher incomes in Europe or Asia, economists know people choose careers based less on the raw salary than on the perceived gap between what they could make in one job versus another. In that sense the growing inequality in the American labor market has undoubtedly hurt the prestige of teaching. In the 1940s, male teachers earned more than half of male college graduates, while female teachers earned more than 70 percent of female college graduates. Today teacher salaries are in the thirtieth percentile for male college grads and the fortieth percentile for female grads. These big pay gaps between teachers and other professionals are unique to the United States. In South Korea, teacher salaries of $55,000 to $155,000 over the course of a career provide 250 percent of the local buying power of an American teacher. This puts South Korean teachers between engineers and doctors in terms of pay.

Another problem is the way teacher pay is structured. Typical pay ladders, known as the single salary schedule, reward teachers for time on the job and further education, forcing a teacher to wait decades to achieve peak pay. High-profile districts like Baltimore and Newark have moved away from the single salary schedule through negotiations with their teachers unions. These cities now reward performance and extra responsibility, like mentoring peers, alongside seniority. This should happen across the board.

Consider this: My first full-time job in magazine journalism paid $21,000. I thought my friends who were public school teachers were rich! Five years later, at twenty-seven years old, I was earning three times my starting salary. Meanwhile, a New York City public school teacher with my same level of education, a bachelor's degree, got a raise of less than $5,000 over the first five years of her career, from $45,530 to $50,153. In North Carolina, a teacher must work fifteen years to move her salary from $30,000 to $40,000. The worst part is that teachers' incomes stagnate in comparison to their college-educated peers just as people begin to think about starting a family or buying a home. This is undoubtedly one reason why some ambitious people leave or never enter the profession, and why teaching is less culturally respected than it should be.

CREATE COMMUNITIES OF PRACTICE

Teaching is not just one profession but several. To understand what I mean, consider medicine. All prospective doctors take the same test, the MCAT, to apply to medical schools. Those schools are certified by a single body, and they move students through a familiar sequence of courses, licensing exams, and clinical rotations. All doctors serve as interns and residents and go through medical rounds at hospitals. Ethically, doctors agree to uphold the Hippocratic Oath.

Education is so very different. Some prospective teachers major in education at teachers colleges; others major in subject areas and earn master's degrees in teaching; still others become teachers through alternative routes like Teach for America or teacher residencies. Some prospective teachers serve as student teachers for a year, others for a semester or not at all. Many teachers believe the goal of their profession should be to close achievement gaps between rich and poor children; others would dispute this, saying that doing so means neglecting gifted kids or is irrelevant in homogeneous, affluent schools. Still other educators would emphasize social-emotional development, critical thinking, or citizenship over measurable academic gains. All these views have relevance and legitimacy and are rooted in American culture and history.

Considering that teaching is more decentralized in training methods and aims than other formal professions, like medicine or law, the Harvard sociologist Jal Mehta and Johns Hopkins political scientist Steven Teles have put forth the idea, still speculative, of "plural professionalism" for teachers, in which communities of practice form around specific pedagogical schools of thought, such as project-based learning or "no excuses." In this mode, teacher prep programs and K–12 schools would work in alliance. They would select a school of thought to emphasize and develop evidence-based best practices that can be shared among researchers, working teachers, and trainee teachers. "Plural professionalism" would give teaching intellectual heft, by inaugurating prospective teachers into communities of practice that use a single vocabulary, share an ethical alignment, and agree on questions like how to assess students.

Today's "no excuses" charter schools have come closest to implementing the plural professionalism model. In New York City and Chicago, a coalition of charter networks launched the Relay Graduate School of Education, which teaches "no excuses" techniques to first-year teachers seeking an alternative certification. There are other legitimate pedagogical practices for teaching low-income children, but they get much less attention. The High Tech High network in San Diego emphasizes connections between school and the world of adult careers, and it now operates its own teacher training program. The Bank Street College of Education in New York City teaches a Deweyite, progressive, learner-centered pedagogy, and it operates a K–12 school where student teachers hone their craft. Other teacher prep programs have a lot to learn from these institutions, which imbue prospective teachers with specific strategies for running a classroom and specific ways of thinking about their work. Since there is no one effective ideology of teaching—but there are many research-backed effective teacher behaviors, like high-level questioning—teacher education should be much more concrete and skills-based than the status quo. Yet it should remain intellectually diverse, since different communities have different expectations of schools, ranging from strict discipline to Montessori. Communities of practice should be able to demonstrate to states that they are rigorous and evidence based. Once they are, they could earn the freedom to choose their own curricula, assessments, and teacher evaluation practices.

KEEP TEACHING INTERESTING

A set of job responsibilities that remains stagnant over the course of five, ten, or twenty years can leave teachers feeling burned out and bored and drives some high performers uninterested in becoming administrators out of the profession. If we expect ambitious, intellectually engaged people to become teachers and remain in our public schools, we must offer them a career path that is exciting and varied over the long term, and which includes opportunities to lead among adults, not just children. In Singapore, after three years on the job a teacher selects one of three leadership paths to pursue, in curriculum writing, school administration, or instructional mentoring. Here in the States, cities like Baltimore are offering teachers promotion opportunities that allow them to remain in the classroom for part of the day, while spending more time leading their colleagues in lesson planning and instructional coaching. Opportunities like these should be available to all good teachers who want them, not just to a handful of administrators' favorites.

The most powerful form of performance pay would reward proven teachers for taking on useful new responsibilities that help other teachers improve student learning. And in a reform climate in which teachers are more and more expected to work together toward school improvement—whether through group lesson planning, peer coaching, or team teaching within the classroom—it makes less and less sense for incentives and pay to focus narrowly on measuring an individual teacher's impact on individual students' test scores.

DEAL WITH THE LEGACY OF THE NORMAL SCHOOL

Susan B. Anthony and W. E. B. Du Bois knew back in the nineteenth century that it was a bad idea for teachers to be educated separately from other college-educated professionals, both for the prestige of teaching and for the good of students. This remains true. During the mid-twentieth century, the old normal schools began evolving into state colleges that granted bachelor's degrees, but their admissions and scholarship standards typically remained low. Since these schools are now producing a huge oversupply of prospective elementary school teachers—in some states, as many as nine times more prospective teachers than there are jobs—states ought to require these institutions to raise their standards for admission or to shut down their teacher prep programs.

That said, high SAT scores or grades should not be the only qualifications teacher-ed programs seek. Preliminary data from New York City linking student achievement back to the universities teachers attended found that graduates of some less elite schools, like Hofstra University and Hunter College, outperformed, on average, the graduates of prestigious institutions like NYU and Columbia. We should not forget Martin Haberman's research showing that long-serving "star" teachers are often from low-income backgrounds, have graduated from non-elite colleges, or are people of faith. Others, like Alex Caputo-Pearl, have somewhat radical politics. What makes these nontraditional teachers special is that they are mission-driven to help struggling students succeed, and they are enthusiastic about holding all children to high intellectual standards. Those are the attributes teacher preparation programs should seek.

FOCUS ON THE PRINCIPAL AS MUCH AS THE TEACHER

There should be a principal quality movement that is as aggressive as our teacher accountability movement has been. Almost every expert agrees that the one ingredient all successful schools have in common is a dedicated, highly respected leader who articulates a clear mission teachers believe in and strive to carry out. A McKinsey study shows that in choosing where to work, reporting to a better principal is just as motivating for top-third teachers as securing more pay. There is also evidence that teachers are more likely to respect and work productively with principals who have been teachers, especially in the same school or neighborhood. It has recently been popular to recruit principals from fields outside education, but this could be a misstep. Instead, effective teachers with exceptional leadership and organizational skills should be identified through the evaluation process and encouraged, after a number of years, to consider transitioning into administration—while acknowledging that becoming a principal should not be the only way for a teacher to expand his or her responsibilities or pay.

And we shouldn't overburden principals with reams of teacher accountability paperwork. As banal as it sounds, paperwork is the major reason that historical attempts to improve teacher evaluation failed. Teacher rating rubrics must get "put on a diet," The New

Teacher Project recommended in 2013. How about focusing on ten effective instructional behaviors each school year instead of sixty?

RETURN TESTS TO THEIR RIGHTFUL ROLE
AS DIAGNOSTIC TOOLS

Americans have always been fascinated by tests, from the phrenology craze to IQ testing to achievement testing today. While we once used tests to draw conclusions mostly about the capacities of individual students, today we believe they tell us much less about the student than about his or her teacher. Value-added research has added immeasurably to our knowledge about what works in education, by measuring teachers' impact on students' test scores in low-stakes settings, in which those scores are used neither to reward nor to punish adults. But there is absolutely no reason to believe that value-added retains its legitimacy in high-stakes settings, when test scores are used to evaluate, pay, and fire teachers and administrators. Leading education researchers like Harvard's Daniel Koretz, a psychometrician, and John Hattie of the University of Auckland, who conducts meta-analyses of education studies, have demonstrated that the most authentic use of achievement tests is to diagnose what students know and can do so teachers can better target instruction toward them. When testing practices are set up to select teachers to fire, educators are incented to raise test scores at any cost, not to use tests to help children learn.

This does not mean that there is no use for value-added measurement within K–12 schools. Given what we know about value-added—that it is more stable at the high and low ends of the teacher quality spectrum than in the mushy middle—principals could target teachers with especially low value-added scores for a more intensive set of classroom observations or other investigations into their practice. Similarly, unusually high value-added scores could be used to identify teachers who are potentially able to serve as peer mentors or evaluators; but again, those rewards would not be distributed without classroom observations, consideration of student work other than tests, and interviews with the teacher in question.

TEACHERS BENEFIT FROM
WATCHING EACH OTHER WORK

The classroom should not be a black box closed to outside scrutiny, especially for novice teachers. Low-stakes value-added research has made it clear that first-year teachers, regardless of how they enter the profession, are learning on the job—and the curve is steep. Ideally, school districts that serve at-risk children would limit their supply of first-year teachers when adequate veterans are available. Another idea would be to change the structure of teachers' workdays so all effective veterans spend some time watching novice teachers work and coaching them. Beginner teachers, in turn, should have time to observe veterans' classrooms and to work with colleagues to plan effective, engaging lessons.

RECRUIT MORE MEN AND PEOPLE OF COLOR

It is important for children to see some of themselves reflected in their teachers. A half century of research and 150 years of practical experience show teachers of color are more likely to hold high expectations for students of color. Yet only 17 percent of public school teachers are nonwhite, compared to 40 percent of public school students. In terms of gender, the feminization of the American teacher corps, begun by the common school reformers in the 1820s, has proven stubbornly consistent. Today only 24 percent of teachers are male.

Making the teacher training process more competitive and intellectually coherent, as well as reorganizing how teachers are paid over the course of their careers, could make the job much more attractive to a more diverse group of workers. Men are more likely than women to value higher pay, and teachers of color are more likely than white teachers to have student debt to pay off. Though there is a perception that alternative certification programs inject clueless white teachers into high-poverty schools, in fact, programs like the Teacher Corps, Teach for America, and urban teacher residencies have always been more successful than the school system at large in recruiting large numbers of nonwhite and male teachers. The small size of those programs, however, means that urban districts may still be experiencing a net loss of teachers of color, as school closings and turnarounds lead to layoffs. That means everyone in the teacher preparation pipeline—teachers colleges, master's programs, and districts—must make teacher diversity a bigger priority than ever before.

END OUTDATED UNION PROTECTIONS

Between 2010 and 2012, 2.5 percent of urban public school teachers were laid off due to budget crises. In some districts a policy known as "last in, first out," or LIFO (pronounced *life-o*), prevented administrators from using performance criteria in choosing which teachers to shed. In 2011, when *The Daily Beast* invited twenty "big thinkers" to suggest a single idea to "fix our broken government," both New York City mayor Mike Bloomberg and Teach for America founder Wendy Kopp named ending LIFO. The term is undeniably powerful, since it conjures up one of the most potent attacks on teachers unions—that they provide incompetents with jobs for *life*.

Until very recently, these seniority rules were fairly uncontroversial. They prevented older, more expensive teachers from being discriminated against during lean economic times. Administrators often appreciated the simplicity of LIFO, especially because there was no consensus on how to best evaluate teachers' performance. Yet LIFO makes little sense as research tells us more about what effective teaching looks like. A sensible layoff policy would use seniority as a tiebreaker between teachers with similar levels of performance on the job. Most school districts are already free to implement such a system if they negotiate it with their unions—there are only twelve states in which the law declares that seniority must be the only factor in teacher layoffs.

The history of moral panics targeting teachers suggests the profession should remain governed by due process. But tenure cannot mean, in practice, that it is prohibitively expensive for a district to fire a bad teacher. If a teacher is judged using fair measures and is found to be consistently underperforming—and if she receives clear feedback and adequate training, yet does not improve within a year or two—her supervisor should have the right to fire her. If the teacher protests that decision, a peer-review board or neutral arbitrator should hold a hearing and make a ruling within a matter of weeks. The process should be swift and certain. To get there politically, teacher evaluation must be based on genuine measures of student learning, such as rigorous, non-multiple-choice tests and sophisticated, holistic classroom observations.

LET A THOUSAND POLICY FLOWERS BLOOM

Teacher accountability policies are not the only levers for improving public education. Just a decade ago the movement to desegregate schools was considered hopelessly outdated; today a growing number of charter school leaders acknowledge the research showing that integration promotes academic achievement and social-emotional growth for all kids. They are opening new schools, like Charles Drew in Atlanta and the Larchmont schools in Los Angeles, that seek to serve diverse student bodies. Even Michelle Rhee, the teacher accountability hawk, noted that in a perfect world, private schools would be illegal.* She actively recruited college-educated parents to enroll their children in D.C. public schools because she knew more socioeconomic integration had the potential to improve education for all the city's children. In 2014 the Obama administration issued new regulations to allow charter schools that receive federal funds to weight their admissions lotteries in order to achieve racial and socioeconomic diversity.

Some other great ideas: At Tech Valley High in Albany, New York, the Linked Learning schools in California, and the MET schools in Rhode Island, teenagers learn not only in the classroom, but also as externs in adult workplaces, so they understand how powerful education is in the real world and become more motivated to make it through high school and college. (Surveys of dropouts found many leave school because they believe it is irrelevant to earning money.) There is also a growing consensus around the cognitive,

* Rhee borrowed this quip from Warren Buffett.

social, and economic benefits of universal pre-K, another priority of President Obama that has not attracted much Republican support in Washington, but is gaining bipartisan steam at the state and municipal levels. In short, teacher evaluation and tenure reform—whether through value-added, peer review, or other means—are only two elements of any agenda to turn around underperforming schools.

BE REAL ABOUT
THE LIMITATIONS OF OUR SYSTEM

Sometimes I worry we are engaged in magical thinking about the American education system itself. We hope the federal government can drive reform, and ideas about school improvement are typically introduced at the national level. Yet, in the words of education historian David Labaree, our school system is "radically decentralized" compared to the systems of our peer nations in Europe and Asia. The United States Constitution never mentions education, leaving it as a responsibility of states, cities, and towns. Today only 13 percent of the financial support for local schools comes from Washington, with the rest about evenly divided between municipal property taxes and state funding.

The federal secretary of education can place conditions on funding in order to encourage favored reforms, like states adopting teacher evaluation systems that encompass student test scores. But he has zero oversight at the level of implementation, where so many well-intentioned social policies—especially education policies—are simply ignored or twisted beyond recognition. This dynamic played out with disappointing results during the Great Society era and again in the Reagan years, after *A Nation at Risk* inaugurated our contemporary federal school reform movement. President Obama's Race to the Top agenda faces similar risks. In a number of states, the administration's policies have already led to the absurd reality of teachers being evaluated based on the test scores of children they have never taught or even met.

Why do national reform priorities keep getting misinterpreted on the ground? The federal Department of Education has no power over state legislatures or education departments. There are no fed-

eral inspectors of local schools to make sure principals, superintendents, and school boards understand how to use complex new tools
like value-added measurement of teachers. Unique among Western
nations, our national government does not produce or select high-
quality tests, textbooks, or reading lists for teachers to use. Lastly—
and perhaps most importantly—we consistently expect teachers and
schools to close achievement gaps and panic when they fail to do so.
But we do not provide families with the full range of social supports
children need to thrive academically, including living-wage employment and stable and affordable child care, housing, higher education, and vocational training, in addition to decent nutrition and
health care.

In the absence of these "bridging instruments" between policy
and practice, I fear American politics will continue to reflect profound disappointment in teachers, and teachers themselves will
continue to feel embattled. But there is hope. If we accept the limitations of our decentralized political system, we can move toward a
future in which sustainable and transformative education reforms
are seeded from the ground up, not imposed from the top down.
They will be built more upon the expertise of the best teachers than
on our fears of the worst teachers. This is how we will achieve an
end to the teacher wars.

Acknowledgments

This book was born in the spring of 2011 at Columbia University, where I was a Spencer Foundation fellow in education journalism. It was Professor Sam Freedman, a masterful writer and teacher, who first suggested that my inquiry into the politics of public school teaching could become a book, and who encouraged me to take a historical lens to the subject. At Columbia, LynNell Hancock and Nicholas Lemann also provided crucial early guidance.

For three years, grants from generous donors allowed me to devote the majority of my working days to this project. I am profoundly grateful to have received a Bernard L. Schwartz fellowship at the New America Foundation and a Puffin Foundation writing fellowship at the Nation Institute. At New America, Steve Coll, Andrés Martinez, Lisa Guernsey, and Kevin Carey were early believers in this project, even before I had secured a publisher. Lisa's research on classroom observation was especially influential on the ideas presented in this book. At the Nation Institute, I was cheered on by Andy Breslau, Taya Kitman, Ruth Baldwin, and Carl Bromley. None of the nonprofit backers of this book exerted an iota of ideological or content pressure over the work itself, nor did they see the work in any form before publication.

My multitalented agent, Howard Yoon, helped me organize a huge mass of research and reporting about education into a workable book proposal, and held my hand along the way. I am incredibly fortunate to have worked with editor Kristine Puopolo at Doubleday. Her trenchant questions and revisions improved every page of this book. Assistant editor Dan Meyer provided probing comments and helped me format the book's photo insert and endnotes. Maggie Carr did what can only be described as the world's smartest copy-edit. *The Teacher Wars* is far more coherent and thoughtful because of her work.

I am grateful to a number of fellow writers who offered me feedback, most especially the razor-sharp Linda Perlstein, who read the entire manuscript and helped me prepare the first draft. My friend Philissa Cramer has been teaching me to be a better journalist since she was a year ahead of me on the staff of the *Brown Daily Herald*. Thank goodness she was available to help me weave the book's major themes throughout its chapters. Greg Toppo, Matt Yglesias, Richard Yeselson, and Adam Serwer were my other trusted and insightful readers.

Since journalists typically lack university affiliations, it is crucial that we have free access to scholarly resources. This book could not have been written without the writers and scholars program at the Schwarzman Building of the New York Public Library, on Fifth Avenue in Manhattan. Much of the work was done in the library's Wertheim Study, which is managed in style by research librarian Jay Barksdale.

Many of the ideas in this book first appeared in my journalism, published in magazines such as *Slate, The Atlantic, The Daily Beast,* and *The American Prospect.* I am a writer who loves being edited, and I've been lucky to work with some of the very best in the business: Ann Friedman, Betsy Reed, Richard Kim, Emily Douglas, Katrina vanden Heuvel, Tina Brown, Tom Watson, Lucas Wittmann, Edward Felsenthal, Torie Bosch, Allison Benedikt, David Plotz, Jess Grose, Kate Julian, and Nicole Allan.

It is profoundly humbling to tackle history and social science as a journalist. A number of academics lent me their deep expertise on topics covered in this book, including Alice Kessler-Harris, Luis Huerta, Larry Cuban, Luther Spoehr, Jonah Rockoff, Doug Harris, Steven Teles, Jal Mehta, Clarence Taylor, and Richard Ingersoll. My love and respect for the practice and profession of history dates back to my time at Brown University, where I was lucky to study with Professors Mary Gluck, Amy Remensnyder, Ken Sacks, and Carolyn Dean.

For pep talks on book writing at key moments when my confidence faltered, I'd like to thank Chris Hayes, Rick Perlstein, Dayo Olopade, and Jeffrey Toobin.

So many friends were unfailingly enthusiastic and supportive as I worked on this book. But I'd be remiss if I did not name two very special people who went above and beyond: Lauren Hinkson and Rebecca Sauer.

For three decades, my parents, Laura Greene and Steven Goldstein, and my grandparents, Carol and Frank Goldstein, have been throwing an obscene amount of love, enthusiasm, and encouragement in my direction. Thank you. Mark Hesse and Bonnie Marmor, my stepparents, are both educators who have not only supported me personally, but have helped me explore the issues in this book.

Virginia Woolf said a woman writer needs a room of her own. But at least for me, a loving home was more crucial. The most important person in my life is Andrei Scheinkman, whom I met just as I was finishing the proposal for this book. Andrei listened patiently to all the twists and turns of this long, long project and pushed me forward when I felt like the work would never be good enough and would never get done. He also made me laugh and reminded me to take vacations. He is now my husband. I am overwhelmed by gratitude and love. Thank you.

Notes

In addition to regular library collections and online resources, I consulted several archival sources. The Massachusetts Historical Society houses the Horace Mann Collection. The Tamiment Library and Robert F. Wagner Labor Archives at NYU house materials from the New York City Teachers Union, including the union's newspaper (abbreviated as Tamiment). The Chicago History Museum houses the Margaret Haley and Chicago Teachers Federation papers (abbreviated as MH/CTF). I conducted my own oral history interviews and also used online oral history archives maintained by the Southern Oral History Program at the University of North Carolina at Chapel Hill (abbreviated as SOHP/UNC), the Center for Oral History and Cultural Heritage at the University of Southern Mississippi (abbreviated as USM), and the *Eyes on the Prize* Interviews in the Henry Hampton Collection, Film and Media Archive, at Washington University (abbreviated as *Eyes*/WU). The term "loc" refers to location in an e-book edition of a work.

INTRODUCTION

2   **Everywhere I traveled as a reporter:** See Dana Goldstein, "The Democratic Education Divide," *The American Prospect*, August 25, 2008. For 2010 Clinton Global Initiative, see Dana Goldstein, "Is the Intra-Democratic Party Edu Debate a War?" (September 22, 2010), http://www.dana goldstein.net/dana_goldstein/2010/09/is-the-intra-democratic-party-edu-policy-debate-a-war.html. For polling on public perceptions of teachers, see http://www.gallup.com/poll/166487/honesty-ratings-police-clergy -differ-party.aspx.

2   **"sitting around, watching the teacher":** Robert C. Pianta and Bridget K. Hamre, "Conceptualization, Measurement, and Improvement of Class-

room Processes: Standardized Observation Can Leverage Capacity," *Educational Researcher* 38, no. 2 (2009): 109–19.

2   **Another study of over a thousand:** Thomas Kane and Douglas Staiger, *Gathering Feedback for Teaching* (Bill and Melinda Gates Foundation, January 2012).

3   **Polls show teachers:** *The MetLife Survey of the American Teacher: Challenges for School Leadership* (February 2013).

4   **"Great teachers are performing miracles":** Dana Goldstein, "Teaching and the Miracle Ideology," *The American Prospect,* July 15, 2009.

4   **In Finland, both men and women:** Pasi Sahlberg, *Finnish Lessons: What Can the World Learn from Educational Change in Finland?* (New York: Teachers College Press, 2011), 73.

6   **Depending on whom you ask:** For more on estimates of the number of ineffective teachers who cannot improve, see chapter 9, especially comments from economist Eric Hanushek and New Haven superintendent Garth Harries.

8   **teachers were fired for cause:** See the Schools and Staffing Survey of the National Center for Education Statistics, http://nces.ed.gov/surveys /sass/tables/sass0708_2009320_d1s_08.asp.

8   **Compared to federal workers:** Chris Edwards and Tad DeHaven, "Federal Government Should Increase Firing Rate," *Tax and Budget Bulletin* (Cato Institute report, November 2002).

8   **But in 2012, companies with over a thousand:** See Federal Reserve economic data, http://research.stlouisfed.org/fred2/graph/?g=q7M. Also Bureau of Labor Statistics Business Employment Dynamics report, http://www.bls.gov/web/cewbd/f.09.chart3_d.gif.

8   **Four percent of all civilian workers:** Richard M. Ingersoll, *Who Controls Teachers' Work? Power and Accountability in America's Schools* (Cambridge, MA: Harvard University Press, 2003), 15.

8   **The National Council on Teacher Quality estimates:** E-mail correspondence between author and Maegan Rees of National Council on Teaching Quality, October 23, 2013.

8   **But the leading teacher demographer:** Richard Ingersoll and Lisa Merrill, "Who's Teaching Our Children?" *Educational Leadership* (May 2010).

9   **According to Andreas Schleicher:** Thomas L. Friedman, "The Shanghai Secret," *New York Times,* October 22, 2013.

9   **"Education is, and forever will be":** John Dewey, *John Dewey on Education: Selected Writings,* ed. Reginald D. Archambault (New York: Modern Library, 1964), 199.

11   **In 2005, the average high school graduation rate:** Christopher B. Swanson, *Cities in Crisis 2009: Closing the Graduation Gap* (Editorial Projects in Education report, America's Promise Alliance, and Bill and Melinda Gates Foundation, April 2009).

11   **International assessments:** OECD, OECD Skills Outlook 2013 (November 2013).

CHAPTER ONE: "MISSIONARY TEACHERS"

13   few truly "public" schools: For summaries of schooling in early-nineteenth-century America, see C. F. Kaestle, *Pillars of the Republic: Common Schools and American Society, 1780–1860* (New York: Hill and Wang, 1983); and Lawrence Cremin, *The American Common School* (New York: Teachers College, Columbia University, 1951).

14   In riveting sermons: Horace Mann to Lydia Mann, April 11, 1822, Horace Mann Collection, Massachusetts Historical Society.

14   "best boy": M. Rugoff, *The Beechers: An American Family in the Nineteenth Century* (New York: Harper and Row, 1981), 314.

14   "irksome and disagreeable": Kathryn Kish Sklar, *Catharine Beecher: A Study in American Domesticity* (New York: W. W. Norton, 1976), 32.

14   "mournful, despairing hours": Ibid., 7.

15   "not a single instance": Mary Peabody Mann, *Life of Horace Mann* (Washington, D.C.: National Education Association of the United States, 1937), 26.

15   "is reputed a lady": Horace Mann to Lydia Mann, April 11, 1822, Horace Mann Collection, Massachusetts Historical Society.

16   "I lie down in sorrow": Sklar, *Catharine Beecher,* 42.

16   "a blank": Ibid., 47.

17   "The heart must have something": Ibid., 50.

17   Litchfield Female Academy: For descriptions of the school Catharine Beecher attended, see Rugoff, *The Beechers,* 43; M. T. Blauvelt, "Schooling the Heart: Education and Emotional Expression at Litchfield Female Academy," in *The Work of the Heart: Young Women and Emotion, 1780–1830* (Charlottesville: University of Virginia Press, 2007); *Chronicles of a Pioneer School from 1792 to 1833, Being the History of Miss Sarah Pierce and Her Litchfield School,* ed. Emily Noyes Vanderpoel (Cambridge, MA: The University Press, 1903); and Litchfield Historical Society, *To Ornament Their Minds: Sarah Pierce's Litchfield Female Academy 1792–1833* (Litchfield, CT: Litchfield Historical Society, 1993).

18   "influence, respectability": Milton Rugoff, *The Beechers,* 61.

18   "Woman, whatever are her relations": Catharine Beecher, "An Essay on the Education of Female Teachers," *Classics in the Education of Girls and Women* (1835): 285–95.

19   "These branches fill young Misses": Frances Huehls, "Teaching as Philanthropy: Catharine Beecher and the Hartford Female Seminary," in *Women and Philanthropy in Education* (Bloomington: Indiana University Press, 2005), 39.

19   "A lady should study": Catharine Beecher, "Female Education," *American Journal of Education* 2 (1827): 219–23.

19   Census figures . . . "ignorant and neglected": Catharine Beecher, "Female Education," *American Journal of Education* 2 (1827): 219–23.

20   The French revolution, she warned: Catharine Beecher, *The Duty of*

American Women to Their Country (New York: Harper and Brothers, 1845).

20   **"energy, discretion, and self-denying benevolence":** Beecher, "Female Education," 123.

20   **10 percent of American women worked outside the home:** Alice Kessler-Harris, *Out to Work: A History of Wage-Earning Women in the United States* (New York: Oxford University Press, 2003), 47.

21   **"I simply ask":** Catharine Esther Beecher, *The Evils Suffered by American Women and American Children: The Causes and the Remedy* (New York: Harper and Brothers, 1846).

21   **"[A] woman needs support only for herself":** Beecher, "Female Education," 114.

22   **Melville "anxious":** W. H. Gilman, *Melville's Early Life and Redburn* (New York: New York University Press, 1951), 89.

22   **Henry David Thoreau:** Lawrence Wilson, "Thoreau on Education," *History of Education Quarterly* 2, no. 1 (1962): 19–29.

22   **"horrible outrage" of the arson:** Jonathan Messerli, *Horace Mann* (New York: Alfred A. Knopf, 1972), 192.

22   **Phrenologists like the:** George Combe, *The Constitution of Man Considered in Relation to External Objects* (Boston: Marsh, Capen, Lyon and Webb, 1841), 268, 415.

23   **his brother Stephen:** Mann, *Life of Horace Mann,* 16–17.

23   **"moral reform":** Arthur M. Schlesinger, Jr., *Orestes A. Brownson: A Pilgrim's Progress* (Boston: Little, Brown, 1939), 40.

24   **"the scantiness of her wardrobe":** Messerli, *Horace Mann,* 226.

24   **Schoolhouses were to be:** Edgar W. Knight, *Reports on European Education* (New York: McGraw-Hill, 1930), 124.

24   **Prussia established normal schools:** Ibid., 171–73.

25   **"I believe Normal schools":** quoted in Frederick M. Hess, *The Same Thing Over and Over Again: How School Reformers Get Stuck in Yesterday's Ideas* (Cambridge, MA: Harvard University Press, 2010), 140.

25   **By 1840, Mann had opened three normal schools:** Knight, *Reports on European Education,* 6–7.

25   **"Twice every day":** Cyrus Peirce quoted in Thomas Woody, *A History of Women's Education in the United States* (New York: Science Press, 1929), 474–76.

26   **many normal schools transitioned:** James W. Fraser, *Preparing America's Teachers: A History* (New York: Teachers College Press, 2007), 151–52.

26   **Most American teachers:** C. Emily Feistritzer, *Profiles of Teachers in the U.S. 2011* (National Center for Education Information, 2011).

26   **In his eleventh annual report:** Redding S. Sugg, *Motherteacher: The Feminization of American Education* (Charlottesville: University of Virginia Press, 1978), 81.

27   **"As a teacher of schools":** Horace Mann, *A Few Thoughts on the Powers*

and Duties of Woman: Two Lectures (Syracuse: Hall, Mills, and Company, 1853), 38.

27   "purified my conceptions of purity": Messerli, *Horace Mann,* 173.

27   the cornerstone of "a cheap system": A. Potter and G. B. Emerson, *The School and the Schoolmaster* (New York: Harper and Brothers, 1842).

28   "Education in this country will never": Catharine Beecher, *Educational Reminiscences and Suggestions* (New York: J. B. Ford, 1874), 49.

28   "The teaching of A, B, C": Horace Mann, *Lectures on Education* (Boston: W. B. Fowle and N. Capen, 1855), 316.

28   "affections outward": Messerli, *Horace Mann,* 443.

28   Between 1830 and 1900: James C. Albisetti, "The Feminization of Teaching in the Nineteenth Century: A Comparative Perspective," *History of Education* 22, no. 3 (1993): 253–63.

28   helped keep men in the classroom: Rebecca Rogers, "Questioning National Models: The History of Women Teachers in a Comparative Perspective" (paper delivered at the International Federation for Research in Women's History conference, "Women's History Revisited: Historiographical Reflections on Women and Gender in a Global Context," Sydney, Australia, July 9, 2005).

28   "Classical studies": Knight, *Reports on European Education,* 213.

29   "the European fallacy": Messerli, *Horace Mann,* 443.

29   "I should rather have built up the blind asylum": Megan Marshall, *The Peabody Sisters: Three Women Who Ignited American Romanticism* (Boston: Houghton Mifflin Harcourt, 2005), 402.

29   Board of National Popular Education: Beecher, *Educational Reminiscences and Suggestions,* 115.

29   young women were dispatched: Sklar, *Catharine Beecher: A Study in American Domesticity,* 179.

30   twenty-one teachers died: Nancy Hoffman, *Woman's "True" Profession: Voices from the History of Teaching* (Old Westbury, NY: Feminist Press, 1981), 56.

30   recruits found that despite their best intentions: Beecher, *Educational Reminiscences and Suggestions,* 120.

30   "Not one can read intelligibly": Quoted in Ibid., 127.

31   In general, he subscribed: E. J. Power, *Religion and the Public Schools in 19th Century America: The Contribution of Orestes A. Brownson* (Mahwah, NJ: Paulist Press, 1996), 87.

31   "Education, such as it is": Orestes Brownson, "Review of 'Second Annual Report of the Board of Education. Together with the Second Annual Report of the Secretary at the Board,'" *Boston Quarterly Review,* no. 2 (1839): 393–418.

CHAPTER TWO: "REPRESSED INDIGNATION"

33   "I should think any female": Alma Lutz, *Susan B. Anthony: Rebel, Crusader, Humanitarian* (Boston: Beacon Press, 1959), 11.

33   **With her $110 annual salary:** I. H. Harper, *The Life and Work of Susan B. Anthony: Including Public Addresses,* vol. 1 (Indianapolis: Bowen-Merrill Company, 1898), loc 1175.

34   **"That salary business":** *The Selected Papers of Elizabeth Cady Stanton and Susan B. Anthony,* vol. 1, *In the School of Anti-Slavery, 1895–1906,* ed. Ann D. Gordon (New Brunswick, NJ: Rutgers University Press, 1997), 57–58.

34   **"penance . . . A weariness":** Ibid., 66.

34   **"I have only to say":** Ibid., 71.

36   **In 1850, four-fifths:** Ibid., 228.

36   **Anthony could no longer sit silently:** Ibid., 226–29.

37   **"Whatever the schoolmasters might think":** Elizabeth Cady Stanton, Susan B. Anthony and Matilda Joslyn Gage, *History of Woman Suffrage,* vol. 1, 1848–1861 (New York: Source Book Press, 1889), 514.

37   **On the conference's last day:** Gordon, ed., *In the School of Anti-Slavery,* 229.

37   **Anthony wrote to Stanton:** Ibid., 319–20.

37   **She had seen her father:** Lutz, *Susan B. Anthony,* 13.

38   **"I am glad that you will represent us":** Harper, *The Life and Work of Susan B. Anthony,* vol. 1, loc 2754.

38   **Ernestine Rose:** Carol Komerten, *The American Life of Ernestine L. Rose* (Syracuse, NY: Syracuse University Press, 1999).

38   **Robert Owen, the Scottish factory owner:** Francis J. O'Hagan, "Robert Owen and Education," in *Robert Owen and His Legacy,* ed. Noel Thomson and Chris Williams (Cardiff, UK: University of Wales Press, 2011).

38   **"I should like particular effort":** Harper, *The Life and Work of Susan B. Anthony,* vol. 1, loc 2694.

39   **her disdain for "schoolmarms":** Ibid., loc 2986.

39   **1880 lecture "Our Girls":** *The Selected Papers of Elizabeth Cady Stanton and Susan B. Anthony,* vol. 3, *National Protection for National Citizens, 1873–1880,* ed. A. D. Gordon (New Brunswick, NJ: Rutgers University Press, 2003), 500.

40   **After a particularly tiring protest:** Harper, *The Life and Work of Susan B. Anthony,* vol. 1, loc 3121.

40   **The women's movement split into two hostile camps:** Ellen Carol DuBois, ed., *The Elizabeth Cady Stanton–Susan B. Anthony Reader* (Boston: Northeastern University Press, 1981), 89–93.

40   **federal commissioner of education John Eaton:** John Eaton, *Report of the Commissioner of Education for 1873* (Washington, D.C.: Government Printing Office, 1874), 133–34.

41   **"The two types of mind":** Sugg, *Motherteacher: The Feminization of American Public Education,* 112.

41   **cautiously addressed The Woman Question:** Charles William Eliot, "Inaugural Address of Charles W. Eliot as president of Harvard College," October 19, 1869, 50.

42 "The average skill of the teachers in the public schools": Charles William Eliot, *Educational Reform* (New York: The Century Co., 1901), 162.

42 "It does not matter whether the trade": Charles W. Eliot, "Wise and Unwise Economy in Our Schools," *The Atlantic Monthly,* June 1875.

42 "weaker than men": Ibid.

43 The wealthier and more developed: William T. Harris, *Report of the Commissioner of Education for 1892–1893* (Washington, D.C.: Government Printing Office, 1895), 545.

43 Across New England, only 10 percent: Sugg, *Motherteacher,* 116.

43 When a teacher took a sick day: Harris, *Report of the Commissioner of Education for 1892–1893,* 546.

43 Dr. E. Schlee, a German principal: Ibid., 534–47.

44 Stephan Waetzoldt, a Berlin professor: Ibid., 567.

44 the "startling heresy": Belva A. Lockwood, "My Efforts to Become a Lawyer," *Lippincott's Monthly Magazine* (1888): 215–29.

45 "odious . . . an indignity": Ibid., 216.

46 H.R. 1571: Jill Norgren, *Belva Lockwood: The Woman Who Would Be President* (New York: New York University Press, 2007), 35–39.

46 she launched a presidential run: Christine Stansell, *The Feminist Promise: 1792 to the Present* (New York: Modern Library, 2010), 99.

CHAPTER THREE: "NO SHIRKING, NO SKULKING"

47 "All of proper age": E. L Pierce to Salmon P. Chase, "The Negroes at Port Royal: Report to the Hon. Salmon P. Chase, Secretary of the Treasury" (1862). Available at http://faculty.assumption.edu/aas/Reports/negroesatportroyal.html.

48 the Port Royal Experiment: Willie Lee Rose, *Rehearsal for Reconstruction: The Port Royal Experiment* (Indianapolis: The Bobbs-Merrill Company, 1964).

48 "There are at Port Royal": Pierce, "The Negroes at Port Royal."

49 a "constant, galling sense": Charlotte Forten Grimké, *The Journals of Charlotte Forten Grimké,* ed. Brenda Stevenson (New York: Oxford University Press, 1988), 111, 140.

50 "that God in his goodness": Ibid., 376.

50 "a strange, wild dream": Ibid., 390.

50 "a constant delight and recreation": Charlotte Forten, "Life on the Sea Islands, Part I," *The Atlantic Monthly,* May 1864.

50 "dreadfully wearying": Grimké, *The Journals of Charlotte Forten Grimké,* 399.

50 she wrote to philanthropists in Philadelphia: Recounted in Forten, "Life on the Sea Islands, Part I"; and Charlotte Forten, "Life on the Sea Islands, Part II," *The Atlantic Monthly,* May and June 1864.

51 Haitian revolutionary Toussaint L'Ouverture: *The Journals of Charlotte Forten Grimké,* 397–98.

51 "Oh, none in all the world before": From John Greenleaf Whittier, *Anti-*

Slavery Poems: Songs of Labor and Reform (New York: Houghton, Mifflin & Co., 1888), 238–39.

51   **"very proud and happy"**: Forten, "Life on the Sea Islands, Part II."

52   **"Schoolhouses are burnt"**: Douglas quoted in Meyer Weinberg, *A Chance to Learn: The History of Race and Education in the United States* (New York: Cambridge University Press, 1977), 43.

52   **"He found . . . that in spite"**: Pauli Murray, *Proud Shoes: The Story of an American Family* (Boston: Beacon Press, 1999), 179.

53   **"one of the happiest periods of my life"**: Booker T. Washington, *Up from Slavery* (New York: W. W. Norton, 1901), 38–39.

54   **In total, the Freedmen's Bureau spent**: Weinberg, *A Chance to Learn*, 43.

54   **southern states spent three times more**: Ibid., 57.

54   **walk five miles**: Ibid., 68.

54   **black teachers to receive only one-third the pay**: W. E. B. Du Bois and Augustus Granville Dill, "The Common School and the Negro American," in the *Atlanta University Publications*, Numbers 16–20 (New York: Russell and Russell, 1969), 132.

55   **"fractions and spelling"**: W. E. B. Du Bois, "A Negro Schoolmaster in the New South", *The Atlantic Monthly*, January 1899.

55   **"touched the very shadow of slavery"**: W. E. B. Du Bois, *The Autobiography of W. E. B. Du Bois* (New York: International Publishers, 1968), 114.

55   **"[T]he fine faith the children had" and "their weak wings"**: Du Bois, "A Negro Schoolmaster in the New South," 102.

56   **Hampton, which taught only the equivalent**: Robert J. Norrell, *Up from History: The Life of Booker T. Washington* (Cambridge, MA: Belknap Press, 2009), 31.

56   **"One man may go into a community"**: Washington, *Up from Slavery*, 72.

57   **Du Bois's bitterness**: see W. E. B. Du Bois, *The Education of Black People: Ten Critiques, 1906–1960,* ed. Herbert Aptheker (Amherst: University of Massachusetts Press, 1973), 28; and *The Correspondence of W. E. B. Du Bois,* vol. 2, ed. Herbert Aptheker (Amherst: University of Massachusetts Press, 1976), 430.

57   **"It was not enough"**: W. E. B. Du Bois, *The Souls of Black Folk* (New York: Bantam, 1903), 73.

57   **Villard fumed in a letter to Washington**: *The Booker T. Washington Papers,* vol. 4, 1895–1898, ed. Louis R. Harlan, Stuart B. Kaufman, Barbara S. Kraft, and Raymond W. Smock (Champaign: University of Illinois Press, 1975), 304.

58   **He responded to Villard**: Ibid., 311–12.

58   **on northern fund-raising expeditions**: Norrell, *Up from History,* 97.

58   **"to cope with the white world"**: Du Bois, *The Education of Black People,* 63–66.

58   **"Washington stands for Negro submission"**: *The Correspondence of W. E. B. Du Bois,* vol. 1, 167.

59   **detailed, practical advice**: Best articulated in his "Sunday Talk" of April 28, 1895, in *The Booker T. Washington Papers,* vol. 3, 1889–1895, ed.

Louis R. Harlan, Stuart B. Kaufman, and Raymond W. Smock (Champaign: University of Illinois Press, 1974), 549–51.

59   **Both men lobbied:** *The Booker T. Washington Papers,* vol. 2, 1860–1889, ed. Louis R. Harlan and Peter R. Daniel (Champaign: University of Illinois Press, 1972), 284–85; and *The Correspondence of W. E. B. Du Bois,* vol. 2, 139–40.

59   **received significant federal funding:** See Donald Roe, "The Dual School System in the District of Columbia, 1862–1954: Origins, Problems, Protests," *Washington History* 16, no. 2 (2004): 26–43.

60   **"missionary spirit":** *The Booker T. Washington Papers,* vol. 3, 552.

60   **"Your real duty":** *The Correspondence of W. E. B. Du Bois,* vol. 2, 8–9.

60   **"My mother was a slave":** *The Voice of Anna Julia Cooper,* ed. Charles Lemert and Esme Bhan (Lanham, MD: Rowman and Littlefield Publishers, 1998), 331.

61   **her application letter to Oberlin president:** Leona C. Gabel, *From Slavery to the Sorbonne and Beyond: The Life and Writings of Anna J. Cooper* (Northampton, MA: Smith College Libraries, 1982), 18.

61   **equal-per-pupil spending:** Robert A. Margo, *Race and Schooling in the South, 1880–1950: An Economic History* (Chicago: University of Chicago Press, 1990), 40, 54.

61   **disenfranchised more than half:** Helen G. Edmonds, *The Negro and Fusion Politics in North Carolina, 1894–1901* (Chapel Hill: University of North Carolina Press, 1951), 211–14.

62   **the state amended its constitution:** Margo, *Race and Schooling in the South,* 37.

62   **Du Bois conducted a survey:** Du Bois and Dill, "The Common School and the Negro American," 32, 50.

62   **In 1899, M Street students:** Karen A. Johnson, *Uplifting the Women and the Race: The Educational Philosophies and Social Activism of Anna Julia Cooper and Nannie Helen Burroughs* (New York: Garland Publishing, 2000), 54.

62   **university presidents and judges:** Gabel, *From Slavery to the Sorbonne and Beyond,* 28–29.

62   **Félix Klein visited Cooper's classroom:** Félix Klein, *In the Land of the Strenuous Life* (Chicago: A. C. McClurg & Co., 1905), 292–96.

63   **"the colored woman's office":** *The Voice of Anna Julia Cooper,* 117.

63   **"The earnest well trained Christian":** Ibid., 87.

63   **"The Solitude of Self":** DuBois, ed., *The Elizabeth Cady Stanton–Susan B. Anthony Reader,* 247–48.

63   **"*I am my Sister's keeper!*"**: *The Voice of Anna Julia Cooper,* 64.

63   **"no shirking, no skulking":** Ibid., 132.

64   **"sympathetic methods":** Johnson, *Uplifting the Women and the Race,* 108.

64   **"Tuskegee machine":** Du Bois, *The Autobiography of W. E. B. Du Bois,* 252–53.

64   **Washington personally intervened:** This incident is recounted by Du Bois

in his 1968 *Autobiography* (pp. 252–53) and investigated in depth by two of the men's biographers: David Levering Lewis, in *W. E. B. Du Bois, 1868–1919: Biography of a Race* (New York: Owl Books, 1994), 168–70; and Robert Norrell in *Up from History* (pp. 225–33).

64   **campaign of character assassination:** *The Voice of Anna Julia Cooper,* 9–13.

CHAPTER FOUR: "SCHOOL MA'AMS AS LOBBYISTS"

66   **"jigger carrier":** Kate Rousmaniere, *Citizen Teacher: The Life and Leadership of Margaret Haley* (Albany: State University of New York Press, 2005), 4.

66   **Michael Haley believed in the promise:** Described in Ibid., 7.

66   **"I don't know Susan B. Anthony":** Margaret A. Haley, *Battleground: The Autobiography of Margaret A. Haley,* ed. Robert L. Reid (Champaign: University of Illinois Press, 1982), 13.

67   **"dear friend":** *The Selected Papers of Elizabeth Cady Stanton and Susan B. Anthony,* vol. 6, *An Awful Hush, 1895–1906,* 239.

67   **$35 per month:** Haley, *Battleground,* 20–21.

67   **Francis Wayland Parker:** Larry Cuban, *How Teachers Taught: Constancy and Change in American Classrooms, 1890–1990* (New York: Teachers College Press, 1993), 39–41.

67   **$40 per month:** Haley, *Battleground,* 22n.

67   **830,000 residents:** Andrew Wender Cohen, *The Racketeer's Progress: Chicago and the Struggle for the Modern American Economy, 1900–1940* (Cambridge, UK: Cambridge University Press, 2004), 19.

68   **"warrants" promising future pay:** John McManis, *Ella Flagg Young and a Half Century of the Chicago Public Schools* (Chicago: A. C. McClurg and Co., 1916), 62–63.

68   **"fads and frills" and Tribune editorials:** Quoted in Herrick, *The Chicago Schools: A Social and Political History* (Beverly Hills, Sage Publications, 1971), 73–74.

69   **freeze a planned $50 annual raise** and **his wife's maid:** Haley, *Battleground,* 35.

70   **"The Federation should have a broader outlook":** Herrick, *The Chicago Schools,* 98.

70   **"lady labor slugger":** This nickname for Margaret Haley was coined by Chicago mayor William "Big Bill" Thompson, a Republican.

71   **"school ma'ams as lobbyists":** Herrick, *The Chicago Schools,* 103.

71   **"Does Unionism Make Girls Masculine?"** Frank G. Carpenter, "Women Taking Part in Labor Movement," *Atlanta Constitution,* May 15, 1904.

71   **"you had to fight hard":** Haley, *Battleground,* 3–4.

71   **half the market value:** Hannah Belle Clark, *The Public Schools of Chicago: A Sociological Study* (Chicago: University of Chicago Press, 1897), 58–60.

71   **$200 million in rent:** George S. Counts, *School and Society in Chicago* (New York: Harcourt, Brace and Company, 1928), 97.

72   **"property . . . loses its moral value":** "Minutes of Mass Meeting of the Teachers Federation at Central Music Hall, October 29, 1900," 27, MH/CTF archives.

72   **"heroic efforts to stem the tide of plutocracy"** and **"You make me think of Moses":** Eliza A. Starr and Lucy Fitch Perkins to Margaret Haley, published in "Souvenir Programme" for CTF fund-raiser, January 18, 1901. MH/CTF archives.

73   **"the plucky little woman":** Wisconsin Teachers Association Meeting Program, December 1903, MH/CTF archives.

73   **"just one human being":** William Hard, "Margaret Haley, Rebel," *The Times Magazine,* January 1907: 231–37.

73   **Harriet Taylor Upton, a leader** and **Haley happily did so:** Harriet Taylor Upton to Margaret Haley, October 19, 1904. MH/CTF archives.

73   **crusading attorney Clarence Darrow:** Hard, "Margaret Haley, Rebel," 234.

74   **his campaign to centralize and professionalize:** Marjorie Murphy, *Blackboard Unions: The AFT and the NEA: 1900–1980* (Ithaca, NY: Cornell University Press, 1990), 7–10.

74   **On Halloween, she booted a formerly truant student:** "Teacher Refuses to Quit," *Chicago Daily Tribune,* November 1, 1902. This incident opens the indispensible Murphy, *Blackboard Unions: The AFT and the NEA,* 7–10.

75   **Andrew Jackson students walked out:** Reported in "Board Suspends Woman Teacher," *Chicago Daily Tribune,* November 7, 1902; and "School Rioters May End Strike," *Chicago Daily Tribune,* November 9, 1902. Also described in Murphy, *Blackboard Unions.*

75   **his client had been targeted in retaliation:** "Calls Teacher a Victim of Plot," *Chicago Daily Tribune,* November 12, 1902.

75   **"the dismal burlesque":** "Like Parents, Like Children," *Chicago Daily Tribune,* November 11, 1902.

75   **"Employment means work":** "Enforce the Decision," *Chicago Daily Tribune,* November 14, 1902.

76   **Liberal magazines like *Harper's Weekly* and *The Nation*:** Cohen, *The Racketeer's Progress,* 136.

76   **"sedition, revolt":** "Teachers of Sedition," *Chicago Daily Tribune,* June 8, 1905.

76   **"teachers are not born":** David Swing Wicker, "The School-Teacher Unionized," *Educational Review,* November 1905: 371.

76   **"the cardinal principle of unionism":** "The Point of View: A Radical Departure in Unionism," *Scribner's Magazine,* June 1903: 763–64.

77   **Helen Todd conducted an informal survey:** Helen M. Todd, "Why Children Work," *McClure's,* vol. XL, 1913: 68–80.

77   **thirty thousand turn-of-the-century Chicago children:** Herrick, *The Chicago Schools,* 86.

78   were so rooted in their ethnic ghettoes: Jacob A. Riis, *How the Other Half Lives* (New York: Charles Scribner's Sons, 1890), 183.

78   "our chief defense against the tenement": Jacob A. Riis, *The Children of the Poor* (New York: Charles Scribner's Sons, 1902 edition), 127.

78   counseling poorly behaved students: Herrick, *The Chicago Schools*, 66.

79   "a constant danger": Jane Addams, *Twenty Years at Hull-House* (New York: Macmillan Company, 1910), 332.

79   "Gentle Jane": Haley, *Battleground*, 103.

79   to keep teachers' evaluation reports secret: Herrick, *The Chicago Schools*, 105–6.

80   she found city aldermen were protecting them: Ibid., 49.

80   discouraged her teachers from assigning homework: McManis, *Ella Flagg Young and a Half Century of the Chicago Public Schools*, 67.

80   she established school baths, and she lowered as many class sizes: Ibid., 92.

80   "melting pot": Ibid., 60.

80   "How to Teach Parents": Ella Flagg Young, "How to Teach Parents to Discriminate Between Good and Bad Teaching," in *Journal of Proceedings and Addresses of the National Educational Association* (Salem, MA: The Association, 1887), 245–48.

80   Young was "endowed with the keenest intellect": Haley, *Battleground*, 23.

81   teachers' book club: McManis, *Ella Flagg Young and a Half Century of the Chicago Public Schools*, 64.

81   including John Dewey and the Harvard philosopher William James: Ibid., 84.

81   "an interplay of thought": Ella Flagg Young, *Isolation in the School* (Chicago: University of Chicago Press, 1900), 17.

81   "automatons": Ibid., 46.

81   "medieval": John Dewey, *The School and Society* and *The Child and the Curriculum* (Minneola, NY: Dover Publications, 2001), 18–19.

81   "When you think of the thousands": Robert B. Westbrook, *John Dewey and American Democracy* (Ithaca, NY: Cornell University Press, 1991), 95.

82   "new education": Dewey's preferred term for "progressive education." Described in Dewey, *The School and Society* and *The Child and the Curriculum*, 24.

82   "direct the child's activities": Ibid., 25.

82   Lab School project: Ibid., 14–15.

82   Dewey worried that turn-of-the-century urban children: Jay Martin, *The Education of John Dewey: A Biography* (New York: Columbia University Press, 2002), 14.

83   she did experience some significant successes: John McManis, *Ella Flagg Young and a Half Century of the Chicago Public Schools*.

83   the "Loeb Rule": Herrick, *The Chicago Schools*, 122–23.

84   "to eliminate men of brain and heart": "Minutes of Chicago Federa-

tion of Labor meeting at the Auditorium, September 8, 1915," MH/CTF archives.

84   "the Interests, the special interests": Ibid.

84   After a long legal and political battle: Herrick, *The Chicago Schools*, 135.

84   founded the American Federation of Teachers: Murphy, *Blackboard Unions*, 83–87.

84   they lobbied the state legislature: Herrick, *The Chicago Schools*, 131–34.

85   The first American teachers to win tenure: For a good short history of teacher tenure see Hess, *The Same Thing Over and Over Again*, 153–57.

85   In New York, the new three-year probationary period: Diane Ravitch, *The Great School Wars: New York City, 1805–1973* (New York: Basic Books, 1974), 118.

85   "I believe that every child": McManis, *Ella Flagg Young and a Half Century of the Chicago Public Schools*, 210–11.

86   Frederick Winslow Taylor: Herbert M. Kliebard, *The Struggle for the American Curriculum, 1893–1958* (New York: Routledge, 1995), 78–83.

86   intricate tables for judging teachers' output: Joseph S. Taylor, "Measurement of Educational Efficiency," *Educational Review* 44 (1912): 348–67.

86   A study by education researcher William Lancelot: William Lancelot et al., *The Measurement of Teaching Efficiency* (New York: Macmillan Company, 1935).

87   According to peer reviewer Helen M. Walker: Ibid., xiii.

87   numeric ratings in largely subjective categories: Taylor, "Measurement of Educational Efficiency."

87   "walking through the rooms": William McAndrew, *The Public and Its Schools* (Yonkers, NY: World Book Company, 1917), 49.

87   "If a principal is unable": McAndrew's 1923 report to the Chicago school board, quoted in Counts, *School and Society in Chicago*, 80.

88   a 1924 "research bulletin": quoted in Ibid., 186.

88   "a training place for cheap labor": "Minutes of Chicago Federation of Labor meeting at the Auditorium," September 8, 1915.

88   "the brand of inferiority": Counts, *School and Society in Chicago*, 188.

89   unions were right to push back: On the history of IQ testing, see Nicholas Lemann, *The Big Test: The Secret History of the American Meritocracy* (New York: Farrar, Straus and Giroux, 1999); Diane Ravitch, *Left Back: A Century of Battles over School Reform* (New York: Touchstone, 2000); and Raymond E. Callahan, *Education and the Cult of Efficiency* (Chicago: University of Chicago Press, 1962).

89   published a study showing: Julius Metz, "IQs and the Underprivileged," *The New York Teacher* 1, no. 4 (1936): 60–63. Tamiment.

89   "antagonizing the bulk of the teaching force": Herrick, *The Chicago Schools*, 161.

89   Haley teamed up with a shady character: see Counts, *School and Society in Chicago*.

89   March 30, 1927, ad: Ibid., 268.

89   Those allegations were false: Ibid., 269–70.

CHAPTER FIVE: "AN ORGY OF INVESTIGATION"

91   **Mary McDowell:** See "Brief for Mary S. McDowell, Respondent" (In the matter of the charges of conduct unbecoming a teacher preferred against Mary S. McDowell before the Board of Education of the City of New York, 1918); "Teachers Who Are Not Loyal," *The New York Times,* November 18, 1917; and "Quaker Teacher's Case Is Argued," *The New York Times,* May 16, 1918.

91   **17 percent of Americans completed high school:** David Tyack and Larry Cuban, *Tinkering Toward Utopia: A Century of Public School Reform* (Cambridge, MA: Harvard University Press, 1995), 47–48.

92   **"a joke":** "Principals Dislike Teachers' Ratings," *The New York Times,* October 19, 1919.

92   **"C or D more accurately reflects":** "Quaker Teacher's Case Is Argued."

93   **"We, the teachers of the public schools":** "Loyal Teachers Urge Internment of Disloyal," *New York Tribune,* December 17, 1917.

93   **all but thirty relented:** "Teachers Yield on Pledge," *The New York Times,* May 10, 1917.

93   **McDowell went on "trial":** See "Brief for Mary S. McDowell, Respondent" and "Quaker Teacher's Case Is Argued."

94   **A jingoistic climate had invaded the public schools:** One of McDowell's colleagues at Manual High School, a German teacher accused of fascist sympathies, was also purged. Across the city from the teens through 1960, language teachers seem to have borne a disproportionate brunt of witch hunts; they were not seen as essential to the social efficiency or vocational curricula.

94   **Alexander Fichlander:** "Won't Promote Pacifist," *The New York Times,* March 29, 1917; "Principals Dislike Teachers' Ratings"; and Alexander Fichlander, "Teachers' Ratings," *Journal of Education* 91, no. 2 (1920): 36–37.

94   **"a sphere for wider influence":** "Won't Promote Pacifist."

95   **"The Board of Education should root out":** "Teachers Who Are Not Loyal."

95   **The Legion was influential:** Marcus Duffield, *King Legion* (New York: Jonathan Cape and Harrison Smith, 1931).

95   **"reds and pinks":** Ibid., 286.

95   **the Legion partnered with the National Education Association:** Ibid., 269–71, 280–87.

96   **William Randolph Hearst:** Murphy, *Blackboard Unions,* 96–98, 137–38.

96   **"an orgy of investigation":** Quoted in Celia Lewis Zitron, *The New York City Teachers' Union, 1916–1964* (New York: Humanities Press, 1968), 173.

96   **Diane Ravitch remembers:** Dana Goldstein, "Diane Ravitch, the Anti-Rhee," *Washington City Paper,* June 24, 2011.

96   **Nelda Davis:** Cheryl J. Craig, "Nelda Davis, the McCarthy Era, and

School Reform in Houston," *American Educational History Journal* 29 (2002): 138–43.

97   **The male share of the teaching force increased:** Thomas D. Snyder, ed., *120 Years of American Education: A Statistical Portrait* (National Center for Education Statistics report, U.S. Department of Education, January 1993), 34.

97   **In New York City . . . an oversupply:** For the process of becoming a certified New York teacher, see Ruth Jacknow Markowitz, *My Daughter, the Teacher: Jewish Teachers in the New York City Schools* (New Brunswick, NJ: Rutgers University Press, 1993), 75–92.

97   **many were disturbingly ignorant:** Howard K. Beale, *A History of Freedom of Teaching in American Schools* (New York: Charles Scribner's Sons, 1941), 247–48.

97   **Three female New York City teachers participated:** Clarence Taylor, *Reds at the Blackboard: Communism, Civil Rights, and the New York City Teachers Union* (New York: Columbia University Press, 2011), 58.

98   **"the exceptional teacher":** Beale, *A History of Freedom of Teaching in American Schools,* xii.

98   **"social movement unionism":** see Taylor, *Reds at the Blackboard.*

98   **Irving Adler always said that his wife, Ruth:** The biographical information is from author interviews with Juliet Relis Bernstein (February 11, 2013), Bruce Bernstein (February 7, 2013), and Ellen Bernstein Murray (February 12, 2013), as well as from Irving Adler's self-published 2007 memoir, *Kicked Upstairs: A Political Biography of a "Blacklisted" Teacher.* Tamiment.

99   **New York City Teachers Union:** see Zitron, *The New York City Teachers' Union.*

99   **dismal physical conditions:** Mark Naison, *Communists in Harlem During the Depression* (Champaign: University of Illinois Press, 1983), 214.

100   **"cautious and conservative":** Zitron, *The New York City Teachers' Union,* 21.

100   **vote for candidates affiliated with the American Labor Party:** See 1945 issues of the *New York Teacher News.* Tamiment.

100   **"The Union's Stand":** See *New York Teacher News,* vol. 1, no. 1, November 1935. Tamiment.

100   **Though Dewey's "new education":** The best review of the evolution (often the nonevolution) of public school pedagogy is Larry Cuban's *How Teachers Taught: Constancy and Change in American Classrooms, 1880–1990* (New York: Teachers College Press, 1993).

101   **Yorkville High School:** Abraham Lederman, Teachers Union president, to Superintendent William L. Jansen, June 11, 1954. Tamiment.

102   **Irving Adler believed:** Irving Adler, "Secondary Education," *New York Teacher* 2, no. 3 (April 1937): 11–12. Tamiment.

102   **In both Bed-Stuy and Harlem, union activists urged:** See "Police, Parents in Joint Program vs. Delinquency," *New York Teacher News,* March 11, 1944. Tamiment.

102   **1950 union study of city textbooks:** Teachers Union of the City of New York, *Bias and Prejudice in Textbooks* (New York: Teachers Union, 1950). Tamiment.

103   **A 1943 TU pamphlet:** Teachers Union of the City of New York, *Safeguard Their Future* (New York: Teachers Union, 1943). Tamiment.

103   **Earl Browder led the American communist movement:** James G. Ryan, *Earl Browder: The Failure of American Communism* (Tuscaloosa: University of Alabama Press, 1997).

103   **six thousand members by 1940:** Taylor, *Reds at the Blackboard,* 60.

104   **"function of a Communist teacher":** C. P. Trussell, "Bella Dodd Asserts Reds Got Presidential Advisory Posts," *The New York Times,* March 11, 1953.

105   **378 New York City public school teachers:** Ralph Blumenthal, "When Suspension of Teachers Ran Unchecked," *The New York Times,* June 15, 2009.

105   **Alice Citron was especially celebrated:** In Morris U. Schappes, "Free Education on Trial," *Jewish Life,* December 1950; and Naison, *Communists in Harlem During the Depression,* 216.

106   **no "proof of any specific classroom act":** Taylor, *Reds at the Blackboard,* 148.

106   **"a teacher who consciously subscribes":** "Report of the Trial Examiner" (In the matter of the trial of the charges preferred by Dr. William Jansen, Superintendent of Schools, against David L. Friedman, a teacher in Public School 64, Manhattan, December 11, 1950), 25–26.

106   **Bella Dodd testified:** Taylor, *Reds at the Blackboard,* 223; Adler, *Kicked Upstairs,* 63; and Trussell, "Bella Dodd Asserts Reds Got Presidential Advisory Posts."

107   **"I love Joe McCarthy":** Adler, *Kicked Upstairs,* 63.

107   **Many purged teachers led illustrious second careers:** "Children of the Black List: Robert Meeropol," Dreamers and Fighters Web site, http://dreamersandfighters.com/cob/doc-meeropol.aspx.

107   **Lucille Spence:** Senate testimony and FBI file provided by the FBI to author via FOIA request, March 13, 2013.

108   **"High school teachers are assembly line workers":** Quoted in Daniel H. Perlstein, *Justice, Justice: School Politics and the Eclipse of Liberalism* (New York: Peter Lang, 2004), 19.

108   **State law said the five thousand strikers could lose:** Richard D. Kahlenberg, *Tough Liberal: Albert Shanker and the Battles over Schools, Unions, Race, and Democracy* (New York: Columbia University Press, 2007), 47–48.

108   **by 1967, 97 percent:** Ibid., 60.

109   **David Licorish:** Quoted in Naison, *Communists in Harlem During the Depression,* 216.

CHAPTER SIX: "THE ONLY VALID PASSPORT FROM POVERTY"

110   "I have seen the impossible happen": David Levering Lewis, *W. E. B. Du Bois: The Fight for Equality and the American Century, 1919–1963* (New York : Henry Holt, 2000), 557.

110   **Ralph Ellison:** Quoted in James T. Patterson, *Brown v. Board of Education: A Civil Rights Milestone and Its Troubled Legacy* (New York: Oxford University Press, 2001), xiv.

111   **"martyrs to integration":** Oliver C. Cox, "Negro Teachers: Martyrs to Integration?" *The Nation,* April 25, 1953.

112   **attacking veteran black educators:** Michael Fultz, "The Displacement of Black Educators Post-Brown," *History of Education Quarterly* 44, no. 1 (2004): 11–45.

112   **"I'm against it":** Johnson, *Uplifting the Women and the Race,* 89.

112   **"The whole matter revolves around":** Zora Neale Hurston, "Court Order Can't Make the Races Mix," *Orlando Sentinel,* August 11, 1955.

112   **A decade after the ruling:** Weinberg, *A Chance to Learn,* 93.

113   **Except in a few high-profile cases:** Ibid., 90.

113   **Previous efforts to expand Washington's influence:** See Gareth Davies, *See Government Grow: Education Politics from Johnson to Reagan* (Lawrence: University Press of Kansas, 2007).

113   **The most lasting Great Society change:** For a good review of ESEA, see Irwin Unger, *The Best of Intentions: The Triumphs and Failures of the Great Society Under Kennedy, Johnson, and Nixon* (New York: Doubleday, 1996), 119–25.

114   **"By passing this bill":** Lyndon B. Johnson, "Remarks Upon Signing the Elementary and Secondary Education Act" (Johnson City, Texas, April 11, 1965).

114   **nine months working as a teacher:** Recounted in Robert Caro, *The Years of Lyndon Johnson: The Path to Power* (New York: Knopf, 1982), 164–73; Doris Kearns Goodwin, *Lyndon Johnson and the American Dream* (New York: Harper & Row, 1976), 65–66; and Robert Dallek, *Lone Star Rising: Lyndon Johnson and His Times, 1908–1960* (New York: Oxford University Press, 1991), 77–82.

115   **"the little baby in the cradle":** Caro, *The Path to Power,* 168.

115   **"a magic cure":** Unger, *The Best of Intentions,* 335.

115   **"wishing there was more I could do":** Lyndon B. Johnson, "Special Message to Congress: The American Promise" (March 15, 1965).

116   **A 1971 report:** *Approaches to Learning Motivation: An Evaluation of the Summer, 1971 ESEA Title I Program of Community School District No. 16, Brooklyn, NY* (New York: The Human Affairs Research Center, September 1971).

117   **"upset our stomach":** Davis, "Elliott Denies Any 'Deals,'" *Tuscaloosa News,* September 12, 1966.

117   **He announced he would use police power:** "Wallace Gives Warning on Negro Teachers," *Miami News,* September 10, 1966.

117   "We got bonded": Eunice Pharr, interview #K-0471, April 12, 2001, SOHP/UNC, 4.

118   "I learned them just like I did": Cleopatra Goree, interview #U-0030, November 13, 2004, SOHP/UNC, 24.

118   First Ward Elementary School: Frye Gaillard, *The Dream Long Deferred: The Landmark Struggle for Desegregation in Charlotte, North Carolina* (Columbia: The University of South Carolina Press, 2002), 144.

119   National Teacher Examination: Fultz, "The Displacement of Black Educators Post-Brown," 27–28.

119   federal Department of Health, Education, and Welfare estimated: Ibid., 37.

119   Willie Mae Crews: Willie Mae Lee Crews, interview #U-0020, June 16, 2005, SOHP/UNC.

119   Heath recalled that the white principal at Glenn was racist: Helen Heath, interview #U-0031, November 13, 2004, SOHP/UNC, 8.

120   "stripped of their excellent teachers": Ibid., 18.

120   "senile" white teachers: Clifton M. Claye, "Problems of Cross-Over Teachers," *Integrated Education* 8, no. 5 (1970).

120   Several surveys of southern teachers: see Thomas H. Buxton et al., "Black and White Teachers and School Desegregation," *Integrated Education* 12, nos. 1–2 (1974); and Mary Victoria Braxton and Charles S. Bullock III, "Teacher Partiality in Desegregation," *Integrated Education* 10, no. 4 (1972).

120   "different values": Buxton, "Black and White Teachers and School Desegregation," 21.

120   "It's not as though we were monkeys": Gloria Register Jeter, interview #K-0549, December 23, 2000, SOHP/UNC, 1.

120   "The Negro Family": Daniel Patrick Moynihan, *The Negro Family: The Case for National Action* (Office of Policy Planning and Research, U.S. Department of Labor, 1965).

120   "Equality of Educational Opportunity": James S. Coleman et al., *Equality of Educational Opportunity* (U.S. Department of Health, Education, and Welfare, 1966).

121   "Just as a loaf of bread": Ibid., 8.

122   "We must not deceive ourselves": Quoted in Fultz, "The Displacement of Black Educators Post-Brown," 45.

122   President Johnson, in a speech: Carol F. Karpinski, *"A Visible Company of Professionals": African Americans and the National Education Association During the Civil Rights Movement* (New York: Peter Lang, 2008), 151.

122   "uniquely important place": Jack Greenberg, "For Integration of Negro Teachers," *The New York Times,* August 21, 1965.

122   one black teacher would suffice: Paul Davis, "Elliott Denies Any 'Deals.'"

123   the number of teachers of color nationwide: See Ulrich Bosser, *Teacher Diversity Matters* (Center for American progress report, November

2011); Sun Times Media Wire, "CPS Teachers Who Lost Jobs File Discrimination Suit," December 26, 2012; and Sarah Carr, *Hope Against Hope: Three Schools, One City, and the Struggle to Educate America's Children* (New York: Bloomsbury Press, 2013), 39. For a review of evidence associating teachers of color with higher student achievement for students of color, see Betty Achinstein et al., "Retaining Teachers of Color," *Review of Educational Research* 80, no. 1 (2010): 70–107.

123   **a program founded two years earlier:** Author interview with Joan Wofford, May 10, 2013.

124   **National surveys showed:** Robert E. Herriott and Nancy Hoyt St. John, *Social Class and the Urban School: The Impact of Pupil Background on Teachers and Principals* (New York: John Wiley and Sons, 1966), 86, 95–97.

125   **James Bryant Conant:** Conant, *The Education of American Teachers* (New York: McGraw-Hill, 1963).

126   **women's section profiled:** Carolyn Bell Hughes, "Peace Corps Teachers Start Here," *Washington Post,* October 13, 1963.

126   **Roberta Kaplan:** Author interview with Roberta Kaplan, April 19, 2013.

127   **As the historian Bethany Rogers has noted:** Bethany Rogers, "'Better' People, Better Teaching: The Vision of the National Teacher Corps, 1965–1968," *History of Education Quarterly* 49, no. 3 (2009): 347–72.

127   **Jane David:** Author interview with Jane David, April 18, 2013.

129   **Beverly Glenn:** Author interview with Beverly Glenn, April 25, 2013.

130   **during the Corps' first three cycles:** Rogers, "'Better' People, Better Teaching," 363.

130   **"Far from being a threat":** "Teacher Corps," *The New York Times,* July 4, 1967.

130   **Ronald Corwin published the definitive evaluation:** Ronald G. Corwin, *Reform and Organizational Survival: The Teacher Corps as an Instrument of Educational Change* (New York: John Wiley & Sons, 1973), 96–97.

131   **"status threat":** Ibid., 389.

131   **"the greater the difference between interns and teachers":** Quoted in Fraser, *Preparing America's Teachers: A History,* 219.

CHAPTER SEVEN: "WE BOTH GOT MILITANT"

133   **Al Shanker biographical details:** from Kahlenberg, *Tough Liberal;* Al Shanker (speech to New York State United Teachers Convention, April 27, 1985); A. H. Raskin, "He Leads His Teachers Up the Down Staircase," *The New York Times Magazine,* September 3, 1967; and Edward B. Fiske, "Albert Shanker: Where He Stands," *The New York Times,* November 5, 1989.

134   **a shortage of public school teachers:** Christina Collins, *"Ethnically Qualified": Race, Merit, and the Selection of Urban Teachers, 1920–1980* (New York: Teachers College Press, 2011), 107–9.

134   the most unionized profession in America: Jal Mehta, *The Allure of Order* (New York: Oxford University Press, 2013), 114.

135   Teachers with collective bargaining rights: Barry T. Hirsch et al., "Teacher Salaries, State Collective Bargaining Laws, and Union Coverage" (working paper, American Economic Association, San Diego, January 6, 2013).

135   UFT co-founder George Altomare's high school economics classes: Author interview with George Altomare, June 21, 2013.

135   Freedom Summer: Sandra Adickes, oral history interview, October 21, 1999. USM.

136   School segregation actually deepened: See Annie Stein, "Containment and Control: A Look at the Record," in *Schools Against Children: The Case for Community Control,* ed. Annette T. Rubinstein (New York: Monthly Review Press, 1970); Doxey A. Wilkerson, "The Failure of Schools Serving the Black and Puerto Rican Poor," in Rubinstein, ed., *Schools Against Children;* and Barbara Carter, *Pickets, Parents, and Power: The Story Behind the New York City Teachers' Strike* (New York: Citation Press, 1971), 9.

137   "Pygmalion in the Classroom": Robert Rosenthal and Lenore Jacobson, "Pygmalion in the Classroom," *Urban Review* 3, no. 1 (1968).

137   "disruptive children": Rhody McCoy, interview by Blackside, Inc., October 12, 1988. *Eyes*/WU.

138   "Even liberal educators view": Quoted in Claye, "Problems of Cross-Over Teachers," 13.

138   "Uncle Tom's Cabin: Alternate Ending": Published in Imamu Amiri Baraka, *Three Books* (New York: Grove Press, 1975).

139   two major organizational backers of community control, CORE and the Ford Foundation: See Karen Ferguson, *Top Down: The Ford Foundation, Black Power, and the Reinvention of Racial Liberalism* (Philadelphia: University of Pennsylvania Press, 2013); and Kahlenberg, *Tough Liberal.*

140   "to destroy the professional educational bureaucracy": Quoted in Lillian S. Calhoun, "New York: Schools and Power—Whose?" *Integrated Education* 7, no. 1 (1969).

141   Stokely Carmichael, a proponent of black separatism: See "Free Huey" and Berkeley speeches published in Stokely Carmichael, *Stokely Speaks: From Black Power to Pan-Africanism* (Chicago: Lawrence Hill Books, 1971).

142   Martin Luther King called this philosophy "nihilistic": See excerpts from King's "Where Do We Go From Here," published in Martin Luther King, Jr., *A Testament of Hope,* ed. James M. Washington (New York: HarperCollins, 1986), 586.

142   In Ocean Hill–Brownsville, an economically depressed neighborhood: See Fred Nauman, interview by Blackside, Inc., April 18, 1989. *Eyes*/WU.

143   these groups had hoped to address the problem: See Rev. John Powis,

interview conducted by Blackside, Inc., November 4, 1988. *Eyes*/WU; Dolores Torres, interview conducted by Blackside, Inc., October 31, 1988. *Eyes*/WU; and Sandra Feldman, interview conducted by Blackside, Inc., October 31, 1988. *Eyes*/WU.

144　**"school officials deprived the community":** Carter, *Pickets, Parents, and Power,* 32.

144　**students enrolled at MES schools:** Simon Beagle, *Evaluating MES: A Survey of Research on the More Effective Schools Plan* (Washington, D.C.: American Federation of Teachers, April, 1969); and Samuel D. McClelland, *Evaluation of the More Effective Schools Program* (Brooklyn: New York City Board of Education, September 1966).

145　**"New Federalism":** Unger, *The Best of Intentions,* 303.

145　**"It was a joy":** Rhody McCoy, interview by Blackside, Inc., October 12, 1988. *Eyes*/WU.

146　**One of them was Elaine Rook:** Les Campbell, interview by Blackside, Inc., November 3, 1988. *Eyes*/WU.

146　**The morning after Martin Luther King's assassination:** Karima Jordan, interview by Blackside, Inc., April 18, 1989. *Eyes*/WU; Fred Nauman, interview by Blackside, Inc., April 18, 1989. *Eyes*/WU; and Kahlenberg, *Tough Liberal,* 91.

147　**"Not one of these teachers":** Ibid., 95.

148　**12 out of 55,000 teachers:** see Carter, *Pickets, Parents, and Power,* 26; and Jason Epstein, "The Real McCoy," *New York Review of Books,* March 13, 1969.

148　**"We've got to make them learn":** McCoy quoted in Calhoun, "New York: Schools and Power—Whose?"

149　**"Teachers have been physically threatened":** Reprinted in Carter, *Pickets, Parents, and Power,* 69.

149　**Art teacher Richard Douglass:** Ibid., 83.

151　**Rivers concluded that the district's accusations:** Published in *Confrontation at Ocean Hill–Brownsville: The New York School Strikes of 1968,* ed. Maurice R. Berube and Marilyn Gittell (New York: Frederick A. Praeger, 1969), 85–99.

151　**When UFT teachers arrived:** Sylvan Fox, "Some Hostility Marks Return of 83 Teachers to Ocean Hill," *The New York Times,* October 1, 1968.

151　**"This is a strike":** Khalenberg, *Tough Liberal,* 97–98.

152　**"You're a racist, Mr. Shanker!":** Maurice Carroll, "Giant City Hall Rally Backs Teachers," *The New York Times,* September 17, 1968; and Robert E. Dallos, "Shanker's Home Picketed by 150," *The New York Times,* November 4, 1968.

152　**"What did they feel about coming to work":** Dolores Torres, interview by Blackside, Inc., October 31, 1988. *Eyes*/WU.

152　**replacement teacher Charles Isaacs:** Republished in Berube and Gittell, eds., *Confrontation at Ocean Hill–Brownsville.*

153　**"it was like someone was filming a movie":** Karima Jordan, interview by Blackside, Inc., April 18, 1989. *Eyes*/WU.

153   "Lots of teachers were pretty racist": Author interview with Peter Goodman, June 3, 2013.

153   "If African-American History and Culture" and "The UFT says NO": Quoted in Kahlenberg, *Tough Liberal*, 107.

156   "To me, the Civil Rights Movement": Al Shanker, interview by Blackside, Inc., November 15, 1988. *Eyes*/WU.

156   socialist, anti-Soviet workshops: Taylor Branch, *Pillar of Fire: America in the King Years, 1963–65* (New York: Simon and Schuster, 1998), 292.

156   "The proposal seems concerned": Bayard Rustin, "Articles on Education, 1942–1987," Bayard Rustin Papers.

157   "sacrificing the needs of the school system": Raskin, "He Leads His Teachers Up the Down Staircase."

157   "Listen, I don't represent children": Quoted in Kahlenberg, *Tough Liberal*, 125.

157   "I'm going to produce!": Quoted in Calhoun, "New York: Schools and Power—Whose?" 21.

157   the years from 1967 to 1969 had been educationally disastrous; "Everyone else has failed": Carter, *Pickets, Parents, and Power*, 55, 164–67.

158   accused of showing standardized test questions: Leonard Buder, "Actual Tests Used to Prepare Students for Reading Exam," *The New York Times,* April 3, 1971.

159   Eagle Academy for Young Men: Information from the Eagle Academy Foundation Web site, http://eagleacademyfoundation.com.

159   not much more successful, in measurable ways: Eagle Academy school data reported by Inside Schools at http://insideschools.org/high/browse/school/1546.

160   The resulting fourteen-week, 2,500-person strike: Steve Golin, *The Newark Teacher Strikes: Hopes on the Line* (New Brunswick, NJ: Rutgers University Press, 2002).

161   Nationally, teachers unions wielded extraordinary political influence: See chapter 9 of Terry M. Moe, *Special Interest: Teachers Unions and America's Public Schools* (Washington, D.C.: Brookings Institution Press, 2011).

162   Central Park East School: Author interview with Deborah Meier, June 4, 2013.

CHAPTER EIGHT: "VERY DISILLUSIONED"

164   "bureaucratic boondoggle": Edward B. Fiske, "Reagan Record in Education: Mixed Results," *The New York Times,* November 14, 1982.

165   President Reagan "may be using me": Terrel H. Bell, *The Thirteenth Man* (New York: The Free Press, 1988), 149.

166   Bell biographical details and Utah merit pay plan: Ibid., 7–13, 79–87.

167   an infamous wall chart: Ibid., 137.

167   A press conference: Reported in the Associated Press, "Bell Asks Schools to Bolster Courses," *The New York Times,* February 17, 1981; and UPI,

"Bell Urges Stiff Tests to Decide If Students Go on to Next Grade," *The New York Times,* April 10, 1981.

167 **with polls showing that by 1980:** Mehta, *The Allure of Order,* 119.

168 **testing programs to evaluate student achievement:** See Ibid., 75–83; and U.S. Department of Health Education and Welfare, *Inside-Out: The Final Report and Recommendations of the Teachers National Field Task Force on the Improvement and Reform of American Education* (Washington, D.C.: U.S. Government Printing Office, 1974), 1.

168 **"competency based" evaluation:** John Merrow, *The Politics of Competence: A Review of Competency-Based Teacher Education* (Washington, D.C.: National Institute of Education, 1975).

168 **California essentially prohibited:** Julie Greenberg, Arthur McKee, and Kate Walsh, *Teacher Prep Review, 2013* (National Council on Teacher Quality report, 2013), 33–35.

169 **"Why Teachers Can't Teach":** Gene Lyons, "Why Teachers Can't Teach," *Phi Delta Kappan* 62, no. 2 (October 1980).

169 **"Bring God back into the classroom":** Quoted in Mehta, *The Allure of Order,* 88.

170 *A Nation at Risk:* National Commission on Excellence in Education, *A Nation at Risk: The Imperative for Educational Reform* (Washington, D.C.: U.S. Government Printing Office, April 1983).

171 **At the American Federation of Teachers:** For Shanker's response to *A Nation at Risk,* see chapter 14 of Kahlenberg, *Tough Liberal.*

171 **"I took it as a personal insult":** Author interview with Dennis Van Roekel, October 7, 2013.

171 **four-day teaching week:** William K. Stevens, "Head of Teachers' Union Bids Locals Push for 4-Day Week," *The New York Times,* November 23, 1969.

172 **Shanker was calling charter schools:** Kahlenberg, *Tough Liberal,* 308–16.

173 **In Japan the average teacher:** David C. Berliner and Bruce J. Biddle, *The Manufactured Crisis: Myth, Fraud, and the Attack on America's Public Schools* (Reading, MA: Addison-Wesley, 1995), 103.

173 **"Basically, no teacher wants to fail":** Fred M. Hechinger, "About Education," *The New York Times,* July 6, 1982.

173 **"The Japanese have invaded":** Quoted in Wendy Kopp, "An Argument and Plan for the Creation of the Teacher Corps" (senior thesis, Princeton University, April 10, 1989), 4.

174 **Two-thirds of the states:** Bell, *The Thirteenth Man,* 139.

174 **"a flawed idea whose time has gone":** Edward B. Fiske, "Education; Lessons," *The New York Times,* August 3, 1988.

174 **studies of merit pay programs:** Samuel B. Bacharach, David B. Lipsky, and Joseph S. Shedd, *Paying for Better Teaching* (Ithaca, NY: Organizational Analysis and Practice, 1984), 28–29, 37–38.

175 **Kalamazoo, Michigan, provides a powerful example:** See Richard R. Doremus, "Whatever Happened to Kalamazoo's Merit Pay Plan?" *Phi Delta Kappan* 63, no. 6 (February 1982); and United States Commission

on Civil Rights, *School Desegregation in Kalamazoo, Michigan* (April 1977).

176 **In Texas, a 1984 guidebook:** Kelly Frels, Timothy T. Cooper, and Billy R. Reagan, *Practical Aspects of Teacher Evaluation* (National Organization on Legal Problems in Education, 1984).

176 **merit pay plans that were popular with teachers:** See Brian T. Burke, "Round Valley: A Merit Pay Experiment," *California Journal* (October 1983): 392–93; Gene I. Maeroff, "Merit Pay Draws Criticism and Praise From Teachers," *The New York Times,* July 2, 1983; Fiske, "Education; Lessons"; and Francis X. Clines, "Reagan Visits Tennessee in Another Swing to Press Education Issue," *The New York Times,* June 15, 1983.

176 **Gera Summerford:** Author interview with Gera Summerford, September 4, 2013.

176 **the merit pay program rolled out in 1982:** Details reported in Robert Reinhold, "School Reform: Years of Tumult, Mixed Results," *The New York Times,* August 10, 1987.

177 **$23,500 per year:** Carnegie Forum on Education and the Economy, *A Nation Prepared* (Report of the Task Force on Teaching as a Profession, 1986), 37.

177 **the Carnegie Foundation recommended:** See Ibid.; and Margot Slade, "Ideas and Trends: Teachers Urged to Face Change," *The New York Times,* August 26, 1984.

177 **Ross Perot, for example, pushed Dallas:** William E. Schmidt, "Economic Issues Spur States to Act on Schools," *The New York Times,* May 5, 1986; Reinhold, "School Reform: Years of Tumult, Mixed Results"; and Linda Darling-Hammond, "Mad-Hatter Tests of Good Teaching," *The New York Times,* January 8, 1984.

177 **formal evaluation programs were too expensive:** Larry W. Barber and Karen Klein, "Merit Pay and Teacher Evaluation," *Phi Delta Kappan* 65, no. 4 (December 1983); and David F. Wood and Dan S. Green, "Managerial Experience with Merit Pay: A Survey of the Business Literature," in Johnson, ed., *Merit, Money, and Teachers' Careers* (Lanham, MD: University Press of America, 1985).

178 **"I always was and still am against":** Edward B. Fiske, "Al Shanker: Where He Stands," *The New York Times,* November 5, 1989.

178 **"The principals were often former gym teachers":** Author interview with Chester Finn, November 11, 2013.

178 **When unions brought this suspicion:** Unlike the NEA, Al Shanker supported the Lamar Alexander career ladder plan in Tennessee, with its complex rating and classroom observation systems. He also supported a similar plan in Winston-Salem, North Carolina. See Linda Dockery and Marcia Epstein, "The Teacher Incentive Program (TIP) of the Winston-Salem/Forsyth County Schools," in Johnson, ed., *Merit, Money, and Teachers' Careers.*

179 **"takes innocent children"** and **"proudest achievement":** Gaillard, *The Dream Long Deferred,* xi.

179   Department of Justice school desegregation suits, 1980 and 1981: John L. Palmer and Elizabeth V. Sawhill, eds., *The Reagan Experiment* (Washington, D.C: The Urban Institute, 1982), 140.

179   **In 1984, Secretary Bell spent $1 million:** UPI, "U.S. Encouraging Merit Pay Plans," *The New York Times,* March 11, 1984; and AP, "Reagan Vetoes a Money Bill for Chicago's Desegregation," *The New York Times,* August 14, 1983.

180   **Bell was even on the record:** Marjorie Hunter, "Bell Will Not Push Lawsuits on Busing," *The New York Times,* March 16, 1981.

180   **In September 1999, Potter ruled in favor:** Gaillard, *The Dream Long Deferred.*

180   **According to research from the labor economist C. Kirabo Jackson:** Kirabo C. Jackson, "Student Demographics, Teacher Sorting, and Teacher Quality: Evidence from the End of School Desegregation," *Journal of Labor Economics* 27, no. 2 (2009): 213–56.

180   **The movement of experienced teachers:** For teachers' mind-sets on student race, see Kati Haycock, "The Elephant in the Living Room" (Brookings Papers on Education Policy, no. 7, 2004), 229–63; and Martin Haberman, "Selecting and Preparing Urban Teachers" (lecture, February 28, 2005, available on Web site of National Center for Alternative Teacher Certification Information).

180   **A second study:** Stephen B. Billings, David J. Deming, and Jonah Rockoff, "School Segregation, Educational Attainment and Crime: Evidence from the End of Busing in Charlotte-Mecklenburg," *Quarterly Journal of Economics,* September 17, 2013.

181   **In a separate paper:** Byron Lutz, "The End of Court-Ordered Desegregation," *American Economic Journal: Economic Policy* 3, no. 2 (2011): 130–68.

181   **One of the most compelling:** Heather Schwartz, *Housing Policy Is School Policy: Economically Integrative Housing Promotes Academic Success in Montgomery County, Maryland* (Century Foundation study, 2010).

181   **In 1980 American school integration reached:** Linda Darling-Hammond, *The Flat World and Education* (New York: Teachers College Press, 2010), 35.

181   **"In the sixties and seventies":** Wendy Kopp with Steven Farr, *A Chance to Make History* (New York: Public Affairs, 2011), 4–5.

182   **he sought to push the standards:** David K. Cohen and Susan L. Moffitt, *The Ordeal of Equality: Did Federal Regulation Fix the Schools?* (Cambridge, MA: Harvard University Press, 2009), 139.

183   **Kati Haycock:** See Karin Chenoweth, "In Education We Trust," *Black Issues in Higher Education* 15, no. 22 (December 1998): 14; and Kati Haycock, "'Five Things I've Learned,'" Pearson Foundation Web site, http://www.thefivethings.org/kati-haycock/#.

183   **The Education Trust distributed massive data books:** New York Times News Service, "Test-Score Gap for Minorities Widening Again, Study Finds," December 29, 1996; Chenoweth, "In Education We Trust"; and

Dale Mezzacappa, "In Poor Schools, Lower-Quality Teachers Abound, Report Says," *Philadelphia Inquirer,* June 22, 2000.

184   **Another issue was:** A good summary of research on class size: Matthew M. Chingos and Grover J. "Russ" Whitehurst, "Class Size: What Research Says and What It Means for Public Policy" (paper, Brookings Institution, May 11, 2011).

184   **"color a poster":** "Alums Making a Difference: Kati Haycock," *GSE Term Paper* (fall 2001).

184   **"semiliterate aides":** Mary Jordan, "Panel Says Poor Children Disserved by School Aid," *Washington Post,* December 11, 1992.

184   **"The polls among black folk"** and **"Twenty or 30 years ago":** Chenoweth, "In Education We Trust."

185   **"Bush's message":** Joan Walsh, "Surprise: Bush Could Be the 'Education President,'" *Salon,* September 17, 1999.

186   **"bridging instruments":** Cohen and Moffitt, *The Ordeal of Equality,* 142.

186   **In Texas:** Ibid., 168.

186   **In 2009 Alabama reported:** See table at http://nces.ed.gov/nationsreport card/studies/statemapping/2009_naep_state_table.aspx.

186   **Perhaps the most lasting outcome:** Alexander Russo, *Left Out of No Child Left Behind: Teach for America's Outsized Influence on Alternative Certification* (American Enterprise Institute report, October 2012).

187   **"I know this is a poem":** Linda Perlstein, *Tested: One American School Struggles to Make the Grade* (New York: Henry Holt, 2007).

187   **Research confirmed:** Jane L. David, "Research Says . . . High-Stakes Testing Narrows the Curriculum," *Educational Leadership* 68, no. 6 (March 2011): 78–80.

187   **In Florida, schools were more likely to suspend:** Tiffany Pakkala, "Study: Suspensions Can Often Help School's FCAT," *Gainesville Sun,* June 14, 2006.

187   **"Texas Miracle":** Michael Winerip, "On Education: The 'Zero Dropout' Miracle," *The New York Times,* August 13, 2003; Rebecca Leung, "'60 Minutes' Report Investigates Claims That Houston Schools Falsified Dropout Rates," CBS News, January 6, 2004.

188   **By 2005 the NEA's:** *The American Public School Teacher: Past, Present, and Future,* ed. Darrel Drury and Justin Baer (Cambridge, MA: Harvard Education Press, 2011), 43.

188   **"The key to measuring is to test":** "Remarks on the No Child Left Behind Act" (speech by President George W. Bush, Philadelphia, January 8, 2009). Available at http://www.gpo.gov/fdsys/pkg/PPP-2008-book2 /html/PPP-2008-book2-doc-pg1522-2.htm.

CHAPTER NINE: "BIG, MEASURABLE GOALS"

189   **Wendy Kopp:** Wendy Kopp, *One Day All Children: The Unlikely Triumph of Teach for America and What I Learned Along the Way* (New

York: Public Affairs, 2001); and Donna Foote, *Relentless Pursuit: A Year in the Trenches with Teach for America* (New York: Alfred A. Knopf, 2008).

190   **"the new idealism," a "yuppie volunteering spirit"**: Kopp, "An Argument and Plan for the Creation of the Teacher Corps," 10–11.

190   **"politicized nature"**: Ibid., 46.

190   **"the brightest minds"**: Ibid., 45.

190   **"the best possible job"**: Ibid., 2.

191   **"break" from "fast-paced lives"**: Ibid., 45.

191   **"send the signal"**: Ibid., 49.

191   **sent her a cautious letter in response**: Reproduced in Ibid., 159–60.

191   **"an emergency response"**: Ibid., 50.

192   **"Something to Think About"**: Flyer reproduced in Kopp, *One Day All Children*, 36–37.

193   **TFA's inaugural class**: Author interview with Alex Caputo-Pearl, February 27, 2011; and Kopp, *One Day All Children*, 50–52.

194   **Of the first class of TFA recruits**: Michael Shapiro, *Who Will Teach for America?* (Washington, D.C.: Farragut Publishing Company, 1993), 189.

194   **"What Teach for America had accomplished"**: Ibid., 75.

195   **"Giving the least experienced teachers the toughest classes"**: Jonathan Schorr, "Class Action: What Clinton's National Service Program Could Learn From 'Teach for America,' " *Phi Delta Kappan* 75, no. 4 (December 1993): 315–18.

195   **Kopp dismissed this suggestion**: Shapiro, *Who Will Teach for America?*, 79.

195   **"a frankly missionary program"**: Linda Darling-Hammond, "Who Will Speak for the Children: How 'Teach for America' Hurts Urban Schools and Students," *Phi Delta Kappan* 76, no. 1 (September 1994): 21–34.

196   **certain types of education classes**: See Linda Darling-Hammond's review of the effects of various teacher qualities and training experiences on student achievement: "Teacher Quality and Student Achievement: A Review of State Policy Evidence" (University of Washington, Center for the Study of Teaching and Policy report, 1999), 8.

196   **10 percent of entering teacher-ed students**: Berliner and Biddle, *The Manufactured Crisis*, 105–6.

196   **"We need an entirely new"**: Samuel Casey Carter, *No Excuses: Lessons from High-Performing, High-Poverty Schools* (Washington, D.C.: Heritage Foundation, 2000), 17.

196   **"Generally, the TFA teachers"**: Patricia Sellers, "Schooling Corporate Giants on Recruiting," *Fortune*, November 27, 2006.

196   **"They work in service of a corporate reform agenda"**: Catherine Michna, "Why I Stopped Writing Recommendation Letters for Teach for America," *Slate*, October 9, 2013.

200   **Teaching as Leadership**: Quotes are from Steven Farr and Teach for America, *Teaching as Leadership: The Highly Effective Teacher's Guide to Closing the Achievement Gap* (San Francisco: Jossey-Bass, 2010); and

the Teaching as Leadership Web site, http://www.teachingasleadership .org/.

201   **The research consensus on TFA:** There have been two randomized control trials comparing TFA recruits to teachers from other pathways, both of which were conducted by Mathematica; they found TFA teachers were more effective at producing test score gains in math. A possible shortcoming of these studies is that TFA teachers were compared not only to traditionally trained teachers, but also to teachers with alternative certifications from other programs, some of which are of very poor quality. A 2005 Linda Darling-Hammond analysis of student-teacher data compared Houston TFA teachers explicitly to teachers who studied education in college or graduate school. It found that students of uncertified TFA corps members were two weeks to three months behind their peers in classrooms with certified teachers. Teach for America teachers who earned certification in their second or third years on the job appeared no different from other teachers, however, and were perhaps slightly stronger in math. See Paul T. Decker, Daniel P. Mayer, and Steven Glazerman, *The Effects of Teach for America on Students: Findings from a National Evaluation* (Mathematica report, June 9, 2004); Melissa A. Clark et al., "The Effectiveness of Secondary Math Teachers from Teach for America and the Teaching Fellows Programs" (Mathematica study, Institute of Education Sciences, U.S. Department of Education, September 2013); Linda Darling-Hammond et al., "Does Teacher Preparation Matter? Evidence About Teacher Certification, Teach for America, and Teacher Effectiveness," *Education Policy Analysis Archives* 13, no. 42 (2005); and Dylan Matthews, "Teach for America's Teachers Are Besting Their Peers on Math, Study Shows," *Washington Post,* April 5, 2013.

202   **A cache of studies:** Andrew C. Butler and Henry L. Roediger, "Testing Improves Long-Term Retention in a Simulated Classroom Setting," *European Journal of Cognitive Psychology* 19, no. 4/5 (2007); Henry L. Roediger and Andrew C. Butler, "The Critical Role of Retrieval Practice in Long-Term Retention," *Trends in Cognitive Sciences* 15, no. 1 (2010): 20–27.

202   **"developing a strong desire to control":** John Hattie, *Visible Learning: A Synthesis of Over 800 Meta-Analyses Relating to Achievement* (New York: Routledge, 2009).

203   **The KIPP schools:** For a fascinating narrative of KIPP's history and role in the contemporary education reform movement, see Jay Mathews, *Work Hard. Be Nice: How Two Inspired Teachers Created the Most Promising Schools in America* (Chapel Hill, NC: Algonquin Books, 2009).

203   **"education can trump poverty":** Kopp, *A Chance to Make History,* 109.

203   **"We . . . control our students' success":** Farr and Teach for America, *Teaching as Leadership,* 198.

204   **"the difference between entry into a selective college":** Testimony of Kati Haycock, President, the Education Trust, Before the U.S. House of Rep-

resentatives Committee on Education and the Workforce, Subcommittee on 21st Century Competitiveness, May 20, 2003.

204　When the older generation: Douglas N. Harris and Stacy A. Rutledge, "Models and Predictors of Teacher Effectiveness: A Comparison of Research About Teaching and Other Occupations," *Teachers College Record* 112, no. 3 (2010): 914–60.

205　Value-added measurement: See William L. Sanders and June C. Rivers, "Cumulative and Residual Effects of Teachers on Future Student Academic Achievement" (Knoxville: University of Tennessee Value-Added Research and Assessment Center, November, 1996); S. Paul Wright, Sandra P. Horn, and William L. Sanders, "Teacher and Classroom Context Effects on Student Achievement: Implications for Teacher Evaluation," *Journal of Personnel Evaluation in Education* 11 (1997): 57–67; and Jim Schutze, "Baby, It's Them," *Dallas Observer,* January 29, 1998.

205　A more sensitive early value-added formula: Heather R. Jordan et al., *Teacher Effects on Longitudinal Student Achievement* (Dallas Public Schools report on research in progress, July 1997).

205　Growth measures that track: For an excellent discussion of the differences between snapshot and growth/value-added measures of student achievement, see Douglas N. Harris, *Value-Added Measurements in Education* (Cambridge, MA: Harvard Education Press, 2011).

206　New York City value-added model: Value-Added Research Center at University of Wisconsin–Madison and New York City Department of Education, *New York City Data Initiative: Technical Report on the NYC Value-Added Model* (2010).

206　Using these methods: An excellent and readable summary of value-added research is Harris, *Value-Added Measurements in Education.* Also see Douglas N. Harris and Tim R. Sass, "Teacher Training, Teacher Quality, and Student Achievement," *Journal of Public Economics* 95 (2011). For teacher quality variation within and between schools, see Raj Chetty, John N. Friedman, and Jonah E. Rockoff, "Measuring the Impact of Teachers I–II: Evaluating Bias in Teacher Value-Added Estimates" (working papers 19424 and 19423, National Bureau of Economic Research, Cambridge, MA, 2013). For evidence that black teachers are more effective with students of color, see Eric A. Hanushek et al., "The Market for Teacher Quality" (working paper 11154, National Bureau of Economic Research, Cambridge, MA, 2005). For the effects of teacher training and professional development, see Darling-Hammond, "Teacher Quality and Student Achievement: A Review of State Policy Evidence."

206　the error rate: Peter Z. Schochet and Hanley S. Chiang, *Error Rates in Measuring Teacher and School Performance Based on Student Test Score Gains* (Institute of Education Sciences/Mathematica report, 2010).

207　two-thirds of teachers who: Harris, *Value-Added Measurements in Education,* 122.

207　five "good teachers in a row": Eric A. Hanushek and Steven B. Rivkin,

"How to Improve the Supply of High-Quality Teachers" (Brookings Papers on Education Policy, 2004).

207   **In a 2006 paper:** Robert Gordon, Thomas J. Kane, and Douglas O. Staiger, "Identifying Effective Teachers Using Performance on the Job" (Hamilton Project paper, Brookings Institution, April 2006).

208   **This reality was demonstrated:** Chetty, Friedman, and Rockoff, "Measuring the Impact of Teachers I–II."

208   **When a separate Department of Education/Mathematica trial:** Steven Glazerman, *Transfer Incentives for High-Performing Teachers: Final Results From a Multisite Randomized Experiment* (U.S. Department of Education/Mathematica Policy Research report, November 2013).

209   **In 2007 Gates met:** For Bill Gates's introduction to value-added research and his early work on teacher evaluation, see Steven Brill, *Class Warfare: Inside the Fight to Fix America's Schools* (New York: Simon and Schuster, 2011), 178–80 and 229–35.

210   **An August 2012 *Vanity Fair* article:** Kurt Eichenwald, "Microsoft's Lost Decade," *Vanity Fair,* August 2012.

210   **Elsewhere in the corporate world:** Greg Anrig, "Chicago Teachers' Strike: What Do We Want? Better Management Gurus Might Help," *Pacific Standard,* September 17, 2012.

210   **Even Japanese schools:** To learn more about lesson study, which is gaining popularity in the United States, see http://www.lessonresearch.net/.

210   **"I am actually really intrigued":** David Herszenhorn, "Test Scores to Be Used to Analyze Schools' Roles," *The New York Times,* June 7, 2005.

210   **She agreed to an experiment:** Marcus G. Springer and Marcus A. Winters, *New York's School-Wide Bonus Pay Program: Early Evidence from a Randomized Trial* (report, National Center of Performance Incentives, Vanderbilt University, April 2009).

211   **One of the hottest tickets:** Dana Goldstein, "The Democratic Education Divide," *American Prospect,* August 25, 2008.

212   **As an Illinois state senator:** Howard Schulman, "Charter Schools Working," *Providence Journal,* August 27, 2004.

212   **he spoke at the launch party of Democrats for Education Reform:** These scenes are re-created in Brill, *Class Warfare,* 131–32.

212   **he was booed at an NEA event:** Ruth Marcus, "From Barack Obama, Two Dangerous Words," *Washington Post,* July 11, 2007.

212   **"wonderful new superintendent":** Jeff Chu, "Obama and McCain Fight Over a Woman," *Fast Company,* October 20, 2008.

212   **When it came time:** Dana Goldstein, "The Selling of School Reform," *The Nation,* June 15, 2009.

213   **"the current research base is insufficient":** "The Promise and Peril of Using Value-Added Modeling to Measure Teacher Effectiveness" (RAND Education research brief, Santa Monica, CA, 2004).

213   **"Let me be clear":** "Obama Speaks to the U.S. Hispanic Chamber of Commerce," March 10, 2009. Transcript available at http://www

.washingtonpost.com/wp-srv/politics/documents/Obama_Hispanic_
Chamber_Commerce.html.

215   **"There's got to be a sense of accountability":** Michael A. Fletcher and
Nick Anderson, "Obama Angers Union Officials with Remarks in Support of R.I. Teacher Firings," *Washington Post,* March 2, 2010.

216   **"Only 7 percent of American workers":** Dana Goldstein, "Grading
'Waiting for Superman,'" *The Nation,* October 11, 2010.

216   **A 2013 AFT study:** Howard Nelson, *Testing More, Teaching Less* (American Federation of Teachers report, 2013).

218   **"There might be good reason":** Harris, *Value-Added Measurements in
Education,* 181.

219   **But in September 2013:** Geoff Decker and Philissa Cramer, "Instead of
Telling Teachers Apart, New Evals Lump Some Together," Chalkbeat
New York, September 16, 2013.

219   **In Florida, Tennessee, and other states:** For information on how "shared
attribution" works, see Laura Bornfreund, "An Ocean of Unknowns:
Risks and Opportunities in Using Student Achievement to Evaluate PreK–3rd Grade Teachers" (New America Foundation study, May
2013). For problems in Alachua County and Kim Cook's story, see Dan
Boyd, "Value-Added Model Has No Value," *Gainesville Sun,* December
9, 2012; and Valerie Strauss, "A 'Value-Added' Travesty for an Award-
Winning Teacher," *Washington Post,* December 3, 2012.

220   **A 2012 survey of ten thousand American teachers:** *Primary Sources 2012:
American Teachers on the Teaching Profession* (poll from Scholastic and
the Bill and Melinda Gates Foundation, 2012); and Terry M. Moe, *Special Interest: Teachers Unions and America's Public Schools* (Washington, D.C.: Brookings Institution Press, 2011), 404–5.

221   **A national poll from Gallup:** Dinesh Ramde, "Wis. Poll: Walker Law
Really About Hurting Unions," *Boston Globe*/Associated Press, April
22, 2011; and Judy Keen and Dennis Cauchon, "Poll: Americans Favor
Union Bargaining Rights," *USA Today,* February 23, 2011.

221   **But polls showed the majority of parents:** Whet Moser, "Poll Shows Sub-
stantial Parent, Racial Divide on Chicago Teachers Strike," *Chicago,*
September 17, 2012.

221   **"a corporate attack":** Jeffrey Brown, "Chicago Board of Education Plans
to Shut Down 54 Schools, Move 30,000 Students" (transcript of *PBS
NewsHour* interview with Karen Lewis, March 22, 2013).

222   **Teach for America emerged as a flash point:** Lauren Fitzpatrick, "CPS
Calls Teacher's Mom to Tell Him He's Getting Laid Off," *Chicago Sun-
Times,* July 19, 2013; Eric Zorn, "Should Teach for America Pack Its
Bags?" *Chicago Tribune,* July 30, 2013.

222   **"There are still places in the United States":** Author interview with Steve
Zimmer, July 22, 2013.

223   **Robert Schwartz:** Author interview with Robert Schwartz, July 19, 2013.

224   **Research from the National Center on Performance Incentives:** Reports

on merit pay in New York, Nashville, and Austin can be found at https://my.vanderbilt.edu/performanceincentives/research/.

225 **In New York City in 2012:** Al Baker, "Many New York City Teachers Denied Tenure in Policy Shift," *The New York Times,* August 17, 2012.

225 **the District of Columbia stuck with its plan:** Emma Brown, "98 Teachers Fired for Poor Performance," *Washington Post,* August 1, 2012; Bill Turque, "Many Teachers Pass on IMPACT Bonuses," *Washington Post,* January 28, 2011; Emma Brown, "D.C. Traditional Public School Teacher Pay Is Higher Than Charters," *Washington Post,* August 19, 2013.

226 **Was teaching improving in D.C.?:** For analysis of teacher evaluation and turnover in District public schools, see Thomas Dee and James Wyckoff, "Incentives, Selection, and Teacher Performance: Evidence from Impact" (working paper 19529, National Bureau of Economic Research, Cambridge, MA, October 2013); and *Keeping Irreplaceables in D.C. Public Schools* (The New Teachers Project report, 2012).

226 **a series of exposés:** For the first piece on adult cheating in D.C. under Michelle Rhee, with links to follow-ups, see Jack Gillum and Marisol Bello, "When Standardized Test Scores Soared in D.C., Were the Gains Real?" *USA Today,* March 30, 2011.

227 **Noyes was not an isolated case:** For investigations of adult cheating nationwide, see Greg Toppo et al., "When Test Scores Seem Too Good to Believe," *USA Today,* March 17, 2011; and *Atlanta Journal-Constitution* staff reports, "From Scandal at APS to Suspicious Scores Nationwide," *The Atlanta Journal-Constitution,* March 30, 2013.

227 **On March 29, 2013:** For the Atlanta cheating scandal, see Michael Winerip, "Ex-Schools Chief in Atlanta Is Indicted in Testing Scandal," *The New York Times,* March 29, 2013; and Olivia Blanchard, "I Quit Teach for America," *The Atlantic,* September 23, 2013.

227 **"The existence of cheating":** Arne Duncan, "Despite Cheating Scandals, Testing and Teaching Are Not at Odds," *Washington Post,* July 19, 2011.

228 **a "tiny" rounding error:** Author interview with Bill Gates, January 30, 2013.

228 **When New York City released:** Fernanda Santos and Robert Gebeloff, "Teacher Quality Widely Diffused, Ratings Indicate," *The New York Times,* February 24, 2012.

228 **Already there is some evidence:** Stephen Sawchuck, "Teachers' Ratings Still High Despite New Measures," *Education Week,* February 5, 2013.

229 **Colorado state senator Mike Johnston:** Dana Goldstein, "The Test Generation," *American Prospect,* April 2011.

229 **"The majority of [American] teachers":** Eric A. Hanushek, "Teacher Deselection," in *Creating a New Teaching Profession* (Washington, D.C.: Urban Institute, 2009), 177.

230 **"We all know test scores":** Author interview with Jonah Rockoff, October 8, 2013.

230 **But as Arne Duncan has acknowledged:** Brill, *Class Warfare,* 422–23.

230 **"I'd seen too many examples"**: Michelle Rhee, *Radical* (New York: HarperCollins, 2013), 154.

CHAPTER TEN: "LET ME USE WHAT I KNOW"

231 **According to a 2013 poll:** *Primary Sources: America's Teachers on Teaching in an Era of Change* (poll from Scholastic and the Bill and Melinda Gates Foundation, 2013).

232 **Polls of teachers who leave:** Laura Bornfreund, "Do Teachers Care About Pay? Yes, but Not As Much As You'd Think," *Slate,* December 7, 2011.

233 **the Bill and Melinda Gates Foundation began a massive study:** Kane and Staiger, *Gathering Feedback for Teaching.*

233 **A 2011 observation:** Stephen B. Plank and Barbara Condliffe, *Pressures of the Season: A Descriptive Look at Classroom Quality in Second and Third Grade Classrooms* (Baltimore Education Research Consortium report, February 2011).

233 **A 2009 review:** Pianta and Hamre, "Conceptualization, Measurement, and Improvement of Classroom Processes."

233 **But research shows:** See chapters 7, 9, and 10 in Hattie, *Visible Learning: A Synthesis of Over 800 Meta-Analyses Relating to Achievement.*

235 **There is nothing new:** For the history of classroom observation, see Robert J. Marzano et al., "A Brief History of Supervision and Evaluation," in *Effective Supervision* (Alexandria, VA: ASCD, 2011).

236 **Danielson wanted to watch teachers work:** Charlotte Danielson interview with author, December 30, 2013.

240 **a district of more than nine thousand teachers:** E-mail correspondence between author and Marcia Vogel, supervisor of special projects, Office of Communications, Montgomery County Public Schools, October 4, 2013.

240 **Journalist John Merrow ran the numbers in Toledo:** John Merrow, "Ohio School District Uses Unique Peer Evaluations to Grade Teachers," PBS NewsHour transcript, December 14, 2010.

241 **researcher Julia Koppich:** Julia Koppich, *Toward Improving Teacher Quality: An Evaluation of Peer Assistance and Review in Montgomery County Public Schools* (Montgomery County Public Schools report, June 8, 2004).

241 **"Maybe the problem":** Author interview with Kati Haycock, October 7, 2013.

242 **few principals can offer struggling teachers:** For information on principal caseloads, author interview with Garth Harries, August 15, 2013; and Jesse Rothstein, "Effects of Value-Added Policies," *Focus* 29, no. 2 (2012). Consultant teacher caseloads in Susan Moore Johnson et al., *Teacher to Teacher: Realizing the Potential of Peer Assistance and Review* (Center for American Progress report, 2010).

243 **Replacing a teacher costs a district:** Johnson et al., *Teacher to Teacher.*

243 **"the powers that be in this country"**: Elisa Crouch, "National Teachers Union Leader Points to St. Louis as a Model," *St. Louis Post-Dispatch*, August 14, 2013.

244 **"If all you do is judge teachers by test results"**: Theodoric Meyer, "An Evaluation Architect Says Teaching Is Hard, but Assessing It Shouldn't Be," *The New York Times*, February 15, 2012.

245 **"Teaching reading is a science"**: Author interview with Caryn Henning, October 8, 2013.

246 **An initial study of the program:** Results provided by the Children's Literacy Initiative to author via e-mail, February 25, 2014.

246 **A 2010 randomized trial:** results available at http://www.cli.org/sites /default/files/OMG%20Assessment%20Summary%201.10%20 -%20FINAL.pdf.

246 **Raj Chetty, Jonah Rockoff, and John Friedman study:** Raj Chetty, John N. Friedman, and Jonah E. Rockoff, "The Long-Term Impacts of Teachers: Teacher Value-Added and Student Outcomes in Adulthood" (working paper 17699, National Bureau of Economic Research, Cambridge, MA, 2011), 4.

247 **Facebook founder Mark Zuckerberg announced:** Details on how the philanthropic dollars were spent are available at http://foundation fornewarksfuture.org/grants/.

247 **"Too much school reform is about blowing up systems"**: Author interview with Jen Weikert, October 8, 2013.

248 **They urged Congress:** Sarah Almy et al., *Preparing and Advancing Teachers and School Leaders: A New Approach for Federal Policy* (Education Trust report, September 2013).

248 **major problems with teacher education in America:** Julie Greenberg, Laura Pomerance, and Kate Walsh, *Student Teaching in the United States* (National Council on Teacher Quality report, July 2011).

249 **"Many in the field"**: Greenberg, McKee, and Walsh, *Teacher Prep Review*, 2013.

250 **An eight-year study:** Matthew Ronfeldt, Susanna Loeb, and James Wyckoff, "How Teacher Turnover Harms Student Achievement," *American Educational Research Journal* 50, no. 1 (2013): 4–36.

251 **When Thomas Kane, Douglas Staiger, and Robert Gordon:** Gordon, Kane, and Staiger, "Identifying Effective Teachers Using Performance on the Job."

251 **a system developed by Martin Haberman:** Martin Haberman, "Selecting and Preparing Urban Teachers" (lecture, February 28, 2005, available on the Web site of National Center for Alternative Teacher Certification Information); and author interview with Christine Brennan Davis of Urban Teacher Residency United, September 25, 2013.

253 **found a mixed record on student achievement:** See John R. Papay et al., "Does Practice-Based Teacher Preparation Increase Student Achievement? Early Evidence from the Boston Teacher Residency" (working paper 17646, National Bureau of Economic Research, Cambridge, MA,

December 2011). Also see http://memphistr.org/2013results/ and http://www.utrunited.org/about-us/research-and-publications.

254 **"very problematic"**: Morgaen L. Donaldson and Susan Moore Johnson, "TFA Teachers: How Long Do They Teach? Why Do They Leave?" *Education Week,* October 4, 2011.

255 **"A lot of UTRs"**: Author interview with Christine Brennan Davis.

255 **At Kingsbury High School**: Author interview with David Montague of Memphis Teacher Residency, November 4, 2013, and author interview with Marcus Clark, October 9, 2013.

256 **Alex Caputo-Pearl**: Author interviewed Caputo-Pearl on six occasions between 2010 and 2013. Author visited Crenshaw High School, where she observed teacher professional development, on May 20 and 21, 2011.

257 **"leftist crazies"**: Erin Aubry Kaplan, "Reviving Education," *LA Weekly,* May 12, 2005.

258 **it was rooted in solid research**: John M. Bridgeland, John J. Dilulio, Jr., and Karen Burke Morison, *The Silent Epidemic: Perspectives of High School Dropouts* (Report by Civic Enterprises in association with Peter D. Hart Research Associations for the Bill and Melinda Gates Foundation, March 2006).

259 **Donald Boyd's 2010 study**: Donald Boyd et al., "The Role of Teacher Quality in Retention and Hiring: Using Applications-to-Transfer to Uncover Preferences of Teachers and Schools" (working paper 15966, National Bureau of Economic Research, Cambridge, MA, May 2010).

260 **Nevertheless, at Crenshaw**: Statistics on race, classes taught, and years of experience of dismissed teachers collected by Alex Caputo-Pearl and Cathy Garcia, sent to author via e-mail on May 5, 2013.

260 **"It is a fundamental right"**: Howard Blume and Stephen Caesar, "L.A. Unified to Overhaul Struggling Crenshaw High," *Los Angeles Times,* January 16, 2013.

260 **achievement data at Crenshaw**: See http://api.cde.ca.gov/Acnt2012/2012GrowthSch.aspx?allcds=19647331932128. Graduation and suspension rates provided to author by Alex Caputo-Pearl.

260 **At Central Falls High School**: See http://infoworks.ride.ri.gov/school/central-falls-high-school; and Kate Nagle, "New Report: Central Falls Graduation Rate Increased 20% in 3 Years," GoLocal Prov Web site, October 19, 2013.

EPILOGUE

263 **But education finance expert**: Bruce Baker, *Revisiting that Age-Old Question: Does Money Matter in Education?* (Albert Shanker Institute report, 2012).

263 **median income**: All figures from the Bureau of Labor Statistics, *Occupational Outlook Handbook,* http://www.bls.gov/ooh/. The figure for teachers was calculated by averaging the median incomes of elementary, middle, and high school teachers.

264   **In the 1940s, male teachers earned:** Eric A. Hanushek, "Valuing Teachers: How Much Is a Good Teacher Worth?" *Education Next* 11, no. 3 (2011).

264   **In South Korea, teacher salaries:** Byron Auguste, Paul Kihn, and Matt Miller, *Closing the Talent Gap: Attracting and Retaining Top-Third Graduates in Teaching* (McKinsey and Company report, September 2010), 20.

264   **a New York City public school teacher:** The UFT salary schedule is available at http://www.uft.org/our-rights/salary-schedules/teachers. For North Carolina, see Emery P. Dalesio, "Report: NC Teacher Pay Slides Against Peer States," WRAL/Associated Press, March 6, 2013.

265   **"plural professionalism":** Jal Mehta and Steven Teles, "Professionalism 2.0: The Case for Plural Professionalism in Education" in *Teacher Quality 2.0: Toward a New Era in Education Reform,* ed. Frederick Hess and Michael McShane (Cambridge, MA: Harvard Education Press, 2014).

267   **In Singapore, after three years on the job:** Rachel Curtis, *Finding a New Way: Leveraging Teacher Leadership to Meet Unprecedented Demands* (Aspen Institute report, February 2013).

267   **a huge oversupply of prospective elementary school teachers:** Stephen Sawchuk, "Colleges Overproducing Elementary Teachers, Data Find," *Education Week,* January 23, 2013.

267   **Preliminary data from New York City:** Reports on New York teacher prep institutions available at http://schools.nyc.gov/Offices/DHR /HumanCapitalData/TPPR.

268   **A McKinsey study:** Auguste, Kihn, and Miller, *Closing the Talent Gap.*

268   **"put on a diet":** *Fixing Classroom Observations* (The New Teacher Project report, November 2013).

270   **Yet only 17 percent of public school teachers are nonwhite:** Data from "Teacher Trends," National Center for Education Statistics, https://nces .ed.gov/fastfacts/display.asp?id=28.

271   **Between 2010 and 2012, 2.5 percent:** From a National Council on Teacher Quality survey of large urban districts, 2011. Results at http:// www.nctq.org/commentary/viewStory.do?id=29568.

271   **there are only twelve states:** Via StudentsFirst, http://www.studentsfirst .org/lifo.

272   **surveys of dropouts:** Bridgeland, Dilulio, and Morison, *The Silent Epidemic.*

273   **"radically decentralized":** David Labaree, *Someone Has to Fail* (Cambridge, MA: Harvard University Press, 2010).

Selected Bibliography

I consulted over five hundred primary and secondary sources while writing this book, most of which are detailed in the endnotes. The works below, arranged by topic, are those I returned to again and again for perspective on the history, social science, and politics of teaching.

GENERAL EDUCATION HISTORY

Callahan, Raymond E. *Education and the Cult of Efficiency*. Chicago: University of Chicago Press, 1962.

Davies, Gareth. *See Government Grow: Education Politics from Johnson to Reagan*. Lawrence: University Press of Kansas, 2007.

Herrick, Mary R. *The Chicago Schools: A Social and Political History*. Beverly Hills: Sage Publications, 1971.

Lemann, Nicholas. *The Big Test: The Secret History of the American Meritocracy*. New York: Farrar, Straus and Giroux, 1999.

Ravitch, Diane. *The Great School Wars: New York City, 1805–1973*. New York: Basic Books, 1974.

———. *Left Back: A Century of Battles over School Reform*. New York: Touchstone, 2000.

Snyder, Thomas D., ed. *120 Years of American Education: A Statistical Portrait*. National Center for Education Statistics. U.S. Department of Education, January 1993.

Tyack, David, and Larry Cuban. *Tinkering Toward Utopia: A Century of Public School Reform*. Cambridge, MA: Harvard University Press, 1995.

EARLY AMERICAN EDUCATION AND THE COMMON SCHOOLS MOVEMENT

Cremin, Lawrence. *The American Common School*. New York: Teachers College, Columbia University, 1951.

Kaestle, C F. *Pillars of the Republic: Common Schools and American Society, 1780–1860*. New York: Hill and Wang, 1983.

Mann, Horace. *Lectures on Education*. Boston: W. B. Fowle and N. Capen, 1855.

Messerli, Jonathan. *Horace Mann*. New York: Alfred A. Knopf, 1972.

THE FEMINIZATION OF TEACHING

Albisetti, James C. "The Feminization of Teaching in the Nineteenth Century: A Comparative Perspective." *History of Education* 22, no. 3 (1993): 253–63.

Beecher, Catharine. *The Duty of American Women to Their Country*. New York: Harper and Brothers, 1845.

———. *Educational Reminiscences and Suggestions*. New York: J. B. Ford, 1874.

———.*The Evils Suffered by American Women and American Children: The Causes and the Remedy*. New York: Harper and Brothers, 1846.

———. "Female Education." *American Journal of Education* 2 (1827): 219–23.

———. *Suggestions Respecting Improvements in Education*. Hartford, CT: Packard and Butler, 1829.

Goldin, Claudia. *Understanding the Gender Gap: An Economic History of American Women*. New York: Oxford University Press, 1990.

Gordon, Ann D., ed. *The Selected Papers of Elizabeth Cady Stanton and Susan B. Anthony*. 6 vols. New Brunswick, NJ: Rutgers University Press, 1997–2012.

Hoffman, Nancy. *Woman's "True" Profession: Voices from the History of Teaching*. Old Westbury, NY: Feminist Press, 1981.

Mann, Horace. *A Few Thoughts on the Powers and Duties of Woman: Two Lectures*. Syracuse: Hall, Mills, and Company, 1853.

Rugoff, Milton. *The Beechers: An American Family in the Nineteenth Century*. New York: Harper and Row, 1981.

Sklar, Kathryn Kish. *Catharine Beecher: A Study in American Domesticity*. New York: W. W. Norton, 1976.

Sugg, Redding S. *Motherteacher: The Feminization of American Education*. Charlottesville: University of Virginia Press, 1978.

Woody, Thomas. *A History of Women's Education in the United States*. 2 vols. New York: The Science Press, 1929.

THE AFRICAN AMERICAN TEACHING TRADITION

Aptheker, Herbert, ed. *The Correspondence of W. E. B. Du Bois*. 3 vols. Amherst: University of Massachusetts Press, 1973–1978.

Delpit, Lisa. *Other People's Children: Cultural Conflict in the Classroom*. New York: The New Press, 2006.

Du Bois, W. E. B. *The Education of Black People: Ten Critiques, 1906–1960*. Edited by Herbert Aptheker. Amherst: University of Massachusetts Press, 1973.

———. *The Souls of Black Folk*. New York: Bantam, 1903.

Gabel, Leona C. *From Slavery to the Sorbonne and Beyond: The Life and Writings of Anna J. Cooper*. Northampton, MA: Smith College Library, 1982.

Grimké, Charlotte Forten. *The Journals of Charlotte Forten Grimké*. Edited by Brenda Stevenson. New York: Oxford University Press, 1988.

Ladson-Billings, Gloria. *The Dream-Keepers: Successful Teachers of African American Children*. San Francisco: Jossey-Bass, 2009.

Lemert, Charles, and Esme Bhan, eds. *The Voice of Anna Julia Cooper*. Lanham, MD: Rowman and Littlefield Publishers, 1998.

Lewis, David Levering. *W. E. B. Du Bois: A Biography*. New York: Henry Holt, 2009.

Norrell, Robert J. *Up from History: The Life of Booker T. Washington*. Cambridge, MA: Belknap Press, 2009.

Washington, Booker T. *Up From Slavery*. New York: W. W. Norton, 1901.

Weinberg, Meyer. *A Chance to Learn: The History of Race and Education in the United States*. New York: Cambridge University Press, 1977.

UNIONS

Berube, Maurice R., and Marilyn Gittell, eds. *Confrontation at Ocean Hill–Brownsville: The New York School Strikes of 1968*. New York: Frederick A. Praeger, 1969.

Carter, Barbara. *Pickets, Parents, and Power: The Story Behind the New York City Teachers' Strike*. New York: Citation Press, 1971.

Cohen, Andrew Wender. *The Racketeer's Progress: Chicago and the Struggle for the Modern American Economy, 1900–1940*. Cambridge, UK: Cambridge University Press, 2004.

Collins, Christina. *"Ethnically Qualified": Race, Merit, and the Selection of Urban Teachers, 1920–1980*. New York: Teachers College Press, 2011.

Golin, Steve. *The Newark Teacher Strikes: Hopes on the Line*. New Brunswick, NJ: Rutgers University Press, 2002.

Haley, Margaret A. *Battleground: The Autobiography of Margaret A. Haley*. Edited by Robert L. Reid. Champaign: University of Illinois Press, 1982.

Kahlenberg, Richard D. *Tough Liberal: Albert Shanker and the Battles over Schools, Unions, Race, and Democracy*. New York: Columbia University Press, 2007.

Moe, Terry M. *Special Interest: Teachers Unions and America's Public Schools*. Washington, D.C.: Brookings Institution Press, 2011.

Murphy, Marjorie. *Blackboard Unions: The AFT and the NEA: 1900–1980*. Ithaca, NY: Cornell University Press, 1990.

Perlstein, Daniel H. *Justice, Justice: School Politics and the Eclipse of Liberalism*. New York: Peter Lang, 2004.

Rousmaniere, Kate. *Citizen Teacher: The Life and Leadership of Margaret Haley*. Albany: State University of New York Press, 2005.

Zitron, Celia Lewis. *The New York City Teachers' Union, 1916–1964*. New York: Humanities Press, 1968.

THE RED SCARE

Adler, Irving. *Kicked Upstairs: A Political Biography of a "Blacklisted" Teacher* (Self-published, 2007. Available at the Tamiment Library, New York University.)

Beale, Howard K. *Are American Teachers Free? An Analysis of Restraints upon the Freedom of Teaching in American Schools.* New York: Charles Scribner's Sons, 1936.

―――. *A History of Freedom of Teaching in American Schools.* New York: Charles Scribner's Sons, 1941.

Dodd, Bella. *School of Darkness: The Record of a Life and of Conflict Between Two Faiths.* New York: P. J. Kenedy and Sons, 1954.

Taylor, Clarence. *Reds at the Blackboard: Communism, Civil Rights, and the New York City Teachers Union.* New York: Columbia University Press, 2011.

PEDAGOGY AND CURRICULUM

Cuban, Larry. *How Teachers Taught: Constancy and Change in American Classrooms, 1890–1990.* New York: Teachers College Press, 1993.

Dewey, John. *John Dewey on Education: Selected Writings.* Edited by Reginald D. Archambault. New York: The Modern Library, 1964.

―――. *The School and Society* and *The Child and the Curriculum.* Minneola, NY: Dover Publications, 2001.

Guernsey, Lisa, and Susan Ochshorn. *Watching Teachers Work: Using Observation Tools to Promote Effective Teaching in the Early Years and Early Grades.* New America Foundation report, November 2011.

Hattie, John. *Visible Learning: A Synthesis of Over 800 Meta-Analyses Relating to Achievement.* New York: Routledge, 2009.

Kliebard, Herbert M. *The Struggle for the American Curriculum, 1893–1958.* New York: Routledge, 1995.

Young, Ella Flagg. *Isolation in the School.* Chicago: University of Chicago Press, 1900.

THE GREAT SOCIETY AND DESEGREGATION

Brown v. Board: The Landmark Oral Argument Before the Supreme Court. Edited by Leon Friedman. New York: The New Press, 2004.

Coleman, James S., et al. *Equality of Educational Opportunity.* National Center for Educational Statistics, U.S. Department of Health, Education, and Welfare, 1966.

Fultz, Michael. " 'As Is the Teacher, So Is the School': Future Directions in the Historiography of African American Teachers." In *Rethinking the History of American Education,* edited by William J. Reese and John L. Rury. New York: Palgrave Macmillan, 2008.

―――. "The Displacement of Black Educators Post-Brown: An Overview and Analysis." *History of Education Quarterly* 44, no. 1 (2004): 11–45.

Patterson, James T. *Brown v. Board of Education: A Civil Rights Milestone and Its Troubled Legacy.* New York: Oxford University Press, 2001.

Schwartz, Heather. "Housing Policy Is School Policy: Economically Integrative Housing Promotes Academic Success in Montgomery County, Maryland." Century Foundation Report, 2010.

Unger, Irwin. *The Best of Intentions: The Triumphs and Failures of the Great Society Under Kennedy, Johnson, and Nixon.* New York: Doubleday, 1996.

TEACHER PROFESSIONALISM AND DEMOGRAPHICS

Etzioni, Amitai. *The Semi-Professions and Their Organization: Teachers, Nurses, Social Workers.* New York: The Free Press, 1969.

Ingersoll, Richard M. *Who Controls Teachers' Work? Power and Accountability in America's Schools.* Cambridge, MA: Harvard University Press, 2003.

Ingersoll, Richard, and Lisa Merrill. "Who's Teaching Our Children?" *Educational Leadership,* May 2010.

Lortie, Dan C. *Schoolteacher: A Sociological Study.* Chicago: University of Chicago Press, 1975.

Mehta, Jal, and Steven Teles. "Professionalism 2.0: The Case for Plural Professionalization in Education," in *Teacher Quality 2.0: Toward a New Era in Education Reform,* ed. Frederick Hess and Michael McShane. Cambridge, MA: Harvard Education Press, 2014.

VALUE-ADDED MEASUREMENT AND
THE ECONOMICS OF TEACHING

Chetty, Raj, John N. Friedman, and Jonah E. Rockoff. "Measuring the Impact of Teachers I: Evaluating Bias in Teacher Value-Added Estimates." Working Paper 19423, National Bureau of Economic Research, Cambridge, MA, September 2013.

Glazerman, Steven, et al. "Transfer Incentives for High-Performing Teachers: Final Results from a Multisite Randomized Experiment." Mathematica Policy Research report, NCEE 2014-4003. National Education Evaluation and Regional Assistance, Institute of Education Sciences, U.S. Department of Education, November 2013.

Gordon, Robert, Thomas J. Kane, and Douglas O. Staiger. "Identifying Effective Teachers Using Performance on the Job." Hamilton Project paper, Brookings Institution, April 2006.

Hanushek, Eric A., and Steven B. Rivkin. "How to Improve the Supply of High-Quality Teachers." *Brookings Papers on Education Policy,* 2004.

Harris, Douglas N. *Value-Added Measurements in Education: What Every Educator Needs to Know.* Cambridge, MA: Harvard Education Press, 2011.

Kane, Thomas, and Douglas Staiger. *Gathering Feedback for Teaching: Combining High-Quality Observations with Student Surveys and Achievement Gains.* Policy and Practice Brief, MET Project, Bill and Melinda Gates Foundation, January 2012.

Lancelot, William, et al. *The Measurement of Teaching Efficiency.* New York: Macmillan Company, 1935.

Ronfeldt, Matthew, Susanna Loeb, and James Wyckoff. "How Teacher Turnover Harms Student Achievement." *American Educational Research Journal 50*, no. 1 (2013): 4–36.

TEACHER EDUCATION AND TRAINING

Conant, James Bryant. *The Education of American Teachers.* New York: McGraw-Hill, 1963.

Corwin, Ronald G. *Reform and Organizational Survival: The Teacher Corps as an Instrument of Educational Change.* New York: John Wiley and Sons, 1973.

Darling-Hammond, Linda. *The Flat World and Education: How America's Commitment to Equity Will Determine Our Future.* New York: Teachers College Press, 2010.

———. "Teacher Quality and Student Achievement: A Review of State Policy Evidence." *Education Policy Analysis Archives* 8, no. 1 (January 2000).

Fraser, James W. *Preparing America's Teachers: A History.* New York: Teachers College Press, 2007.

Greenberg, Julie, Arthur McKee, and Kate Walsh. *Teacher Prep Review, 2013: A Review of the Nation's Teacher Preparation Programs.* National Council on Teacher Quality, 2013.

Haberman, Martin. "Selecting and Preparing Urban Teachers." Lecture available on the Web site of the National Center for Alternative Teacher Certification Information. Delivered February 28, 2005. http://www .habermanfoundation.org/Articles/Default.aspx?id=32.

Papay, John R., Martin R. West, Jon B. Fullerton, and Thomas J. Kane. *Does Practice-Based Teacher Preparation Increase Student Achievement? Early Evidence from the Boston Teacher Residency.* Working Paper 17646. Cambridge, MA: National Bureau of Economic Research, December 2011.

TEACH FOR AMERICA

Clark, Melissa A., et al. *The Effectiveness of Secondary Math Teachers from Teach for America and the Teaching Fellows Programs.* Mathematica Policy Research, National Center for Education Evaluation and Regional Assistance, Institute of Education Sciences, U.S. Department of Education, September 2013.

Darling-Hammond, Linda. "Who Will Speak for the Children? How 'Teach for America' Hurts Urban Schools and Students." *The Phi Delta Kappan 76*, no. 1 (September 1994): 21–34.

Darling-Hammond, Linda, et al. "Does Teacher Preparation Matter? Evidence About Teacher Certification, Teach for America, and Teacher Effectiveness." *Education Policy Analysis Archives* 13, no. 42 (2005).

Farr, Steven, and Teach for America. *Teaching as Leadership: The Highly*

Effective Teacher's Guide to Closing the Achievement Gap. San Francisco: Jossey-Bass, 2010.

Foote, Donna. *Relentless Pursuit: A Year in the Trenches with Teach for America.* New York: Alfred A. Knopf, 2008.

Kopp, Wendy. "An Argument and Plan for the Creation of the Teacher Corps." Senior thesis, Woodrow Wilson School of Public and International Affairs, Princeton University, April 10, 1989. Seeley G. Mudd Manuscript Library.

———. *One Day All Children: The Unlikely Triumph of Teach for America and What I Learned Along the Way.* New York: PublicAffairs, 2001.

Kopp, Wendy, with Steven Farr. *A Chance to Make History: What Works and What Doesn't in Providing an Excellent Education for All.* New York: PublicAffairs, 2011.

Schneider, Jack. "Rhetoric and Practice in Pre-Service Teacher Education: The Case of Teach for America." *Journal of Education Policy* (August 2013).

Shapiro, Michael. *Who Will Teach for America?* Washington, D.C.: Farragut Publishing Company, 1993.

THE STANDARDS, ACCOUNTABILITY, AND SCHOOL CHOICE MOVEMENTS

Bornfreund, Laura. "An Ocean of Unknowns: Risks and Opportunities in Using Student Achievement Data to Evaluate PreK–3rd Grade Teachers." *Early Education Initiative,* New America Foundation, May 2013.

Brill, Steven. *Class Warfare: Inside the Fight to Fix America's Schools.* New York: Simon and Schuster, 2011.

Carr, Sarah. *Hope Against Hope: Three Schools, One City, and the Struggle to Educate America's Children.* New York: Bloomsbury Press, 2013.

Cohen, David K., and Susan L. Moffitt. *The Ordeal of Equality: Did Federal Regulation Fix the Schools?* Cambridge, MA: Harvard University Press, 2009.

Mathews, Jay. *Work Hard. Be Nice.: How Two Inspired Teachers Created the Most Promising Schools in America.* Chapel Hill, NC: Algonquin Books, 2009.

Mehta, Jal. *The Allure of Order: High Hopes, Dashed Expectations, and the Troubled Quest to Remake American Schooling.* New York: Oxford University Press, 2013.

Perlstein, Linda. *Tested: One American School Struggles to Make the Grade.* New York: Henry Holt, 2007.

Rhee, Michelle. *Radical: Fighting to Put Students First.* New York: HarperCollins, 2013.

Index

About the Author

Dana Goldstein comes from a family of public school educators. She received the Spencer Fellowship in Education Journalism, a Schwartz Fellowship at the New America Foundation, and a Puffin Foundation Writing Fellowship at the Nation Institute. Her journalism is regularly featured in *Slate, The Atlantic, The Nation, The Daily Beast,* and other publications, and she is a staff writer at the Marshall Project. She lives in New York City.